Tony Gibson's

The Power in Our Hands

Neighbourhood based — *World* shaking

This is a book for strap-hangers, and washing machine-watchers and people in queues. So it is marked out in many small sections that can be read between-whiles. (Even in the Airport Departure Lounge, waiting for the plane.)

It is meant for all those people who are fed up with the blundering and blethering of the powers-that-be.

It's also for those insiders in government — local, national, world-wide — already doing their damnedest to get results, but frustrated by the systems they have to work, needing to supplement inadequate resources by unearthing the buried skills within the community.

Some politicians and academics see ordinary people as voters and taxpayers who have to be coaxed or intimidated into handing over power and money so that others can do the job. It turns out that they can't do it properly, on their own, any longer. But here and there in the world, people have found ways to take a hand in doing what needs to be done, and when that happens, things change.

At first in very small ways. Eventually, on a mega-scale.

It has happened in the past. It is happening now.

THE POWER
IN OUR HANDS

Neighbourhood based – *World* shaking

by Tony Gibson

Foreword by Lord Scarman

JON CARPENTER

Acknowledgements

To those *moving spirits* named in the book, many of whom I have worked with, and others who have told me of their work

To Jonathan Bean whose travels off the beaten track in far-off places, and collaboration in *Planning for Real* from its inception, make his drawings come to life.

To others who have helped my researches and looked over early drafts, including Richard Adams, Joel Bolnik, Nellie Wee Bonsall, Pat Conaty, *Deus ex Machina*, Anita Hobday, Glenn Handley, Tazeen Hossein, Dr Obi Igwara, Carol Riddell, Liz Shephard, Louanne Tranchell, and John F. C. Turner.

To those who have helped knock the text into shape, including Christina Nash, Marion Olusoga, Ann Parnell and Veronique du Vergé; and to Emma Must who followed up the contacts in Appendix 3.

To fellow members of the Neighbourhood Think Tank, and colleagues in the Neighbourhood Initiatives Foundation, much of whose work is reflected in the book at large and particularly in Appendix 1.

To my family who have put up with it all and made the work worthwhile.

First published in 1996 by
Jon Carpenter Publishing
The Spendlove Centre, Charlbury, Oxfordshire OX7 3PQ
☎ 01608 811969

© Tony Gibson 1996

Drawings © Jonathan Bean

ISBN 1 897766 28 9

Printed in England by J.W. Arrowsmith Ltd., Bristol

Contents

Foreword by Lord Scarman   vi

1	Here and Now	1
2	Neighbourhoods no Longer?	11
3	Moving Spirits and Microchips	21
4	Just the Job	41
5	Ganging Up	57
6	Breaking Out	80
7	"Here lies the only hope for our society"	104
8	Must the Talkers Always Win?	121
9	Four Weddings and a Funeral	142
10	Family Feeling	167
11	The Mean Machine	189
12	Time and Money	203
13	Sources of Power	227
14	Self-Evident Truths	242
15	Common Ground	258
16	Mind Blowing	270

Appendix 1 — Using the tools to make it happen   293
Appendix 2 — Targets : *The Real World*'s UK hit list   299
Appendix 3 — Work mates   300
Appendix 4 — Further reading   311

Foreword

by Rt Hon Lord Scarman

How does one describe this book? It is the tale of Tony Gibson's voyage of exploration amongst the people of Europe, Africa, Asia, America and many other places as well. But it is more than a traveller's tale: for Tony develops a philosophy. Is it also a treatise? Yes and no: his purpose is not didactic, but is to explore and display the undiscovered strengths and skills in ordinary people.

The style is abrupt, surprising and often very witty. He hits his target, and does so in a manner the reader can never forget. This is in very truth an epic, not of war but of exploration..

Yet pacific though this epic of today is, my exhilaration as I read it was such that I suddenly saw Tony as a twentieth-century Homer *and* Odysseus. To be sure Tony is neither poet nor wandering hero. The story he tells is of an enthralling journey in the course of which he came face to face with the magical capacity of ordinary men and women, if only they be given the chance, to exercise their own skills and talents.

The magic he discovered was their community enterprise. He has shown himself an inspiring and tireless worker in the development and support of the community enterprise of ordinary people. His successes have been many and he is still at work. Odysseus told his tale after he was safely home: and Homer, who immortalised the tale, did so when all was done. Tony is still hard at his self-imposed task. His journey is not yet ended. This book is not the final chapter in the story of community enterprise.

Yet it is invaluable — as well as a joy. I find it inspiring: and I believe all who read it will feel as I do.

Let us ensure that the homeless and neglected are guided and aided so that they may build their homes and — like Odysseus — reach a happy conclusion to their endeavours. Tony Gibson will be not only their guide: he will also tell their magic tale.

Scarman
August 1996

Here and now

This is about the fine mess we've been landed in, and the way to get ourselves clear. Or at least make a beginning.

Looked at from Outer Space, the world is chock full of useful resources, more than enough to keep most people busy, well housed, well fed, with a bit of time left over to have fun.

One of the most useful resources is the human race itself, swarming over the planet, brimful of curiosity, up to every kind of trick, not content to take No for an answer. But we've reached a point in time when the questions themselves are world-shattering. In less than a lifetime the world's population has doubled. Women are showing that they have as good a claim as men to whatever jobs are going. Electronics have invaded supermarkets, craft workshops, offices, the factory floor. Expert information is at everybody's fingertips. A few can do the work that used to be done by many. And we have a problem: there aren't enough jobs to go round.

Correction: there aren't enough paid jobs to go round. Childcare, education, health, public transport, protecting the environment, treating crime — apparently we can't afford the extra workers needed to do these jobs properly. So children are at risk, medical treatment is delayed, houses decay, traffic pollution increases, the shopping malls by day and the streets at night are no longer safe to wander in.

There's a mismatch. Plenty of work that needs doing, but millions of people, worldwide, who are denied the chance to do it.

We can't afford that, either.

It's not much use expecting Them — the governments, the high powered experts — to solve these problems entirely on their own. For most of this century they have been slugging it out to determine whether State power or Market forces can deliver the goods. That conflict has left the Soviets disintegrating and America and its allies knee-deep in debt, with their arms salesmen off-loading weaponry to every well-heeled State villain they can find.

Neither side has managed to stop the fighting or to protect air, earth and sea from creeping pollution. In most countries the gap between rich and poor is widening. People in the bottom third of the population are nearing the end of their tether, and beginning to make the better off shit scared of the consequences.

We have floods of technical expertise on tap. There are professionals everywhere, knowledgeable about what could be done. But they can't gear their knowledge to the job in hand, to make things work on time. They find themselves walking through treacle, or something rather worse.

What clogs their activities has to do with their dependence on systems which were originally devised to ensure democratic accountability. But the tendency is for the procedures to zombify, creating a tyranny where they should be liberating their users to make better use of their own commonsense and creativity. For the most part, these systems work by numbers, and the number-crunching ignores much of the capacity of people to get things done on the spot, in their own way; and get some job satisfaction out of it.

 Waste of people, waste of money, waste of space, waste of expert knowledge — to match the waste of raw materials which everyone is now beginning to recognise as crucial to human survival.

But there is a difference. **One system destroys the rainforests, pollutes the sea and the air. The other destroys initiative, saps confidence, grinds down hope and self-respect.**

There's a widening confidence gap. The important people have been saying *Leave it to Us.* But this no longer works. When results fail to match promises and expectations, everyone says *It's all Their fault. They are the ones to blame. It's nothing to do with Us.* So in our turn the rest of us are labelled as *apathetic, indifferent, uncommitted.*

And yet… there's a gut feeling that, between us all, we could make a better fist of it, given half a chance.

Half a chance

Half a chance? How you react to that depends on how you see that bottle on the shelf. Half empty? or half full?

Half full people make the best of a bad job, look on the bright side — and get slagged off by the half empties for being too wet behind the ears to know that high hopes get you nowhere, and there's no such thing as a free lunch.

The key question is: can anyone do anything about it?

On this I am at least a 50 percent enthusiast. If you are ever in danger of drowning and there is half a chance of reaching a bit of driftwood floating by — you become very enthusiastic about getting to it. Only a 50 percent chance of success. But what's the alternative?

Our time is like no other. In less than a lifetime, there have been almost as many technical advances as have happened over the previous 4,000 years. These changes are coming thick and fast; much faster now than most of us can take them in. We have more resources within our reach, and have the means to do more with them, for good or ill, than any other generation since history began. We are at a turning-point. We don't have to plod on along the same old routes. The old paths have petered out. The map is out of date and we have to improvise our ways across unknown territory.

Our immediate future — say, the next ten or fifteen years — holds more threats and more promise than any of our ancestors ever had to face. We know more of what's going on around the world, good and bad. We know a little about Eskimos and Hottentots and Latin American gauchos, and they know a lot about us — they see it on TV, like everyone else.

We take for granted what shows up on that magic mirror — the heights and depths of human achievement: space conquests, universal music, record-breaking athletes, microchips, transplants — alongside man-made famines, smart missiles, *ethnic cleansing* and breaching the earth's ozone shield. **We ourselves are much the same**.

Choices

At times, there doesn't seem to be much choice about what hits us next, good or bad; but we still have to choose what to do about it when it happens.

Long ago, during World War II, British troops were overrun by the Japanese advancing through the Malayan jungle. They lost touch with their regiments, and had to fend for themselves. One of them, Spencer Chapman, wrote a book about it afterwards. He said that some soldiers went in fear of

"man-eating tigers, deadly fevers, venomous snakes and scorpions, natives with poisoned darts, and a host of half-imagined nameless terrors."

They lost hope, gave up and soon died. For others, the jungle

"teems with wild animals, fowls and fish which are simply there for the taking."

They kept going. Same jungle, different responses. The jungle is neutral, he said, what mattered was the attitude of mind.

Two choices:

☞ Go on or go under

☞ Get together or go it alone.

We have to understand the jungle — the threats and promise of the new world as it's taking shape around us; our own mixed motives; our fears and suspicions; our job satisfactions; and, sometimes, the kick we get from belonging to something outside ourselves, from joining in with other people.

Across the world and back through time, we have had to adapt ourselves and our surroundings in order to survive.

A lot depends on whether we choose to resist the pressure to grab whatever is worth having, including our nearest and dearest, arm ourselves to the teeth, wall up in our private cave, and say, *I'm all right, Jack, so sod off!*

Civilisations take shape when in spite of their fears and suspicions, people begin to see the point of acting together. We drained the marshes, ploughed up the land, crossed the seas, shaped dynasties or overthrew them. It happened, and here and there in the world it is still happening. So now we need to look around us, and maybe cast a backward glance as well, — to see how it's done.

This book is about such happenings, past and present, far away and close at hand. It's a patchwork of many people's first-hand experience, for the most part people with next to no outside resources: *ordinary people* who have surprised themselves by doing **extra-ordinary things**.

For most of my life, I have been working alongside such people: here in Britain, and in China, parts of Africa, western Europe and the Soviet bloc, the Caribbean and briefly in Australia and the USA. In their ways of doing things and in their words to me, I have heard echoes of others in times past who brought the same human resources to bear, for good or ill, on their surroundings and their way of life.

Not particularly knowledgeable people, not wildly enthusiastic. But no longer content to let things drift.

What is it in human nature that brings that about?

You can't change human nature!

That's often said as if it were a minus. Actually, it's a plus, if you count the human capacities that have kept us going over the last half-million years.

First and foremost, it's our ability to *"see oursels as ithers see us"*, or at least to glimpse the way we really are. And you can't help feeling a bit self-critical. As a human race, we're falling short of our full potential, and it bugs us. That nagging dissatisfaction makes the difference between us and all the other species on the planet. It's the bit of grit in the oyster, round which a pearl could form.

Hold on! What makes us special is more than that discontent with things as they are. It's the fact that, sooner or later, we do something about it. Maybe break new ground. Maybe regain lost ground. Maybe tear the place apart. Mostly, this isn't a lone response. We get together, gang up.

There are four ingredients in the human make-up which are especially worth considering. (There are umpteen others, and umpteen other ways of classifying the way we think and act; but I've picked these out because they are there to hand, commonplace capacities that we take for granted.)

☞ There's the **DIY feeling**, the job satisfaction that gets a kick out of making things work, achieving a personal best.

☞ **The staying power that comes from belonging to a group**, which you have chosen, which accepts you and which you can rely on.

☞ **Our inborn curiosity** — our habit of asking **Why**? It's one of the first words that comes into any conversation with a two-year old. With luck, it's coupled with the question **How?** — and once you catch on to how it's done, it's likely that you'll want to do it. Children are born with this very capacity — the will to try things out — that society requires to get itself out of the mess we're in. But, too often, their upbringing and their schooling allow these capacities to atrophy from lack of use.

☞ **And a feeling of identity** — having roots in a family, a place, a country, a race, a set of beliefs in which we were brought up, which we can fall back on when the rest of the world seems strange and alien.

What's so special about all that?

These half-hidden capacities are what makes us members of the human race. Without them, we'd be useless, unable to handle resources within reach, buffeted by natural disasters, driven this way and that by forces outside our control.

Maybe that describes the way we are now — at the mercy of other people's egotism, greed, exclusiveness or violence. Failing to make sense of ordinary life, watching the world go sick.

Two things to bear in mind:

☞ Human capacities, like the jungle, are neutral. Under the pressure of events, we are capable of destroying; but we've survived so far because we are just that little bit more capable of creating. **It's a matter of choice.**

☞ At work on their own, each of these capacities gets a modest rating in the human make-up. But when people come together and begin to pool their resources, there's a difference.

It's the difference, as every baker or bomb-maker knows, between a

mixture and a compound. In a mixture, each ingredient stays unchanged, with the same properties as before. But when they interact to form a compound, something new is created. Something with properties — capacities — of its own which the original ingredients did not possess.

Once the cave-dwellers got together, quarried tin and iron, made fire, they could create a new compound, bronze, with a cutting edge: a ploughshare or a sword.

Moving spirits

What is it that prompts people to become doers, to create something new?

At street level, it's what I call the **moving spirits** among us. They are not necessarily the leading lights in any community. Charismatic leaders may help to blaze the trail, but it's obscure, *unimportant* people among the rank and file who say to themselves *Enough is enough*, make a move and persuade the rest of us that after all something can be done, here and now.

They are the invaluable earthworms who move around to break up the soil. They are the yeast that makes the dough rise. They scarcely get a mention in the National Curriculum; but they are the history-makers.

History is made, worldwide, when, maybe only once in a lifetime, some outside force — television, war, famine, new technologies — opens people's eyes. They discover that they are no longer isolated and incapable. As a class, a generation, a gender, a religious following, they suddenly see themselves as *agents, not victims*.

☆ ☆ ☆

It's tempting to stay up on Cloud Nine, talking about these changes in general terms. We need to come down to earth to understand how they work out in practice. We have to see ourselves as part of a process which is taking place all over the world. Women in Indian villages, landless peasants in Latin America, dissident students in China, middle-class environmentalists in the Home Counties, homeless squatters in South Africa, the *underclass* in American cities, religious fundamentalists in the Middle East, ethnic minorities the world over — there's the same dawning self-awareness, and the same capacity to become self-propelled.

What lessons can be learned from this? What are the obstacles which everyone encounters and how, across the world, are people managing to overcome them? How do small-scale initiatives build up to create the power and the momentum for the big changes which will determine our future?

Alongside this, how about the people known as *Them*? Who might be allies within the ranks of the experts and the politicians? How can their work reinforce what the *unimportant people* are beginning to do?

How do we get the balance right between what the professionals tell us and what ordinary people get up and do? How do we create working relationships in which decisions can be reached and acted on, not lost in a wilderness of talk?

Showing what you mean

People who were onlookers become doers. Somehow, they have to hack their way through the verbal undergrowth which stifles ideas worth having and pursuing.

If that last sentence sounds to you like a patch of verbal undergrowth — that's part of the problem.

We have come to think that words themselves are performers, that analysing a problem makes it go away, that you can talk yourself out of a crisis — when what's needed are deeds, actions, behaviour, attitudes — which tempt onlookers to have a go themselves.

Turning the talk into action means being able to **explore** possibilities, **sort out** options, **rank** priorities, **share out** responsibilities. Those words describe visual processes, which allow people who aren't particularly good with words to deal on level terms with the fluent talkers.[1]

We also have to communicate, not just within a particular group but between many groups scattered far and wide, sharing experience, pooling information on what is going on behind the scenes, concerting action.

In earlier times news spread and ideas caught on: set down on back room printing presses, spread abroad from hand to hand, carried on horseback to far off places. Now, in the 80s and 90s, infotech has transformed this process. Words spread at a speed and on a scale that was never dreamed of in the past. The **Network** is accessible to ordinary people, not just to financial tycoons and media moguls.

Some politicians and academics see *ordinary people* as voters and tax-payers who have to be coaxed or intimidated into handing over power and money so that others can do the job.

It turns out that they can't do it properly on their own, any longer.

But when ordinary people become doers instead of onlookers, things change. At first in very small ways. Eventually, on a mega scale.

---

1 We have developed tool-kits such as Planning for Real which people in many countries use to cut the cackle, streamline decision-making, develop an agreed plan of action. More about this in later chapters.

pieces and link them up to make a frame. Within it, other pieces begin to fall into place:

☛ **How *infotech* can disseminate grassroots experience and give it global impact.**

☛ **How children's upbringing can unearth their buried talents — their innovatory skills, their built-in ability to work things out together.**

☛ **How sorting out options and reaching decisions can be done by *showing what you mean*, not just talking about it.**

☛ **How professionals can adapt to new roles, forge new relationships with the rest of the community.**

☛ **How between them, they can change the false economy we live in into the real economy which matches human resources to basic human needs.**

And how, for much of the time, to make it fun.

This patchwork process is happening on the other side of the world as well as on our doorsteps. People who are nearing the end of their tether — up against political corruption, commercial exploitation, civil war — are being forced back on their own resources, shaping their future with their bare hands.

We need to understand and to compare their experience with ours, for at least two reasons:

☛ Their situations, and their response, can't be quarantined, even if the rest of the world wanted it that way. Their problems and their opportunities interlock with ours.

☛ We haven't yet reached the point where we too are forced to rely on ourselves with nobody else to sort things out, to get the pattern right. But there isn't much time left.

So it's not too early to learn from those far away people, as well as from the moving spirits already at work right under our noses.

I can't claim to complete the picture. There are gaps in my understanding which your own experience may fill. I'm not putting forward academic theories; just some rules of thumb to tackle the work we must now take in hand. Work which starts small, not too intimidating, within our reach, and ends in changes that could overtake the world.

The starting place is where we are now, in our own surroundings, where we feel at home. The neighbourhood, good, bad or indifferent. It's the place where the moving spirits first operate. It's the crucible in which we fashion the tools of recovery or the weapons of self-destruction.

2 Neighbourhoods no longer?

Neighbourhoods? What makes anyone think they have a future? Why bother about the people next door when the *infotech revolution* will put us at the end of the line to anyone else in the world?

Besides, half the world's population have turned into city people. And cities which once were patchworks of local life are becoming anonymous dwelling areas where people keep themselves to themselves for fear of each other.

More and more of us spend our time away from home, commuting to work or the football match or the disco, staggering back to flop in front of the TV and fall into bed soon after.

And yet...

Neighbourhoods have roots. People remember. And when you probe further, to find out what it feels like to be living in a neighbourhood, time and again the same story, or almost the same, comes out. On stress estates and leafy suburbs in the West, in shanty towns and villages in far away countries, some old person talks about the days when she was young. Or some youngster repeats the story heard from an Auntie or a Gran. It is often about the letterbox, with the string through it attached to the latch inside. When someone was poorly, the neighbour could pull the string to enter, take the children to school, make a cup of tea, do the shopping. But now, people say, it's so *different*.

Neighbourhoods and neighbourliness are no longer quite as they used to seem.

How would you reckon these neighbourhoods compare?

1. *Chernobyl*

When part of the atom plant blew up, in 1986, the plume of contamination generated by the disaster was wind-blown across the plains of Byelorussia. Over the next few days thousands of people took flight — and were received and looked after by those living just outside the contaminated area. Some had relations they could stay with, others came as strangers. All might be carriers of the contamination. But people opened their homes, sometimes to fifteen refugees in one small house.

There was no exclusion then. Afterwards, things changed. Six years later, I went with a handful of British and Americans to meet Byelorussians who were trying to cope with the situation which was spiralling out of control. The break-up of the Soviet Union had sparked off civil wars in some of the newly independent States. The Byelorussian republic was holding together, but at the receiving end of refugees from the wars next door. There was nowhere for them to go but into the still contaminated area, to squat in deserted homes and scratch a living. The area was a refuge for drug peddlers and criminals on the run, using it as a base to grow opium poppies, to prey on the less contaminated areas, and to sell what they could loot on the new "free market". Some of the original inhabitants still stayed on where they had always lived, although the food they cultivated and the air they breathed was still giving geiger counts of up to 50 curies. (That compares with 0.5 registered by the UK Met Office as the contamination drifted across Welsh farms at the time of the original explosion; that was enough to decide the government on compulsory slaughter of livestock.)

Five of us went into the 50 curie area where whole villages were apparently deserted, with grass growing in the streets, and birds nesting in the rooms. And suddenly, a neat house with lace curtains in the window, a pot of geraniums on the windowsill, and 74 year old Hannah at the kitchen door, beside her supply of home grown pumpkins and her pig scratching in the back yard. She had fading photographs of her grandchildren and great grandchildren on the living room wall, without a hope of their ever returning to see her. She said she had lived there all her life, and intended to die in her own place, within walking distance of a few old neighbours, and some younger ones, who said the same.

Officially no one was allowed to stay on, and the government provided transport and resettlement allowances. But some who had gone as refugees and been resettled had decided to return, because the people in the resettlement areas now resented them.

They were accused of taking homes and competing for jobs, when housing and jobs were in short supply. So though they looked and spoke the same, and had been born into the same country, they were seen as immigrants, and rejected by people who wanted their own place to remain theirs, without intruders.

2. Philadelphia

In the 80s Norris Square was called *Needle Park*: soaring drugs and crime rate, residents mostly *Latinos* without enough English to make the authorities pay heed to leaking water pipes, faulty gas mains and festering garbage. People who could afford it started moving out. Not so 57 year old Tomasita Romero who persuaded friends and neighbours to hold candlelit all night vigils — anything from 10 to 20 people standing on the street corners right beside the drug dealers, and gradually edging them out. Then she got on with her gardening, which included the unofficial greening of Norris Square.

Meanwhile Pat DeCarlo and other residents in the Norris Square Civic Association had managed after nearly 10 years' campaigning to get the City Corporation to release 2 derelict buildings, rat-ridden eyesores and fire hazards. The *dream which crystallised* in December 1989 was to recruit jobless men, some with prison records, to form their own self-governing *Workers' Crew* (officially the *Norris Square Economic Development Corporation*), converting the buildings into low-rental apartment blocks. They were trained on the job by a retired building contractor, with English language tuition thrown in to improve their chances on the job market. Housing officers sniffed at the mere idea of such a hotch-potch achieving results. The Crew squabbled periodically amongst themselves, threw out one member for fighting, then allowed him back: but gloried in the completion of *a nice job*, on time. Work began on converting a funeral casket factory into homes for the living.

The City Fathers began to see the neighbourhood in a new light. Some public services suddenly improved. Residents made their own surveys, block by block, to find out everyone's concerns and priorities; ran advice services on mortgage negotiation, setting up business enterprises and dealing with police brutality; and began negotiations to turn the Park into a play area. In the middle of all this the Working Crew, now an independent construction co-op, fell apart under the stress of personality clashes, and had to be painstakingly re-constituted, all over again. But in April 1996, 350 volunteers cleaned up the Park and equipped it as a play area, to the designs of local children, and opened for business.

As yet, no needles.

3. London

A while back when I worked for the BBC, I decided to do some programmes about neighbourhoods, centred on the way teenagers saw them. So I went to Bethnal Green to meet a bunch that used to hang about on the street corner just off Bethnal Green High Road. They always met there after work, and then decided where to go, to the pub or the park, depending on funds, and usually up West at the week-end. Always the same rendez-vous, just up the street from their primary school, going right back to when they were kids.

They used to come across each other during the week; I recorded the girls window-shopping and glad-eyeing one of the lads behind the counter inside. They knew every inch of the neighbourhood, and where they could find each other.

It was only when I began to put the programme together, and asked for everyone's address, that I discovered that none of them lived there any more. They had been dispersed to fringe housing estates, where there was no such thing as a neighbourhood. They came together where they knew they still had roots.

People hang in together because of the things they all know about, the memories they share. Or sometimes, because of what they want to do together. Today, on the other side of the Thames, the Peckham Young Boys, who scribble up their initials — PYB — in the places they rob or vandalise, have grown up on estates that are not very neighbourly, and chosen to become a clan family of their own, loyal to each other, with their hands against the rest of the world.

4. *The two faces of Rodney Street, Jamaica*

Downtown Kingston is a patchwork of poverty-stricken neighbourhoods — Tivoli Gardens, Craig Town, Concrete Jungle, Tel Aviv, Spoilers, Dunkirk, Jones Town — each one dominated by one or other of the political parties which bicker over Jamaica's dwindling resources. Jones Town when I first saw it at the end of '95 had 22 *dons* (short for Don Carleones) godfather-type leaders of varying power each recruiting and protecting local youngsters, starting as lookouts, ending as gunmen. The don of dons, 30 year old Ian Scott, nicknamed Stella, had his base on Rodney Street. Two days before I got there he quarrelled with his No. 2 over a dead man's gun, shooting it out inconclusively from either end of the street. Next day Stella was mown down by police gunfire and his lieutenant fled, for the time being, to the hills.

A bunch of youngsters had their *corner* at one end of Rodney Street. They had taken over a derelict site, cleaned it up, raised funds by running domino games at 2 Jamaican dollars a throw, and laid out their own miniature park — trees, shrubs, ornamental paths, a cook house, a community veg. garden, and — on the way — a fish pond and a children's play area.

One boundary fence had its own mural: TOGETH- ERNESS. Another had WELCOME TO THE RODNEY RAIDERS, with everyone's names below. One of them summed it up:

"It's the closeness of the people which count ... so you go up the road and pass it around that we are going to Do something. We go from yard to yard. If a person can't support by giving his or her labour, them assist financially. The older people willingly give because they see the productiveness of the youth. ... those youths see their labour, and each take pride when someone passes by and say 'That park is pretty, man'. And that alone kind of build him up from inside. We find that we get more people all the time because people are seeing an end product. They feel competent and they feel nice the way it is. Tell the truth, me myself feel good too."

Same street. Same people?

5. *Uzuakoli*

I was working in Nigeria and had some leave due. An Igbo friend in the capital offered me the chance to live with his country cousins.

So I drove away from the supermarkets, the tower blocks, the High Life dance halls, out across the Carter Bridge jam-packed with smart cars, bus-loads of commuters, heavy goods trucks, bikers with bulging cycle panniers — down the main trunk road to the East. At the end of a two-day journey, turning off the macadam road, bumping across miles of one-lane track, ridged with red laterite dust, asking directions of wayside peddlers, until at last I reached the village where my friend's family lived.

My host greeted me under the eaves of his small mud-brick house, and to show me honour, he broke a small cola nut and shared it.

The next day, having eaten and slept well and gone the rounds meeting the rest of the family, he took me out *to see what the young people were up to.*

A short cut through the forest, a glimpse of bright water in the distance, drumming, laughter, many voices singing. It sounded like a picnic.

Maybe *works outing* would describe it better. Where the river banks shelved to the water's edge, there was a crowd of young men, some chest-high in the water, holding on by a rope, shouldering timbers and passing rocks from hand to hand as they built their bridge. It was theirs because they were celebrating their coming of age by building it in a day. They had something of the controlled zest which can be seen here and there in Britain when Jehovah's Witnesses get together to pool their skills and build a Kingdom Hall.

This bridge building was not a religious expression. The builders and the young women supporting them with food and drink were proving themselves

to the rest of the world. Their parents had celebrated by building a school, a church, a clinic. Two generations further back, the way for your generation to make its mark might have been by raiding another village. Today they were building something which would last, as a memorial to themselves, and a gift to the rest of the community. Something they would be proud to live with.

I have never seen, before or since, such work and such workers. Not a chain-gang, not a production line, but working as one. Building as if desperate to avert some imminent catastrophe. Building for their lives, and making fun of it.

6. Belfast

In the Falls or the Shankill Road, what began as loyalty to a family religion has become a defence of the patch. Jimmy Creighton's patch, as a community worker, is Glencairn:

"It's a community turning in on itself. It's young people bored out of their minds because they're bundled out of school with no real education, no prospects of jobs, where 63% are unemployed. Some drop into a life of crime. From there, it's only a step to the paramilitary."

the kids. It happened gradually. They were good kids and they used to go on the street and play football, but then they were beginning to do odd things. I couldn't put my finger on it and I thought 'what is happening?'

Then the mentally ill were getting shoved out of the hospitals, the cuts started in the Social Security, and this is when I really saw the place go downhill. People were using any means to be able to live to get their daily bread. There was nothing for the children. And then it started. At one time you could leave your door open, people wouldn't venture to go in and steal, but now whether your door's open or shut, they need money to survive and it's the same with the children. The shoplifting, the aggression, the anger. I have never seen anything like it."

Nancy Peters grew up on Merseyside, moved to Tyneside, settled in on the Meadow Well Estate, with children and eventually grandchildren, helped to set up the best Credit Union in the North-East, got on well with children in the street, and stayed unflustered when those youngsters' anger and frustration boiled over in the Meadow Well riots.

Turning point

Some outsiders — the media, the political pundits, the social scientists — looking in on trouble spots like Meadow Well are inclined to say that the *fabric of society is coming apart.* Young people who feel betrayed can become destroyers; in their way, as powerful as the destroyers of the rainforests and the polluters of the atmosphere. The destruction **could be** allowed to continue until human and material resources are no longer enough to sustain the human species. Or those resources **could be** salvaged, re-cycled, painstakingly put back into use. Nancy doesn't talk about the fabric of society but she is one of those who have begun to show that things can be turned, as you might do if you couldn't afford a new shirt and wanted to reverse a frayed collar.

The point about a neighbourhood is that, like an old shirt, you are used to it. It's familiar ground. Even at night, when muggers are about, you know where you are.

It's here that you can see results — feel them in your everyday life. If government policies are rubbish, you can see their effects as Nancy Peters sees them on everyday life in Meadow Well. If the residents lose hope and self-respect and chuck their own rubbish on the streets and open spaces — that too strikes home. Short of a package flight to Benidorm, you can't get away from what's happening. If it's good, you share the local pride.

If not...

Others besides Nancy puzzle out what has gone wrong. They see those wasted human resources, young and old. Here and there, someone decides that there is a choice. Things have reached a point when something has to be done to stop the rot. If we don't get together to do it *now,* it will be too late. That's the choice. And someone has to make the first move.

Break-through

The starting point is seldom *up there* amongst the established leaders and the media personalities. They may come in useful later on, telling the world that what is happening on the ground is a sign of the times, a signal for change.

But someone, somewhere, has to set the example, get things moving, show what's needed, not just talk about it in the abstract.

Once in a while, these small beginnings catch on, nationwide, worldwide, almost of their own accord.

Almost, but not quite.

The difference is that today's moving spirits are learning how to use the old and the new technologies to tell the world in their own way.

Which brings us to Chrissie Maher, a moving spirit if ever there was one.

3 Moving spirits and microchips

Chrissie Maher started out in Merseyside, where Nancy Peters comes from. Nowadays, she lives and works in New Mills, back of beyond, off the beaten track, and likely in winter to be reached through snow. It's on the Derbyshire High Peak, by Kinder Scout and Edale, where generations of city-dwellers have broken loose to roam free in daylight and sing and dance the nights away. (Well, at least until Lights Out at the Edale Youth Hostel.)

> *I'm a rambler, I'm a rambler from Manchester way...*
> *I get all my pleasure the hard moorland way ...*
> *I've sunbathed on Kinder, been burnt to a cinder...*
> *I may be a wage slave on Mondays,*
> *But I am a free man on Sundays.*

Amongst those free men, at weekends with his girl, was John Axon, one of the last of the engine drivers in the age of steam. There was a famous Radio Ballad about him, when he won a posthumous George Cross; he met his death, on the footplate; wrestling with a jammed steam pressure valve as his engine  chugged up the steep climb out of Buxton and ambled over the crest with the guard running alongside begging him to jump clear. But he wouldn't give up, and stayed on as the train rocketed out of control downhill from Dove Holes to the station in Chapel, far below.

Chrissie Maher got a medal recently for her kind of heroism; unsung as yet, perhaps because the disasters she grapples with seldom hit the headlines.

Her working life spans the gulf between the railway age and the day of the Information Superhighway.

She moved up to the Peak a few years back, but she was born and bred in Scouseland, the next to youngest in a family of six. Her father, a coal heaver, died when she was seven. From then on, she was her mother's mainstay. By the time she was sixteen, she knew a lot about life, but hadn't had time to learn to read or write. There wasn't a book in the house, she said.

When I met her in New Mills, there were plenty of books around. She lives in an old farm house. You get into it via a porch squatted by a peaceful mother cat surrounded by a patchwork quilt of black and white kittens, about fifteen of them. Then through the kitchenette into what was once the farm house kitchen. Two enormous sofas, moulded into hospitable shape by many bums. Also present — five desks, two telephones, a photocopier and fax machine. Open plan! Four others beside Chrissie, all busy, Scouse accents mingling with Oxbridge.

To discover what they are about, you have to go back to Chrissie as an illiterate teenager, desperately looking for a job.

> *"Nobody was working in our house, five brothers and nobody was working. I was like Yosser Hughes from The Black Stuff, 'Go on, giss a job, I can do that'. And when they asked me if I'd got any qualifications, I said, 'No'. Then I told them my background and the boss said, 'OK, but only if you go to night school. I'll pay for English, maths and book-keeping.' So I did, and I copped myself a job in his office, God bless his cotton socks. He used to let me polish his car as well for cream cakes and a few bob pocket money, 'cos me mum took all the pay. I used to walk to work, there and back."*

Flash point

Over the next few years, Chrissie learnt to put herself across on paper as well as by word of mouth. Then she married, and took stock of the place her children would grow up in.

> *"I'd grown up in an area where the drains were always blocked and the kids' swings had concrete beneath them so that when they fell off, they got massive big bumps. Our bins were never emptied on time; there were rats and mice in the streets. I see my children having the same problems during the summer, trying to play out in the street with the terribly smelly blocked sewers, and if you put them to play in the back entry — that was the back of the house — there was always loads and loads of rubbish there: old beds thrown out and suchlike.*
>
> *Part of the problem lay with the people themselves and part of it lay with the council who wouldn't come very often and empty the bins, and didn't brush up after them. Left all kinds of rubbish all over the place.*
>
> *So one day, you just snap, and you say 'ENOUGH IS ENOUGH!', and you take your bin round to the local councillor's house and you dump it on his doorstep. Tip it up and say 'See how you like it!'.*
>
> *I took it round on two occasions, because the first time it didn't work. The second time I did it, they got quite angry, but that's the whole idea. You get across a gut reaction of what it's like to live with that sort of thing."*

☆ ★ ☆

Quite a lot of neighbours got involved, through mums chatting in the school yard when they fetched their kids. The word got around that Chrissie was a doer, she knew where to look for the form you needed to get a grant, or the person to contact with a complaint. Particularly the complaints.

"You start shouting at the local papers.

We said to one paper 'What are you doing about the bins, and the fourteen foot high rubbish tip?' And they did one or two stories, sort of for the glare value."

But news isn't news any longer when the novelty wears off. And besides that…

"You learn later on, of course, that the big newspapers have contacts with councillors and they need to keep good friends with them.

And I said, 'ENOUGH IS ENOUGH! We'll do our own newspaper!' I thought I'd like to know about what our local bobby was doing, and what our local Scout group are up to, and where the nearest jumble sale is. Most of all, I want a paper to shout at councillors, to tell them to go and get the bins emptied and the improvements made.

There were about seven of us, friends and mothers with kids at the school. And they said, 'It's never been done, a community newspaper as you want to call it. They sat around gasping, 'You can't do that, you'll get locked up. We're ordinary people who have never ever taken action before.'

And suddenly, they think, 'Yes, we can, come on, let's have a bash.' And we sit around in the back room like a bunch of Christians waiting for somebody to come and knock on the door and nail you to the nearest piece of wood. You shiver in your shoes, but you do it.

People said, 'OK, how do we finance it?' I said, 'Like the big papers, let's look at adverts. But we don't want our mouths shut because the big advertisers dislike what we are saying.' So we handpicked the local fishmonger and the local butcher, because nobody had any complaints about them. And at 3p for each copy and the advertising money, with a print run of 2,000, we could just pay the litho printers' bill. Over the past years, we'd built up relationships with two or three reporters that were on the Liverpool Echo, and we got them to come down and give us a hand. You know, just tell us if we're writing the right sort of thing. They said, 'Yes, we'd love to' and told us 'This is what you should do', and of course great arguments broke out, because we wanted to use our own language in our own way to tell the council to get off their backsides, and that wasn't journalism to them. You're expected to put it more nicely, a little bit more flowery. Whereas we wanted to get out there and call a spade a spade. But they were good for us, they did teach us a few skills, layout design and suchlike, and it really went on from there."

Spreading the word

The first edition, 2,000 copies, hawked round from door to door, sold out in two hours, and the *Tuebrook Bugle* never looked back.

WHO OWNS THE BUGLE?

The short answer is that nobody owns the Bugle. In fact, it's a very different kind of newspaper from those you've been used to.

Most papers are started to make money for the owners, but the Bugle was started by a group of Tuebrook residents concerned about the future of their area.

This paper has no editor and no paid staff. Anyone interested in helping to run the Bugle can simply come along and join the editorial committee.

The *Bugle* is not going to be packed with adverts as some papers do in order to make vast profits. Of course, we need adverts to help pay our way, but once we've got enough for that, we'd rather fill the rest of the space with news about Tuebrook.

In the next column but one — the other side of the glamour pic of Tuebrook's own beauty queen —

OUR HOMES ARE IN THE BALANCE!

Halfway down New Road in Tuebrook, there's a monument to what Liverpool Corporation have done to the area. There isn't an inscription, but it speaks for itself. It's as big as two houses. And in fact, that's just what it is — two houses, with doorways and windows bricked up, and the roof missing. ... The houses stand there, an eyesore and a disgrace.

... Uncertainty hangs over everyone's head. ... The Corporation have said nothing to anyone. They haven't tried asking residents what they want. ... The Corporation haven't told anyone what they intend to do with the area.

The reason the Corporation haven't told anyone is simply that they haven't a clue what to do with the area.

The people of Tuebrook can kill two birds with one stone. First, they can put an end to the uncertainty by telling the Corporation what they'd like to see done to the area.

Secondly, they can make the Corporation put into practice their declared policies of letting the people really participate in planning.

The Corporation are undecided, so the Bugle is going to make sure that the people of Tuebrook decide for them.

Further down the same front page, there's a bit about a Radio Merseyside programme in which Chrissie was on a chat show with the city's Chief Planner, Jim Amos, and the Director of Recreation and Open Spaces, Mr P. McCormack. She invited them to *come and see what it's like to live here. And being on the air, they just couldn't do anything but accept.*

They didn't actually get round to fixing dates on the radio, but the *Tuebrook Bugle* intends to see that this is done. And when we find out when they're coming, we'll make an announcement, so that everyone can have a word with Mr Amos and Mr McCormack.

That was just the start, and the *Bugle* continued, month after month, going from strength to strength, for nine years, until the whole area was redeveloped.

☆ ☆ ☆

It wasn't easy at first. Some people objected to spreading news about the state of the place. It might worsen reputations and bring down values.

"We got bricks through windows, human excrement through letterboxes. People didn't like you telling the world that they had rats. It lowered the value of their properties."

OUR OWN WORST ENEMIES

Dear Readers,

I do hope you felt something if only disgust at our environment that I spoke about in last month's issue…

Don't get me wrong — some people severely criticised me, saying my column painted the district black. (I did. It is black.) But most were kind and saw, through the paper, the hard work, the facts and figures, the enthusiasm that went into producing the Bugle.

People said it was good, and they hoped we would carry on. …

I found that people were their own worse enemies. In some roads, we saw holes and when we asked "Have you tried to get them filled in?" — "No" was the answer…

It's going to be a battle. We will have to show someone that we mean business…

It is a case of the people helping the people to help the people, so it turns out it helps you to help yourself.

Sort that one out if you can.

Best wishes to everyone,

CHRISSIE

Back-up

The hard work, the facts and figures and the enthusiasm came from a rich mixture of *Bugle* helpers.

There was a pensioner, my mother actually — all the Pensioners' Club wanted a hand in it, so she gathered all their news. Then there was someone who knew how to cook; we'd put a little simple recipe that didn't cost the earth, and with ingredients you could go out and buy. Pat wanted to do Your Stars, and she made them up, and that was a good laugh. And her husband Sid did a few bits and pieces, going round and speaking to people, but didn't really want his name on anything.

And there was Moira — fifteen years old, fantastic, lovely kid who came in her little hot pants, God bless her, and stuck with the Bugle throughout and is still with us now. She did everything, wrote bits — went round and got the adverts, visited old ladies and got their stories, wrote a few poems. Dead keen she was, and she sold most copies. The local kids, they all used to earn pocket money by selling the paper as well, a penny a copy out of the sale price.

They kept up the campaigning, beginning with the Lister Drive Tip. Rubbish where the kids ought to be playing. A thousand children living between Lister

Drive and West Derby Road. The Corporation's idea for a suitable playground had been Rathbone Road.

Good idea! If it wasn't for the four main roads the kids would have to cross, and the hour it would take to get there. ...

So they costed the Corporation's plan and compared it with what could be done for the same money on their own patch by clearing up the Lister Drive rubbish, levelling, seeding and fencing the site, with space for football pitches as well as the adventure playground.

Pinching every penny, the Corporation could give our thousand children a decent play area, safe and clean, for just over £10,000. If we all stay here for only another five years, that makes it £2 a year per child for the play area. It's cheap at the price. The solution to vandalism, and all that is staring the Corporation in the eyes. What about it, Mr Amos?

In the April issue, the *Bugle* is promoting plans to set up a street football league for children under twelve.

And the first thing they'll be wanting is local pitches, so the children don't have to travel far afield.

Still no word, though, from Mr Jim Amos, Chief Planner, and Mr P McCormack, the Head of Recreation and Open Spaces. The last thing we heard was that clearing the land was the responsibility of the Department of the Environment.

What have Mr Amos and Mr McCormack done about this? Have they been on the phone to the Ministry? Or are they still dawdling?

A better understanding

Three months later, with the *Bugle* blaring away —

AT LAST — A CHANCE FOR THE KIDS

At last the Lister Drive Tip we are always moaning about may soon become known as the Lister Drive Recreation Area. Work has started by workmen organised by Mr David Pullen for the City's Projects Officer...
I hope this will be a small step in the right direction of a better understanding between ourselves and the Corporation as to what our needs really are.

Meanwhile, those needs and preferences are being surveyed, under the Bugle's lead, by residents themselves going door-to-door to find out about housing —

Who owns your house? Is it worth saving? Do you want to stay in your house as it is now? Would you like to stay in it if it was improved (but this might affect your rent)? If your house is knocked down, where would you like to live?

Not only that — but who are you willing to let live? What happens when the neighbourhood threatens to become an exclusion zone?

There was a *furious meeting* to discuss a proposed gypsy encampment. One resident threatened *open warfare* if the gypsies stopped over. The *Bugle* faithfully reported the anger, and then flanked the account with —

THE CASE FOR THE TRAVELLERS

Mr and Mrs Candle have roamed England for the past ten years.

They are, at present, camped with four neighbouring caravans on one corner of a debris site at Everton Road. On an adjacent blank wall are scrawled the words, **Tinkers get out**.

Mr Candle and some of his neighbours work as labourers, tarmacking the roads. In his spare time, he deals in scrap metals and antiques.

Outside their quaint, but ageing, little caravan, along with refuse normally found on a tip, are little heaps of carefully stacked scrap metal and a Corporation dustbin.

A little fire blazed merrily, and rows of freshly-washed clothing swayed in the breeze.

Inside, everything was neat and spotlessly clean. Their only real luxury, a small portable television set.

As soon as we convinced them that we were fair-minded, we found them anxious to answer our questions.

They explained that they had been visited by reporters before, but their resulting stories were far from the truth.

We found the Candle family to be a simple but genuine people — religious, hard-working and clean-living. ...

Factfinding, and opinion-forming. Lots of opinions. Especially within the editorial committee.

"There is always squabbling, fights and fisticuffs, tears and laughter. There's always far more written than can be put in. You've got to make a decision, and that's what democracy's all about. But that's where, for the first time, you learn democracy can work against you. People put their hands up and say you can't have your column in. And then you can't have your column in.

Community newspapers are very passionate. You're battling with people's emotions and their feelings. But after you've all squabbled and fought and carried on, it's great, because you sell a newspaper and it does what you wanted it to do. There's lots of laughter as well, and somehow it seems to cement the group together."

Ripple effect

The *Bugle* call sounded across Merseyside. People from other estates came asking for their needs to be trumpeted. The answer was always, *Go and start up your own paper.* And they did. In a year or two, Chrissie reckoned, there were over 90 community papers on the go.

So the ripple effect continues, and here and there begins to make waves.

Chrissie's column attacks *the Moguls who run Liverpool* for their lack of ideas and inspiration on housing.

> Their ideas on housing have been all wrong and dated — splitting families and thrusting them into great skyscraper blocks of flats that hold them like prisons.
>
> Especially the old, parents with young children, and people who are ill with rheumatism and the like, who can't move out of their flats once a lift stops working (which is quite often these days). These flats that echo every noise from one to the other due to the lack of soundproofing and paper-thin walls...
>
> The reasons for this are quite plain. Quantity without quality, and economics ...
> To sum up ... the Liverpool overlords are that busy building roads, motorways and huge office blocks (for whom and what purpose, I really wonder) that they have forgotten human beings live here as well.

The planning overlords were a prime target. Liverpool University students helped to direct the fire.

> *"We heard the news that planners from all over the world had been invited to Liverpool for a conference and to see the delights of Liverpool.*

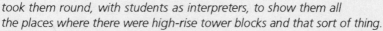

> *We wanted to show them the **blights** of Liverpool. So we got a bus to arrive at their hotel at the same time that the official bus had been ordered, or just before. We took them round, with students as interpreters, to show them all the places where there were high-rise tower blocks and that sort of thing.*
>
> *But when we made the first announcement to the visitors, they were terrified because they thought we were underground people who were going to shoot them. Then the interpreters from the University explained what we were going to show, and they settled down. When they got off the bus, they all put money in the hat to pay for the bus trip."*

There were two objectives. One was to enlighten the professionals, get through to them the effects of what they planned, and what people really wanted. The other was to penetrate the smokescreens of officialese, so that people could see how to get things done, how to use the system.

Clearing the air

Chrissie and co. opened up what they called The Benefits Shop to give advice on government forms, what they meant, and how to fill them in. The target was official gobbledegook.

> *"At that stage, along comes Lord Young, he was Michael Young then, and he'd just got the Government to set up the National Consumer Council, and he said 'We've heard about what you're doing, do you fancy being a National Consumer Councillor?' And I said, 'I'm not a committee lady, I don't know nothing of agendas, I like to do things.*
>
> *'What would you like to do?' So I said 'I'd like to find out why there are £600 million in welfare benefits that never get taken up, and I think it's because of the forms.'*

And he said 'How would you do it? And I said 'Go to a big supermarket, get every-body coming in, ask questions about form-filling, find out what's wrong, make recommendations, and if the forms need to be simplified, that's what we should do.' He said 'I like you. Come and join us.' And he gave us £50 a year which went into the community Benefits Shop funds."

The first enquiry was staged in the Salford market. And what came out of that was the *gut belly reaction to all the garbage and gobbledegook* that the professionals produce.

"Very highly intelligent people, it seemed the forms bamboozled them as well. I've been there. I have felt the humiliation of those ten foot walls, those words that isolate you, stop you from getting benefits, stop you from cooking, stop you from mending your car, leave you having to sign leases and agreements and say you understand them and will abide by them, and yet you're never in with a fighting chance of ever doing so."

With a bit more help from the National Consumer Council, they got in touch with the Department of Social Security.

"They threw 30 forms at us and said 'Go on, see what you can do with that.' So we took the forms away and rewrote them and showed it could be done. And then nothing happened. So I thought — THIS IS NOT GOOD ENOUGH! We collected all the government forms we could find, from other Ministries too. And about half a dozen of us got a van and a lot of cardboard boxes with the forms inside, tied up with red tape, and we took a paste table and set it up in Parliament Square. There was no other way left open to us to bring the message home to Parliament — whilst it was sitting — that what they were doing was churning out rubbish.

I was quite prepared to go to jail because I was fed up. But we got quite a nice reception. The world's press were there, and the bobbies when they came along were really nice. I had my hands joined together — 'Go on, take me.' As it happened, the Riot Act, which they read out, was about 150 words long, and at the end of it, I said 'Does all that mean Please move on?' And the world's press had a lovely story."

Nobody was locked up, and Mrs Thatcher wrote them a lovely letter, and said she was setting up an enquiry, and invited them to meet the Chairman of Marks & Spencer, who was in charge of it.

"He was very sympathetic, not patronising, he actually felt sorry for us and he knew what we were after, and he quite agreed that his job was to put it right. So they saved £250 million in costs by getting rid of unwanted forms, and improving the forms that people fill in incorrectly. We got Forms Units set up in every government department. And that's the way the Plain English Campaign took off.

I honestly, truthfully, thought it would all be done in three years. Now, 25 years later, I'm still here, and with the EEC and Maastricht, there's another ten foot wall to climb."

In those 25 years, the Plain English Campaign has made its mark wherever there is gobbledegook to be sought out, ridiculed, and put right. It has a commercial arm that rewrites, redesigns, trains and publishes. No charity handouts — just money down for services rendered, and the profits go to the Campaign.

"We don't like grants. You start taking grants, that's when you start compromising."

So now there are six or seven hundred volunteers feeding prime cuts of gobbledegook to the team, no longer in Chrissie's sitting room but in a three-storey building in New Mills, already bursting at the seams because the campaign is now running courses in plain English for school-leavers with a diploma at the end — about a thousand during 1996 from all over the UK, plus four from Ghana, all set to go back and spread the gospel as 'soldiers in the field'.

"We can get the skill into a marvellous growth market — kids will be able to get jobs in banks and building societies and insurance companies. And they'll be able to go abroad, with English being the nice world language. Plain English is a skill that has to be taught; and we're going to teach it."

A success story so far. In spite of the odds.

"Most people are apathetic. But today, when people whinge to me and say 'This government does nothing, I say 'What have you done about it? And they say 'What do you mean?' They never ever believe they can do anything — 'People like us don't do things like that'. 'Why not?' 'I can't be bothered.' And that's the truth of it. I'll never have any sympathy with anybody who can't be bothered. So you have to go back to those few who have got the guts to stand up and do something.
You're in there, you know what's wrong, you feel it, you've had to live with it. So that's what makes you a real campaigner. You have that gut reaction. And you know that it's not just for you, but for many millions of people out there who feel it just the same.

*You can actually pass on that feeling, the passion of what it was like, and what it **could be** like. And they join in, and they take the flag and fly with it."*

Passing on the passion seldom figures in official guidelines or academic analyses. Yet it's that gut feeling which strikes home with the rest of us — once there's a basic communication system to link us up.

Multipliers

ENOUGH IS ENOUGH was Chrissie Maher's gut reaction when she first took off on Merseyside. In 1993, it was a headline in *Alarm Bells*, the newsletter of ALARM UK, the National Alliance Against Roadbuilding, as it reported the battles of Twyford Down, and the Preston Southern and Western Bypass, and the East London River Crossing at Oxleas Wood, and the 230-mile South Coast corridor from Folkestone in Kent to Honiton in Devon.

 Transport 2000, an independent research body, has given a helping hand. Stephen Joseph, its director, also has a talent for soundbites (the Government's line on public roads enquiries *is not to ask whether eating babies is wrong, but whether you like them boiled or fried*). He put together the BBC television programme, *Car Sick*, which broke all records with 44 mailbags of supporting letters from 20,000 viewers.

ALARM UK's moving spirits include gentle, undemonstrative people like John Stewart, with a knack for involving the media, working behind the scenes to gather and collate the information fed back by phone and fax from those at the fighting front. Among these in the early days, 27-year old Emma Must, joining the first protesters on Twyford Down after her day's work as children's librarian in Winchester. Padlocking herself to a bulldozer, imprisoned for two weeks in Holloway, giving up her respectable job to work full-time in the downtown office of ALARM UK. Local groups were springing up overnight like mushrooms. They can't be dismissed as a travelling rent-a-mob. Not rabble-rousing, but working out practicable alternatives. A year later, the hard-nosed *Economist* reported:

> In the past 18 months, anti-roads protesters have scored an unprecedented string of successes. A new Thames crossing has been dropped because it would have ruined Oxleas Wood, a historic clump of trees. Local anger has forced plans for a bypass around Hereford back to the drawing board. Two new link roads to the M62 have been shelved. The Department of Transport is now considering an expensive tunnel under the scenic Devil's Punchbowl in Surrey rather than a road across it.
>
> The anti-roads lobby is growing in size and in diversity. ... ALARM UK, an umbrella organisation for angry locals, has recently brought together about 250 groups from around the country. And in December, MPs set up the first Tory backbench anti-roads group. ... At public enquiries, retired brigadiers take the same platform as New Age travellers. ...
>
> Lobby groups are proposing coherent alternatives... Road-pricing, special lanes for cars with more than one occupant, and encouraging commuters to travel off-peak. Friends of the Earth argues that investment in rail brings greater economic benefits. Increased rail travel, it says, will free the roads for freight. New rail lines, it claims, help to regenerate inner city areas, whereas new roads suck economic activity into the countryside.
>
> The protesters are becoming politically cannier. Once, Friends of the Earth would lobby ministers and MPs privately. Now, it also deploys the undeniable powers of mass protest. ... Groups are honing their media skills.

Media skills have meant skills in penetrating the media which others control. All sorts of moving spirits, outside the establishment and within it, worm their way through the corridors of power and entice the media workers out to see for themselves what is going on.

People power

The *showing* that the protesters were making, in the flesh and on the media, had sufficiently *shown up* the government's road policies to bring about the scrapping of the Oxleas Wood ring-road and the widening of the M25, with well over a third of the Government's Roads Programme scrapped indefinitely, only 2 out of 22 new road schemes begun in 1994, and roadbuilding almost at a standstill in 1995. To cap it all, Emma Must was named as one of six of the world's *environmental heroes*, and awarded £47,000 from the Goldman Environmental Foundation in San Francisco.

"It's been a whirlwind couple of years, really. Not what I expected to be doing. What I found out was that, if you want to change something, you can. It just requires two or three other people with a similar burning desire and you've got a nucleus which is capable of doing anything. You may not change the first thing you set out to change. (The bulldozers won on Twyford Down). But the change may happen further down the line. What I've learned is the power of people when they operate together. The immense strength that you have in a group of people all wanting to do things to effect that change.

I don't think committees are the way to do things. Very often, they can be restrictive rather than helpful. Working groups seem to be more effective. Corridor alliances (like SCAR — South Coast Against Roadbuilding) have so far been just wonderful. The corridor is a chain of local groups, each opposing one section of a much larger road scheme. They've operated not by having fixed Chairs and committees, but by setting up working groups when something needs to be done — organising stunts, making traffic surveys, getting out a Report — moving the meetings along the corridors, hosted by different groups each time, operating by consensus.

They are quite loose structures which you might think would be very fragile, but in fact they're extraordinarily strong because so many people are involved in them. They resist take-over bids. Everyone puts in a lot of effort and they're buggered if they're going to let someone come in and run it for them. They resist people trying to use them for their own ends or imposing their own agendas. But if anyone wants to take a back seat for a while, there are always others to take their place."

Q 'And when the going gets almost too hard?'

"I suppose my worst experience of working with other people was what happened after Twyford Down as we tried to set up a group to network direct action on roads nationally.

We'd put our all into trying to stop this road, and didn't manage to do it. Had about 4 hours' sleep a night for about a year. We were exhausted, half of us had been in prison, we were being sued for £1.9 million, we'd been followed by private detectives and security guards, there were Special Branch files on us, our phones were tapped, we were absolutely knackered. And this small group was being careless of itself. Too few people trying to do too much. We weren't taking enough care of each other, and things were quite rocky for a while. There were a few bust-ups, various individuals having to leave and maybe come back later."

Second wind

But the moving spirits are in their turn sustained by the people they got moving in the first place.

"The basic strength was still the local campaign groups. It didn't matter what happened to those of us who were trying to push things nationally. Those groups were going to survive anyway."

Up among west Yorkshire's hilltop farms and industrial towns, the most active campaigners have been long-term unemployed, retired people and those made prematurely redundant by factory closures. They linked up and put paid to a threatened motorway link (M1-M62) along the Calder Valley, with a 20,000-signature petition backed up by a 6,000-household survey which showed that only 6% were in favour.

"One of my favourite examples is the Bursledon Rights of Way and Amenities Preservation Group from near Southampton. They were rather respectable local worthies, all of them retired, all with grey hair. According to their chairwoman, they'd traditionally spent their time planting azaleas and dredging the village pond. Then they joined SCAR and they had a candlelit vigil at the local railway station at six in the morning and handed out leaflets to commuters, arguing for a switch in resources from road to rail. And they began making banners and lighting bonfires with other groups in SCAR — all along the South Coast to ward off the second Armada — the invasion of the Road-builders."

Opposition: proposition

The keys to ALARM UK's success so far have been this decentralising to local groups, coupled with working alliances with national bodies — Transport 2000, Friends of the Earth, Greenpeace, the Rail Unions, and rail users' groups, Nature Conservation, WorldWide Fund for Nature, the Royal Society for the Protection of Birds, the National Trust. Some more cautious than others about direct action, but all helping to gather information, analyze, publicise, and get there first to negotiate with the authorities on the basis of practical, expertly researched, alternative schemes.

"You eventually get through to people — in the local councils, people in quite senior government positions, the junior Minister even, and a very senior member of British Rail offering his services openly and voluntarily. People in positions of power within the established structures actually assisting the grassroots groups, and other experts working on our ideas to get them into a form where they are implementable. What I find most exciting is that we have created this climate; and we're beginning to feel that we're pushing at an open door.'

Moving spirits like Chrissie Maher and Emma Must learned how to prise doors open with nothing more than their passions, to begin with. It communicates. And the media grapevine spreads it far and wide.

Their starting points may be the kitchen table (for ALARM
UK), backed up by computer-wise young volunteers co-ordi-
nating their direct action on their bulletin boards, making waves.
In the woods threatened by the Newbury By Pass the protesters'
tree houses are linked by CB radio and mobile phones via their
own P.R. office to the world's media.

☆　☆　☆

Chrissie and co. have moved a few mountains of gobbledegook from her farmhouse kitchen in New Mills. They're not in the least isolated, although in
America, the Colorado Centre for the New West talks about Lone Eagles, the self-
propelled professionals who stay home and do everything at arm's length. Chrissie
doesn't belong to the professional class, and she's used to teamwork, so her eyrie
is usually pretty crowded. But each member of the team can be in daily contact
with everyone they need to know. Well, almost everyone: they nipped over
recently to seek a face-to-face encounter with US Vice-President Al Gore, and are
still in pursuit. They want to sort out with him how his $2 billion scheme for the
Information Superhighway could become a through route for Plain English.

The telecottage

What do Chrissie and co. want from the Information Superhighway that
they haven't got already?

Their computer can sort out and store their data, their takings, their mail-
shots. It can shift their money around electronically without the need to handle
a bank note or write a cheque. Their fax machine can put them in touch with
whoever they want to impress. Their phone line links them to the global market,
and their information bank can tell them where to look.

They can pursue a home lifestyle — like two or three million others in the
UK, part-time or full-time, self-employed or subject to a distant employer. It's
partly a throwback to the life that the farmer's wife might once have had when
Chrissie's living room was her farmhouse kitchen. It probably had a desk to do
her accounts, and the farmer's wife was in charge of the chickens as well as the
children and the housekeeping.

In the telecottage, as they call it, there's no need for
commuting apart from an occasional trip to the local
market. Flexitime suits the job and the time of the year.

It doesn't suit everyone. The graph for home-working
started to climb steeply in 1988 as the recession threw people out of permanent
office-based jobs. Many solitary workers have had to set up shop from scratch,
without much going for them. There are no more human contacts at the coffee
break. Being out of touch with others in the same situation makes people dependent on the buyer of their services who may save anything up to £3,000 of office

overheads per employee, and finds it pays to shop around for cut-price deals with outworkers, short-term.

But Chrissie's lot are different. They're used to rubbing ideas together in a friendly way and they have a track record for doing what nobody else so far has got round to doing so well. So they are into *the nice world market*, a growth market, at the end of their telephone.

The same goes for pressure groups like ALARM UK — piecing together information on environmentally hostile road planning, working out environment-friendlier alternatives.

The moment you begin to investigate alternatives, the creative juices begin to work. The boundaries of convention no longer hem you in. Unexpected possibilities are revealed. Computers are pedigree retrievers, off in a flash to fetch what you are after. But you can never be quite sure what else they might bring back to lay at your feet.

Free riders

The word, good or bad, gets around. The Information Highway will spread it further and faster, and as they get wise to the system, people like Emma and Chrissie can, if they choose, use it to wake people up and spur them on. They can give an upbeat slant to events, and combat narrow-mindedness and hostility. They can be antibodies resisting infection, like the *Bugle* challenging its readers to see the gypsies they hated in a different light.

Sometimes people stop their ears because, as Chrissie puts it, *they can't be bothered.* But nowadays, when established views seem fly-blown, almost anything fresh has the edge. New networks take shape. Desktop publishing is already streamlining the production of fanzines celebrating the worship of soccer heroes. The desktop may be based in anyone's back room, producing news and views on paper, to be distributed just as Chrissie and co. got out the Tuebrook Bugle, or as Emma Must tells the world about threatening road plans. It won't be long before such networks go electronic. Whether the results circulate on paper or on disk, they can reach their target audience in a matter of hours.

The basic methods of communication have been around for a long time. The pioneer workers in telephone, telegraph, sound recordings, films and video have always been Do-It-Yourselfers possessed by the possibilities of the medium, experimenting in all directions, dimly aware that they were on to something momentous.

Their work gets taken over by the media moguls, busily assembling and controlling the means of distribution, staking out their own Tom Tiddlers' Ground, doing in their own field what Rockefeller did in the oil industry (more about him later). So access to parts of the Information Highway is likely to become restricted.

Already Rupert Murdoch has acquired a monopoly on the decoder that sits on top of the TV and is needed to access satellite television. As big businesses scoop up rights on information or entertainment they will be able to make us pay to get it.

Meanwhile the users, rather than the commercial providers, are running the show. Anyone who can afford a modem as well as a computer, and who has learned to drive, will have free range to put out, or take in, whatever they choose.

Overnight, almost, the moving spirits are reaching out to the rest of the world. And the rest of the world, good, bad and indifferent, is on the line back to them.

The technology is flexible. It gets through to people via the media networks and the Internet; by telephone trees and fax. It responds to a fingertip touch, and **almost anyone can have their finger on the button.**

Power lines

Chrissie's telephone line will shortly change from copper wire to gossamer-thin *optic fibre*, researched initially by British scientists but about to be developed with Al Gore's $2 billion research programme over the next five years.

The fibre line can stretch from end to end of any country, and pass under the sea to link every nation. It can carry encyclopaedic information almost instantly in either direction. The multinational cable and phone corporations who want the contracts to build the network are likely to charge anything from $100 billion to $400 billion for the job. Once the network is installed, the actual cost of operating it is next to nothing.

An alternative to the fibre network is also in prospect. Thin air. A satellite system based on the redeployment of 840 small satellites left idle from the Star Wars. Bill Gates, who built Microsoft from nil to £4 billion in ten years, is teaming up with Craig McCaw to spend $9 billion on developing a system which it is claimed would *include all the world's citizens and put ... a Bedouin in touch with his cousin in Los Angeles.*

These schemes are, as they say, in the pipeline. Estimates on cost and completion dates may be even wider of the mark than those for the Channel Tunnel. But sooner or later, for better or worse, they will be with us, as we work at home, or move around, mobile phone pack at the ready.

❖   ❖   ❖

The network is a source of power which no-one has yet learned to tap with maximum effect. But a lot of people are beginning to find out just how far they might be able to go.

Already, there is the INTERNET: fully-functioning, a global network of computer networks that grew out of the cold war links made in 1969 between the Pentagon and American research institutions. The idea was to disperse the suppliers of research information so that there was no central point which a nuclear attack could take out and destroy the system.

For a few pounds a month, almost anyone can join. You tap into the *World Wide Web* via a regional service centre and can learn to track down anything, anywhere, that is publicly available on computer disk. A robot doctor's diagnosis. Shakespeare's plays. A shopping catalogue. The Watergate documents disclosed under the US Freedom of Information Act. The Dead Sea Scrolls. The Trans-Siberian railway timetable. News pooling groups on almost every subject you can think of. Computer games. The lot.

All sorts of interaction can develop. There are shoulders to lean on for those who are victims, under stress, alone. There are shared jokes, sidelong looks at what is going on inside and outside the world of technology. There is ample room for special interests — soccer enthusiasts, weather experts, cancer victims, birdwatchers, film buffs, the gun lobby.

Getting through

People are thirsty for information, and no-one has yet found how to stop them drinking when they get the chance that technology can offer. That goes back to the first European printing technology, used by William Tyndall to put his English translation of the Bible within reach of *the boy behind the plough*. The Establishment disliked the idea, seized copies and burned them, and eventually burned Tyndall too. But they could not get complete control. So all their efforts at censorship eventually failed.

The range of technology available now is much greater. It includes the audiotape recordings which brought exiled Ayatollah Khomeini to power in Iran. Hardly anyone knew who he was or how he wanted to challenge the powers-that-be. But there were enough supporters to get audio cassettes of his recorded sermons, and to distribute them secretly so that they were available under the counter in every city street.

Official channels can be by-passed. Burma's elected leader, Aung San Suu Kyi, displaced and restricted by a military junta, has been able to appeal direct to the July 1996 meeting of the European Parliament in Strasbourg by a videotaped interview smuggled out of the country earlier in the month.

Governments can exclude anything they dislike from the screens they themselves control, as happened in South Africa for three generations, and as still happens in China now. They can attempt to halt the flow of anti-government propaganda from outside by banning satellite dishes, as happened in Iran, Saudi Arabia and Malaysia. Transmission by satellite costs a lot, and only a well-heeled opposition can afford it. But efforts to block the message may be short-lived, as the size of satellite dishes begins to shrink. Already, a satellite dish the size of a wrist-watch is in prospect. When that happens, the technology will outflank the censors.

You can receive what anyone likes to throw at you, including a constant flow of irrelevant rubbish. There is a lot that is entertaining, informative, a shot in the arm. (Bill Gates has bought up the rights for electronic reproduction of a substantial chunk of the world's art.) And, seeping in here and there, relatively unimportant as yet, there are the carriers of infection

Shit hits the fan

In the spring of 1994, someone discovered that the Web was allowing child abusers access to an illicit porno video library service organised by one enterprising researcher and concealed within the Metallurgy Department at Birmingham University. Meanwhile, an American bulletin board was offering 12 sets of porno pics a day. (You pay to get the code, and it's all perfectly legal). Neo-Nazis in Germany and the USA were circulating times and places of meetings, racist propaganda, the addresses of opponents and details of how to make a bomb. In 1995, the Oklahoma massacre threw a lurid light on the networking of the right-wing militia and the gun lobby. How many such poisons are circulating in the system right now is anyone's guess.

✧ ✧ ✧

The flow of information through the Web is said to be doubling every year. In 1995 it had 30 million users in more than 50 countries. One estimate put it up to 35 million, with more than a million logging on to the network every month.

So what use will all that be to the likes of Chrissie? The group can set the computer to shop around, fishing for facts in every one of the world's great libraries, during the course of one afternoon. They might land choice items of gobbledegook to feed the media; more important — track down the sources of gobbledegook: the government officials, the business management pundits, the dodgy manufacturers who window-dress to camouflage the facts.

Locate the sources of pollution: weasel words, industrial effluents, planning blight, exhaust emissions, nuclear waste — and then alert others to the need to clean them up. Fax the findings singly, or set up a mini-network with others scattered round the globe who have a common interest and can share their results.

They can have discussions with each other via the screens on the best way to get the message across — tapping out *bulletin board* ideas, gossip, financial information; listing contact points and target areas — all for the price of a quick phone call.

It's a two-way network, outsiders getting through to people whom their governments have tried to quarantine; insiders telling the world what is happening.

Telling the world

As a successful journalist, novelist, writer of children's books and top-rated comedy sitcom writer for Nigerian TV, Ken Saro-Wiwa knew a lot about communications networks. Throughout his adult life he had been concerned about the treatment of his own people, the Ogonis, living in the oil rich Niger Delta. Although Ogoni land had produced $30 billions of oil revenue over the thirty-five years since Anglo-Dutch Shell began to exploit the oil field, precious little of the profits went back to the people themselves. Their own living standards have stayed below the national average whilst (According to the European Parliament Resolution on Human Rights, 1995) they *have experienced an ecological nightmare: spills, pipelines driven through farms and villages, brutal suppression of any protest.*

In 1990, he formed and led a non-violent protest — the Movement for the Survival of the Ogoni People, demanding civil rights and a better economic deal.

On *Ogoni Day*, January 4 1993, 300,000 people out of a population of just over half a million took part in peaceful village marches throughout Ogoni land. The military government responded by covert attacks — 750 dead and 30,000 homeless — followed in 1994 by a campaign *to restore order,* imprisoning Saro-Wiwa without access to lawyers for nine months, and then putting him on trial on a trumped-up murder charge, and finally hanging him with eight other Ogoni leaders in November 1995. Nineteen others have been put on trial by the same Army-dominated kangaroo court. Yet in spite of this destruction of most of the Ogoni leadership, and the efforts of army and police to suppress the protest movement, Ogoni Day January 1996 brought people out on the streets of the state capital and the village squares to show their continuing support.

Inside Nigeria, news has been censored. But, in the words of Nigeria's Nobel Laureate, Wole Soyinka,

> "In spite of all the obstacles, in spite of the entire might of the Nigerian military, and in spite of their land being turned into a militarised zone from which all prying eyes are banned, the Ogoni people under Ken Saro-Wiwa's leadership have managed to sustain the struggle and to present their case before the conscience of the world. … (This is) the first organised movement in the oil-producing areas in Nigeria to demand reparations for destroyed natural resources. … What Ken Saro-Wiwa has done has been to mobilise them in a way that has never been done before."

The pollution and the protests against it have been videoed, and the cassettes smuggled out to find their way onto the world's media. Amnesty made Saro-Wiwa a Prisoner of Conscience, two awards (the Swedish Right

Livelihood, and in the USA the Goldman Foundation Environmental Hero award) have been widely publicised and a worldwide campaign has been launched on the Internet. Media teams arrived to cover events on the spot. In his last months Ken Saro-Wiwa managed to revise his diary account of events, and smuggle it out, a few pages at a time, to be transferred to computer disc and sent secretly to London for publication.[1] It was edited, printed and published within a couple of weeks, even as the death sentence was being carried out.

In spite of the military crackdown the Movement set going by this moving spirit has taken on an international life of its own.

Two weeks in Holloway jail for Emma Must doesn't compare with Ken Saro-Wiwa's martyrdom; any more than the ravaging of the Ogoni countryside by the international oil industry compares with the impact of motor traffic on English towns and villages. **But the determination that moving spirits find they possess moves onlookers to become participants, and makes their participation news. And the news spreads on electronic wings.**

Guerrilla army

In Mexico, Rafael Sebastian Guillen Vicente, aka Subcomandante Marcos, the *hi-tech Robin Hood,* is a University lecturer with a first degree in communication science. He took his computer with him into the Lacondona jungle and began building a guerrilla army of landless Mayan Indians. In 1994, he began to confront an ailing government that still can't catch up with him.

Everyone else knows what's it's all about, because over the last few years, Marcos and his Zapatista Movement have used the Internet to tell the world about the 66% of the country's population who live below the poverty line, and the threat to their future posed by American agribusiness.

In 1995, the *Guardian* carried a report that when Mexican police raided Zapatista safe-houses, *more floppy disks were captured than guns.* But the information campaigning is succeeding. Two years running, in Mexico City itself, there have been 100,000-strong demonstrations in support of the Zapatista rising, chanting *We are all Marcoses.* Their placards say, *MARCOS IS THE PEOPLE.* Early in 1996, Comandante Marcos was invited to the government's mediation commission, with his arrest warrant on terrorism charges suspended and the army and police ordered to protect him; so that in his words *The path of dialogue should remain the only possible way of resolving the war.*

Not just one moving spirit, but many.

---

1 *A Month and a Day.* Ken Saro-Wiwa. Penguin Books, 1995.

Staying power

The Internet is there for almost anyone to use. Like the jungle, it is neutral, but it offers the moving spirits the means to reach out beyond the frontiers of their own neighbourhood and to tap into the feelings of others like themselves. **To share in what Chrissie calls** *the passion*.

That passion is what keeps the moving spirits going. Their commitment begins to rub off on the rest of us. So we sign petitions, turn out in support. So far, so good. But that could leave the moving spirits on their own again, once the first flush of enthusiasm fades.

The feeling of inertia which Chrissie calls *apathy* **can overtake us unless there's something solid, practical, to get our hands on.**

There are other kinds of motive power which figure in later chapters. But the first, usually quite unspectacular, is **the urge to do your own thing, better.**

The DIY instinct.

4 Just the job

The birth of DIY in the 1950s was a surprise all round. It caught the commercial people unawares.

The surprise began with the introduction of the Wolf Cub, the first of the electric power drills to meet the needs of the amateur enthusiast. Its makers had picked up the German idea of a compact electrical hand tool, and when I met the Managing Director of the British firm he explained that they had thought there might be a modest market in Australia, selling to homesteaders in the outback. No-one was likely to want such tools in the UK, so they were to be for export only.

But no longer: I was recording the interview with him in the firm's canteen, which was being hurriedly converted in order to extend the production area so as to cope with the spiralling demand — not from Australia but from the home-steaders of Essex and Manchester and the Scottish Highlands and the West Country.

I went on to see the editor-in-chief of the Newnes publishing group which specialised in magazines for the home hobbyist — *Practical Wireless, Practical Gardener*, that sort of thing. He told me that his Board had decided there might be a little profit to be had from a new publication that dealt with the interests of what were becoming known as *Do-It-Yourselfers*. After the firm's experts had researched the market, it seemed there was a good case for a steady circulation of around thirty thousand. As usual, the firm launched its new periodical with a generous print run to catch everyone's eye on the bookstalls. The print order of eighty thousand sold out on the day of publication and they went on reprinting during the next week, settling down to a regular print order in hundred thousands. Before long other magazines started up and there was a total monthly circulation of two million.

Meanwhile all sorts of teenagers were going in search of tea chests and thrumming on wash boards with their mother's thimbles, setting up their own skiffle groups. Others were into cycle speedway. Not motorbikes. People in those days hadn't the money, so they fell back on pedal power. Pedal cycle speedways took shape on bombsites all over the country, with an unassumingly sexist division of labour between dads who fixed up starting gates and helped to bank the course, and mums and sisters who knitted scarves and bobble hats in the sporting colours of the rival teams. Within a year of the craze beginning there was a rough and ready pedal cycle speedway league exchanging visits with teams from the continent.

The Wolf Cub tools and their costlier and only slightly more reliable successors, were an answer to the handymen, and soon the handywomen, who were moving into their first homes, in the desperate housing shortage after World War Two, partitioning off the in-laws, converting sheds and garages, pushing out extensions, liberating attics. But it did not stop there.

DIY is something people like turning their hand to even when it is no longer a question of homesteading.

What is common to skiffle and pedal cyclist speedway then, and the sunburst of pop groups in the seventies, break-dancers in the eighties, and rappers now? Like DIY, **they let loose the old Adam in us and maybe the older, creative Eve, the mother of us all, unstoppably determined to do our own thing.**

Lifestyles

The kind of thing we take for granted as worth doing seems to have been changing. In the 1990s, studies in the US show as you would expect that the almighty dollar matters most to people at the bottom of the pile, desperate to make ends meet. But above the poverty level the survey showed that what makes people feel good is not money, but friendship, a loving family, enjoyable spare time — and work itself. Robert Lane reported that the University of Michigan survey revealed that people enjoyed work more than watching TV. The only things that ranked higher were talking to their friends and playing with their children.

For a long time people have been changing their lifestyles to suit such preferences. In 1979, a generation after the DIY craze first caught on, a Norwegian professor, Johan Galtung, working for the UN, had found that in many western countries people were tending to opt out of the rat race in favour of work which gave them more time. For what? — for DIY, and family and friends and mutual help among neighbours. Harford Thomas, commenting in his *Guardian* column, said:

> It is a social change which is most noticeable among young people in the 'over-developed' countries of northern Europe and north America. It is happening almost unnoticed by governments ... it could make a nonsense of the Thatcher theory of monetary incentives. ... the dynamic behind it will be the recognition that today's dominant lifestyle is no longer rational or workable.

✧ ✧ ✧

I cut out these comments and carried them around with me during the early years of Mrs Thatcher's reign. They came in handy when I met Harford Thomas and about a hundred other experts whom the Town and Country Planning Association brought together in a series of workshop sessions to discuss whether there ought to be another Garden City.

The Town and Country Planning Association was all in favour of community planning, and a lifestyle freed from the rat race. Its founder, Ebeneezer Howard had wheeled and dealt with the authorities to acquire land at the turn of the century first in Letchworth and then in Welwyn. By some very fast talking he managed to attract investors who allowed a team of planning experts to design each new city from scratch, and then to welcome prospective inhabitants in.

Top-down?

For his time this was a fine piece of creative thinking. It meant seeing the needs and the possibilities of a city as one whole, separating factories from homes, giving people elbow room and a breath of fresh air. But he and his collaborator Francis Osborn ruled from the top down, as *vigilant managers*. They had no patience with the excesses of do-it-yourself:

sheds, fowl houses, rabbit pens, amateur designed porches, unauthorised trellises etc. require constant vigilance. They spread like a rash and once established are difficult to clean out.

Prospective residents were expected to accept what had been provided for them; and on the whole, they did.

So there we were, half a century later, meeting periodically over two years, to decide whether that way of going about things still applied. Did the top-down approach really work any more? And was planning best done on the scale of a city? Some of us, including the Chief Planner for the Telford New Town Development Corporation, thought otherwise. We argued that planning cities was all very well when it came to working out how to get round them or through them and where to put the factories or shops. But the people coming to live in them deserved something a bit more — what was the word? — *neighbourly*. What's more it ought to be a mixture with opportunities to work at home, or near it — rabbits and chickens, a craft workshop, and all. And the homes and the workshops could be *self-built*.

This view won through and the Telford Chief Planner thought that a patch of land, on Lightmoor, twenty two and a half acres to begin with, might be available to try these notions out.

Some of us tramped over the site with him and with a member of the Development Corporation Board. The site was just down the road from Coalbrookdale, where Abram Darby had built his family fortunes round hard graft and wrought iron and ushered in the Industrial Revolution. All that was left was rough country, and the crumbling embankment of the steam railway which used to freight the iron ore, the coal, the bricks and the tiles that made a living for the people who once lived there.

On the edge was a derelict building, the Poplars. On the 1850 maps it was shown as a *house and shop* serving a thriving community working mostly for themselves in brick works, foundries, nail making, family sized mine shafts, raising livestock and vegetables — now all vanished but for the mounds of pit spoil.

Now the land lay empty. The commercial developers passed it by and that helped us persuade the Corporation that they could do worse than let someone else have a go. They said,

"If you can get the people, and the money, we might, just possibly, lease it to you on affordable terms."

Bottom-up

On January 1 1984 I found myself committed to set up a project for a self-built community, with no money, no people and no firm promise of the land. I talked about a **belt-and-braces economy**. People coming together to build, literally, their own neighbourhood, and hopefully their livelihoods as well, was a bit of novelty. Especially with the media. Our slogan, *A computer in the kitchen and a pig in the back yard*, caught on. The *Sunday Times* wrote us up with a cartoon of the pigs operating the computers in the kitchen. Other nationals, and the BBC and the local press gave us a kind of Silly Season space. I went everywhere in the neighbourhood to ask local people what they thought of the idea, and persuade them to wander over the site.

Weekend after weekend I sat on a wall beside the Poplars to meet all comers. People came from near and far and wanted to meet the committee and study the plan. I explained that as yet there was no committee, and no plan. I asked everyone to look around, case the joint, and size each other up.

We built a rough 3D model of the site with moveable wooden houses and a bootlace for an access road. Prospective residents sorted out the possibilities, with one or two experts from the Corporation on hand to consult. At one point we took the model onto the middle of the field and people strung out along the contours to see where the access road might go, and what the view would be if they got the plot they wanted.

There was a lot of choosing, but nothing sure. The Nationwide Building Society, and later the Halifax, might, or again might not lend the money. The Development Corporation might have other plans for the land. The people who came and went and returned again dared not commit themselves without something hard and fast and down on paper.

One-off

After nearly twelve months one couple, cooped up with a family of four in a tiny council house, decided to break the log-jam.

"We hadn't got any front garden at all. We had a patch called a back garden so tiny that you walked out your back door and you could practically put your arms out and touch your next-door neighbour. It was that close."

There was no space for Brenda Cooksey to raise the livestock she wanted or for her husband Dave, a bricklayer seasonally unemployed, to grow his vegetables.

"We had to travel two miles down to Horsehay to milk the goats we had, twice a day. We spent an awful lot of time on the allotment, but you couldn't leave your spade or your fork on the site because of vandalism, and then you had a good twenty-minute walk, pushing a wheelbarrow-load of vegetables down the main road.

*The talking about Lightmoor seemed to go on for months. We went through a bad patch. And I got this panic within myself that **it's got to work, it's got to work**. Not just for myself, but there was something about the idea that it had got to work. One particular day I'd been really depressed, a panic sort of depression. And Dave came home, walked through the door and I said 'Do you want it or don't you? Are you willing to chance it?' He said 'Yes, I want it as much as you' and I said 'Right'."*

So they bought a second-hand caravan for £200, dumped half their furniture in my lodgings, and in the teeth of winter moved onto the edge of the site.

"On the coldest day of the year! — the best day to pick to move! It has been hard graft living in the caravan. It took us, oh, four or five months to get used to it. With four of the children and no modern conveniences! We had a lot of trouble with condensation, everything went mouldy, but I'd got my animals near to me, and when I opened the caravan door, I was outside, but really outside, nobody looking at me through their front window. I felt at home."

We were still negotiating for the site and had no legal title. But the Corporation turned a blind eye. The first building to go up on the site, long before we had money or title to the land, was Brenda's livestock shed and we all helped to build its foundations. Dave planted his fruit trees, built a chicken shed and a rabbit hutch, began to get the ground dug up by his pigs, and marked out the vegetable plot. Brenda tended her goats, and brewed innumerable cups of tea for everyone who came to see.

For another year, whilst endless discussions went on and the paperwork went to and fro between the government, the Development Corporation, the District Council, the Building Society, and the lawyers, the livestock sheds were all there was to show.

But the Cookseys were there, in their caravan, confronting the talkers with a bit of reality. Others in the group began to make up their minds. Gerwyn Lewis was a craft teacher who had set his heart on building his own house. On their first visit, his wife June was undecided.

"I thought the Cookseys were a very nice couple living in very difficult circumstances. It was a cold wet night for a start, and they were in a sort of gaslight, with a black and white television crackling off what I think was a car battery. I suppose I was just entrenched in the old ways and had forged a little niche for myself and the thought of uprooting and starting in this rather strange project was a bit daunting."

June decided to give herself time to think about it. Without saying a word to Gerwyn, she sneaked off to explore the rest of the site for herself and spent four weeks digging out local maps and plans from the Development Corporation and a file full of background information. One Sunday evening the conversation turned round to Gerwyn's dream of building their own house. No mention of Lightmoor. So Gerwyn said *'Obviously there are some subjects in this house which are absolutely taboo'. 'Like what?' 'Well, Lightmoor.' 'Really?' 'Well, have you got their telephone number?' 'Might have it somewhere'.* So she went upstairs and got this rather large file with all the Lightmoor information and placed it in front of him along with the date of the next business meeting of the group. And he said *'You crafty little bugger, after fifteen years of being married you can still amaze me'.* And from then on, they were in.

By the spring of 1985 a core group of eight families were willing to sign away their future. Lightmoor New Community Ltd was registered, with approvals by  the local authorities and the TCPA. Nine more months of negotiation ending in a Christmas party that brought everyone together, with all sorts and sizes of children, largely unknown to each other, whose existence had up to now seemed almost incidental. And then, on New Year's Day 1986 the building society money came through.

Getting down to it

We all got to work, first to build an access road, then to dig deep to create the Black Hole to receive the sewage treatment plant. The soil was deceptively soft on top, but nine inches down we found impacted clinker from an old foundry which took Kango hammers to break up. We man-and-woman-handled the enormous septic tank and the treatment tank to the edge of the hole, gingerly lowered them into position, put back the surface soil and allowed the grass to grow back. Then we got on with digging the drains — trenches seven or eight feet down for most of the way across the site.

"I enjoyed doing it somehow. I enjoyed doing all of it. Often frustrated but you can't go through all this bad weather, swamps, mud and freezing snow, and not rub off on one another."

When newcomers turned up they usually met most of us at the bottom of the trench. One local couple had heard about the project and dropped in to get some copy for a magazine article.

"Everyone was working, we were introduced, one by one, and they each went on with what they were doing. We thought this obviously isn't the kind of place where everyone stops and has a chat and reads you a book about the project. So we hoped we wouldn't get in the way and we started barrowing gravel."

They applied to join and were accepted.

The group had grown to thirteen families and one eligible bachelor. Everyone, women as well as men, got into the act. Besides the wheelbarrows there was a second-hand tractor and something called a powerfab and looking like a small sci-fi space vehicle, that could be used to excavate a trench for water pipes and the power cable. Wives and daughters rode the powerfab like a bucking bronco. Once the road and the sewage system were out of the way and the mortgage monies were coming through, each family could get on with its house building, occasionally making use of each other's special skills. For the most part they were at best rudimentary DIY skills, practised on the job, and gradually improving.

Local people dropped in to see how the work progressed. With the road and the sewage system completed, people could build at their own pace, and largely to their own design. There were brick bungalows and timber frame houses, with a great deal of insulation and careful positioning to make the most of the sun. There was no universal bulldozing, trees were preserved, and the plots were beginning to yield vegetables and nourish livestock even whilst the building went on.

Free range

The site was full of children, twenty or so, who saw it as the perfect adventure playground. To outsiders that seemed a dangerous situation — deep trenches, machinery, amateurs at work. But most children came from places where you could no longer play in the street because of the traffic, and you had to look out for yourself for fear of molesters. Free-ranging on the site they learned the basic do's and don'ts and everywhere they went they were within site of honorary aunts and uncles, able to tick them off if need be, without the prospect of a parent coming to tell them not to interfere.

The children made their own dens and hideouts.

"I was standing on the roof the other day. Our kids were playing in the dirt at the bottom and I shouted down 'What are you doing Bryn?' 'The foundations' he said. 'What's next?' 'Well were are putting in the joists, and then the rafters. I'm building a house and Mary is building a bungalow.' There they were mimicking almost at

your feet, in the time honoured tradition of children learning their skills from their own grown ups. All the kids have found a new freedom here. At holiday time they can disappear out of the door at nine o'clock in the morning and we literally don't see them until it's dusk. We don't have to set up situations to keep them amused or ferry them around to friends, or any of those artificial scenarios we got involved with in the past."

The kids have grown up along with the Lightmoor village itself, seeing their parents at work, not just in house building but also, part time or full time in developing their own livelihoods. Ideas catch on without the need to tell anyone what to do. Twelve year old Steve Cooksey borrowed his Dad's rotovator to dig up his own personal veg plot. Other children laid out little gardens of their own. During one summer, a ten year old, without any adult prompting, set up a summer school for the toddlers, the real thing, not a charade. A three days wonder with other children joining in to help.

Pressures

It wasn't all easy. There were horrendous meetings to reconcile conflicting interests. But decisions couldn't be dodged.

"Each individual family and each individual person is experiencing a new way of basic living which has put pressure on them. That causes tension within the person them- selves, therefore within that particular family. So if there is anything that is causing friction in the group, things can explode. But you're in a situation where you have to see the other person's point of view because we have to reach decisions that are not going to upset people. So I think it has made me more concerned about other people's wishes, perhaps more considerate, you might say a better neighbour."

The Cookseys' next-door neighbours surprised themselves.

"I still can't believe it. I didn't realise I had it in me to do the things I do here at Lightmoor. We had to pioneer, living in a very small caravan while we built. All my married life it has always been an electric fire or a gas fire, all nice and clean, and there was me going for buckets of coal, and going out to clean the Portaloo outside. I had such a comfortable life in the past but in fact it has done me good to do this pioneering. It gives me a feeling of well-being. We have just grown very fond of all the people who are building here. We are all different, even racially. We are all from different backgrounds and different age groups — students up to middle-aged people and even grandparents. And I think that is the magic, the magic of Lightmoor."

The youngest plot holder in the scheme, at twenty-five, was the last to join and had a fresh view of everyone else. He liked what he saw:

"It wasn't just high idealistic people. That was one of the things that made me decide to come down here. Because it was ordinary people who you might meet in the street."

Ordinary people confronting an extraordinary range of possibilities, without being quite sure what they were letting themselves in for.

One surprise was the National Award delivered by the Prince of Wales, for the *outstanding community enterprise of the year,* in the scheme sponsored by *The Times* and the *Royal Institute of British Architects.* For a year or two everyone felt they were living in a goldfish bowl, featured by the media, quizzed by other organisations at home and abroad wanting to see how they did it. Two years after the award the Prince turned up with his entourage which we managed as tactfully as possible to sidetrack so that he could get round the houses without fuss. He overstayed his schedule, and took up the cudgels with some of the bureaucrats to speed up the next phase of the development (it didn't make much difference, but we appreciated the effort).

After the dust had settled from the royal visit and the media follow ups, everyone on Lightmoor breathed a sigh of relief mingled with satisfaction, and settled down to enjoy the working neighbourhood they had created. The space earmarked for the village green got a few saplings planted, the bellmouth entry from the main road was — rather slowly — completed. But for a year or two most families were content to concentrate on their own homes and plots and workshops. Fixing up the inside of the house demanded another set of skills, but that still left time for trying out some livestock and getting the vegetable supply under way. And in the fullness of time another cluster of self built houses has gone up and is in occupation. More long drawn out negotiations are underway for project number three, catering especially for young singles and couples at risk.

A proper job

About this time Bill Forsythe's film *Local Hero* got its general distribution. There's a scene on the Scottish island which is being reconnoitred by a high powered young man from the American company which may decide to transform the place with an oil rig or two. The locals are chatting with the young man and they ask him what work he does. He explains that he is a research executive or some such and they say *Yes, and what else?* They can't get used to his reply that that's all he does.

"Here you have all sorts of things you need to be doing, like being the postie, and keeping some chickens, and cultivating the smallholding, with a bit of fishing thrown in, and whiles, playing in the local band."

All that adds up to a proper job, which makes the most of you.

Lightmoor people have something in common with those Scots. Some have conventional outside jobs, part time or full time, but that's only part of the work they do, and like doing.

Recently, having got the basics done on houses and plots, some have been exploring fresh worlds to conquer. There's the patch of marshland just over the hill which borders the housing area. It's part of the land they own and it's been waiting to make a fresh challenge. It will take time for everyone to draw breath and make this new assault, but it probably wont be long. There's no money in it, but it is likely to be rewarding.

Meanwhile several people went along to a big local meeting where they heard from the man himself, Michael Linton, who invented a scheme which he called LETS. He had gone to Canada to live, and hopefully to work. In Courtney, in the Commox Valley near Vancouver, he found a lot of people unemployed, with no way to use their skills. So he got a group together to set up something called the *Local Exchange Trading System*. A scheme of brilliant simplicity. Many people are used to doing an occasional favour for a friend or neighbour, as a straight swap. *I'll dig your garden if you teach me Spanish.* That's fine provided the Spanish speaker wants his garden done. Michael Linton introduced two new elements — the Register and the Directory of what's on offer. Anyone in the scheme can have their skills listed in directory; and perhaps products, too. The offers range far beyond what you might find in a conventional Job Centre or trade directory. *I'll bake your birthday cake … or repair your bike … or clean out your shed, … or do your accounts, … or hem your curtains … or provide you with genuinely new laid eggs.*

Swapping skills

That's already the sort of thing that Lightmoor villagers do for each other by mutual arrangement and there's usually some favour you can do eventually that will repay what someone has done for you. But Michael Linton's Registry puts a different slant on the situation. Anyone can contact someone in the Directory and bargain for the cost of the service or the product they provide. The cost is calculated in local units — in Canada it was *green dollars*. Since then as the idea has spread to New Zealand, Australia, US and now in Britain, it's in *Acorns*, or *Stones*, or *Trugs*, or *Creds*, or *Olivers* (that's in Bath), whatever name the local group cares to invent as its own equivalent to the conventional pound or dollar.

They don't have to pay anything on the nail. They don't even pay each other direct. The Register takes care of all the transactions and marks you up for how much you owe, or how much is owed to you, in respect of each deal you make. But the debt or the credit is with the System, not any particular individual. You can buy a lot of services or goods from people inside the scheme, and work off your debt to the system by selling what you have to offer to all sorts of people over what may be quite a long time, sometimes as much as a year. The system can take it because there's no money involved, no interest to pay — and no point in hoarding your credits. The only way they are any use to you is when you spend them on services and goods you buy from the others in the group.

LETS has caught on all over the place. In 1996, 15,000 people in 350 networks in the UK alone.

This success seems to be because people feel good to have something to offer that other people value; quite apart from being pleased to be able to shop around and get all sorts of little jobs done without too much hassle, and without paying an arm and a leg to a middle man. The Register is in the middle, and it charges a tiny percentage, marked up as a debit to each party for each transaction. Those proceeds are enough to pay someone to do the book keeping (as it used to be) and nowadays the computing, to keep everything up to date and all the information available to all concerned.

So now Lightmoor people are promoting their own scheme which runs on *Wrekins*, to suit people in and around Telford, and to please the Wrekin District Council which has helped with publicity to give the project a proper send-off. The Council has seen the point in an area of unemployment where there are a lot of skills going to waste, along with a great many bright ideas.

LETS have mushroomed. Are such schemes a passing fad like skiffle or pedal cycle speedways long ago? Or do they answer needs which most of us have, but may not recognise? The experts that people employ to tell them how to get the most out of their workers have figured it out. The workers will work better when they know what they're making, and have a hand in deciding how to make it.

Job satisfaction

But that's barely the half of it. The other half is what we do with the rest of our lives, and what that offers apart from being a couch potato. Increasingly, people work for money to buy time in which to work at things they want to do and for the most part these things can't be bought with conventional money.

There was one housing estate which badly needed a facelift, but the local Council was strapped for money. It scraped together enough to buy a lot of shrubs, but the Council workforce had been cut back and it could only be spared to plant two thirds of what was needed. The Council put the situation to local residents and got them to plant the remaining third.

… And it came to pass that there was a great drought in the land. And behold the shrubs that the Council planted withered away. Whereas those that the residents had taken on — they thrived…

Because the residents were not content to stand by, and they went out most evenings and watered them. No money involved, just satisfaction.

Job satisfaction.

✧ ✧ ✧

The second time I went into the Chernobyl contamination area in Byelorussia I met people who were building their own houses in a hurry. They looked like ordinary houses, but they were used only in the Spring and Summer months. Everyone came out on bicycles and buses and trains from the cramped flats they occupied in towns and cities. The new houses and the plots were called *dachas*, which comes from the Russian word for gift. It's been a tradition for fifty years or more for an outfit like a local library association, or a hospital, or a state-run factory to be given land by the State to dish out to its members, in small plots, at low cost or sometimes free. In Soviet days there were more rules about the size and shape of the house than there are nowadays, but the basic condition is the same: you get your patch of land and the opportunity to build on it — on condition that you use the land to grow things. If you don't it is taken away and given to somebody else.

In Byelorussia the Regional authorities in Gomel City handed over a lot more land in an increasingly desperate attempt to cope with a rising food shortage. So there, on a site where maybe fifty plots were being developed, the *developers* were individual families, with parents and kids dividing their time between building a house in which they could take refuge at weekends and over holiday periods, growing supplies to take back to overcrowded tenement flats and having fun improving and decorating their own houses to their own tastes. No money to spare for insulation to tide over the winter, or a *civilised* plumbing system, but precious time lavished on beautifully fretted, brightly painted door frames and window shutters.

The older ones mostly got on with the job without going outside the family for help. There might be an annual party with people clubbing together to provide the food and drink, but *community* had become rather a dirty word. It had become an excuse for top-down directives, that set out what the authorities decided was good for everybody. Being done good to gets to be exasperating.

Some of the younger ones, particularly young couples just cobbling a life together, seemed to have a different view. They went in for more parties, and they helped each other almost as an extension of the party-going, on the site. They did not call this *community co-operation*. They just did what comes naturally in a generation that is more used than any previous generation to getting around together without unnecessary fuss.

Creative drive

Given half a chance, people get a kick out of making something work for them, personally. Call it the **creative drive**. It's a part of human nature that you can't do without.

What you do with it — that depends...

✧ ✧ ✧

There was this lad, son of a small-time trader in lumber, salt and patent medicines. At seven years old, young John was using his pocket money to deal in turkeys for Thanksgiving. At sixteen, he was learning the commercial ropes as a shipping office clerk. Four years later, he set up as a trader on his own account, with a partner whom he bought out when he was twenty-six. By the time he was into his thirties, he could afford to buy a palatial home, with a fireplace of red glazed bricks to his own design, and woodland where he could plant his own trees.

That wasn't quite enough to satisfy the creative urge, so in his forties he bought a bigger place, up in the hills, where he

"directed the landscaping, contrived the views, and worked at laying out new roads himself, with stakes and flags, sometimes until he was exhausted."

Meanwhile, he was spending the rest of his time beavering away to become the richest man in America.

John D Rockefeller's riches flowed from the world's first big oil strike, on a poor farm in a hick township called Titusville (population 125) in north-west Pennsylvania.

He had nothing to do with actually locating the oil or with inventing the distillation process that turned it into kerosene, the universal lamp oil which burned brighter and sold cheaper than any other illuminant on the world market.

What John D understood better than anyone else was what he liked to call the Great Game: the financial numbers game calculated to a third decimal point. Others saw it as a racket run by *a gang of thieves.*

The trick was to work behind the scenes — *to expose as little surface as possible*, he said — making secret deals with the railroads for preferential freight charges at the expense of his competitors, monopolising the production of wooden barrels needed to store the oil, using front companies to buy into rival firms, *making a fist* at retailers to persuade them not to deal in rival products.

As a strict Baptist, Rockefeller doled out a percentage of his profits to charity. When these grew to millions, some people hesitated about accepting *tainted money*; he hired some expensive PR people who restyled his image, and all became well.

By his mid-forties, his Standard Oil Trust had survived exposure by a courageous investigative journalist, and a series of challenges in the law courts. Standard Oil had become part of the American scenery, too widespread to root out.

It was another kind of landscaping: *upstream*, controlling the sources of the crude oil; *mid-stream*, transporting it by rail, sea and pipeline; *downstream*, refining it, warehousing it, getting it onto the world market.

New technology — the invention of the incandescent light bulb — almost put paid to kerosene as a lamp fuel; but then its by-product, gasoline — which was being sold off at 2 cents a gallon or poured away as waste — suddenly came into its own with the development of the internal combustion engine.

Standard Oil became a multinational Great Power, overtaking rival interests in Russia, Venezuela and the Middle East. Then in Rockefeller's last years, getting together with the Middle Eastern interests in a Scottish castle to fix prices and carve up the market worldwide. (That was in 1928, just one year ahead of the stock market crash from which, surprise, surprise, the richly self-sufficient oil interests emerged almost unscathed).

Getting your own way

Rockefeller nearly always managed to get his way, to have things just so. He set a pattern which others have followed. The oil men have wheeled and dealt with each other to control the oil flow to suit their *corporate interests*: first as buyers on their own terms from the oil producing States. Then, when the Organisation of Oil Exporting Countries became stroppy and set its own terms, getting in cahoots with them to take a generous share of the difference between the oil production costs and the sale price. The Rockefeller estate (and charities) continue to benefit.

Since liquid oil and/or gas-fired electricity generation have become the world's prime energy resource for transportation and industrial power, the half-hidden influence of the oil tycoons has overturned governments, or underpinned them, and marked up the price of nearly everything we buy.

As President Roosevelt once said:

"The trouble is, you can't win an election without the oil sector, and you can't govern with it."

The richest oil corporations, the *Seven Sisters*, are known by name: two British — Shell and British Petroleum; five American — Exxon (the renamed Standard Oil of New Jersey), Standard Oil of California, Texaco, Gulf and Mobil. Those who run them prefer, like John D, to stay outside the limelight — *to expose as little surface as possible*.

What is it that drives them?

The money? Far more than anyone can manage to spend on themselves. Power? Certainly — but power to do things the way they want to do them. It's the same creative drive which motivates the graffiti artists and ram-raiders on Tyneside, and the self-builders of Lightmoor and Byelorussia. All of them, Do-

It-Yourselfers, sorting out what to do, getting kicks from seeing it done.

Rockefeller had to be creating something — a fireplace to his own design, a wooded landscape, country roads, a financial juggernaut which overrode or undermined every other enterprise or institution which stood in his way. Perhaps he never felt the difference.

But we do. So we shall not be too starry-eyed about it.

DIY is the adrenalin that gets us out of the rut. Where you head for from then on: that depends.

People who go it alone may make their mark as artists, writers, musicians, press barons, explorers, oil tycoons, gardeners, mathematicians, serial killers, philosophers, bomber commanders — you name it.

They may have to make use of other people, but fundamentally they are self-propelled. They do their own thing, whether they are modest and self-effacing, or aggressively self-assertive.

The personal pronoun they use most is I, not We. There's nothing wrong with this. It applies to all of us at times. It's a piece of self-expression that can work for us even when the job is mainly routine — provided there's some scope to decide how to go about it. It turns you on because you can put a bit of yourself into what you're doing.

Your personal hairdo, the fine-tuning of your hot-rod, the way you make your music, your garden, your home, your business, your career. Your personal best.

It's there in all of us, waiting to be released. For good or ill, like the Genie of the Lamp.

✧ ✧ ✧

Fitting it together

Let's recap on the argument so far.

The human species has got by until now because people who didn't see themselves as particularly gifted or important have shown an astonishing ability to hang on, and adapt.

The obvious starting point for us now is the place where we are within reach of each other: the neighbourhood. Somewhere in it there will be moving spirits who say, ENOUGH IS ENOUGH!, make the first move, and then coax or nag or jolly the rest of us into joining in.

It's as much human nature to be up and doing as it is to be a couch potato. But getting us off our butts depends on the scope there is to make something of ourselves, to show our mettle, make our mark as heroes or villains or something in between.

Those moving spirits work on us, individually, by saying

"You, and you, and you, and you. Look at what any one of us could
be doing, here and now.
Yes, you. You could be building your own house, for instance."

And then, collectively,

"Look at what this mixture of skills and experience could achieve between us.
*We could **create our own neighbourhood!"***

 From Do-It-Yourself, on your own, to **Do-It-Ourselves**, *together*.

◇ ◇ ◇

The first two corner pieces of the jigsaw are *Job Satisfaction* and *Ganging Up*, which is what the next chapter is about.

Ganging up? That sounds a bit rough. Wouldn't *Group Work* be more … respectable?

Back in the 1980s, long before Hillsborough and Heysel and Dublin, sportsmen joined with academic researchers at a conference in Rome to consider what the *hooligans* were doing to soccer.

They reckoned that bad behaviour on the terraces was not just mass hysteria sparked off by some faulty decision by the referee. The behaviour was pre-planned. Groups worked things out beforehand, with clear objectives in mind, and they kept to the rules they set themselves and made the most of the media limelight to show what they felt about the rest of the world. They had their own rituals, their own war cries. Manchester United fans went marching down the streets chanting, *We hate humans.*

The researchers called them *deviant groups*, but said they were much like any *non-deviant group* in the way they depended on each other, and shared certain beliefs in common.

What makes the difference between one kind of group — deviant or non-deviant — and another is their **staying power**.

A group may come together for a while to get something done which individuals can't manage on their own. There are more new houses built by groups  of self-builders than all those put up by private firms or government agencies. But in most self-build schemes, when the houses are up, the front doors shut fast. The members of the group have survived the pains of collaboration and with a sigh of relief, they retreat within their respective caves.

There are lots of such groups which form round a common interest. They are good whilst they last, but they don't last long unless the chemistry begins to work: that interaction which binds people together and gives them a new identity — good or bad — and the power to do together what none of them could have done alone.

Let's take some samples to see what it is that makes that power last.

 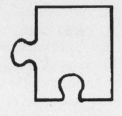

5 Ganging up

It is the Friday night of one of those residential weekends when a lot of officials, politicians and welfare workers, most of whom scarcely know each other except at the end of a telephone or the signature to a memo, get used to bedding down together (occasionally, literally).

Most of those arriving are paid to attend, obliged to come away from more attractive weekend activities, and put up with a lot of boring, if well-intentioned talk.

The subject, this time has to do with World Development. Everyone has a bad conscience about it, without necessarily knowing what it really means.

It seemed a good idea to break the ice with something that people were not expecting. So after they had dumped their bags and eaten their supper, they find themselves queuing up outside a large empty room. In the doorway is a poster which reads:

Self Preservation Act

WARNING

It has been officially confirmed that A DELUGE IS IMMINENT.

SURVIVAL KITS are being issued as quickly as possible.

You are advised to complete the construction of your personal or family **ARK** WITHIN THIRTY MINUTES.

PERSONS WITHOUT ADEQUATE MEANS OF SUPPORT WILL DROWN.

By Order:

Ministry of Inundation

As each person is admitted he or she is issued with their *possessions* and their *dependants*. Some have no dependants and great possessions. Others have families to consider (one or more small, weighty figures fashioned from old torch batteries). Possessions might include a sum of money (not the same for everybody) and various kinds of materials to make an ark; balloons, Squeezy bottles, lolly sticks, bits of fabric, string. In one corner of the room, otherwise bare of anything that might have been commandeered to eke out these possessions, is a small washing-up bowl attended by an official from the Ministry armed with blank Buoyancy Certificates. Before you can try out your ark in the bath and, if successful, gain your buoyancy certificate, you have to pay a small fee and fill out a very long application form. *Don't ask why. It's the regulations.*

 Resources are unequal. You couldn't balance your dependants on a single squeezy bottle or balloon; some sort of raft is needed and the means to hold everything together.

At first, it is everyone for him or herself.

This is where the man with the ball of string — let's call him Sheikh Maxwell ibn Murdoch — finds he has the edge. Far more string than he will ever need, but he's selling it by inches and charges at least a balloon a time, to say nothing of folding money he could use to buy extras for his own craft.

For everyone it is a race against time, to think out what to do with the resources they have, and how to market them in exchange for what they lack. It is a **Me** culture, get up and grab whilst you can.

There are some exceptions. Twenty minutes in, six poor people have got together, and are able with some hard bargaining to amass four balloons. Then they have to get the string to tie them. They can't afford enough for the necks of the balloons as well as the lashing together. But one technocrat makes a breakthrough and shows how if you stretch the neck of the balloon you can tie it without needing a bit of string. They lose one balloon in the process because someone's nails were too sharp but they get their lash-up and it supports all their families.

Means of support

So where did all this happen? What better place than Rochdale — which has attracted people from all over the world. The attraction? Well in the '30s it was Our Gracie, Gracie Fields who sang her way to stardom through the Depression, as the Lancashire lass who looked on the bright side even though she walked in the shade, and who made people laugh at trouble:

> There's a shop called the Co-op in the High Street, By Gum! It's a great idea.
> For what you spend, you get a dividend. Three times, ev'ry year.
> When Ma takes two shillings for her share, she shouts, feeling like a millionaire,
> Stop and shop at the Cwop, the Co-op shop.

What a shop is the Cwop, the Co-op shop!"
You can buy from a chop to a prop or a mop,
Or a bottle of ginger pop, at the Cwop shop.
They have tripe, nice and ripe, at the Cwop shop.
Pink pills, powder puffs, pork pies,
Paraffin and jam, carbolic soap and ham, clothes pegs and glass eyes.
And pigs' heads all grinning in a row will join in this chorus, sweet and low,
Stop and shop at the Co-op. What a shop is the Co-op shop!

She always got a big laugh when she sang the praises of the Co-op shop, which is the other reason for making a pilgrimage to Rochdale.

People have been coming from a long way off to see the stamping ground of the **Rochdale Pioneers**.

Not a great deal to see when you get there. A little shop still preserved at No. 31 Toad Lane, which was once T'Owd Lane. It had its opening night on Saturday December 21 1844, after a long search for premises cheap enough to rent. James Daly, a joiner, fixed up shelves. All the stock in trade they could afford didn't take up much shelf room. But it cost all of 16 pounds, 11 shillings and 11 pence which David Banks and John Hill spent on:–

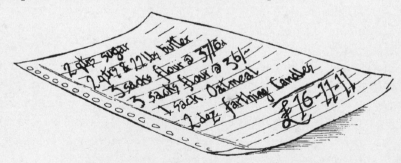

The candles were mainly for illumination at the grand opening. James Smithies aged twenty-five took down the shutters, nineteen year old Sam Ashworth was the salesman, twenty-two year old Billy Cooper, *a roistering sort of lad with red hair that stuck up like a mop*, was the cashier — all paid at the same rate, 3 pence per hour (but only if the shop broke even).

They were anxious and inexperienced and opened an hour late, with a gaggle of teenagers taking the piss out of them for the limited stock on offer — *You could get all yer stuff on a wheelbarrer*, plus the fact that Sam hadn't yet learnt to fill a paper cone with sugar without spilling it.

Among the jeering onlookers were local shopkeepers — the *badgers*, loan sharks who had got away with high prices by hooking their customers on easy credit.

Pioneers

The Pioneers had the last laugh. At the end of the day, Miles Ashworth, the old soldier turned watchman, Sam's Dad, locked up. They had almost sold out. Mr Holt carried the takings home for safety and entered a modest profit in the books.

On Sunday afternoon, everyone turned up at James Smithies's house in Lord Street to take tea and celebrate. There were over thirty involved, twenty eight as members of THE ROCHDALE SOCIETY OF EQUITABLE PIONEERS and a few others who were not allowed to have any money interest, so that they could be independent *arbitrators* to watch out for anything dodgy. Young Smithies from Huddersfield had recently finished his apprenticeship as a weaver and set up on his own. Someone said of him afterwards, *he laughed the Society into existence*. He was full of fun and *radiant enthusiasm*. His home was nicknamed *Henland*, because that was where people with ideas came to roost and to hatch out plans. None of the group claimed to be anything special. There were two shoemakers, a tailor, a cotton block printer, a couple of joiners, a cabinetmaker, two hatters, a warehouseman, a clogger, a street hawker *with the loudest voice in Rochdale*, and the rest were all in the weaving trade.

Haves and have-nots

Years before all that Rochdale had become rich on the wool trade, until the Americans put up tariffs, and put a third of the Rochdale hand-loom weavers out of work. That was back in 1828. In November 1829, the Association of Rochdale Weavers addressed their fellow citizens saying that the manufacturers *have openly declared that they are determined to destroy the market and the unions and that trade will then be under their sole direction and control.*

Who were these manufacturers? They were Rockefeller types, on their way up from small beginnings,

> ... men who have risen from a state of indigence and poverty and now that they are raised to a state of affluence are vaunting their own selfish and diabolical designs ... to sacrifice the interests of men who are only employing their own means in a manner consistent with what they themselves have always enjoyed.

The nub of the complaint was that the manufacturers were cutting rates by twenty percent, and even the rates they paid for a 16-18 hour day were being trimmed by all sorts of deductions, so that a so-called *Christian manufacturer* owing 17 shillings and 6 pence for a week's work to a poor woman with a family to keep up, would leave her with 10 shillings take home pay. All over Britain, times were hard and getting harder. City syndicates with sure-fire schemes to build railways were going bust, with the work unfinished and the workers jobless. Wages were being pared down whilst food prices soared.

Two nations

An up and coming young Conservative MP, Benjamin Disraeli, who supplemented his pay by churning out novels, rather like Jeffrey Archer's but better written, took the trouble to visit the wool towns in Lancashire where some people could not afford even the blankets they produced, and slept on straw. In Rochdale alone, there were over 3,000 people living on between sixpence and two shillings a week.

> A spirit of rapacious covetousness, desecrating all the humanities of life, has been the besetting sin of England for the last century and a half …

> There are two nations between whom there is no intercourse and no sympathy; who are as ignorant of each others' habits, thoughts and feelings as if they were dwellers in different zones, or inhabitants of different planets; who are formed by different breeding, are fed by a different food, are ordered by different manners, and are not governed by the same laws…

Two nations … *the Rich and the Poor.*

Setbacks

Even while Disraeli was writing these words, some of those poor people in Rochdale had already formed their club, fifty strong, and raised enough cash to subscribe to three London papers. They were readers as well as thinkers. But for years they got little success. The Association of Rochdale Weavers (John Scowcroft, the street hawker among them) tried withdrawing their labour but were forced back on the manufacturers' terms. Half a dozen got together in 1833 to buy a few goods wholesale together and re-sell them. The scheme failed, like many other experiments in co-operation before it.

The customers were poor people, buying on credit, long drawn out, and there were bad debts. Miles Ashworth and his son Sam went to a big meeting in the theatre in Toad Lane, to hear Feargus O'Connor making a speech about getting back to the land and growing food for yourself. So they packed up and joined a colony down South in Oxfordshire. They planted potatoes but could not sell them because of a boycott by local traders and Sam came home to Rochdale with his Dad following soon after.

They met up with some of their mates in the Weavers Arms in Yorkshire Street but they couldn't see an answer to their problems, until James Smithies turned up and jollied them into making a fresh attempt on that old idea of co-operative trading.

The problem they saw was credit, and slow repayers, or people who defaulted and dropped out. But if you stopped offering credit, what other incentive was there to shop at the Co-op? Charles Howarth kept thinking about it and the story goes that, in the middle of the night he woke up his wife and said *I've got it!* In the morning he went round to Billy Cooper, and then on to John Best the tailor, and that evening they all came round to the Smithies' in Henland. The break-through, enshrined in rule 22 of the Rochdale Equitable Pioneers, was that every quarter the profits should be divided and paid out to all the members in propor-tion to the amounts they had purchased in the shop. All purchases had to be for cash on the nail, but the more you bought, the bigger your dividend would be.

The group bought one sack of flour and divided it amongst themselves, at cost, for cash, and it worked out less than the local shops demanded. They had no previous experience in the grocery trade. They drew up their Rules, registered themselves as a Friendly Society, called a meeting to plan ahead — nobody turned up — tried again, with better notice, and began to collect tuppence a week for the fund that would rent premises and buy stock. Total collected — £28. Premises — several attempts which failed, and finally that small warehouse in Toad Lane owned by the local doctor, disused and *sadly out of repair.* Upstairs was the Bethel Chapel, rented by a radical offshoot of the Methodists, with a good deal of hymn singing filtering through the floorboards. After some bargaining — £10 a year on a three year lease for the ground floor, but a quarter's rent demanded in advance as the landlord *did not know the Society or anything about it.* (James Bamford, shoemaker in better times, detailed to spread a layer of cinders on the mud floor in time for the grand opening night.)

Opening out

After that glorious opening just before Christmas, the shop went from strength to strength. In January, they decided that business was good enough to justify buying the salesmen green aprons and sleeves. By the spring, in spite of attempts at boycott by local traders, they had opened up on weekday evenings and Monday afternoons. In a year, the membership had more than doubled.

The shop was part of a bigger plan. Besides selling provisions and clothing they intended to purchase or build houses, to *commence manufacture of such arti-cles as the Society may decide upon, for the employment of such members as may be without employment, or who may be suffering in consequence of repeated reductions in their wage.* And they would go on to buy an estate or estates of land *which shall be cultivated by members who may be out of employment or whose labour may be badly remunerated.*

They set up a Corn Mill Society, had a bad first year and sacked an incom-petent manager, survived and went into profit. They sparked off the Rochdale Co-operative Manufacturing Society, *to carry out in common the trades of cotton and woollen manufacturing.* Shares of five pounds each, paid off at a shilling a week, with anyone defaulting fined a penny a week unless the management committee waive it because of *sickness, distress or want of employment.* Long before local authorities got down to it, they had opened their own Turkish Baths.

One day they would build or purchase houses for the members, not as a far away retreat, but as a *home colony* in the heart of Rochdale. Meanwhile, in the bad winter time of the Hungry Forties, they let their back room at tuppence per meeting to the Short Time Committee.

What sort of people were they? A visitor, who eventually wrote them up, thought that *human nature was different in Rochdale to what it was elsewhere in England.* The get-togethers continued every Sunday afternoon at the Smithies, with everyone taking turns to provide hospitality, and all the children sent up to the attic to play together or read. Downstairs the grown ups cracked jokes, talked shop — and planned ahead.

Hard-headed thinkers

They were hard-headed thinkers, without cosy illusions, practical men of vision who understood what it takes to break new ground. From the outset, they put aside ten percent of profits for education. In 1849 they took on the room above the Toad Lane store and got James Daly making benches so that discussions could be held. Later, it became a *News room* with a subscription to the *Manchester Guardian*, and a school for 14's to 40's on Sunday afternoons.

They collected books — all sorts, romances, crimes, tracts, lumped together in a big box in the middle of the room.

The first hundred or so included: *Half Hours with the Telescope; An Afternoon of Unmarried Life; Indoor Plants and How to Grow Them; Twelve Sermons on Unjust Judges, Gaming, Forbidden Marriages, Parsons and Tithes, and the Rights of the Poor; Christian Beliefs and Living; Young Laundress of the Bastille; The Boys' Own Book of Sports and Pastimes; Art of Cookery; Freaks of Cupid; Ancient Philosophy (Pythagoras, Socrates, Xenophon); History and Science of the Game of Cricket; On the Combustion of Coal and the Prevention of Smoke;* Tom Paine's *Age of Reason,* and a translation of the *Koran*.

In ten years, they had 5,000 books, and provided their librarian with a pair of slippers, *owing to his noisy clogs.*

They got outsiders in to talk, about everything under the sun. There was a Professor Stuart from Cambridge, lecturing weekly about astronomy. They rigged up a telescope on the roof for everyone to see what he was talking about. One week he left some of his wall charts behind. There was some doubt that they would be a distraction for the co-operative's business meetings in the same room. Not so. They argued about the charts and the upshot was that they asked the professor to come early on his next visit so that he could answer questions. Everyone enjoyed *a good heckle.* They had invented the granddaddy of the University Extension Class, where you were not content with just listening, but could join in an educational conversation, and help tease out the truth, together.

Harmony

The talk was to the purpose, but wide ranging. It was resolved

"That every member shall have full liberty to speak his sentiments on all subjects when brought before the meeting at a proper time and in a proper manner and all subjects shall be legitimate when properly proposed."

To underline this freedom of speech anyone who interrupted another member, and persisted after cautioning by the Chair was fined threepence.

The doing and the talking went hand in hand. In 1856, they published their annual Almanack, headed by an advert for the range of goods and services they could now offer (not quite as many as Gracie Fields mentions, but doing well).

Rochdale Equitable Pioneers
ALMANACK for 1856
PROVISIONS, GROCERIES, BUTCHER'S MEAT, LINEN AND WOOLLEN DRAPERY, HATS, CAPS, SHOES, CLOGS AND COALS * TAILORING, SHOE-MAKING, CLOGGING * ORDERS AND REPAIRS EXECUTED WITH DESPATCH

The Rise and Progress of the Society

"Now in business for 11 years with a success never before equalled by any distributive co-operative association."

"... The doubts heretofore entertained as to the practicability of working men carrying out any extensive projects for the amelioration of their condition are now, as far as Rochdale is concerned, set at rest."

"The uninterrupted harmony that has existed among the members (which numbered upwards of 1400 in December 1855) may be fully understood by the fact that the arbitrators of the Society have not yet been called upon to exercise the functions appertaining to their office..."

Harmony was a favourite word.

It had stayed in members' minds from way back in the days of the 1827 Address by the weavers of Rochdale.

They wanted to get the balance right: **the individual job-satisfaction (with a living wage), matched by mutual enjoyment of what they achieved together.**

Bearing each other's burdens

They had grown up in the aftermath of wars, revolutions, and religious upheavals.

Rochdale was one of the places where John Wesley's Methodists had taken root in the previous century. But fifty years after his death, some of the things he had planted were turning out differently from what he might have expected.

He and his brother Charles were thoroughly sober, respectable young men who had set up a small study group nicknamed the Holy Club, in Oxford. All told, there were 12 on the first Thursday night, 40 the next, 100 soon after. The group was inward-looking, opening up about themselves to each other, at first shrinking from what was going on in society around it: the sloth and self-satisfaction of many church people, the self-indulgence of the rich, the anger and despair of the poor.

His mission was to call sinners to repentance, in this life, so that they might be saved in the life to come. The Church of England in which he was an ordained priest disapproved of his enthusiasm. Enthusiasm was a dirty word. It meant going beyond the comfortable limits of conventional church membership, getting worked up, going to extremes. In 1738, cold-shouldered by the establishment, he joined a little group in London *to share ideas in entire openness and the avoidance of any kind of reserve*. He became converted for the second time. From now on, he felt himself driven to venture outside the safe circle of conventional church life and to make the world his parish. When he was no longer allowed to preach 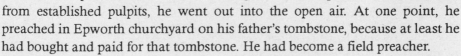 from established pulpits, he went out into the open air. At one point, he preached in Epworth churchyard on his father's tombstone, because at least he had bought and paid for that tombstone. He had become a field preacher.

He spent fifty years on the trot, a quarter of a million miles, ambling on horseback throughout the country, drawing crowds wherever he stopped, because he had the words that plucked at people's hearts. And his brother Charles wrote words and music to make them sing for joy at the prospects of salvation. Not salvation now, but in the afterlife.

Among the crowds there were converts, sheep needing shepherds to keep them on the right track. Wesley, being very methodical, was sure that people had to be led and organised, and that cost money. Regular funds were hard to raise.

They were discussing this one day in Bristol when a certain Captain Foy suggested there should be regular collections, half a penny a week per member. And if they were too poor? Then, said Captain Foy,

"Put eleven of the poorest with me, and I will call on them weekly, and if they can give nothing, I will give for them as well as for myself."

The group idea seemed an answer to prayer, and they called the groups *Classes*. Nothing to do with schools, it just meant dividing people up into manageable numbers. But then the idea took on a new shape; two of the collectors, or class leaders, reported that they had found one member quarrelling with his wife, and another drunk, whereupon Wesley thought,

"This is the very thing we wanted. The Leaders are the persons who may not only receive the contributions, but also watch over the souls of their brethren!"

These Methodist cells came to be known as *society classes*. They allowed the leadership to have everyone *under inspection*. Wesley was a *top-down* man if ever there was one. In the last year of his life, still trying to take in the shocking news of the French revolutionaries, he wrote:

"As long as I live, the people shall have no share in choosing either stewards or leaders among the Methodists. We have not and never have had such custom. We are no republicans, and never intend to be."

Group dynamic

A curious thing began to happen which put Wesley's intentions on the back burner. Within each society class, there were all sorts and conditions of people. Miners, farm workers, fisherfolk, beggars, occasionally the well-to-do, even the Countess of Huntingdon. Mostly, they were lay people and the class leader had no more than the authority of his appointment by Wesley, or by some senior officer whom Wesley had appointed.

There were no hard and fast rituals to set the leader apart from the rest. Some vigorous hymn singing, often to Charles's words and music. Plenty of free-ranging, spontaneous prayer. And that still left time for *holy conversation*.

Once you start conversational exchanges in a mixed bag of people, all sorts of things come up. People's feelings of exhilaration or despair, the physical problems posed by the wife-beater and the heavy drinker.

People could talk things over in an intimate, informal, friendly way, and this fired members' confidence in themselves and in each other. **They could come clean with each other, challenge each other, comfort each other, confide.** And this makes for

confidence within the group. **They learned from each other and could size each other up. There wasn't much room for dominating leaders.** There was plenty of scope for people who could inspire others and get them on the move, shoulder to shoulder.

This is what happened when four Methodists, two of them the Loveless brothers, local preachers, were among the six men of Dorset who were sentenced by the local magistrates to transportation because they met together in the village of Tolpuddle to swear an oath of union solidarity, to promote the interest of their fellow farm workers. They were convicted on a technicality, the oath-taking. In hindsight, that says something about the strength that possessed them. They were not swearing fealty to a leader, their loyalty was to each other in the group.

That's where the chemistry comes in, and why John Wesley's society classes turned out to be models for bottom-up political action, quite unlike the top-down pattern he favoured.

Four years after Wesley's death in 1795, one society class leader, Alexander Kelham, published his own pamphlet on *The Progress of Liberty*, which argued that Methodists should be self-governing, democratic. Others like him became a breakaway group increasingly concerned with what should be done about fellow human beings here and now, as well as hereafter. They called themselves the *New Connection* but were better known as Tom Paine Methodists.[1]

One of their stamping grounds before long was Rochdale, where in 1839 the newly-formed Chartist movement had a *tumultuous conference*. The Chartists demanded a democratically-elected Parliament — secret ballot, free choice of MPs, manhood suffrage — and they set about collecting a million and a quarter signatures in support, with local fund-raising groups based on the system of the Methodist society classes.

The Chartists were crowd-pullers, like Wesley, at their best in public denunciations, making rallying-calls to ever increasing crowds. They were the nearest thing in England to the revolutionary movements which were taking place elsewhere in Europe. They scared the English establishment, but somehow they lost momentum and Chartism fizzled out. What was happening inside those Chartist classes? A great deal of talk about what should be. Not very much action to provide a taste of what it *could be* really like.

Comparisons

Twenty years on, Billy Cooper, the *roistering* red-haired socialist, wrote to an enquiring professor, to explain how things began with the Pioneers:

---

1 Tom Paine was not quite the sort of man of whom Mr Wesley would approve. He served in his teens under Captain Death on a privateer vessel, The Terrible, worked for his dad as a stay-maker, got a job as an excise man in Sussex, lodging with a tobacconist, married his land-lord's daughter, wrote articles against slavery and the subjugation of women, and emigrated to America. His pamphlet, Common Sense, which sold 120,000 copies (partly subsidised by himself), helped to launch the American Revolution. He carried a vital dispatch for the revolutionaries by boat under British fire. He went to France and helped to stir things up there, risking his own head trying to save the King from the guillotine, but wrote his book in defence of the revolution, *The Rights of Man*, which has been a textbook for independent-minded people ever since. More about Tom Paine in Chapter 14.

"It happened in Rochdale — as in most other towns — that there were Societies of Chartists, Teetotallers and Socialists, and each of these pleaded theirs was the best plan for bettering the position of the working classes…"

Most of the men who became the Rochdale Pioneers belonged to at least one, some to several at the same time. Billy and some other unemployed weavers turned up at a joint meeting of the three main groups,

"to discuss and talk over their several remedies for the evils of Society … The Chartists would have people agitate until they got the six points of the Charter, when, they said, having universal suffrage and the Government in their own hands, they would remove and remedy wasteful and class misgovernment."

The Socialists saw it a different way:

"Their idea was to establish communities of each for all and all for each, where the property should be held in common."

There were also some strong teetotallers present, who said,

"Now if the working class saved the money spent on drink, they would become well-off, almost independent."

Billy and his mates took all this in but, he explained, they concluded:

"All men could not be persuaded in a day to become teetotallers; that the ruling classes would be a long while before they granted the Charter; that competitive society could not be converted into communities of united interests in a reasonable time; (so) this question arose, What can and shall be done? And several persons said, Let us become our own shopkeepers."

Working model

They ignored the Chartists who attacked such *half-measures* and who thought the working class could never afford the cash to do anything for themselves. They made sure that everyone kept up their subs, just as Captain Foy had recommended to the Wesleyans. They expanded their shop, moved to new premises, inspired others to build houses, schools and workshops.

They showed what they meant, as well as talked about it. In the best Methodist tradition, they fashioned **a working model**.

When they talked about the harmony of the universe, they used the image of the steam engine to explain what it was all about. They wanted balance, precision, so that power could be effectively harnessed to do what was needed. **Their motive force was their commitment, their solidarity, their staying power.** Getting used to each other, putting up with each other, making the most of each other, created **a working relationship** in which that power could become effective.

Put it another way. **They were visionaries who knew where they wanted**

to go, and they were used to tackling things in a workmanlike fashion, producing results which you could see and celebrate. So there was a double lock.

What they dreamed of enriched what they did. Their dreams began to come true because they made *common sense* **in Toad Lane, bang in the middle of everyday life.**

ALMANACK 1857

… One case is as good as a thousand. What one company can do, a thousand other such companies may do. It matters not whether the shareholders be a thousand or a million, whether they may be rich or poor, educated or not, so that they have the common sense to adopt the ordinary machines of such concerns. People discourage you, by telling you that the thing has been attempted before and failed. There were many failures before the steam engine would act satisfactorily, but it acts now…

Does it still *act now?*

Guerrilla attack

In Hull, a few years back, a bunch of single youngsters, footloose and jobless, and cheesed off with the existing system, began to make a guerrilla attack on the housing problem.

Some had been students and dropped out because they reckoned their courses were blind alleys. Some, like Linda, were breaking away from broken homes:

"My Mum and Dad split up when I was eleven or twelve. My old lady moved out to London so either I went with her, or went to live with my Dad. We moved on to this housing estate and my first experience was walking to school and seeing someone being stabbed. It freaked me out — vandalism, sex crimes, tons of drug problems.

Dad and I lived in a maisonette and the quality of the housing was just crap. Damp, 30 ft-long living rooms with glass windows that weren't insulated properly. The architecture of it, totally ridiculous.

They put loads of single parents there, disadvantaged people — just bung them on the estate and then start whinging about people getting into trouble because they've got nothing to do. It's not surprising that a lot of people there are drug addicts and crime is rife. If you're not into crime up there, you know you stick out. You've got to be into drugs, you've got to beat your wife up — it's that type of thing to be normal.

And on the high-rise estate next door, flats are filled with young kids out of detention centres. They aren't giving them adequate money to help them pay for these flats, so these people are getting into trouble with the bills. They're also putting single parents on the fifteenth floor, and pensioners too. The lifts are broken, and there's pensioners that can't go out because they daren't go in a lift and they obviously can't walk down the stairs. It's just barmy.

Anyway, after a few years with my Dad, he got a new girl-friend and I had to leave — I got chucked out at seventeen, so basically I was homeless."

That was when Linda bumped into the four lads, and one lass, who had squatted in a derelict terraced house, away from the new housing estates. They had managed to buy another house cheap, partly with the help of a mortgage (in the name of a respectable ally) and partly by some creative uses of credit cards. They gave Linda a tenancy of one of the rooms in the house they owned. She dropped in occasionally to help them fix up the houses they were working on. Then she decided to travel around for a bit and left them to it.

Giroscope

They opened up formal negotiations to buy the house they were occupying, without actually mentioning that they were the same people who were squatting in it, and thereby lowering its value. In the winter of 1986-87, with another mortgage agreed, they gutted the house, replaced the old windows, rewired and replumbed, did some plastering and *sort of learned quite a lot, though we were pretty crap, pretty slow.*

They lived off Giro — which meant that they had to pay themselves less than £50 a week in order to qualify for benefit. They charged low rents to the single tenants of the first house they had bought, and invested the money in the work they were doing on their own house. They formed themselves into a Workers' Co-op, GIROSCOPE, and decided they weren't into having permanent leaders, so the Chairperson would rotate from meeting to meeting.

✧   ✧   ✧

They were visited by one sympathetic councillor, ignored by all the others, and quizzed by the Environmental Health Officer:

"The first time we met her, we both started shouting at each other for about an hour. We actually ended up getting on quite well, but the shouting did sort of

establish our independence. Now, we're probably a bit more pragmatic about it. We know there are certain things we've got to give way on, and other things we don't. Over the years, we've found various people in the council who we can deal with, and that can be quite useful."

Down to business

Very early on, the group decided to meet every week in a formal way, with Minutes. Meeting by meeting, there are echoes of the Rochdale Pioneers...

First meeting, March 5, 1986 — duration: 2 hours. Organisation of the kitty — will it run to a midday snack as well as supper and porridge in the morning? ... Some antagonisms... Problem of bad working atmosphere... Decided that if everyone is working on the house simultaneously, then a better atmosphere is produced. K Cram complained of the foul condition of the bathroom due to people washing up paintbrushes in sink, bath, etc., then not cleaning the porcelain.

Second meeting — ... K Cram explained why he had not cleaned the bathroom and his reasons were accepted... Seeds were planted in the garden but serious work deferred until work on the house is completed. Plans for kitchen garden and allotment discussed... After a short debate, it was decided that none of the tenants should answer the door in the next three weeks unless they were certain that it wasn't the Fair Rent man knocking. ...

Agreed to get a kitten to add to two existing cats... Should be female.

Sixth meeting — ... To make matters worse, P Gower then interjected in the proceedings, demanding to know whether he could move into the downstairs bedroom. He was told he could. He replied he didn't want to, as he liked the bedroom he was presently in, and then (writes the long-suffering Minutes secretary) he metamorphosed into a cloud of radioactive illogicality and promptly drifted off to pollute the North-East.

Eight meeting — D Salmon gave a financial review which was even grimmer than usual.

Ninth meeting — ... M Newman said he had re-roofed the outside toilet, a feat which had obviously filled him with joy... It was agreed to either purchase or make a wheelbarrow as soon as possible.

Tenth meeting — ... A rather shocked but nevertheless delighted M Newman articulated the meeting's general pleasure in, for once, actually doing most of the things we were going to do at the previous meeting... An impromptu maths class revealed a float of £15 after everyone had been paid, and this could be given to the co-op. It was agreed that everyone's wage level should be £30 per week.

Twelfth meeting — ... Any other business: the general view of the meeting was that greater effort to be at work early should be made.

Fourteenth meeting — ... It was generally agreed that the co-op is not a set of 8 individuals, but a group of 8 people who should be working together as a group, and the group as a whole should decide the level of commitment collectively. Each individual should be aware of their responsibility to the group and if they are not pulling their weight, it is the group they are letting down.

It was decided to have group dynamics at every meeting; this will involve constructive slagging off in most cases, and negative slagging off in the case of a complete and utter bastard.

Fifteenth meeting — Agreed to explore the possibility of making trailers for the push-bikes to carry tools in etc.

Eighteenth meeting — Those responsible for working at the house on Glencoe Street admitted they had been appalling and had done very little work... After group criticism of the Glencoe Street workforce, they agreed to pull their fingers out.

Nineteenth meeting — Work report: R Amesbury cursed the weather but informed the meeting that he had started painting the walls with Snowcem.

Marking time

With the work finished on the base, there was an unwished-for interval — six months' negotiations with a very cautious Co-op Bank manager before money was released to get on with the group's master plan — to cover the cost of the first five houses, renovate them, and make them available at low rents to single homeless.

So they were in the doldrums for a while, with nothing much to do apart from look around for more properties which one day they might find the money to acquire. And they went on meeting, and occasionally getting across each other.

Twenty-fifth meeting — Group dynamics: our relationships are complex due to us being friends who also live and work together and spend most of our free time with each other.

Twenty-seventh meeting — Financial review: ... Regarding the patter of tiny feet, it was decided to give M Newman £40 per week and G Mann (his partner) should get about £40 per week on one-parent benefit... It was also agreed to meet travelling costs incurred due to the sprogg's impending birth at Beverley Hospital.

Thirtieth meeting — Group dynamics: D Salmon was not prepared to be in a worker co-operative with someone who was both unwilling to work and to co-operate... P Gower said that perhaps part of the problem was that he had come recently from a job where he was not really expected to show much motivation, and therefore you only did as much work as necessary. ... The debate concluded that everyone in the co-op would have to do jobs they don't like from time to time, and that everybody should accept that and not be disillusioned about it.

Thirty-fourth meeting — Financial review: ... The credit card repayments can probably be left for another month, unless S Wheatley receives a nasty letter in the meantime.

Thirty-fifth meeting — Work review: ... It was agreed to operate a baby-sitting rota (so that the baby's mum can do some of the renovation work).

It was decided to see how Giroscope might possibly make an impact on the Hull housing scene in this Year of the Homeless.

Work structure: G Mann (the baby's mum) proposed a structured working week and the filling in of timesheets as a check to ensure that everyone is pulling their weight.

... It was decided that the minimum hours should be 35 a week. A number of those present stressed that during periods of renovating houses, Giroscope members should be putting in a lot more than 35 hours per week and that figure shouldn't be viewed as a deadline to reach and then stop. Those who work less than 35 hours per week would be accountable to the weekly meetings.

Thirty-sixth meeting — Plumbing: ... Agreed to attend a 40-day course... One person in Giroscope should have an overall plumbing knowledge as this is one area in which we are presently almost totally deficient... Everybody felt it was important to get training and develop as many skills as possible...

AOB: G Mann to collect £2 a week from everyone's wages, deducted at source, for the holiday club.

Group dynamics: ... There is too much talking and not enough listening if the Chairperson isn't severe enough. ... G Mann said we ought to be more easy-going with each other, and less excitable... The solution is that we try to talk to each other more (about problems) outside the meetings.

Good vibes

By the time Linda had come back from travelling around, the loans had come through and everyone was working again.

They threw a party to celebrate completing their fifth house, invited the neighbours as well as the local officials and voluntary workers. They had worked all through the night, and didn't finish painting until an hour before people arrived for the afternoon party. But there was food and wine, and a slide show, and speeches. The neighbours dropped in for the drinking session, on speaking terms this time, though in the past there had been shouting matches when they fiercely objected to the noise the group made when they worked through the small hours.

"Some of the older women in the streets have got a lot of sway and we sort of got in with them, and although there's been trouble sometimes, they've gone around and given us good publicity."

The Press were invited, and turned up trumps. There were bits in the *Hull Daily Mail* and the *Yorkshire Post*, and later on a good article in the *Guardian*:

"The Guardian article got us into the 6 o'clock News — you know, the skateboarding duck item, the freak item they usually put at the end."

Coming into the limelight after beavering away entirely on their own, they discovered that charities might be interested:

"We got a knock on the door while we were working, and there's this guy, 30-ish, really top notch clothes, and he said: 'I've just been sent down to reconnoitre you.' And we stood there covered in plaster and crap... And the cheque came... £20,000."

All that in the first year.

Vision

Since then, more loans from the banks, some charity money, and house after house bought and converted. The co-op has stayed small. There are six Directors and three, including Linda, on three months' probation before full acceptance.

Everyone continues to pay themselves £35 per week (or £40 for the mums and dads). There's a co-op shop that Gracie Fields would have approved of, and an office, and negotiations under way for workshop and storage space to pre-fabricate building components. One member says she wants part of one workshop to run a course in motorbike maintenance and conversion. There's a printing co-op from Birmingham planning to move up and join in.

The original baby-sitting scheme soon turned into a creche as more sproggs arrived. First, it was just to free parents to get on with the renovations. Now, it's open to neighbours, and a good way of keeping relations happy.

House no. 19 is a bit special: it's the *ecology house*:

"We went to visit the Alternative Technology House in Leicester and we adapted what we saw to fit our house. We wanted to do it up in a way that normal people could afford, so most of the things we built in can be done reasonably cheaply. It's got solar panelling, that's quite expensive, but it's also got a heat exchange system which isn't expensive. All the walls are insulated, and the windows are double-glazed. It's been draught-proofed inside and we've got thermostats on all the radiators."

There's been a change of mind, maybe even a change of heart, among some politicians who felt for a long time that what Giroscope was up to was actually a threat to what the Council was doing. Giroscope reckoned the Council might be well-intentioned, but was pretty old-fashioned. They were dead against *multiple occupation*. Their idea of housing need was suiting the nuclear family. But these ex-squatters were fixing houses up to be shared by single persons, quite contrary to Council policy.

Five years on, the Council has revised its policy. Sharing as an idea has at last become respectable. (The nearest the members of Giroscope had ever got to respectability was to put on a clean pair of jeans when they went to the Council offices.)

Every so often, there's an Annual General Meeting, not every year, but when there's real progress to report. I went to one of the earlier ones in the top floor of a pub, crammed tight with 50 others in their late teens and early twenties, all wanting places of their own.

The Giroscope Directors were explaining themselves to everyone, not that much explanation was needed. It made such common sense.

Staying power

No question, Giroscope has the staying power that comes from job satisfaction:

"We've always been renovating houses. It was quite clear why we were doing it — you're renovating this house to house someone. I feel really privileged — you do something that you want to do and at the same time it helps people as well. To make a living, help people, do something you enjoy — and also be able to buck the system at the same time — I don't really see what more you could want."

It's what used to be called vision. Not a pipe dream — but the ability to see a long way ahead, to work out in practical terms what could be, and to plan accordingly.

In their way, they stand comparison with those young men in Rochdale who set up shop in Toad Lane.

You could say that the Co-op members have grown in wisdom as well as in clout. Shuttie, one of the earliest members, reckons that it's the sproggs that have made the difference:

"I've got two kids now, and the thing about kids is: you realise that, whatever we do, we're doing for the next generation really. It warms your politics up. It's not a sort of cold, black and white sort of politics. You've got your kids, and you're doing it for a reason besides the 'greater good and the struggle', you know what I mean, you've got your sproggs."

As in Rochdale, the first efforts of the pioneers were contemptuously dismissed by the powers that be. The normal generation gap was made much worse because of the bitterness this engendered. Neither side had anything good to say of the other. This rejection forced the group back on its own resources. There was little or no money to put down on the table. So the group took risks with credit cards, and by persuading respectable friends to put their names to mortgage applications.

It was a buccaneering approach, which paid off because of the dogged determination that underlay it. The group worked out its own constitution, which was relatively easy, largely a matter of taking a set of rules off the shelf. It also established its own working rules, distilled from many heated meetings; and they stuck to low wages and shared resources, so that any profits could be ploughed into furthering the work.

Over the years, they have been as faithful to their free-ranging Rule as any monastic order, or as any Methodist society class.

Their own rules, not someone else's system that they have had to fit into. There is something special about any group which sets out to do something, and creates the way to do it.

Developers

The last Annual General Meeting I went to was as crowded and lively as ever. There were visitors from Leeds and Manchester and Grimsby, wanting to pick up ideas. It was Shuttie's turn to give the progress report. He pushed a hand through his blond dreadlocks, climbed into the pool of rainbow light on the disco stage, apologised that he was no speech-maker, and wowed his audience through six close-typed pages of his script — a sight more penetrating, accurate and imaginative than your average property tycoon is likely to come up with in a month of Sundays.

In their first seven years, Giroscope fixed up seventeen houses, three flats and a shop, won a National Housing Award, appeared on radio and TV, linked up with housing projects in Germany, Belgium and Portugal, notched up half a million pounds in assets against £150,000 of liabilities, provided accommodation for months or years at a time for 250 young tenants (average stay: 17 months), and contributed 16 sproggs of their own to the creche. All on £35 a week, less £2 holiday savings. Next steps — 3,000 sq. ft. of work space.

In comparison, one Council scheme has taken five years to build three hostels with a total of 30 beds at a cost of a million pounds.

Shuttie:

"Whilst I recognise the need for more hostel accommodation, surely more imaginative and cost-efficient ways can be found... What we want to see is more co-operative housing in Hull... Projects that allow young people to create and control their own housing... Decent housing is a basic human right. There is so much potential in housing to change things, to get people involved and give people confidence. By all means, build hostels and keep people off the street, but let's put the same resources into projects that cure the disease rather than just treat the symptoms."

❖ ❖ ❖

Afterwards, I had to say my guest speaker piece, quoting some of the bits about the Rochdale Pioneers that I've put at the start of this chapter. I said that Rochdale and Giroscope matter, because they *showed* what they meant, not just talked about it.

When the formal meeting ended and the party was well under way, Mowt, another of the founding members, sat down beside me. The night before, in Chapeltown, Leeds, two young men had been shot up, chased to the hospital and shot up again. Two other young men have been arrested and charged with attempted murder.

"Well," said Mowt, *"it's been happening on Moss Side in Manchester, as well as Leeds. How long before it gets that way in Hull? Ninety percent of young people hereabouts are saying that these days you've got to solve things with a gun. Not*

us. But we got Giroscope going in the second half of the 80s. It's the 90s now. Will they think we are 80s people and write us off?

How do you rate our prospects?"

Rocking the boat?

Mowt and Shuttie, in the nineties, are perplexed by the pace of change; the prospects for their sproggs.

All of a sudden, it seems, our cities have become infected with industrial pollution and organised crime. We are in the middle of a drug culture that is worldwide, and lethal. Just as we thought that jobs were for life, we discover that there isn't job security to be had any more. Outside our borders, there is an advancing tide of the displaced, dispossessed, victims of racial and religious intolerance. Countries we used to think of as picturesque and rather primitive are suddenly overtaking us in commercial production, flooding our markets with their products instead of the other way round.

What's the explanation?

The new technology?

✧　✧　✧

I was asked to do something about a hundred bored technology students whom the authorities had scheduled for a liberal education on Wednesday afternoons when they would really have preferred outdoor games or indoor snogging.

We booked the college Assembly Hall which had a platform at one end and double doors giving on to a foyer and the street at the other. I spent the previous evening stapling together strips of yellow card to make up what looked like an enormous toilet roll. It was marked out in divisions to represent the passage of the years, an inch to a decade. It started on the stage and was thumb tacked the length of one side wall, back again to the foyer entrance and out. If we had lengthened the time-strip a quarter of a mile down to the traffic roundabout, we could have placed a marker: perhaps a stone, to represent the first efforts of homo sapiens to fashion — what? A millstone? A tool? A weapon?

On some big tables in the middle of the room we spread scores of small cards. Each had the name of an invention, from man-made fire via the printing press, the zip fastener and the safety pin to the computer, the space craft and the ball point pen.

As the students arrived, they were asked to pick any invention that they fancied. Each card had its date written on the back. Everybody had to pin their cards at the right points on the timescale. So they all moved over to the wall strip that went the length of the hall and into the foyer.

And then suddenly, most of those hundred students found themselves crowding together on the narrow platform, all trying to fit their invention cards onto the last few inches on the timescale.

❖   ❖   ❖

Those were students of the sixties, the parents of Mowt and Shuttie's generation. Suppose that timescale exercise was to be tried out now, three inches longer to bring it bang up to date?

Within those three inches, how much room would there be for the myriad changes in this generation's own lifetime?

Microchips with everything from smart bombs to supermarket checkouts. Innovations spreading like Beijing 'flu. There is a buzz word for what is happening:

Each change triggers off many more.

Every younger generation properly feels unique, a step or two ahead of the worn-out assumptions and the fly-blown achievements of the oldies. But today's younger generation, and their parents, are something else.

Take all the changes, technical, political, psychological, that we can recall within living memory: they add up to more than all the changes which have occurred before this century, going back half a million years.

So feeling extra special isn't something we shall grow out of as we grow older.

So much has happened, for good and ill, that, whether it's a threat or a challenge, it's difficult to respond.

One reaction in Britain, parts of Europe and the USA, is to try to damp things down, more law and order, no more interference than you can help. It's stability that matters. Don't rock the boat!

If you're up the creek without a paddle and stuck in sleaze, then **rocking the boat** is the best way to get back into clear water. Chuck out the right-of-centre government, put in the left-of-centre government. Don't lean too far or you might capsize.

But our situation is becoming rather different.

We're finding ourselves far from land, rocked by forces outside our control. If you're in an open boat on a choppy sea and the outboard engine conks out, you unship the oars and row like mad in order to make some headway. In the process, although you may go up and down a bit, there's a lot less of that queasy heaving from side to side.

At all costs, you don't just drift. Get out those bloody oars! Give us a breathing space to get the engine working properly.

We are in that situation now, needing to improvise, innovate; to win time whilst we knock some sense into the top people; get to grips with the new technology, and make it behave.

● **Those moving spirits I described earlier can only get us going so far.**

● **We can develop some momentum for ourselves if there's scope for some personal job-satisfaction.**

● **Getting together — ganging up — we can drum up some mutual reinforcement.**

But all that may fail unless we overcome our fear of the unknown, and draw on our capacity to adapt, to break new ground.

Deep down, that's part of human nature, too. A buried talent waiting to be released.

When was that talent buried?

One answer is — **in our upbringing, the attitudes and habits of mind we picked up at home and in school**.

Of course, there are exceptions, but for most of us, life's earliest lesson was that **parents, on the whole, were old hat, and school was a bit of a drag**.

Neither did much to prepare us for the tidal waves of change.

If that was even partly our experience, then, what might today's children make of us, and the schooling they are getting, now?

And what *could be* done about improving matters?

Come to that, what's the evidence that here and there, once in a while, those buried talents have already been unearthed and brought back into satisfying use?

How's it done? And who can do it?

6 Breaking out

Who's going to make a start? *Don't look at me,* you might say, *I don't mind backing you up, eventually, but I'm not into taking the initiative. Hardly any of us are.*

Not now, we aren't. But go back to ourselves at the age of two, what then?

Any two-year old takes the world for granted — no worries about what it is or what it will be, compared with what it was. What it is, here and now, is a Tom Tiddler's ground to explore. Two-year-olds are good at wondering Why? And, soon afterwards, How? If there's no-one else around to give an explanation, pat — then wondering soon turns into finding out by experiment; suck it and see for yourself.

Growing older means that for most of us this inner urge to wander off the beaten track, to work things out from experience, gets rusty for lack of use. We're all too busy doing what we're told is best for us.

Yet it's still there, deep down in all human beings, like seeds beneath the snow, that capacity to strike out, take the initiative: to make changes for ourselves — not just put up with changes imposed on us from outside. To adapt ourselves — in order to set about adapting the world we live in. That has been people's experience over the whole span of history — from the time when we changed from being hunters and gatherers to being farmers and boat-builders and smiths and story-tellers and artists.

If it's true that this capacity to innovate and adapt is really part of our make-up, inbuilt — what holds us back? What's the evidence that five-year-olds and seven-year-olds and fifteen-year-olds and twenty-year-olds can respond? And what has our upbringing to do with it?

There are success stories, here and there. In Balsall Heath, Birmingham, once notorious for prostitution, crime, drugs and despair, a handful of workers in the St Paul's Community Project opened up a school for pupils rejected by the mainstream schools. They were mostly teenagers who could scarcely read and write, who had given up any idea that schooling could be of use to them. In turn, their schools had given up trying to educate them.

Some teachers from the mainstream schools gave time to work in a different way with the youngsters at St Paul's and by 1994 their pupils were scoring high by conventional standards — next to no truancy (a 91% attendance rate), 100% passes in GCSE exams, and ranking sixth out of 68 Birmingham secondary schools.

Success depends on teachers finding how to convince pupils that they have within them that unexpected capacity for change.

Two continents away, in Bangladesh, the same thing has been happening — nationwide.

In the 1980s the Government primary schools had a drop-out rate of about 75%, mainly the girls. BRAC, the *Bangladesh Rural Advancement Committee*, was set up in the '70s in the aftermath of the War of Independence on the initiative of one moving spirit and by the '80s had become the most influential voluntary organisation in the country. It worked by holding *village organisation meetings* to sort out what residents really wanted for themselves, beginning with adult literacy. In one, a woman said *What about the literacy of our children who cannot read or write?* A few determined teachers came together and persuaded BRAC to look more closely at what was going wrong in the primary schools. Children dropped out from the government schools because they were needed to help their parents in the fields. And anyhow, schooling had lost its glamour and seemed to have lost its relevance to real life.

So BRAC came up with an alternative, worked out with the parents themselves. In each village, they were asked to find space for a school of their own. It might be one room in somebody's house, rented at a reasonable cost to BRAC. Or it might be a patch of land on which a bamboo hut could be built for next to nothing.

BRAC set up crash courses for local villagers, particularly younger women, in order to learn about teaching. It isn't just a question of ramming texts down children's throats. There is room for songs and dances, home-made plays, sports events. And it all happens free, including the books, paid from the limited funds raised by BRAC, as a charity.

One parent said she had a problem with her two children. The elder girl was still going to the government school, and had to be pushed hard every morning to get her there. She complained that the teacher took no interest in the children. He would set everyone to learn multiplication tables, and then go to sleep at his desk. The younger daughter was going to the BRAC school, and you couldn't stop her, rain or shine. The school premises were primitive, the children had no desks or chairs and sat on the floor. But the teachers were friendly, and all the things that were going on outside the lessons were fun. Even the lessons were bearable.

The timetable varies to suit the parents and the time of the year, so that the children can help on the farm when most needed. The teachers themselves might be lending a hand, because they live in the neighbourhood. They make up for the limitations of their training by their knowledge of the children and their surroundings. There are no outside exams, the teachers can see and judge best how each child is progressing. Classes are kept small and the same teacher continues with a class for three years for the basic course and two years for the follow-up. The children call their teacher *Apa* which means sister, and this relationship is part of the secret of a breath-taking success.

> In the past ... it was believed that parents did not value education for their children enough to make sacrifices. [Now] parents' attitude toward education is apparently changed ... Children and their parents have come to value education and are willing to sacrifice in order to continue.
>
> From Catherine H. Lovell's research report on
> *The BRAC Strategy*

The first 22 experimental schools were launched in 1985, aimed mainly at children who had never been to school, or had dropped out early on. Over the next ten years, this *Non-Formal Primary Education* took off, and by the mid 90s there were upwards of 50,000 schools, a million children in them, daily attendance 95% and a drop-out rate of less than 1%. BRAC has got the backing of the United Nations Children's Fund, and its example is being followed in Nepal, India and Vietnam.

Exceptional results, which leave some people asking what it is that makes the difference.

Exceptional children? Exceptional teachers?

Or something else?

Compare the situation in the San Lorenzo slum in Rome at the turn of the century.

Maria Montessori had been studying Italian children who were classified as *feeble-minded*. She managed to bring together a selection from all the schools in Rome, to see whether after all they were capable of more than other people thought. She managed to get them on her side by devising ways to make learning exciting and demanding. She found that then they pegged level in reading and writing tests with *normal* children. She pointed out to everyone that this did not mean that normal children were no better than the feeble-minded. It was simply that traditional schooling was not fulfilling. It failed to make the most of what any of those children could offer, because it underrated their capacities to learn for themselves.

About this time the housing administration for the city of Rome had set itself to pull down slum housing and build *model* tenements.

Eduardo Talamo, the Director General of the Rome Association for Good Building, invited Madame Montessori to repeat what people were calling the *miracle* of her work with the *idiot children*, and to set up infant schools for the children of the families coming into the new tenements. Between them they decided that the school should be inside the tenement, because, as Maria said later:

> "The school is put within the home ... leaving under the eyes of the parents the whole life of the teacher in the accomplishment of her high mission. ... The idea of the collective ownership of the school is new and very beautiful and profoundly educational."

The first of these little schools — each one called the *Casa dei Bambini*, the Children's House — was opened at 58 Via dei Marsi, in the San Lorenzo slum. It was to be free for the children of parents who had to work for their living and could not give the daytime care the children needed. The parents had to accept conditions: the children must arrive *clean and punctually* and everyone must give due *deference* to the Directoress, and co-operate with her in the education of their children. At least once a week the mother must talk things over with her, giving her information about the child's home life, and *receiving helpful advice*.

The photographs in her book show Madame Montessori as a rather imposing, stately figure. *Deference* was certainly in order. But she listened and watched as well as instructing her teachers in the way they should go about their jobs. She contrived a range of play materials which children of three years and upwards could use in order to learn skills for themselves, beginning with dressing themselves and coping with the elaborate lacing and buttoning that used to involve. She helped them to create a new kind of classroom order in which every child had its own place, but was free to leave it in order to do things with other children, and return to afterwards without being told.

Children were being taught to get up and do things for themselves — even to leave their desks on their own initiative. *Montessori methods* became popular in many playgroups and infant schools. Madame came to London every year in the early days of this century to run courses. She made even the hard graft of the three Rs enjoyable, with numbers and letters as cut-outs in bright colours, so that children could sort them out for themselves and learn to make sense with them.

Hand-outs

Further up the school ladder, such notions took much longer to catch on. The teachers continued to chalk and talk and to keep pupils in attentive rows, **learning to do as they were told**. Education continued for the most part to be built round what the teacher handed out. As a ten-year old, I got my printed date card from our class teacher and was told to memorise the battles and the reigns of the kings and queens that were listed. The date card stopped short well before World War One. But our teacher liked to make his number with us by reminiscing about his own schooldays in Belfast when he *went to school in an armoured car for protection from the IRA*. We remembered those three capital letters, but who they represented, or why they existed — we hadn't the faintest.

SQUARING THE HIPPOPOTAMUS

Later on, in secondary school, we were much better off. Our teachers had time to talk to us and were very well informed. But our job was, as usual, to write up our history notes, copy the diagrams from the physics book, dissect the frog, describe the characters of Macbeth and Lady Macbeth, list Shakespeare's uses of the supernatural, and memorise the proof that the square on the hypotenuse is equal to the sum of the squares on the other two sides of the triangle. All sound stuff, and you felt it was doing you good.

There was one attempt to change course, when the Labour government of Ramsay MacDonald commissioned the Hadow Report on primary schooling, published in 1931 just as the Conservative-dominated government took over.

The Report said:

> The school is not merely a teaching shop. It is a community where children learn to live... to be themselves, and to develop in a way and at a pace appropriate to them... It lays special stress on individual discovery, from first-hand experience, and on opportunities for creative work. It insists that knowledge does not fall in separate compartments.

Some hope. Most teachers were prisoners of their classes, 40 or 50 children boxed up with them in their classrooms, with precious few resources apart from the blackboard and the chalk. In the secondary schools, particularly, knowledge stayed in separate compartments. Subjects were tied to the timetable, with the curriculum neatly arranged like clothing mothballed in the chest of drawers.

Then came World War Two and people no longer did what they were used to doing. When the air raids began sedate city dwellers took to sleeping under the stairs, or sitting out the raids five feet below ground in a damp garden trench with a corrugated iron roof, or bedding down with a hundred strangers on the floor of a church crypt. Families were scattered by evacuation and by war service, far and wide. When they came together again as the war ended, people who had put up with changes for the worst were ready to change things for the better.

Stirrings

The Labour government came to power with the peace, and at last put up the money needed to do justice to a new system, based on a new Education Act, put through the year before. It opened up secondary education to a wider age range, and gave more resources to the grammar schools that already existed.

Back from the war came demobbed warriors with their minds liberated by the wartime education courses that had helped fill up the time when there was nothing else to do. They went into Emergency Teacher Training schemes, rushed courses because there wasn't time to give them more than a grounding. But their eyes were set on bringing about some of the things that the war was supposed to have been fought to achieve. They remembered how they had been taught as children in pre-war classrooms, which most had found pretty boring. But now, having been out and about in the world, they felt that they could put themselves across as rather more interesting personalities than the old hands.

There were some new resources that were becoming more widely available — film strips, instructional films, schools radio. Some of the teachers, old hands and newcomers, felt a bit *threatened* by these resources. Others found them useful to give everyone a breather between bouts of nourishing chalk and talk.

◇ ◇ ◇

I got a writer/producer job with the BBC, beginning with schools and going on to launch a clutch of programmes for teenagers, broadcast nightly on the Light Programme (the forerunner of Radios 1 and 2). For one programme I went the rounds of seventy teenagers — today, they're young granddads and grannies. Then, they were just emerging from school, and had a lot to say about their teachers.

Their schooling had been less disturbed than nowadays by drugs, joyriding, playground knifings and fourth form pregnancies. On the whole, they had the opportunity to learn without too much interruption.

How were they taught? For the most part, during the war years and on into the peace, it was by the same old chalk and talk, latterly gingered up by the anecdotes their teachers brought back from the war.

I met such kids again and again, in my forays all over the country to record exciting actuality on teenagers' doings. They were all quite philosophical about their school days. They took their teachers as they came — not too bad on the whole, certainly well-meaning — much as they took the subject matter of the teaching. It was something to get you a job. So long as you could read, write, cope with sums and take orders, the jobs were there. I came across one school leaver who had had six different jobs in as many weeks, with the choice of more if he felt inclined.

Resources for learning

Experienced teachers could put their children through their paces like circus ring masters or the keepers in the zoo. There was very little chance to learn what children might be capable of outside the cage — all the difference perhaps between a chimpanzee tea party and Diane Fossey's studies of gorillas in the wild. The Hadow Report's concern with *activity and experience rather than knowledge to be acquired and facts to be stored* was all very well. So long as you stayed carefully on the beaten track.

We were now in the sixties, with a Conservative government that could see value in what people were calling *progressive* teaching. It set up a couple of committees, one under Sir John Newsom concerned with *13-16s of average or less than average ability* and another under Lady Plowden on *children and their primary schools*. Each produced reports commending the work of teachers who were moving away from chalk and talk and getting a different quality of response from their children.

The teachers who were actually breaking new ground were still a small minority. The BBC *Discovering Science* series featured the work of a rather maverick Scandinavian in a well-heeled Cambridge prep school where there was enough money to have small classes and give teachers time to prepare effectively. So Gerd Somerhof had his children making miniature robots, hot air balloons, wind pumps. On the telly, he showed everyone else how to make such things work, and how to figure out why they worked as they did.

One reason for success was the presence of teachers like Somerhof who had room to get their own ideas across and enthuse their classes. The children's work might be taking place all round the classroom, but it still centred on the teacher.

Taking the initiative

I presented another BBC TV series aimed at parents wanting to understand more about children's *Growth and Play*. Most of the programmes showed children on their own home ground, how they responded to each other, how they used their surroundings to create worlds of their own, all by themselves.

Later on, I took video cameras to record children in their classrooms, so that afterwards teachers could stand back from their normal teaching jobs and observe small children's unexpected staying power. In one primary classroom, someone brought in a live locust found in a crate of bananas. *The* Locust, not just any locust, dominated the children's work for weeks, drawing, describing, seeing for themselves. What had seemed to be the dullest child in the class turned out to be the only one who spotted just how the locust's tummy moved when it breathed. So we brought in the video camera and the children themselves used it to show the locust's tummy filling the screen, and the way the locust moved and ate. They called the shots and edited the sequences. Some of them were no more than seven years old.

In another school, I kept the cameras in the background. There were 3 four-year olds on their own in a Wendy house. They had a dummy telephone and spent nearly thirty minutes using it to organise imaginary help for a broken leg (one of them had recently been in hospital), and they went on from that to visit an imaginary doctor, and to do some shopping with another group on another side of the room behind a dummy corner shop counter. The teacher was there, out of earshot, but within reach; but the children had become self-propelled.

Being *progressive* was now the thing. But not for everyone. In 1969, a group of educationists brought out the first of the series of *Black Papers*. They couldn't abide the people who were pushing progressive teaching down everyone's throats. They admitted that such methods sometimes worked

> *"with younger children, particularly those drawn from overcrowded homes in drab surroundings... The duller pupils are surprisingly happy and the brighter make remarkable progress. But this was because there were exceptional teachers, provided with an exceptional amount of space and equipment — usually able and ingenious enthusiasts who had themselves devised the techniques they practised. But when copied by the young teacher, fresh from college, the outcome, more often than not, was utter failure."*

What made these teachers *exceptional?* What about the children? Were they *exceptional* when they responded? What was it that made them self-propelled?

Many of the teachers I saw in their classrooms had the long hair and the trendy clothes that made you think they really were *hip*. But when you looked at what they were doing, it did not seem greatly different from what the old chalk and talkers used to do. They might split the kids into groups, but they were not so much groups as clusters of children, each one filling in one of teacher's worksheets, occasionally peeking at each other's work, and doing teacher's bidding as best they could.

The classroom was often open-plan to allow children to move around as their interest changed or developed. Once their imagination was captured and they began to concentrate on a *Project*, they could become purposeful. They might be allowed to stray into the school library and do some *finding out*, hunters and gatherers collecting materials to assemble as a *Topic*. Some of this project work looked really good, but as teachers used to say to me, *you had to make allowances*. There were the bright children you could rely on, and the others (whom the *Black Papers* people called *the duller children*) — they were the *passengers*. From these *you couldn't expect too much*.

Experiments

I got together a group of teachers, a cross-section from infant teachers to university lecturers, all attracted by the possibilities of 'ETV' — educational television. At first, everyone wanted to make video programmes to back up their normal teaching work: to substitute the television screen for the blackboard, to give maximum impact to the teacher.

It turned out, however, that ETV, rather more than other *audio-visual aids*, could become a sort of Trojan Horse, entering the classroom and almost displacing the traditional teacher. When that happened, the focus shifted to the children.

One experiment was sparked off by a proposal to make a programme about Sir Christopher Wren. How as a boy he liked making models; and as a grown-up was commissioned to design a replacement for the burnt-out St Paul's; how his first design was turned down by the bishops; and he went back to the drawing-board to produce what we can now see at the top of Ludgate Hill.

Instead of making the programme all as one chunk, we split it into sections, and took the video out to a selection of schools where, as usual, the teachers were used to distinguishing between the *bright* children and the *passengers*.

Along with the video, we provided an odd selection of cardboard boxes. The first part of the video invited children to follow Wren's example and experiment with putting the boxes together in different ways as model buildings. With the next section of the video, each teacher was asked to show the class a copy of the site plan Sir Christopher had to work on in his first attempt. The children set about contriving their versions. Then they had the third part of the video showing what Wren had come up with, and how it failed to please the bishops. So they too went back to the drawing-board to make their revision of Wren's first design. Finally, they could compare their results with his.

The feedback from the teachers set everyone thinking. They'd all had to lengthen the intervals between showing each section of the video because the children were giving so much time and effort to contriving their own designs. The *attention span*, said the teachers, was much greater than they had expected. The whole class, *passengers* included, had become *self-propelled*, not whizzing off in all directions, but purposefully aligned to going one better than Sir Christopher Wren.

So we went a little further, and took another theme, the neighbourhood, with a video designed to encourage children to re-design their own *Living Space* — home, local estate, city, landscape. Just one seven-minute video, coupled with a selection of bits and pieces which children could arrange and re-arrange in order to work things out for themselves. A dozen different group activities, including:

- The layout and decor of a living room (4 hinged cards to make the instant room with a selection of fabric scraps, a paint card, a moveable door and window to work out where to put the telly).

- A long frieze representing rolling countryside on the edge of a town, with pin-on houses, farms, trees, tourist venues, in order to deal with competing claims on the countryside.

- A green belt layout representing the countryside around a small village, with a selection of little wooden houses to be laid out in such a way that the incomers and the village residents would be able to get on with each other, and make the most of what open space could be preserved.

- The dingy brown layout of a derelict inner city site with matchbox houses to make a housing estate with lengths of tape and coloured wools to design an access road and the most economical layout for power lines and water and sewage. The teacher was briefed to issue rather fewer matchbox houses than the number of the children in class. So when everyone was invited to apply for a house on the layout, there was a housing shortage, which that particular group had to solve, by negotiation with one of the others.

Decision-making

The *Living Space* pack, with these and other group assignments, was taken to a few local schools, along with the seven-minute videotape. Once again, the feedback was thought-provoking. The children's motivation — right across the age and ability range — was much stronger than the teachers expected. And the video, quite attractive so far as it went, was becoming almost as marginal as the teacher. The children wanted to get on with working out their own ideas. Within each group there did not appear to be much need for *leaders*. They were egging each other on, picking up ideas from each other, not content to leave the decision-making to any one individual.

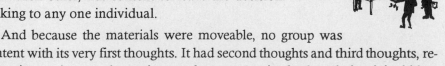

And because the materials were moveable, no group was content with its very first thoughts. It had second thoughts and third thoughts, re-arranging, trying out alternatives, perhaps even going back to their original idea.

The reactions of the classroom teachers were as interesting as the children's. They, too, were beginning to have second thoughts — about the *passengers*. Perhaps — like the teachers from whom Madame Montessori borrowed the *feeble-minded* children — they had been overlooking that half-hidden capacity which in children is nearer the surface than in most adults:

The kick to be had from making up one's own mind.

I managed to get an interview with Dr W D Wall, who had just completed a spell as the Director of the *National Foundation for Educational Research*. At the end of our session, which I had thought would be just a one-off, he said, *Come back again*. And this went on, over several weeks, as I reported the progress of the *Living Space* experiment. He ended up by saying this was something special, and it ought to be taken very much further. I launched into what turned out to be a four-year stint, funded partly by the Social Science Research Council, and eked out by a BBC series I did at week-ends on *The Decision-Makers* (politicians, captains of industry, media moguls) whose attitudes compared interestingly with the fresh thinking of the children using the *Living Space* pack.

Taking soundings

I began by going to schools in eight different local education authorities in England and Scotland, interviewing over 300 Junior, Middle and Secondary schoolteachers to find out how they saw their jobs, and their classroom clients — the children. The teachers, surprise, surprise, were very good at talking. (Later, I made a book for Penguin based on a trunkful of the tape transcriptions of the interviews.) They unburdened themselves, free-range.

Afterwards, I went through the transcripts and began to sort out what seemed to be each teacher's preoccupations — the problems and opportunities that engaged her or him most.

Some talked often about the need for orderly behaviour, no noise, trouble-makers kept in their place. They were concerned about planning their children's work for them, setting specific tasks, vetting results. They had a lot to say about the information they were giving out, the standards of behaviour, the correct procedures. Most of their time was spent in telling and showing.

For them, *learning by doing* still meant **learning to do as you're told**. They didn't expect much from the *passengers*, but there were always a few others who made it worthwhile — who responded to encouragement and always put up their hands when teacher asked a question, and nearly always wrote *a full page*.

About one in four teachers was less traditional. More concerned with tapping into the children's own experience, helping them to enlarge it through the information they gathered from grown-ups, at home and on project visits, prompting them to form their own judgements.

For these teachers, *learning by doing* meant **learning in order to do** — working out first principles, not being afraid to try something out which perhaps had not been tried in quite that way before.

These teachers were those the *Black Papers* had set apart as *exceptions* to the rule.

Nearly everyone talked at some point about the need for structure, authority, discipline, the acquisition of useful skills and important information. Also about understanding children's own interests and drawing on their own experience.

What made the difference between what seemed to be broadly two classes of teacher was the number of times that they talked about this or that. I sorted out those teachers who talked often about what they *put into children* and how children could be *fitted into* the teaching pattern; and those teachers more concerned with *drawing out* children's hidden capacities, *building on their experience*, and their ability to work things out for themselves.

I double-checked with a questionnaire to teachers, so that they could set out their priorities without having me in their way. Their answers confirmed the rough division I'd made. So I went back and persuaded just over 200 teachers in Junior and Secondary schools to spare time — a minimum of 60 minutes — to try out a *neighbourhood pack* in class.

Neighbourhood change

There were two kinds of pack, actually, roughly corresponding with those two teaching styles. One, *Living Space*, in line with the teachers concerned mainly with *drawing out* or *eliciting*. The other pack, on the same theme of changing your surroundings, reflected the more traditional approach, *handing out* or *instilling*.

I set off to distribute the packs, one for each teacher, without saying anything about the styles of teaching they were meant to represent. I went the rounds like Father Christmas dropping a parcel down the chimney, to schools in sedate Fenland villages and market towns, to rumbustious classrooms in London's East End and in downtown Glasgow, to remote one-teacher schools in the Highlands and the Western Isles, to the children of jobless Merseysiders and of commuter parents in the Home Counties. One hundred and eighty-eight experienced teachers and 16 student teachers, each with one pack, undertaking 220 class-room trials (some using their pack in more than one class). No-one obliged to use the pack for more than 60 minutes.

Only 2 teachers chose to stop after 60 minutes — one because he didn't like the pack, the other because she was poorly. All the others said they liked the look of the materials — varied, colourful and easy to use, and the children took to them eagerly.

Then the reports I tape-recorded on my return visits began to differ. Some teachers said the project had gone quite well, maybe a shade better than usual, but then came to a natural halt. Other teachers became progressively more gobs-macked at the response their children were making. The children were getting the bit between their teeth. One Junior teacher told me,

"When I opened the pack, I could see it was too advanced for them."

Q: *"So you stopped?"*

"No. It's been going six weeks. They were coming in for more in their lunch hour. I should have been very unpopular if I hadn't let them keep going."

Such teachers continued using the packs not just for a few weeks, but for months, a term or more, even a whole year. There was the same involvement by the whole class, the same feelings of *surprise* and *amazement* in the teacher's account of the *unexpected* increase in self-reliance, self-discipline, co-operation within groups and between them, the same impression that for once in a while, what the *Black Papers* people would call the *duller pupils* were really ... **thinking**.

Two sets of results. The difference both in the response of the children and the reaction of the teacher, depended on the matching — or the mismatching — of the teaching style of the packs to the customary teaching style of the teacher. Those who got a pack on the lines of what they were used to got much the usual result. The interesting difference occurred between those who got packs that were contrary to their usual practice.

The teachers who were keen to *draw out* children's experience, and who were landed with a more traditional pack, set about adapting it to give more scope for their children's initiative, and got much the sort of results they were used to getting.

The crunch came with the more traditional teachers who were given a *Living Space* pack, designed to liberate the children's capacities to figure things out for themselves, try out alternatives, reach their own conclusions. Most of these teachers were so impressed by their children's unexpected response that they chose not to alter the pack to suit their own styles, but to let things rip.

Counter-attack

It took nearly four years to get round to each teacher on my carefully weighted list, issue a pack, re-visit at intervals to hear what had happened.

 About half-way through these trials, another enquiry got under way led by Neville Bennett, based at Lancaster University and backed by the head of his department, Professor Noel Entwistle. They had begun by sending questionnaires to 871 primary schools in Lancashire and Cumbria. Like me, they wanted to find out what teachers were up to. The answers on the questionnaires, like the tape-recorded interviews I had conducted, showed that the majority of teachers, long after the days of Plowden, were spending most of their time in talking to the whole class, or in setting and vetting tasks given to groups or to individuals. Less than one in five were using what the Lancaster team called *progressive* methods.

They sorted out the answers to their questionnaires into three main categories of teaching style, with variations, — *informal*, *mixed* and *formal*. Then they followed up just 37 teachers, drawn from these three categories and got them to agree to have their children tested in the basic skills — broadly, the three Rs. One set of tests at the beginning of the new school year, another at the end of the year.

Comparing the tests revealed that by the end of the school year, the children taught by *formal* teachers were several months ahead of those taught by *informal* teachers. They concluded that

"a number of pupils cannot cope effectively in a less-controlled setting, and are unable to accept the responsibility of self-directed activity..."

In America, at about the same time, other studies produced similar results. And this was said to show that many children *would find an open classroom, that operates successfully for some children, extremely threatening and anxiety-provoking.*

Game, set and match to the authors of the *Black Papers*.

There was one notable exception to the trend amongst the 37 teachers whose classes were tested in the Lancaster experiment. She was a teacher in her mid-thirties with ten years' teaching experience, working in a school in a new town. Her children spanned a wide range of ability. Her classroom was open plan. She was one of the group classified as *informal* and her children's results matched or surpassed everyone else's. Her children spent more time on maths and English than many formal classes; at the beginning of the year, they groaned at the prospect of maths, at the end of the year they loved it. And they had lots of scope for the other two Rs — creative writing, stories, topic work.

As Neville Bennett said in his report,

... It requires a special sort of teacher to use informal methods effectively — one who is dedicated, highly organised, able to work flexibly, able to plan ahead and willing to spend a great deal of extra time in preparatory work. How many teachers do we have that could meet these specifications?

Unexceptional teachers, surprised by unexceptional children

Whilst the Lancaster team was writing up their experiments, I was pressing on with the rest of mine. Most of the 84 Secondary classes and the 128 Junior classes had a mixture of abilities. Some ranged from IQs of 135, which is pretty bright, to below 70, which is regarded as educationally subnormal. But at every age level from nine-year olds to sixth-formers, one or other of the same two packs was used, without changing a word or a picture. And the traditional teachers continued to find themselves witnessing the response of children to what might be called *progressive* teaching methods, right under their noses — impressed as time went on to such an extent that many chose to adapt their own teaching styles in future.

Unexceptional teachers with *unexceptional* children who they were used to controlling, directing, pushing along; now finding the very same children becoming self-disciplined, self-propelled.

One grammar school teacher of 20 years' standing reported,

"Great excitement, great noise which died down ... it died down of its own accord. I didn't have to quell it. One of the things that I've learnt is that I've underestimated their powers of thought and organising themselves ... before it all came from me, now it's coming from them. It's a different role for the teacher from the one I'm used to ... they are having to think out and solve problems instead of being totally dependent on me, and I find that this is a good thing."

Primary teachers landed with this unfamiliar teaching approach showed the same sense of wonderment as the secondary teachers:

"Children who have achieved very little in their time at school, achieved something in this. It's amazing really."

"A hundred percent better than I expected ... quite abnormal interest."

"Staying power very good indeed, above average ... more co-operation ... more logical thought than I expected."

"There was a sense that they were teaching themselves."

"A better quality of work ... it was more to satisfy themselves than to satisfy me."

"One boy, it"s about the first time I've ever known him to achieve something and finish it completely on his own."

"They are taking care ... going to the trouble to find out the mistakes they are making."

"They wanted to carry on, even though they found it hard."

 Other teachers told me that children were coming in early to school, staying in over play time, working unsupervised when their teacher was called away, reluctant to go home. In some secondary schools, those who had begun to truant came in on the days the pack was in use.

Norfolk dumplings

There was one school where there were two teachers in next door classrooms each teaching children from the same year. One told me

"It's a pity you've come this year. Last year's class was a joy to work with, but this lot, well I call them Norfolk dumplings. Pleasant enough, but lethargic, and I don't expect much from them."

The teacher next door was quite pleased with the children in his class that year. When I went back, a few weeks after the launch, he told me that the children were responding well, much as he would expect from this lot, maybe a shade better than usual. The pack materials fitted in well with his usual style of teaching. Three weeks in, he said, the brighter children were still going strong, as you might expect, but the others' interest was beginning to sag, and he figured that in a week or two the project would reach its natural end, much as he found such projects usually did.

Later on I went back again to hear how it had ended, and found it was still going strong. There had been an upturn, he said, various children had offered ideas for developing the work, and persuaded him to let them develop these ideas in little syndicates. *We seem to have got a fresh lease of life* which was rather surprising.

Next door the Norfolk dumplings had also surprised their teacher. Neither she nor they were used to the kind of work the pack materials promoted. But the children were responding enthusiastically, and showing more purposefulness, greater staying-power. They were self-propelled, but not veering off in all directions. She was not at all used to this kind of lesson, and certainly not used to this response, least of all from this year's bunch. But she really liked it.

What made her Norfolk dumplings so unlethargic? And, even more intriguing, why did the children next door stop sagging, and give their project fresh life?

The answer was in the playground at the lunch break, when the Norfolk dumplings were telling their neighbours about what they were doing with their pack (the *Living Space* one). Their excitement and commitment rubbed off on the brighter children next door who had been issued with the traditional pack. They got the message from the Norfolk dumplings and smuggled in the new ideas under the nose of their teacher, to transform the work they were doing.

The *Living Space* pack had turned out to be a Trojan horse, invading the classroom citadel, not laying it waste but transforming it, to the teacher's and the children's great satisfaction.

The children were showing their teachers a thing or two about themselves. It was the *discovery method* turned upside down.

Basic skills

I had been worried that teachers would take *Living Space* as a breathing space between serious work on the three Rs. I needn't have bothered. About a third of the trials took place in Scotland. One day I was rung up by the Chief Inspector of Scottish Schools who said his Inspectors had been coming across the wake left by the *Living Space* experiments, not always present during the lessons when the packs were first used, but seeing and hearing what the packs seemed to be doing to the children. The reports were good, so how about undertaking some seminars for senior teaching staff in schools and training colleges to ram the whole thing home? Fine.

And which teaching disciplines would be represented?

"Oh, the English teachers, of course."

This took me aback. After all, the whole point of the packs was to favour children who weren't much good with words. No, it had to be English teachers, because what the Inspectors were reporting was that the packs were promoting *language development*. Those kids who couldn't talk were talking nineteen to the dozen as they handled the materials, because when they were short of words, they could **show** what they meant, and they were picking up words from each other as they went along.

Geographers and maths teachers were quite happy too, because their children were finding that they needed the mapping skills and the number skills in order to work things out and solve the problems they had themselves created. They had acquired the motive power to learn. Even from teachers who could hardly be called *exceptional*.

✧   ✧   ✧

This doesn't seem to have been a fluke result. There has been more evidence since those four years' *coal-face* enquiries with the packs in the 220 classrooms. The *Living Space* pack used in the experiments aroused so much interest that we had to set up a small publishing unit to make more available, at cost, and to respond to requests for new packs, some for schools, some for adult communities — which have multiplied over the years. One of the later schools packs was piloted in a comprehensive school where the teacher reported that children who were legitimately at home, poorly, were **truanting from home to school** in order to take part.

Would this approach only work with the seasoned teacher? I wondered about the *Black Papers'* comment that for *the young teacher fresh from college*, the outcome of trying to be *progressive* would be *utter failure*.

Student power

Twenty-four students, a complete first year intake in a training college, volunteered as guinea pigs. Nearly all had been taught as children by formal teachers. Most, like the majority of student teachers elsewhere, came straight from school and university into the training college. A few had escaped to earn their living in the real world and now came back to learn. Most of them afterwards said they hadn't really known what they were letting themselves in for.

 Student teachers tend to be rather scared of their first school practice. It's like jumping in at the deep end. Our idea was to provide some homemade floats. The students had a good look at the *Living Space* materials, and were then asked to invent their own mini-packs which they could take into the classrooms as a means to get the children moving under their own steam so that the students could watch them and learn from them.

Each student was assigned to a small group of children at first. Later on they took on more groups, until they had the whole class — I was going to say, doing their bidding. But that was not the object. They had set the children going along lines the children themselves developed. The materials they had provided were the ingredients, not the recipe. The children could work out what needed doing, and they got a kick out of working out how to do it between them.

The students saw how the children responded to each other and to the materials. Back at base, they compared notes, plundered each other's ideas and experience, and then returned to give a new twist to the mini-projects in hand.

The experienced teachers were watching too. The Heads of the schools concerned reported that their own staff wanted to keep up the good work. The largest school put in a bid to the training college to repeat the scheme with double the number of students next year.

The student group went on pooling their experience and testing it against the theoretical work that took up the rest of their time back in college. They had created their own momentum. As they neared the end of their first year, they began to lobby the college administration, proposing that the experiment should continue in their own second year, and that the new first year intake should get the same chance that they had had. The tutors in the education department saw what the experiment was doing for their students and backed them up in a resolution to the top brass. One tutor, with ten years' experience of the established methods in the college, said he had never come across any student response that remotely compared with this one.

The top brass admitted that the scheme was a success. Continuing it was another matter. What would it do to the timetable? Where did it leave the training responsibilities of the college? What would it do to traditional subject divisions? However, to let everyone down gently, once the scheme was wound up, there would be a working party to *diffuse the benefits of the experiment*.

This did not satisfy the students. Unprompted, they got together and drafted a memorandum to the Academic Board. It said that the course

> had led to a deeper understanding of the child and his needs, the teacher and his role, and the value of resource materials in the classroom. It has given us confidence and … expanded our capacity to consider and think.

They were backed up by the Director of Studies at the High School where part of the classroom work had been done. He said the scheme was *a realistic and relevant reform of teacher education*.

The College administration was bombarded with the students' memorandum on three separate occasions, and at length conceded that the next year's group might be allowed to tackle some aspect of the scheme. But that was as far as it went.

What made the difference between the behaviour of teachers and children in the 37 classes that Bennett had carefully researched, and the responses we got from the 220 classes undertaking the neighbourhood packs' experiments; plus the 24 raw student teachers who followed in their wake with the materials they devised themselves?

More to the point, what was the difference in the behaviour of the children they all tried to teach?

There's nothing to suggest that any of the teachers or any of the children in any of the experiments was exceptional — apart from that one experienced woman teacher whom Bennett singled out as being the *exception* to what seemed to be the rule.

There is more to learning than doing the teacher's bidding, whether it is *Do as I say* or, more or less, *Please yourself.*

It has something to do with those deep-rooted motives we all share. The job satisfaction that comes from getting something right which is exciting and challenging to do; and the group satisfaction that comes from doing things together, egging each other on. An instinct to find out, try out, think out for ourselves.

Charles Darwin had a lot to say about instinct, which has helped the human species to adapt and survive.

If it were only a protective instinct, we might have stayed as we were a million or so years ago. But our evolution has come about **because we have been able to cope with change, worry things out, revise our ideas as we go along.** And this is the way, said Darwin, that children learn. They only learn when

"their interests are enlisted and ... learning is self-originated, arising from some instinctual source within them."

Resources for learning

Remember those technology students a generation back in the '60s, jam-packed round the last few inches of the time-scale?

Finding umpteen more changes to adapt to in their lifetimes than any other generation had had to face since the dawn of human history. They were suddenly discovering that they themselves were unique: as their children find themselves now.

In the 50s and 60s, we were still sorting ourselves out of the mess left by the war, grappling with the first effects of *Automation* and the *Infotech Revolution*. Like those hundred technology students, we had to admit that change was in the air, and wondered rather excitedly, *Whatever next?*

In the '70s, when the first *Living Space* experiments were taking place, some of that excitement was turning sour. Some changes seemed a bit threatening. At home and overseas, we could see the divide between the well-heeled haves and the footsore, jobless, have-nots. The gap was widening.

If ever there was a time when we could have done with a shot in the arm, a re-charging of batteries, a re-tooling of resources — this was it.

And, talk about the unexpected! We struck oil in the North Sea.

Enough to overhaul our ageing industries, convert from the dead-end arms race, expand the peacetime manufacturing base.

Enough and to spare for the upbringing of the next generation (at home and at school in the '80s) that could fit them to deal with the changes we know now.

Enough of those oil revenues to buy *time*.

Time for would-be teachers to get around, see the world (as their grandparents did in World War II), explore the hidden lands of the spirit, acquire zest for learning and doing that could one day rub off on the kids they teach. Time also for their tutors to spend in schools and in the community, understanding more about what children are up against and how they choose to cope.

Teacher/pupil time, with classes small enough to allow teachers and pupils to get to know each other properly, and generate the staying-power you need to build a firm foundation in the basic skills.

Time to give to parents, letting them in on what teachers are trying to do, seeing their own children through others' eyes; opening up more resources outside school hours for parents and children to enjoy doing things together.

In 1979, the hard graft of installing the first North Sea oil rig was over. The oil bonanza had begun. It was all there for the taking. And Margaret Thatcher, the true-blue millionaire oilman's wife, blued the lot (on our behalf), year in, year out, on the arms race and tax cuts for the comfortably off and unemployment benefits for the jobless.

Rather late in the day, we wonder why classrooms breed frustration; why many children, and some teachers and some parents, have given up trying.

❖ ❖ ❖

Opportunities

Living Space is not a substitute for the hard-won knowledge and experience that teachers and parents can pass on. The trouble is that for most teachers, there has not been enough time to enrich their own experience, let alone convey it to their children. They probably got where they are, at least in part, because at school they filled out their worksheets; put their hands up when asked for a recap of the broadcast or the textbook or whatever it was that teacher told them recently; and always wrote *a full page*.

On teacher training courses, they have been at the mercy of too much second-rate experience — mugging up other people's educational theories, but starved of the opportunity to do as most theorists once did — to study children in the raw, inside and outside the classroom; to try things out with them; to learn what really makes them tick.

As for their own exploration of those hidden lands  — arts, sciences, politics, growing things, caring for birds and animals, travelling far and wide to see how other people live — well, if you're going to pay your way, there simply isn't the time, these days.

What's true for teachers is doubly true for parents. If both of you are out of a job, there's not the money to go in for all that culture stuff. And if you're both earning full-time to pay off the mortgage and the video rental, bringing up the kids with the help of a paid childminder or an au pair, there doesn't seem much of your time left to spend with them and share their thoughts and feelings.

Children need the chance to make up their minds: to suss out problems together, try out solutions, make comparisons, see what works; and if it doesn't, go back to the starting point and try things out afresh without losing face or falling out with each other in the process.

Below the surface, it's still there, in our children, in ourselves — that hidden capacity to be up and doing. Waiting to be tapped. If not by Them, it had better be by the likes of Us.

LESSON FROM OIL CREEK

Upbringing means more than schooling. This isn't merely an academic point. If we are to bring up children, at home and in school and on the street, to become the agents of change, not just its victims — we have to go further than the three Rs and the events on the history chart and the places on the globe. Further even than being able to shovel all this information into the computer, and dig it out again on request.

Our children, like the rest of us, need opportunities to hone their skills in adapting to the unexpected.

Children have always been better at this than their elders, and they can teach us a lesson, just as with the *Living Space* packs, they began to teach their teachers.

It's a comprehensive lesson about the human capacities we all share.

We *can* get a kick out of DIY; and ganging up; and breaking out to try something new for the hell of it.

We *can*. The capacity is there, waiting to be recognised.

We don't know what we're missing.

✧ ✧ ✧

Take a backward look at Oil Creek, Pennsylvania, which made his first fortune for that man with an unerring eye for the fast buck, John D. Rockefeller. He was the man who made the most of the resource that nearly everyone else had overlooked.

In the early days all that anyone knew about Oil Creek was that you could make a modest living out of the oil puddles that lay on the surface of the land. People used to sop up the oil with rags, wring it out into medicine bottles, and sell it at fairs as Rock Oil (or Seneca Oil, after local Indians). Rub it on, swallow it down, sniff it up, it's the all-purpose remedy for *headaches, toothaches, deafness, stomach upsets, worms, rheumatism and dropsy.* It's guaranteed to make you feel good (or at any rate, better than you were before you tried it).

Not even Rockefeller as a smart trader knew what he was missing until an oddball called George Bissell, ex-professor, ex-high school teacher, ex-lawyer, ex-journalist, and in poor health, happened to take a second look. He got the oil analysed and found, as he suspected, that it could be processed to become a winner, as lamp oil and engine oil.

But how do you get enough of it to make a killing? In his wanderings, he had come across an advertisement for drilling equipment used to get hold of rock salt, deep down. He borrowed the money to set up a very small drilling operation, on a patch of poor land. First attempts — nil result.

Then, on August 27, 1859, 69 feet 6 inches down, they struck oil. Rather more than the surface puddles. An oil lake, which nobody had realised was there.

✧ ✧ ✧

The deep springs of motivation in most of our children are still largely untapped. We occupy them with information gathering, spiced with praise for those who sop up most and follow our advice in how to apply it when they have squeezed it out and bottled it up.

Sample drillings like the *Living Space* experiment show how much more is there, across the age and ability range, awaiting the means to bring it to the surface.

Bringing it out in our children is one thing. It *could be* done if we choose to change some of our own priorities. But that depends on recognising our own capacity to make changes for good instead of hanging around until bad ones are forced on us.

Here at home, the technological changes are coming thick and fast. We are dimly aware that this is a moment in history unlike any other. Many small changes multiply to create inexorable change, worldwide. (We couldn't accept that this really happens, until we heard about global warming.)

We can recognise that the world is changing. It's difficult to believe that we can change the world.

And yet...

Our children can remind us of the hidden resource we share with them, the capacity to explore new possibilities, to make a fresh start.

It's deep down in our human nature; it comes to the surface when people — a class, a gender, an ethnic group, a religious following, a generation — suddenly see themselves in a new light; and recognise that *they have it in themselves* to be the agents of change.

The results, for good or ill, can be more creative, more devastating, than all the novelties of new technology put together.

This is happening, for the most part, on the other side of the world from us. We used to think of nations to the South as backward, underdeveloped countries. Now their upheavals and their transformations impact on our own development.

Where did all these changes begin? And who helped bring them about?

Running through the web of change like a scarlet thread is the response of young people. Mowt and Shuttie's age group, and younger. Child soldiers in the service of warlords in Liberia, Rwanda, Somalia — are not all conscripts. Some have joined up because they, too, want to make their mark and show their mettle.

In Afghanistan in 1995, over a period of about four months, a student movement, Taliban, suddenly emerged from almost total obscurity, a core of 800 among the refugees from the recent war, schooled by fundamentalists in Pakistan, growing to an estimated 25,000, marching 300 miles from Kandahar to Kabul, having taken over the southern third of the country for Islam. The Washington Post reported of Taliban that

its members have stopped highway robberies in the provinces under their control, and they have reportedly executed drug dealers and have burned thousands of acres of opium poppies. Women apparently are not allowed to work and must wear veils.

One expert observer said, *Nobody knows where they came from or where they are going. We only see them moving.*

Every new generation has it in itself to challenge what the oldies have done. To assert independence against the powers-that-be. To carry its ideas and enthusiasms, its loves and hates, far and wide.

One thing most have in common — the grapevine. The faculty every younger generation has to communicate almost instantly, without fuss. To convey a feeling — a craze even — more often than a doctrine. A sense of identity.

This collective self-awareness can possess students in particular because they come together with thirsty minds, absorbing new ideas like a sponge, one moment bone dry, the next soaking wet.

"Here lies the only hope for our society"

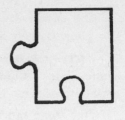

The pace of events has quickened. We expect the unexpected. We know that things ain't what they used to be, but we're still not sure whether that's a plus or a minus.

There is a kind of groundswell. Looking out to sea, a surface movement unlike what was there before. Something is happening a long way off, which we cannot easily identify. All we know is that change is on the way, and it has something to do with the way people view themselves. In particular, young people. A world-shattering self-discovery.

So this chapter is a sort of hinge to the book. In it, we trace the paths of three young Chinese — in a country which over the next ten years, if its economy doesn't overheat, could become the most powerful in the world; somewhat before anyone has really come to grips with what that could mean for the rest of us.

- 1 -

The first, who became a student teacher, was born into a society where everyone knew his place. *Between the four seas, all men are brothers.* They belonged to the largest culturally consistent population in the world. War, famine, pestilence could not disturb the natural order. It was summed up by Kan *Fu Tze*, Dr Kan (known to us as Confucius):

> *"First, the scholar, because his mind is superior to wealth, and it is intellect that distinguishes man above the animals ...*
>
> *Second, the farmer, because the mind cannot act without the body, and the body cannot exist without food ...*
>
> *Third, the mechanic, because ... the man who builds a house comes next in honour to the man who provides food.*
>
> *Fourth, the tradesman, because as society increases and its wants are multiplied, men to carry or exchange or barter become a necessity. (But his occupation tempts him to dishonesty, so his grade is low).*
>
> *Fifth and lowest in the list — the soldier, because his business is to destroy and not build up society. He consumes*

Confucius, he say this...

what others produce, but produces nothing himself that can benefit mankind. He is, perhaps, a necessary evil."

Every child's baby cap had embroidered on it the four words of good fortune: *Jung Min Fu Gwei* — the same written characters that any other child in China might wear to honour the written word, whether or not he could ever read anything else. The educated Chinese scholar knew some 20,000 Chinese characters. They were a direct link with the past and a universal bond throughout the land. Anywhere you went, if you were literate and met an educated stranger who couldn't understand your accent or dialect, you scribbled the Chinese character with your forefinger on the palm of your hand and what you wrote was recognised and understood.

For at least 2,000 years, the natural order could be taken for granted — much as ours was during the half-century or so when the British Empire seemed about to last forever.

But in his teens, this particular student teacher found that nearly every part of society was under threat. He stayed on at college, reading, reading, reading: the works of the ancient Chinese philosophers matched with the latest books from the West. He became part of a student protest movement. Their targets were the imperial régime, and the foreign powers, western nations and Japanese, to whom that régime seemed to be selling out.

He had grown up during the thirteen attempts by the revolutionary Sun-Yat-Sen to topple the dynasty of the Manchu emperors. The thirteenth, in 1911, set up the Republic, but without the clout to cleanse China of government corruption and competing warlords.

As a teenager, still at school in Jangsha, devouring everything he could read about Western reformers and revolutionaries, he came to the conclusion that

"There is an unchanging law … There must be the sacrifice of the individual for society, and the present for the future."

After six years in teacher training college, he moved on to Beijing and a dogs-body's job in the library of the University, read ten hours a day and kindled to the words of Professor Jen Tu Hsiu, China's most influential and adventurous academic

"I hope those of you who are young will be self-conscious and that you will struggle. By self-consciousness I mean that you are to be conscious of the power and responsibility of your youth, and that you are to respect it. Why do I think you should struggle? Because it is necessary for you to use all the intelligence you have to get rid of those who are decaying, who have lost their youth. Regard them as enemies and beasts…

O young men of China! Will you be able to understand me? Five out of every ten I see are young in age, but old in spirits. Nine out of every ten are

young in health, but they are also old in spirit. When this happens to a body, the body is dying. When it happens to a society, the society is perishing. Such a sickness cannot be cured by sighing; it can only be cured by those who are young, and in addition to being young, are courageous. We must have youth if we are to survive, we must have youth if we are to get rid of corruption. Here lies the only hope for our society."

Those words struck home first and foremost to students, who saw themselves not just as scholar guardians of the past, but as liberators, redeeming the sloth and corruption which had grown up round Sun-Yat-Sen's revolution.

The first great challenge to the old ways took place on May 4 1919.

In Tiananmen Square.

Ten thousand students of Beijing University assembled at the gates, and then marched in protest against three government ministers accused of secret sell-out dealings with the Japanese. Thirty-two students were arrested and this sparked off student strikes which spread to Shanghai and Nanking, and won support from railwaymen and shopkeepers and factory workers. The authorities gave in. The students were released, the three 'traitor' Ministers escaped to Japan.

Half a lifetime later, a student teacher no longer, Mao Ze Dong looked back at that student show of strength and called it

"the greatest and most thorough cultural revolution in Chinese history."

The honey bees

In his twenties he had been part of a student movement which really saw itself as *the only hope for our society.* They did not see themselves as an intellectual class apart, an élite.

In the towns and cities, they exposed government corruption and financial domination by foreigners, and began to involve city workers in their protest strikes.

They carried their knowledge into the countryside to share it with the *lao bei shing* — the old hundred names, the Smiths and Joneses and Robinsons. A YMCA worker named Jimmy Yen persuaded students, first of all in Shanghai, and then in other universities, that they had a special role, an obligation. Confucius's reverence for learning made it so valuable that it had to be reserved for the scholars. Jimmy Yen, honouring the ideals of Sun-Yat-Sen's revolution, set about making learning available to everyone. He could not see formal Western education working in Chinese society, especially the peasant society, with no money for schools and teachers. So he set to and sorted out from 20,000 Chinese characters just 1,300 which he arranged as the *Thousand Character Lessons.* Step by step, each lesson added a few new written words. Countrymen's words, concerned with homes and crops and livestock.

Students were the carriers of the new learning, like honey bees, going out to the villages as amateur teachers helping illiterate Chinese peasants to acquire this basic knowledge inside four months.

The lesson materials could literally be traced out on the hard-packed earth of the threshing floor. The first lesson goes like this:

Shia-Tze K'u — The blind suffer

Bu Shih Tze-Ti Yeh K'u — The letter-blind also suffer

For the letter-blind, the lessons are eye-openers in a double sense. They teach more than literacy. Sentence by sentence, they explain how villagers can use their own skills to transform their lives. First to better themselves, then to better each other. Tree planting to check soil erosion, street cleansing to check disease; credit co-ops to defeat the loan shark.

Mao, sizing up the experience of the European revolutionaries, saw villages as more important than towns. Not Lenin's sailors and factory workers, but farmers. The key for him was *land to the tiller*, land reform which re-distributed the land of the former landlords but still allowed them a share.

The revolutionary party founded by Sun-Yat-Sen was meant to follow out his Three Principles — *Independence*, *Democracy* and *Livelihood*. But for many of his followers, national independence was the only one that mattered. Others, like Mao, saw in communism the necessity to transform working conditions and provide a better standard of living. So *Livelihood* came first. In between these two objectives, that word *Democracy*. Not with the meaning Westerners understood, just unquestioning acceptance of Party rule — the Nationalist Party, the *Guomindung*.

> *"Members of the Party should possess spiritual unity... If the individual would sacrifice freedom, then the whole Party will have freedom."*

Not so far from Mao's own belief in *the sacrifice of the individual for society*. So for a time he stayed within the Guomindung. But to Sun-Yat-Sen's heir, Generalissimo Jiang Kai Shek, the Communist members of the Party were a threat which he tried to neutralise by a surprise military coup. The Communist survivors were forced to retreat across China, harassed by six successive military campaigns, on the Long March, six thousand miles to the northwest and the little town of Yenan, where they had their backs to Russia. They left the rest of China to the increasingly corrupt rule of the Nationalists.

The *Little Teachers*

In the fastness of Yenan, they began, under Mao's influence, to work out their version of the good society. Former students were the driving force in a new kind of mass education. Once again, it worked through villagers. The

Thousand Character Lessons got a new life. The Communists began to run winter schools, making use of the time when farm work slackened. They kept the new learning fresh in people's minds by wall newspapers — blackboards in each village edited by the local teacher, writing up the latest news to reach him  through the government newspapers. The words used on the blackboards were carefully limited to those learnt in the winter schools. The teachers themselves were served by a monthly magazine which ranged more widely, drawing on local talent in essays, short stories, poems and colour wood-cuts. But this *new writing* was built round local situations, and included local dialect. Literature, not as a private domain, but designed as part of everyday life.

Mao drew on his reading of the old Chinese poets and story-tellers, and the traditional songs and dances that celebrated marriages and harvests. The *Yang K'o* were turned into campaigning playlets which were fun to perform.

Southwards the Generalissimo's Nationalist government adopted the student mass education movement as a six-year programme aimed at wiping out illiteracy for everyone below 45. Then came the Japanese invasion, and all such notions were blown to smithereens. Nationalists and Communists made an uneasy truce in order to fight the Japanese. In the north, Japanese troops could occupy territory only by establishing strong points. There were few pitched battles, and the outside world knew very little of what was actually happening. Gradually, it emerged that the Chinese Communists were fighting most of the war, as an army — the *Eighth Route Army* — made up of guerrillas. They had a song:

> *We have no weapons*
> *We have no ammunition*
> *Never mind*
> *The enemy will provide them.*

Villages supplied the food, the information on Japanese troop movements, and the part-time fighters, who could make surprise attacks, and then fade back into the countryside. The network worked because there were those *cadres,* the Little Teachers, teaching war as well as re-development. Western military observers, dropping in on Yenan as representatives of the Grand Alliance against the Axis powers, were impressed by this co-ordination, and towards the end of the war with Japan, began to supply communications gear to help things along.

Mao and his closest colleague, Jou En Lai, made overtures to the Americans — but were rejected. With the Japanese surrender, the fragile alliance between Nationalists and Communists began to fall apart. The Nationalists seemed to have decided that now was the time to crush the Communists with the help of the military supplies received from the US to fight the Japanese.

Chinese students had been evacuated in the face of the Japanese advance across north and central China to the far southwest. Whole universities, students and professors, had taken to the road and set themselves up as *bush universities* in and around the city of Kunming in the southwest of China. Now those students reacted to the fresh stirrings of the civil war.

The students of three exiled universities organised a general strike, attempting to repeat the pattern of that Tiananmen protest a quarter of a century earlier. They almost succeeded, but were finally beaten by Nationalist military and police. Three students and one teacher were killed.

And that brings us to the second student, whom for safety we'll call Zhou Wen.

- 2 -

Zhou Wen's father was an army officer, often away from home fighting for the Nationalists in the power struggle with the Communists, and later against the Japanese. As a child at school, each day for Zhou Wen began with the singing of the national hymn to celebrate the *San Min Ju Yi* — Sun-Yat-Sen's Three Principles. His family believed in the Nationalist Party's role to bring China towards *Democracy* and *Livelihood* by way of *Tutelage*. That meant telling everyone what to do and how to think. There were *Thought Control* forms to be filled out at regular intervals, to make sure everyone toed the Party line.

He was accepted as an agricultural student in Nanking, but almost at once his university took to the road. Far away in the southwest, he and his fellow-students did their best to pass on their agricultural knowledge on the visits they made to green-fingered peasant farmers (who already knew more than all the students put together, but were far too polite to say so).

Then he came across an odd collection of young men and a few young women, some Chinese but most British or American. During most of the Japanese war, they had been trucking medical supplies, and operating a few surgical units at the battlefronts. But as the war with Japan neared its end, they were beginning to turn their hands to other work. They were pacifists, funded mainly by Quakers, who thought the best way to express their beliefs was to get as close as possible to war and then do something constructive to point the contrast. As an officer's son, brought up in the Nationalist military tradition, all this came as a surprise to Zhou Wen, but an increasingly attractive one. He dropped out of the bush university and joined the group, which was called the Friends' Ambulance Unit, later the Friends' Service Unit in China.

That is where I first met him. It was just after the Japanese surrender, during a lull in the Civil War and I was coming from service with the Unit in the Mediterranean, en route to a city on the North China Plain, which had suffered a double attack. It had fallen to the Japanese invaders; and it had been devastated by the flooding of the Yellow River.

A drowned city

When the invading troops were sweeping across the Plain, the Chinese decided the only way to block the Japanese advance was to blow the dykes at a place called Hwai Yang K'ou. As a result, year after year, at flood time, the river flowed south-eastwards, writhing every year on a different course, leaving great tracts of bog and marshland where no boat could move. Ten thousand villages were drowned by the river waters or devastated by the silt the river left behind — dry volcanic dust, brought down from the hill country in the far north-west. As that lifeless silt dried out, it drifted into great sand dunes, moved continually onwards by the wind, engulfing villages like lava from a volcano, turning farmland to desert.

Forty miles further down the present course of the river, there had once been the city of Jungmou. But a year or two ago the river, in one of its convulsions, had sliced through it and laid it waste.

In its heyday, Jungmou was a thriving city with its own bath-house, theatre, prosperous merchants' houses of red brick and green tiles, and, on rising ground, the magistrate's *Yamen*. There had once been ten thousand people living within the boundaries of its city walls. Now all that was left were the mounds on which the walls had been built, and on one flank, the east gateway. Outside it was the eastern suburb, Tung Guan, a huddle of makeshift huts which had been recently rebuilt by families who had fled when the floods approached. Now they had come back to their family lands, and the gravemounds which showed above the sea of mud.

Once the river was put back on its old course, the city could revive.

Four of us, two Chinese and two English, camped out in a mud hut eight miles inland from the drowned city and worked with the villagers of Shih Li T'ou to set up a clinic (the only medical resource within a fifty mile radius), a school, a textile co-operative, and soon afterwards, a livestock breeding scheme, resourced by a Berkshire boar, a Holstein bull, some Leghorn chickens and a he-goat, which we had acquired in a variety of devious ways. The great thing was that the patients attracted to the clinic began to bring with them their sows and cows and she-goats to be serviced whilst they queued.

We'd had a brief look at Jungmou city on our way in, and negotiated for the use of the only surviving building — the magistrate's Yamen, noting the scope for at least a five-a-side football pitch on the land between it and the river's edge.

Six months later, reinforced by Zhou Wen and others, we prepared to set up a second base, in order to follow the same plan, this time city-wide, and, thanks to Zhou Wen, with rather more attention to animal husbandry.

When we unloaded our bedrolls from our ancient ox-cart and looked around the city, we found there was no longer space between us and the river for a football pitch. Not even a cricket pitch. The waters were rising, undercutting the banks, shearing away the soft yellow earth to carry it 1,000 miles south-east to the Yellow Sea.

We were not the only incomers. Downstream, on the opposite bank of the river, a camp had been set up by a section of railway engineers. They were beginning to build a new bridge to replace the one that the river had destroyed. We watched from our clinic window through the winter as the bridge progressed. The engineers worked along it, with their supplies inched forward on railway wagons. By the spring, it was almost completed. Great timber piles supported a single railway track with planks laid across the gaps between the sleepers to make a path for pedestrians.

Diverting the river

Back at Hwai Yang K'ou, the old dykes which had been destroyed in the war had now to be rebuilt, against the full force of the River.

It was happening because a quiet-spoken *moving spirit* called Donald Faris, a Canadian pastor, had hired a boat to drift across the mile-wide Gap in the dyke to take soundings. (He gave me his pencilled diagram as a souvenir.) On the strength of this, he persuaded UNRRA, the newly-formed United Nations Relief and Rehabilitation Administration, to send Todd Almighty to supervise the diversion of the river back onto its old course.

Mr Todd was an American engineer, a get-up-and-go man, bristling with determination, who had got his experience, his nickname and his reputation careering about Asia in a guerrilla war on untamed rivers. He and General Jao, the Government's representative, made a marvellous pair — this compact bundle of American energy and his massive, slow-moving opposite number, as placid-seeming as the river itself.

Between them, they had worked it all out. There would be a fresh channel dug out to the north, so that when the dyke had been mended, the waters would flow naturally back along their own course, through Communist territory. The Communists were also to be supplied with money and equipment so that they could restore the wind-eroded dykes in their own territory. And it was all going to happen within a year.

Seven, nine, finally eleven thousand village labourers were mobilised, with creaking wooden wheelbarrows and panniers slung from *tiao* poles swaying on their shoulders. They ferried earth from the surrounding fields, and the few lorries available brought loads of stone blasted from a quarry thirty miles away.

On either side of the mile-wide gap, soldiers and villagers operated towers of timber like mediaeval siege engines, shafting tree-trunks topped with stones.

They hauled on ropes that raised the trunks and then let them fall to drive wooden piles deep into the yellow earth. Around them, fresh layers of earth were thumped down hard by gangs of villagers moving in a sedate dance circle. Each man held a cord attached at its other end to one great stone on which they could all pull together. The foreman chanted, the gang hauled, the cords jerked, the stone rose high in the air and came down hard on the surface of the earth. The gang side-stepped, moved six inches forward, swayed back and hauled again. Foot by foot, the Gap narrowed.

Then, the flood season.

The waters rose. Foot by foot the river edge in Jungmou came nearer to the foundations of our clinic building. One night, the rhythm of the river changed. In the moonlight, we could see the surface throbbing, with little crests like the scales on a dragon's back. And the sound it made was like the hum of turbines, or the roar of the Great Fire of London, or a fleet of bombers overhead. Next morning, we saw the centre piles come loose like a child's milk teeth. Then half the bridge went, and with it the wagons and the pile driver and ninety workers. Within another hour, all that was left were a few jagged stumps above the raging waters.

Meanwhile, the uneasy truce in the old Civil War was shredding away. We were getting occasional gunshot wounds in the clinic. Not many, because the river itself was in this part of China the main barrier between the Nationalists and the Communists. Once it was diverted northwards, the way would be open again. But which way? Nationalists advancing north, or Communists advancing south? For the time being, the Nationalists were still regrouping, bringing up their troops from the southwest. With them came more *Thought Control*.

Zhou Wen decided to re-join his university, which had now come back to its former base in Nanking. More and more students were coming together to oppose the resumption of the Civil War. Some were moving on into Communist territory. Zhou Wen stayed put; and at risk as one of the key student leaders.

Another visitor to Nanking was Todd Almighty. By this time, with the flood season over, the noose around the River Dragon's neck was almost tight. A swaying wire footway, twenty metres long, spanned what was left of the Gap. The whole force of the river, fathoms deep, thundered between the two sides of the dam. And at long last, the United Nations had managed to get some of the supplies out of the Shanghai warehouses, to complete the job.

But no supplies had gone as yet to repair the dykes in the Communist territory. Until that work was done, there had to be a halt. Otherwise, when the river rose again, it would burst out of its old course, and create new devastation.

At this crucial moment, there was an *important conference* which had taken Todd Almighty conveniently far away to Nanking. And whilst he was safely out of the way, the placid but devious General Jao got his orders from his government to pull the noose tight and force the river down the entry channel prepared for it.

At first, a gentle flow. But in a few weeks' time, the ice would melt far away in the north-west, the mountain streams would pour down to swell the River to its full ferocious strength.

Counter-attacks

The Nationalists were ready to counter-attack, with the River Dragon at their head.

Donald Faris, the Canadian pastor, decided to get there first. In the gentlest possible way, he raised hell with the UN and got the promised money for the Communists' share of the repair work. A convoy formed to take it into Communist territory, twelve trucks needed because the Nationalists had changed the money into very small denominations, and backed this up by strafing the convoy as soon as it reached Communist territory. So it had to come back.

More patient negotiation. We got forty trucks, loaded this time with wheel-barrows, netting and hand tools, spent five hours in the Nationalist Governor's headquarters getting past his administrative underlings to his inner office to find him immaculate in riding breeches and high polished boots, and emerge at last with a fresh set of safe-conducts.

This time, we were unmolested. We crossed the river's old bed and the no-man's land beyond it, followed the crumbling dykes within which the river was beginning to flow, and three days later reached our destination, the headquarters of the Communist *Yellow River Commission* — a cluster of villages, one a hospital, another set apart for visitors, nothing permanent so that in six weeks or so, everyone might shift to fresh billets in new villages to foil the Nationalist air raids. The only modern communication system was a single strand telephone wire, slung on willow poles, that meandered alongside the river.

Our cargo was dispersed overnight. A day later, a Jeep turned up with two men in faded uniforms without insignia. One was the Chairman of the Yellow River Commission, responsible for an area of 20 million people. The other was his driver, who smoked in the doorway whilst the Chairman and Donald discussed how best to persuade the UN to tackle its Rehabilitation job once the Civil War was over.

Returning on the dirt road next day, we could see the precious supplies already in use, with village teams at work on the double line of dykes where the river had already begun to lap near the vulnerable edge.

The diggers and *tiao* pole carriers attacking the dykes, unlike the conscripts at the Gap, were operating guerrilla fashion, free-range, with local decisions left to local people. But when the waters rose, the dykes had been raised by over a metre for 360 miles on either side. The onslaught of the river was contained.

✧ ✧ ✧

The Civil War had flared up. In Nanking, the student protests mounted. There were killings, beatings, disappearances. Their street demonstrations were increasingly backed by their professors. But it was the students that posed the greatest threat to the Nationalist government. Zhou Wen, as a student leader, was in danger. By this time, I was on my way home. And when I got there, I gatecrashed my way round Whitehall, pulling every string in sight to get him over to England on a study grant.

Over the next eighteen months, the Chinese Communists went over to the offensive, generously supplied with captured Japanese and American equipment.

They spread southwards like the Yellow River in flood, and scoured their way across China.

Zhou Wen pursued his studies, not only agricultural. He looked at us in England, and found us wanting. He went back to work in the new, Communist, society, where it seemed that a new world was dawning.

The young dancers

In Beijing, after the civil war had been won, a foreigner watched a procession winding down the city streets. The sidewalks thronged with people, middle-aged, elderly, very small children. The road is filled with youngsters in a procession unlike anything seen before. There are no officials to set the pace or keep the ranks, everyone on the road is dancing, girls and boys pirouetting, skipping, matching the rhythm of their singing in leaps and bounds. They wave bright scarves and banners in the wild abandon of a gypsy dance, or the joy of spring lambs in the sunshine.

The foreign onlooker was a Christian missionary who said afterwards that the nearest way he could describe that *Yang K'o* was by comparing it with the picture he had in his mind's eye when he read about the early Christians in the Acts of the Apostles.

What are they celebrating?

As volunteers, they have just completed the cleansing of the old city's open drain, a running sore which had defeated the efforts of everyone else for centuries past.

Where else could you find young people dancing triumphantly in the streets to celebrate a piece of sanitation?

Mao, the ex-student teacher, never forgot that youngsters in schools and in the Red Army were the life blood of the Communist revolution — in Jen Tu Hsia's words, *the only hope for our society*.

They were the Little Teachers who knew better than those oldies *who are decaying, who have lost their youth*.

Zhou Wen wrote back to his friends in England and told us to stop writing. He wanted nothing more to do with us. He got on with the work that was to hand — back in the university teaching and researching to speed the agricultural revolution.

All over China, youngsters were coming into their own, no longer subservient to their elders, owing their loyalties at first to the Party; before long entirely to Chairman Mao. It was in its way a youth religion which began to take over the whole of life. The Word was spread by press and radio under Mao's personal control. He became its prophet, almost its god.

Which brings us to student number three.

- 3 -

Jung Chang was born in those days of joy and achievement, her parents long-serving committed Communists, who had endured the perils and privations of civil war and the war with Japan. Her schooling was centred on reverence for Mao, and by the time she was in her teens, her most important textbook was the Little Red Book containing the *Thoughts of Mao*.

In the early 1950s, the makers of the revolution were villagers, the guerrilla workers who repaired the dykes, reclaimed the land, harnessed local hydro-electric power. They built the railway system, section by section, which put everyone in touch and fed the cities.

The pace quickened. People flocked to the towns and cities for the jobs that were going in the new factories, the railway marshalling yards, the ports. The cities mushroomed. At the same time, the power generated within each village began to be transmitted through the village *cadres*, to strengthen the power of the district, and then the region, and ultimately the grip of central government. So what had begun as the Great Leap Forward, decentralising to village level, 'bottom-up', had turned into a 'top-down' control of everyone and everything.

Mao forced the pace through national campaigns to increase food production, kill the sparrows that stole the crops, search out every bit of old iron to feed the steel furnaces. The Great Leap Forward was to achieve everything at once, and those that got in the way were *enemies and beasts*, heretics who denied the true faith.

Believers

It was more than most people could take. Production figures were invented to satisfy the high priests of government. Villagers hung on to food supplies. Famine killed off millions. Mao's lieutenants, amongst them the Secretary of the Party, Deng Xiao Ping, managed to slow down the campaigns and the economy began to recover.

Mao felt himself sidelined. He blamed the Party officials, the self-styled experts, who were *going down the capitalist road*. Remembering his younger days, he put his trust in villagers. They were the best teachers. The so-called experts should be made to learn from them. Everything that was going wrong was the fault of people in power, apart from himself. He had to undermine that power in order to put things right.

So he made his appeal to those who are always inclined to oppose authority — the young. He went over the heads of established officials, academics, army officers, and launched his *Cultural Revolution*. He was remembering his own feelings back in 1919 when the Peking students came out on Tiananmen Square for what he had believed was *the greatest and most thorough cultural revolution in Chinese history*. Now he called into existence the new young revolutionaries, the *Red Guards*. Young people, everywhere in China, were encouraged to see them-

selves as cleansers of society, to make a clean sweep. They could do this whilst they were still at school, by exposing the shortcomings of their teachers (a doddle, really!). In the universities, they took on their professors, and the administration which had installed them, as if they were village landlords brought before a mass trial. They marched anyone they disapproved of through the streets with placards round their necks describing their *crimes*. The movement caught on almost overnight, like a Crusade or a Jihad. And it grew in violence.

Fourteen-year old Jung Chang was swept along with her classmates as a Red Guard, pledged to *submit ourselves unquestioningly to the control of our Great Leader, Mao*. It was an outpouring of love and loyalty, carrying everything before it like the River in flood.

Afterwards, in her book *Wild Swans* (HarperCollins Publishers Ltd.) she tried to analyze what had happened.

On 9 January, the *People's Daily* and the radio announced that a January Storm had started from Shanghai… Mao called on the people throughout China to … seize power from the capitalist-roaders.

'Seize power!' This was a magic phrase in China. Power did not mean influence over policies — it meant licence over people. In addition to money, it brought privilege, awe and fawning, and the opportunity to take revenge. In China, there were virtually no safety-valves for ordinary people. The whole country was like a pressure-cooker in which a gigantic head of compressed steam had built up. There were no football matches, pressure groups, law suits, or even violent films. It was impossible to voice any kind of protest about the system and its injustices, unthinkable to stage a demonstration. Even talking about politics — an important form of relieving pressure in most societies — was taboo. … So when Mao launched his call to 'seize power', he found a huge constituency of people who wanted to take revenge on somebody. Although power was dangerous, it was more desirable than power-lessness, particularly to people who had never had it. Now it looked to the general public as if Mao was saying that power was up for grabs.

Mao had given youngsters belief in themselves, and in their power to do whatever they saw fit. Always provided it could be done in his name. They knew things had gone bad — that was obvious to everybody. Mao, who more than any other had been the creator of the new China, had star quality. They were his fans, loyal to him alone.

They gave him back absolute power and he used this to consolidate his position as the one person who knew best. So anyone who differed, or might differ, was suspect. Millions found themselves under threat. Some, relatively lucky, might be sent far into the countryside so that they might *learn from the peasants*.

Heretics

Zhou Wen, being always rather independent-minded, was denounced as a *rightist*, deprived of his job in the university, sent with his family far away to a remote inhospitable valley. (Resourceful as ever, he managed to win over local farmers who found he could give them good advice on horse breeding.) He was one of the luckier ones. Many other dissidents were sentenced to aid the industrial revolution in forced labour camps, churning out cheap goods for the Western trade. Many others died in slavery.

For six years, the Cultural Revolution arrested China's development. The economic juggernaut which had been created in the early years of the Revolution had spawned new industries at a faster rate than anything that Europeans had achieved. But the Great Leap Forward that Mao brought about was really a lurch backwards. By 1970, the hangover had begun. Centralisation was a recipe for corruption and inefficiency.

Some of the most passionate of the young Red Guards began to use wall posters to reclaim first principles, and indirectly to criticise the personality cult fostered by Mao's Yes-men.

Jung Chang like Zhou Wen in her turn was getting a shade too critical of the régime. She was sent away to learn from the peasants. She became a *barefoot doctor*.

Then, during the seventies, towns and villages began to be encouraged to fend for themselves, once more. Millions of villagers were on the move to the big towns and cities, seeking work in offices and factories. But Mao was old and sick, and those who became his successors were admitting that *the biggest problem in the nineties will be in the countryside*. With the death of Mao, the state system began to swing round like a giant oil tanker on a fresh course — to decentralise and allow country people more scope to work things out for themselves, away from the swollen cities.

Jung Chang was accepted back in her home town and after some nail-biting uncertainty, nominated for a scholarship in England. In the 1980s, gathering information for her book, she went home on yearly visits, and saw the rise in standards of living as Mao's successors began to reverse the centralisation, and restore initiative to *Town and Village Enterprises*, mostly family-based. Even whilst the labour camps continued and dissidents were persecuted, there were signs of growing independence. In the cities, students were putting up more wall posters, floating new ideas as well as old ones, none of them conformable to the régime.

Zhou Wen managed to get back to his research and teaching work in the city. The political pressures lessened and he became respectable again.

A generation on from his first trip abroad, escaping from the Nationalists, the government allows him to attend an interna-  tional conference. He comes to England and we spend a day together visiting the Lightmoor Village. He talks pigs with some of those who had built it and were beginning to develop their own smallholdings. There are reminders, he thinks, of the village outside Jungmou where we first worked together. But as the day ends, and he prepares to return home, he says to me, *It's going to be worse before it gets better.*

He goes back and before long communication stops once more.

Chinese students, once again, are proving troublesome. This time, they're organising themselves in protest, much as Zhou Wen and his generation did in the middle of the civil war. They concentrate their efforts, in memory of the students of sixty years back, on Tiananmen Square.

This is a fresh generation, the children of the Red Guards of the 1960s, but no longer brainwashed. Students have always felt themselves a kind of fraternity, sorority, having more in common with each other than with the older generation. So they come in thousands in Tiananmen Square to show their strength.

They time it for the visit of Gorbachev in 1989, the one time when the authorities have at all costs to keep face. Their banners claim *Glasnost* and *Perestroika* for China too. It's about as big a humiliation for the régime as anyone could imagine. Older people, at first sympathetic, hold back whilst the tanks roll in to flush out the students, away from the television cameras, to be hunted and killed in the streets outside.

Zhou Wen comes back from a field trip to find empty streets. The city has retreated behind doors, watching, waiting, numbed but not cowed.

Many students survive, some to lie low, others helped by unexpected sympathisers escape abroad to fight another day, one day.

The universities, especially Beijing, continue to be seedbeds for change. Six years after the Tiananmen massacre, when the government makes its usual security checks against disturbance, the University district is sealed off with armed police keeping foreign journalists away. But 45 leading academics and political activists, brought together by Professor Ding Zi Lin and her husband, of Beijing University, signed a petition on behalf of political prisoners:

"I'm very glad that so many people dared to sign their names. It's the first time," she said.

She also gathered 27 signatures for a petition to the People's Congress *to enquire into the truth* of the Tiananmen massacre. Meanwhile, dissidents are circulating a new edition of the pro-democracy *Peace Charter*.

Jung Chang sums it up:

"The course of liberation is irreversible. Yet Mao's face still stares down on Tiananmen Square."

Zhou Wen comes abroad again for an international conference and I meet him in the USA. *It's beginning to get better*, he says.

Step back for a moment. What is special about the stirrings I have described in this chapter? Jimmy Yen's *education movement*, the Chinese Communists' *winter schools*, the *guerrilla campaigns*, the *Democracy Wall* posters, the *student strikes*. People are seeing themselves in a new light.

Zhou Wen and his fellow students were following in the tradition of those who had first demonstrated, back in 1919, on Tiananmen Square. By the time he had reached middle age, students and schoolchildren were out again in the streets, making their mark as Red Guards.

To outsiders, the Red Guards were mindless fanatics with an appetite for violence that was going out of control. Generations of students before and after were by comparison high-minded, non-violent.

What all of them have in common is their belief in themselves, and their willingness to sacrifice themselves, individually, for a greater cause.

This self-discovery is easily exploited by corrupt politicians or religious bigots, but it seldom begins as the result of a system or a structure.

You can't spot a particular moment or a place where it all started. There is a stirring which releases a force of nature, *human* nature, like the melting of the snows in the spring that swells the waters of the Yellow River.

The River grows in strength and power from many tributaries. You can't pick on one and name that as its source. All you can say is that **there is a season when the flood waters rise**.

You can channel them to irrigate the crops and power the turbines, or blow the dykes to devastate the countryside.

Transmission

If the Yellow River gets star treatment in this chapter, it is because living beside it — attempting to cross it in the engineers' high-powered river launch, carried on the River's back a mile downstream — I felt its strength.

. And stayed on to see it tamed, almost bare-handed, by *people power*.

At first, it seemed the River Dragon of Chinese legend, almost omnipotent; just as Jung Chang in her Red Guard days saw the godlike person of Great Chairman Mao, *Chairman Mao is the red sun in our hearts!"*

It doesn't do to romanticise power, make a mystery of it — any more than to confuse those who hold power, for the time being, with power itself. That has been the mistake of many history books, and of the media personality hypes which take their place today.

Power grows from very small beginnings, as rivulets become streams and streams become a mighty river.

And the power to control power? Those Chinese dyke workers working with scarcely more than their bare hands, changed the Yellow River's course, and finally contained it. How do you rate that?

Our concern is with the process whereby unimportant people become powerful; not just as individual Do-It-Yourselfers and moving spirits, or as ginger groups like Giroscope or the Rochdale Pioneers, but as a floodtide that carries many others with it.

Mobilising people's power depends on being able to transmit that power effectively: getting the river to work the water-wheels and the turbines. Or, to bring that transmission idea nearer home — it's a matter of linking pedal power to the bicycle wheel. A bike is a marvel of economical, adaptable, satisfying energy application. But only if the chain that links the pedals to the wheel is tight and strong.

At present, the mechanism for translating intentions into action is — *talk*. And as umpteen encounters between Us and Them have demonstrated, talk alone simply doesn't stand up to the strain.

We need an alternative...

8 Must the talkers always win?

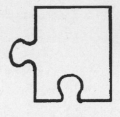

We have communication problems.

Are any of these situations familiar?

What's to be done about them?

Talk shop number one

There's to be a public meeting in the local hall. Could be about vandalism, or the new dual carriageway, or muggings, or drug abuse, or housing repairs. Main thing, it's called by the Council so there's a chance to get at them and find out what they are up to.

The Chairman has a suit and a tie and about fifteen minutes after the meeting was due to start he decides no one else is likely to turn up.

"Well, I am sorry we haven't got more here this evening, but I do congratulate those of you who have managed to come along.

*Now what we want to do is to **consult** you. With me here we have Alderman Mrs Bagwash, and the Chief Assistant to the Assistant Chief. And our very good friend who has prepared some of the information you can see [he indicates large maps in bright colours and rather small print]. And there are brochures which I hope you will take with you as you leave.*

Now, we want to give you the broad picture of the situation, as we see it — it's all right, Sir — there will be an opportunity for questions, later on."

If you are sitting on the sidelines you notice, as the meeting grinds on, that the front row — the prominent residents — are giving appreciative nods — just to show they're really with it.

In the middle rows they are just nodding.

And at the back of the hall, as the talk goes on and on, a latecomer can contain himself no longer, gets up and shouts:

"WHAT ABOUT MY BLOODY **GUTTER!**" [Or whatever else the Council should have done something about but hasn't.]

At this point real communication has ceased.

The meeting goes on for a while. Some other comments, more or less emphatic, and then everyone disperses, in time to get in before the pubs close.

In the Saloon Bar over the gins and tonics, the platform party tell each other,

"It's always the same. You never get much sense from these people. Some of them are as thick as two planks… They don't appreciate the trouble one takes, all that material, the brochure, the display… One simply wonders whether it serves any useful purpose — apart from the public relations aspect of course."

Further down the road, in the Public, some of the people who were at the back of the hall are making their pints last, and filling in time being rude about the meeting.

"Typical, really. The only time they got near anything practical was when Ernie mentioned his gutter. And all that wanker on the platform could do was say he wanted to consider the broad picture. Don't catch me going to another meeting like that. And what's more, that lot get paid for coming here!"

Talk shop number two

Someone else is being paid to be an *animateur,* a *facilitator.* She comes in as an outside worker to bring key residents together and help them to express themselves.

She has a flipchart, and seats everyone in a circle. So there is no question of hierarchy or anything like that. Except that she is the one with the coloured felt pens. She winkles suggestions and complaints from those present; she writes them briskly up, as they come, with her own adjustments to make them more relevant or less confusing.

It's a bit like one of those teacher-led discussions sessions in the classroom, although colours are better than chalk on the blackboard. She is not in the least patronising, she doesn't talk posh, she is genuinely anxious to get people's ideas, and to help them to work out how best to put them across to whatever authorities or charities might take notice. All the same there is a lingering feeling amongst those who have once been Brownies or Wolf Cubs that they are ranged around a Brown Owl or an Akela. And that the end product should be an expression of enthusiasm that sounds a little bit like *Dyb, Dyb, Dyb* from the leader; and *Dob, Dob, Dob* from the rank and file.

Anyhow they have to rely on her to do her best on their behalf in any dealings with influential outside bodies.

Talk shop number three

The Action Group is meeting, at short notice, in someone's flat. The Chair is late, but hurries in with a bulging folder.

"Is this all of us? I thought more had promised. Oh well, let's get stuck in. I've written to the Council as we agreed. And to the police. And Tricia has been doing some telephoning. She'll report on the results as soon as I've gone through the

letters. And I've got some points to raise that I think we should all consider. It's alright Ernie, we'll have the discussion a bit later..."

The meeting goes on and on and one or two remember appointments they have which means they have to leave before closing time. So finally, there isn't a quorum when it comes to summing up and making decisions.

At the next meeting there are not so many present. And the one after just has the Chair and Tricia as Secretary and someone who has come in because it is warmer. The Chair and the Secretary turn to each other:

"All this we've been doing, your telephone bill, it's a fortune I've spent in stamps alone. And there's just no support. People don't realise how important it all is for them. How much longer are we breaking our backs on their account? It's the apathy, the indifference."

Three unkind caricatures. They're 2D, not 3D. They don't tell you all that's going on beneath the surface. But what's common to all three is that when you describe them like that to professionals or to residents, they say, *Yes, it's true, it happens. That's what we are all up against.*

Not the only thing we're up against, but the first.

Killer talk

It's the talk that puts people off at the very start. **Killer talk.** It's the fluent talkers who make the killing. They keep going long after the rest have shut down or moved out. So in the early stages the talkers win. But it is a Pyrrhic victory. In the long run, everyone's lost out. The talkers haven't won over anyone to the extent that people want to join in and believe they can do something.

Maybe the worker with the flipchart gets nearest to arousing people, because it is their ideas, mainly, that she writes up. But when it comes to putting all the ideas together, and presenting them to the outside bodies, she carries the can. Everyone else is fairly content that she should, because after all, she knows how to put things across. So she ends up as more than a messenger.

She has to translate a lot of rather fuzzy, even random ideas into an acceptable form. A form which **she** finds acceptable and hopes the outsiders will see fit to take on board.

Everything depends on these talkers, because they are the ones who deal and bargain on the rest of the community's behalf. So feelings of dependency — which are aroused because people are having to live on benefit, or plead for jobs, or put up with poor housing — these feelings of dependency are reinforced.

Another thing which makes it difficult for anyone without the gift of the gab is the need to speak up in front of everybody else. In a public meeting pent-up feelings may make you blurt things out in a way that puts the platform off and doesn't argue your case. Or you might make a positive suggestion, but not put it very positively, being unused to this kind of public speaking. The Chair thanks you and invites the meeting to comment. There is rather a long pause. No one likes to push themselves forward and speak up, even though some might actually agree with what they *think* you're saying. The Chair looks around for a glimmer of response ... then thanks you again, rather too effusively, for your suggestion; and moves on to other matters. Catch you sticking your neck out like that again!

Personalities

Egos dominate. There is nothing you can say that doesn't carry your image with it. Could be that everyone thinks you are marvellous, charismatic, honest as the day is long. So whatever you say, they swallow it whole.

It is more likely, however, that one personality is another's *bête noire*. Anything that so-and-so puts forward is likely to be a load of codswallop. Or if it isn't, it masks a vested interest. Nothing dishonest, necessarily. But

"We all know where she comes from on the estate, and it always seems to be her patch that gets the support, somehow. They shouldn't be let get away with it again."

When it comes to differences of opinion, everyone sticks up for their own idea: through thick and thin, because if you give way, you lose face and people won't take so much account of you or your ideas, next time. So it pays to be single-minded and whilst everyone else is blethering, to keep putting your point across, even if it has to be dragged into other parts of the Agenda. Even if that means that the rest are staying quiet because they are gradually being turned off.

Single-mindedness also makes it difficult to see things whole. Banging home one idea all the time leaves little scope to consider the ways a proposal might affect things we had already decided. Or might have to decide about in the future. It's all too easy to latch on to one simple proposition that gets considered in great detail, and mops up the time so that the rest of the Agenda goes hang.

Talking things into the ground goes a long way back.

"For my part I am butt a poore man, and unacquainted with the affairs of the Kingdome, yett this message God hath sent mee to you, that there is great expectation of suddaine destruction; and I would be loath to fill upp that with words."

Trooper Everard was one of the rank and file soldiers elected to take part in the *Putney Debates* held by Oliver Cromwell and his generals at a turning point in the English Civil War. The top brass and the Other Ranks were for once almost on a level footing, faced with the possibilities of defeat. For most of the proceedings the man who took notes of the discussion did not know the Trooper's name from Adam, and wrote him down simply as *Buff Coat.* They were there to settle on *the future constitution of England* and in the end because the likes of Buff Coat managed to cut some of the cackle, they emerged more or less of one mind.

Three centuries or so later, another rough diamond was on the Committee to negotiate the first really successful housing co-operative north of the Border. It was taking the best part of a year to reach a watertight agreement between the incoming tenants and the City officials handing over to them.

A good man, everyone said, and a shrewd one. But he told me,

"I go to the meeting and I know what I want to say. But sometimes it is thirty minutes before I can find the words."

Missing

In such situations, the fluent talkers carry on regardless. And all that common sense, local knowledge, intuitive understanding, lying below the surface — wasted. They may not even realise what they are missing.

People attend a public meeting to see what can be done, usually about their own surroundings — what's happening to homes, or children, or the landscape or the prospect of a job.

Or they might have seen something on TV that creates a bond with people far away faced with danger or oppression which the viewer can recognise. People see what it is like, feel it for themselves, they are in the picture, but they don't find the words to say what they mean.

Other people — the platform people — have got where they are because they find words dead easy. They were the ones in the junior school who always wrote a full page; in the secondary school they joined in teacher-led discussions. They did well at interviews for college. They know how to take minutes, rig the Agenda, write reports, handle the telephone, draft press statements.

They're pretty good at number work too. They can quantify needs, apply measures, cost benefits, grade performance indicators and count up outcomes.

In the Ministry, they like to talk about *taking a view,* as an issue is passed from one desk to another, down the corridor and back up again. They make field trips and are taken round — by the local platform people — to see for themselves. But they fit their findings into the systems that guide their working lives. Their perceptions tend to be different from those in which the people at the coal face see and feel and think things out.

On their own ground, local people have their own kind of word power. They come across on TV, full blooded, from the heart. For the most part they are saying

"Look.

Look at what you have done to us. Can't you see what is happening? When are you going to pull your finger out and do something about it?"

This makes great TV, and the ones who are always good for a furious sound-bite get asked back whenever some vivid colour is needed to liven up the programme.

What's missing is a meeting of minds.

Whichever side of the Us and Them divide you happen to be, it's all too clear where the problem lies. It's with Them.

"It's not our fault," say the platform party, *"that our Award-winning schemes get vandalised."*

"What are we paying taxes for?" comes the response. *"You've got a bleeding cheek to blame us for your cock-ups. Earn your pay, for a change!"*

When resources permit...

Crime, drugs, truancy, joblessness increase the pressures. The gulf between Us and Them is becoming more difficult to bridge. Resources are scarcer. Feelings are higher. Attitudes harden.

The Council goes on saying, *Leave it with Us.*

The residents go on saying, *It's all Their fault.*

The talking shops continue. The reports multiply, with more and more descriptions of the problem which gets wrapped up with layer upon layer of paperwork. Each official adds another wrapper, as if everyone were playing pass-the-parcel in reverse.

Hardly anyone disagrees about what needs to be done, sooner or later, *when resources permit.* But those resources already include disused buildings, derelict space, and all the disregarded talent and experience of the people who live in the place.

Somehow, the connection isn't made.

One mind?

Dr Roger Sperry, American scientist, won his Nobel Prize for research on the brain and the two hemispheres which make it up. It divides like this:

LEFT SIDE		RIGHT SIDE
speech,		spatial perception,
writing,	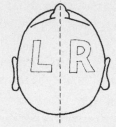	pictorial recognition,
number,		intuitive thought,
logical analysis		non-verbal communication

Suppose there is an accident, or a surgical operation? The two hemispheres become disconnected. What happens? It is as if there are two individuals, each in partial control of the same body, neither aware of the existence of the other, neither able to deal properly with what the other does best.

Does that situation sound familiar?

At this point, I have to get you back to Chapter 6 and the *Living Space* experiments in schools. Some people in the Department of the Environment heard about the results, in particular the way the so called *passengers* in the classrooms had responded. They figured that there were passengers on housing estates whom the authorities wrote off as *apathetic.* They might in the long run turn out to be as hostile as those children in the classroom who found traditional teachers a write-off.

Dummy runs

The *Living Space* trials showed that in an average school classroom, youngsters, with and without the gift of the gab, could use the pack materials to work things out together and make sense of real neighbourhood problems. Why shouldn't the method work with grown-ups?

I was commissioned to find out.

What seemed to do the trick in the classroom was to have things in 3D, with the chance to shift them around in order to work out how to transform a situation. Not so juvenile, after all, if you consider what Rommel and Montgomery got up to with their sand-trays in the Western Desert.

I came across a raw, new estate outside Oban in west Scotland where tenants had just moved into rows of houses on three sides of a rectangle, and low-rise flats on the fourth. They had a problem. The police were lining up their children and taking names and addresses in a forcible way because the kids were playing football where they shouldn't. This was because they couldn't play football where they should. The space enclosed by the housing was piled high with builders' junk, left behind when the contractor moved on.

So, as usually happens, mums took the lead, formed a tenants' association, bearded the local councillor with a petition (press photographer alerted to be in attendance), and established that the contract required the builder to remove his junk.

The Council made the builder behave, and then challenged the tenants to decide for themselves how they wanted to use the open space now available.

That challenge seemed to me just what many other neighbourhoods could be considering. Meeting it required consensus between all sorts of different interests within the community. The process of sorting those out ought to involve Us as well as Them.

So we made a pack which included a 3D layout, with the open space and a selection of every kind of option that anyone could think of, shown as cut-outs which could be placed on the model, moved around, thinned out as people gradually established priorities. The *Open Space* pack was published for neighbourhood groups to use as dummy runs, working out how they might tackle problems if they took on the roles of those real Scottish people.

It was a kind of game, and the players were invited to represent different interests — the caretaker's concern about access for the refuse trucks, and the problem of arson in the basements; teenagers wanting a five-a-side pitch plus somewhere to meet without elders breathing down their necks; the tenants' association committee, briefed by their local councillor, that there could be a grant, but only for something everyone is ready to accept; council officers with a memo from the Chief Executive saying *Do something, but it mustn't cost much*; patient members of the local Advice Bureau, trying to get a hearing from all parties, and maybe coax sense into them.

One of these packs went particularly well when it was used to launch a week's course for a variety of professionals, planners, social workers, housing officials, all sorts. From the very first day, the pack took over, and for the rest of the week, the groups were interacting, with increasing zest, and at times anger and frustration. Some 'tearaway teenagers' went up and down the corridors of the college where the course was taking place, shouting slogans, intruding on the anxious discussions of the 'tenants' association committee', plastering the walls with slogans. The keenest member of this particular group was an elderly magistrate's clerk. Meanwhile, the 'local government officers' had locked themselves in and were refusing all approaches from the other parties, whilst they tried to *frame a policy*.

For real

By the time the course dispersed, it was clear that *Open Space* packed a punch. Some of those involved introduced it to a real residents' group, in Dalmarnock, eastern Glasgow. They quite liked the look of it. *Ah,* they said, *Very interesting. But where's the place it's all about?* I said it could be anywhere, it was meant to be a situation everyone could recognise.

*Not good enough, at all, at all. We want it **for real** so that whatever we work out will suit Dalmarnock, and give us a chance to get something done.*

We made a new pack, with materials that could be arranged to suit whatever neighbourhood the users belonged to, beginning with Dalmarnock. The model was made over a long week-end, put together and spread out on table-tennis tables, big enough to dominate the biggest room in the social club.

Twelve feet across, it left no room for a platform party and an audience in rows. Along the wall, we hung freezer bags of the option cut-outs so that anyone could shop around, pick whatever they preferred and plonk them on the model, wherever they chose.

The residents' group set a date in February 1977 and invited all comers within Dalmarnock to take part.

At this point, there was heated discussion about *Them.* Should outsiders be invited along? A BBC *Tonight* team had been filming various public meetings where feelings had been so strong that Us and Them had come to blows. Could we accept the risk of bloody noses round the model?

Hoping for the best, it was decided to take the risk, but to hedge bets by labelling each visitor with name and job, offering a cup of tea, and then quietly mentioning that *the rules of the house are that anyone wearing a label should keep their mouth — **shut** until spoken to.*

The visitors — local councillor, regional planners, district planners, housing officers, the secretary of the Citizens' Advice Bureau, the police superintendent — all told about 15 of them, clustered rather near the door, eyeing the possibility for a quick exit. But within minutes, they were sucked into the proceedings.

Eyes on the ball

 Residents, busily placing option cut-outs on the model, were button-holing the visiting experts to check up on legal, technical, financial possibilities and constraints. They were able to do so conversationally, because everyone was milling round the model, rubbing shoulders, with a tendency to talk to each other out of the sides of their mouths while fixing their gaze not on each other's faces but on the subject matter itself — the place and what might be done to it.

The traditional consultation process was turned on its head. Instead of the professionals coming in to *consult you,* the residents, and then going away to decide unilaterally what might be best for them, it was the residents who were consulting the experts to tease out the range of options that might be open in dealing with any issue.

The BBC team turned up. David Jessel interviewed some of those who had taken part, and called it,

"a scheme which at a stroke of childlike brilliance put reality into the lazy jargon of community participation."

Reality. Not dummy runs. Fun, everyone agreed, but not a game. Part of the realism came from people being able to recognise familiar landmarks. I over-heard an old lady, as she leant across and fingered the sides of a tower block, counting upwards until she reached one particular window, turning to her companion, *That's my flat!* she said. It was only a sheet of A4 folded up and spiked onto the polystyrene model base with sausage sticks. The model making didn't run to providing the building with a top. But for her, it was, in a sense, real, just like the vandalised garages below and the rubbish-strewn ground where the back greens should be.

Take up

So we called the new pack *Planning for Real,* and now it has been in demand at home and abroad for nearly twenty years. The range of option cut-outs has trebled as more ideas have come in from later users. Packs have found their way to Australia, Africa (east, west and south), the US, India, Russia, Italy, Belgium, Holland, East and West Germany, Indonesia, the Caribbean, parts of Latin America and other places we don't even know about until someone gets up at a meeting and says, *Oh yes, we've been using one of your packs for ages.*

The packs seem to attract all sorts of people. What they have in common with the rest of us may have something to do with that Laurel and Hardy approach I mentioned earlier. **The urge to put things together, shift them around, try out alternatives until eventually they come right.**

On one estate outside Nottingham, the generation gap had become so desperate that almost any adult had become a target for teenagers who were in and out of court and custody. They particularly disliked the police. The estate had nothing for them — apart from a patch of waste ground. Then they were offered an old Portakabin and a chance to adapt it to their own designs, worked out beforehand on a model of the building, with a bigger model of the site to show where the building should go. They showed the models around, and suddenly their image changed. They were no longer written off as antisocial tearaways. They became acceptable and began to tackle the job itself without losing any of their zest and independence. They formed their own action group and chose to reinforce it with adults, including a local policeman.

Success did not always come so easily. In one city, the first *Planning for Real* was officially declared out of bounds by the Council leadership, perhaps feeling threatened by what the residents would come up with. (We were taking videos as the exercise went on, and had to edit out the faces of local government offi-cers who sneaked out of their offices in order to join in.) Next year, another *Planning for Real* in the adjoining ward — and this time the Local Authority was all smiles. Maybe it no longer felt threatened; or perhaps it could not afford to stay clear.

Conflict and consensus

In Sheffield, the authorities cottoned on to the idea from the start, gave their support, but didn't try to dominate. The area covered by the model was a red-light district. As usual, there were follow-up groups to sort out priorities on particular issues. The *Housing* group tackled the problem of empty houses from which tenants had flitted, which were then occupied by prostitutes and their pimps. The residents knew all about this, but it was news to both of the outsiders joining in, a policeman and the housing officer. Between them all, they worked out a system to alert the housing department so that it could house families from the homeless list the moment the residents signalled that a house was vacant.

The *Transport* group worked out an ingenious traffic circulation system which still survives and makes it very difficult for kerb-crawlers.

Then a third group took shape, on *Prostitution,* pure and simple. The groups were meeting in each other's houses, and this one grew quite heated. The elderly, on the whole, simply wanted the prostitutes *Out! Out! Under somebody else's carpet!* Some of the others in the group, mainly the younger ones, wanted to tackle the roots of the problem, the shebeens, the single parents on inadequate benefit. One night, two members of the group grew so angry with each other that one went outside and kicked the other's car headlights in.

And what happened afterwards? They went on meeting. One member commented,

"It's like a family quarrel. You don't just give up."

The interesting point was that no-one was blood-related. There were also ethnic divisions, and yet when a permanent body was set up to see the joint plans through, a mainly white population elected an Asian as their Chair.

Afterwards, the Leader of the Council commented

"Planning for Real is an example of residents changing the Council's mind and thereby saving their area from demolition."

✧ ✧ ✧

Remember Nancy Peters, on the Meadow Well Estate on Tyneside,[1] talking about the time, ten or 15 years back, when the place started to deteriorate? She was one of the moving spirits who tried to stop the rot. They could see that the children were getting out of hand partly because the surroundings were no longer good places to play in. So a few, mainly women, began to agitate for a children's playground on a derelict site. The Council had a fairly progressive reputation elsewhere in the Borough, but it wasn't going to be badgered into

---

1 Page 18

changing its priorities. So the agitation continued and feelings got worse. Eventually, the project came up for decision, the funds were allocated, catalogues of commercial play equipment were flourished, and the Council's workforce set it all up. *Over to you,* said the Council.

The local action group, unpaid, hard up, which had already put a lot of effort into persuading the Council to do something, reckoned it was the Council's responsibility to see the job through and provide supervision and maintenance.

No such luck.

So the children, well used to running wild, took over and the older ones gradually took the place apart, whilst everyone else looked on. This put relationships between Us and Them at a new low.

Many of the same residents were running a Rights Centre designed to get everyone wise to what they were entitled to from the authorities; and to back them to the hilt in any arguments with Council departments that might result. The Rights Centre soon acquired a mixed reputation. Residents were all for it, the Council appeared to be increasingly against it and began to find reasons for terminating the Centre's occupation of the disused corner shop in which it was based.

Meanwhile, as more jobs were lost, the vandalism and the aggro increased. Council officers began to feel that money spent on Meadow Well was money down the drain. Everyone was obsessed by the lack of *resources,* by which everyone meant money put into the community by outside bodies such as the Council (which in the long run was partly money taken out of the community in taxes). Nobody had much to say about the biggest resource of all, the untapped capacities of the residents themselves.

Drilling for oil

I began meeting with a handful of residents in what was then thought to be the most drug-ridden and crime-ridden patch on the estate. They were interested in the idea of *Planning for Real,* and used it to work out, for the benefit of the Council's architects, a system of security fences to hold muggers at bay. Then we went a stage further with a device that had long been in use as part of the *Planning for Real* strategy: the *Neighbourhood Talent Survey.* Like the model itself, the questionnaire was fun to look at, quite unlike an official form, and used simply as a starting point for a wide-ranging chat about all the skills and interests buried in the household: far more talent than people themselves realised, until they looked at the list, and began ticking off their hidden skills.

The survey, as usual, was done house-to-house, face-to-face, by a few residents themselves, initially visiting 47 houses picked at random from the 220 houses in five streets. One out of the 47 didn't want to know and slammed the door. The other 46 were eager to tell about the skills and interests they had.

When the results were put together, it was a surprise for everyone. This trouble spot, written off as a dump for no-hopers, was brimful with untapped talent.

The handful of moving spirits drew on this to get a few activities going for different age groups, learning by tempestuous experience on the job how best to cope with free-range five-year olds in temporary premises; organising excursions and parties for older people, improvising a snack bar.

The word got around the rest of the estate, and led to the forming of a Working Party to do something drastic about a much bigger patch, the site of an old reservoir, with a solitary community building on it, badly designed, and not well run, where the youngsters for whom it was intended spent more of their time throwing half-bricks at the incomers than participating in the old-style activities on the programme.

There were more *Planning for Real* models, of the building itself, and of the area around it; and an ambitious neighbourhood talent survey of over 1,000 households, which as before, surprised everyone by the wealth of buried talent it revealed.

The Working Party was reinforced by a sympathetic officer from the Council, which was just beginning to revise its ideas. (Although one senior officer was overheard to say, *Those fuckers couldn't plan a pram shed!*). A little Council money had been spared to fund the Working Party which now put together a fifty-page Report, *A New Heart for Meadow Well,* with plans and costings provided by the Newcastle Architectural Workshop to a detailed brief put together during the *Planning for Real* sessions. There were proposals to convert the discredited youth centre and make it the base from which the wasteland surrounding it could become what later was called the Community Village.

But even whilst the Report was being drafted, government cuts persuaded the Council to close the building down.

Words and deeds

The authorities quite liked our Report when it was published in the spring of 1991. It said that if improvements weren't made soon, there would be more trouble. And then, for five hot summer months, the paperwork went around and around. A galaxy of sub-committees came into being, each with the benevolent inclusion of community representatives to make sure that they could have a say. To begin with, there was a lot to be said, just reminding the powers-that-be that here was a viable scheme overdue to be put into effect. Then, as the talking shops continued, the residents began to drop out, to attend to the rest of their hard days' lives.

In September, the younger generation expressed their view of the youth centre's closure by burning it down.

Two days and nights of riot forced the police on the defensive, with potshots at a helicopter cruising above and other fires which burned out a corner shop and laid many houses open to the sky.

The September riots forced everyone to think afresh. Members of the Rights group took turns to sleep in the Rights Centre and in a nearby church centre to keep them safe. One elderly lady who had stayed home for three nights ventured out to walk up the debris-littered street, *shaking,* she said, because everything seemed to have fallen apart. But, like others, who had dropped out of the talking shops, she went into action, got hold of a disused hut on the premises of the local school, brought children together to form and run their own club. The members of the Working Party renewed their efforts, and focused them now on the replacement of the burned-out building by a new, all-purpose, community building (with, of course, a *Planning for Real* model to start it off).

At long last, there was money in prospect to get the work done. But this time, the Working Party said, the initiative would have to come from within the community. They decided to hold estate-wide elections, and to form a nine-member *Community Development Trust* which could then negotiate with all the outsiders — Council, government departments, charities, well-intentioned private firms, the lot.

The Trust made use of the priority charts which form a part of most Planning for Real exercises. The charts were divided horizontally:

and vertically under headings that distinguished between what WE CAN DO ON OUR OWN, what WE CAN DO WITH A LITTLE MONEY AND ADVICE, what WE CAN DO JOINTLY WITH OUTSIDERS, what WE EXPECT OTHERS TO DO BECAUSE WE CAN'T DO IT OURSELVES.

Most of the Trust members were unused to committee-mongering, and many were suspicious of each other's special interests in the estate, but they got round some of the aggro by putting detailed suggestions on to cards which could be spread out on the table and then transferred to the chart. The moment the cards left the writer's hand, they became anonymous, because no-one had to know whose suggestion it was, and anyone could place it on the chart. If there was any disagreement about the placing, all you had to do was unobtrusively to turn the card face down, showing the word *Disagree* on the back. Even that could be relatively anonymous.

The process was fun. It began with the everyday chaos of everyone's notions jumbled together.

> *"The priorities are — Now, Soon, Later — and by putting your ideas on cards, then everyone gets together and you chat about it... This is the first committee I have ever been on and the first time I'd ever seen the other members of the Trust was at the first meeting... I got to know them as the weeks went by. I could see what we were trying for... I'd say we're all after the same object in the long run. It's just that some have got good ideas, and some have got better ideas...*
>
> *We've had a couple of squabbles... but not anything that's really out of place... I wouldn't say it's been easy-going, we're still struggling to a certain point, but reaching some objectives...*
>
> *People are less likely to fly off the handle... At one stage (one Trust member) had assumed more power than was reasonable... and he was quite firmly put in his place by the Group... and there seemed to be no hard feelings. And that seems to be a learning occasion, for everybody... I think there is more sense of humour... (He's) very serious in some things, but it's easier now for people to rack him a bit, and he's more likely to laugh at himself... People are less frightened about making a decision."*

The jigsaw pattern began to sort itself out.

The *Planning for Real* model had shown roughly *Where* things might be improved. The priorities chart helped people to work out realistically *When*. The neighbourhood talent survey showed among all the wasted skills and experience *Who* might be willing, paid or as a volunteer, to take part.

Filling in time

Council officers, at first rather doubtful about the capacity of these *inexperienced* residents, began to think again.

> *"I'm very impressed by their professionalism, their commitment, which I haven't seen in other community groups. They're able to put aside their own individual needs for the good of the community, which is quite difficult to do... They've managed to put aside things that happen on their own doorstep and see things in a much broader view, which is quite unusual.*
>
> *They've grown from strength to strength, and they realise that they needn't be intimidated by outside agencies, that they're just as good as anybody else."*

This gradual attitude change helped to get most of the Trust's proposals accepted by the authorities.

Meanwhile, as the paperwork circulated in search of one endorsement after another along the corridors of local and central power, everybody waited.

Youngsters, in particular, were unaware of the ins and outs of bureaucratic procedure. The night after the press was headlining the murder of Jamie Bulger by two ten-year olds on Merseyside, I came on to the empty Metro platform on the edge of the Meadow Well Estate. There was a child's bike, almost brand new, on the rail tracks. Sprawled over the roof of the platform shelter were other ten-year olds, plus or minus, who had placed it there, eagerly waiting for the train to smash it up.

Another time, residents had organised a Fun Day, with a bouncy castle, and hamburgers, and a raffle, just to keep everyone happy. Some professional community artists set up a display of their own. All day, they cut and hammered old floorboards to fashion a work of art: a great big heart-shaped arch, to celebrate the proposed *New Heart for Meadow Well*. They kept everybody off whilst they did the job, and then welcomed a bunch of ten-year olds to group themselves within the heart and be photographed. They looked as good as gold. Then, when the photograph was taken, the ten-year olds took over, and smashed the heart to pieces. Afterwards, one of the visitors found children busily breaking into his car, and had a job to drive off without them.

The Trust members, meanwhile, were following a slightly different strategy. An empty store-room, number 40 Avon Avenue, had been taken over by the Council to provide temporary youth facilities, where at first there was modified

mayhem. The Trust raised a little money to employ a local community artist to work with some of the teenagers to decorate the façade of the building. A set of graffiti boards, and the security shutters over the windows, covered the space from the pavement to the roof.

Forty-Odd emerged in dazzling colours. On the Fun Day when everybody celebrated this achievement, an elderly resident told me, *It won't last the week-end. They'll mess it all up, they always do.* Year after year, I go back to see. So far, it is still there, intact.

Works of art

That small success encouraged the Trust to stage the new *Planning for Real,* this time for the design of the community building to replace the one burned down in the riots. *Forty-Odd,* now resplendent inside as well as out with more graffiti artwork, was the venue.

The morning was reserved for the younger generation to build up their idea of a multi-purpose centre, on a layout representing the affordable space that might be available. One lad who had dropped in was a reputed ramraider. (A newly-transferred police inspector, trying to get the feel of the place, said he had to admire the way the young ramraiders went about their work. Everything thought out so well beforehand, the details, the timing, the teamwork — *a real work of art!*)

The reputed ramraider spent all morning with other teenagers experimenting on the layout and stayed on in the afternoon to argue things out with the architect the Trust had brought in, and to swap ideas with the older residents. He wanted to get it *right*: for all parties, not just the young ones.

In the early days, the Trust met every week, come what may. With luck, and a taxi when things overran, I could attend the evening meetings and still catch a train to another scheme south.

It's all yours

The taxi driver tells me he is twenty-five, and his family always lived here. He likes the look of Forty-Odd but he says *I can better that.* When he was fifteen he was trying for an O level in Art, which was generally considered to be a doddle. There were ten in the art class and one day they started talking about the dead-boring appearance of the bus shelters, particularly the one on the promenade in Whitley Bay, which was just an uninviting expanse of brick.

Uninviting? They decided to do something about it. When no-one was looking, they measured it, and one night they primed it. They had got together to design a really interesting mural, in which each had his own bit to do in his own way, but blending after a fashion with the others. They bought their paints (at the school discount) and began at 11.30 one night, with two taking turns to watch out for the police, completed the job at 7.30 am and went straight on to school, feeling a bit tired.

The local paper called it MINDLESS VANDALISM and the Council threatened to whitewash it. But a local reporter did a mini-survey and found that 85% of local readers actually liked what had been done,

"though some said we should have asked first. So we actually sent a reply in to the paper which they didn't print of course, pointing out that if we had asked the Council's permission they would have replied 'Sod off!' It's still there, ten years on. Every time I pass it in the taxi, it gives me a boost. Got me an O level too, just scraped in with a D. I'd do it again like a shot, and so would the others, and enjoy it.

My three-year old son has been drawing on the sitting room wall. So I stripped the wallpaper off in his bedroom, gave him some more felt pens and said, 'Carry on. All yours!'

It becomes a question of ownership.

It took a year to build the new community building, hopefully the first in the proposed Community Village. The Trust negotiated, to and fro, between charities, and *support agencies,* and the Council, and the regional representatives of central government. Out of all this emerged a scheme centred on a handful of young people who would get training on the job, and afterwards set themselves up as a construction enterprise, all ready to tackle more building work as the Village takes shape.

There was another Fun Day, indoors as well as outdoors this time, to celebrate the completion of the building. Everybody packed in to hear a few words from visiting VIPs. One of them, representing the Council, said that the building work was in a special sense unique. This building, *unlike every other building scheme in the Borough,* had taken shape from day one to completion *without a single case of vandalism or theft.*

Hands-on

People safeguard what they have helped to create.

In Meadow Well, the lads who built the new centre were at the leading edge of a process going back through the riots and the earlier *Planning for Reals,* and the first Rights Centre, and the Credit Union, and the Action Group for the children's playground. At each stage people were coming together to **show** what they meant, showing to themselves as well as to the outside world. Showing more often by visual means rather than by words.

They were underlining the lessons taught by the children who took part in the *Living Space* experiments. There was one housewife, working on a housing scheme in another part of the country, who summed it up. She was one of a group that were working out their own house designs for a new development, with a couple of architects on the sidelines, watching to see what these amateurs came up with. In particular, how they coped on the model layout, with moveable walls, doors, windows, sinks, cookers, fridges — to design their kitchens.

> *"We saw what we were doing. You could translate words into action… Just as two people who live together can start a sentence and you know the rest of it. You look at the model and say 'Let's try this'. So we tried it. If it was wrong, we changed it. Then objections were raised — so 'Alright, let's try it again another way'. And this is where we came to a consensus.*
>
>
> *It was like speaking your thoughts. You visualised each other's thoughts… We got to a state in the end where we didn't need to speak."*

The watching architects, commenting afterwards, were at a loss. An hour or so's work by the prospective residents, and they had come up with all the ergonomic problems, and devised all the right solutions.

The professionals had nothing left to add.

On top or on tap

So the professionals are destined for the scrap heap? Everything is up to Us, and we no longer have to depend on Them?

No-one seriously doubts that the changes we need to make have to be made together; in some sort of combined operation which makes effective use of different sorts of knowledge, skill and experience. Neither side can do without the other.

The way they interact with each other, however, that's something entirely different.

For a start, it may mean taking a fresh look at traditional roles.

My Uncle Frank was more an onlooker than a doer, but he didn't miss much. He just scraped through his exams as a surveyor, so that made him a professional onlooker, but he never got a proper job until the air raids. Then he became a bomb damage inspector at ten pounds a week walking from 'incident' to incident to assess claims for War Damage.

At the time I was working my way through a hospital to pick up enough experience to be useful, one day, in China. I used to come over to Uncle's on my nights off, and give him the inside dope on the way the hospital ran. It was short of staff and so welcomed ten of us as orderlies, polishing floors, emptying bedpans, chatting up the living and laying out the dead. In return for this, and if we were good, we might rise to the heights of the operating theatre, and crown our efforts by scrubbing up and assisting the surgeon in taking out somebody's appendix.

The theatre sister was a purposeful redhead whose standards never dropped, on duty. We sweated it out, day and night, but never dared loose a drop of perspiration in her immaculate theatre. When the time came to assist the surgeon, he was equally exacting and made me change my sterilised theatre gown because it once touched a non-sterile surface.

At Christmas one grateful patient, who kept a pub, sent us all a case of his best and when it was the turn of our theatre to close down we decorated it with strips of bandage dipped in acraflavine and gentian violet. Towards the end of the party, I noticed the redhead had apparently passed out on the theatre floor.

But when the next door theatre was suddenly landed with more bomb casualties than it could take in, she woke herself up, re-opened for business, and, professional to her gloved fingertips, sailed through the next operation undaunted.

Telling Uncle about such things made me a medical expert in his eyes. He was attending the out patients department in another hospital because of a little trouble incurred in his walks around the bomb damage. Perhaps it was his legs, or just possibly his waterworks. He wanted to know what the doctor thought was wrong, but the doctor was always in a hurry and just asked him to keep coming back. However Uncle managed to glimpse his Case History sheet two days running and told me at the weekend what he had seen. On the first day the doctor had written

P.U.O.

The day after he had added below it

N.Y.D.

Neither of these diseases was known to my uncle and he asked my advice. I explained that the first meant *Patient Under Observation* and the second meant *Not Yet Diagnosed.* The doctor, good professional though he might be, was clueless. But as a professional it didn't do to let on.

Anyone who has invested years of study to get professional qualifications needs to feel that all that time and money were well spent. More than that, it's important that other people should feel the same about one's special knowledge. You have to be right most or all of the time.

Until recently this also meant that no one expected you to go asking advice from the patient. Information, of course. But the consulting room was meant to house a one way consultation process.

This applied just as much to professionals in other walks of life. Knowledge is power, and it is tempting to hoard it. In the Middle Ages people talked about the *mysteries.* Each craft was a mystery in its own right, you served a long apprenticeship, and were gradually admitted to the mystery, much as a London taxi driver painstakingly acquires *the knowledge* which distinguishes him from the drivers of mini cabs.

There is also a feeling that if ordinary people know too much they may become aware when you, good professional though you are, happen just for the moment to be clueless.

In Oxford, the nineteenth century Master of Baliol College would never have allowed himself to be thought of as a role model. But his example lingers.

My name is Benjamin Jowett
What is knowledge, I know it.
What I do not know, is not knowledge;
And I am the Master of this college.

Civil servants and local government officers have tended to say *Leave it with us* (because, although it's left unsaid, *We know best*).

Professionals are knowledgeable. But are they in the know about what's really needed? Do they know what they don't know?

Once in a while, one of these professionals has a hunch that some of the residents know what some of the professionals don't know. And maybe are able to do something that the professionals haven't been able to do.

Once in a while, residents begin to see that the professionals are not invariably bloody-minded, and may even know what they're talking about.

It's one thing to reach this mutual understanding. It's another to survive the hard knocks of living and working together.

Which brings us to —

9 Four weddings and a funeral

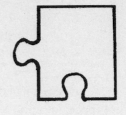

Working out the right relationship between Us and Them takes some doing.

Earlier, we have considered the ways in which the moving spirits among communities persuade the rest of us to get a move on; how groups come together to back each other up; how ideas take shape.

In all these situations, the professionals get a mention, but the part they play is often left in the shadows. Sometimes, a working relationship emerges and endures. Sometimes not. So now, consider more closely the way these marriages of convenience or inconvenience work out.

1 • Birkenhead

When *Planning for Real* was launched in Birkenhead, Philly was in her early twenties and saw most of it from the sidelines. The model, 24 feet long and about 6 foot across represented a mile long strip, the spine of the city. When they were making it the residents began to point out that this was not one locality, but about seven. You could work out the invisible boundary lines by the pubs people called their local.

Philly's family was scattered around a central section, quite close to the Birkenhead park, designed by the same man who thought up the Crystal Palace. It used to be a great place for the kids. Nowadays less so, because of the dog turds and the abandoned drugs syringes.

The *Planning for Real* exercise was reasonably successful: it created ripples of interest, and some of the proposals shown on the model went through the committee cycle and turned into fact. But now, it was over.

Not so. A year after the first sessions began the Chief Executive rang me up to say, in effect, that the vibes were still good. *Planning for Real* had brought residents, officials and even a few politicians milling together round the model, talking to each other in a different way, conversationally, not as if they were at a public meeting.

They had even got to using first names, which at that time was unusual. And it had gone on like that. A resident would ring up an official to slag him off about a load of rubbish left behind by a contractor's gang, and they would be talking to each other as members of a family would when someone complained about a sinkful of unwashed dishes.

The Chief Executive was retiring anyway and felt more inclined to innovate in his last year. So he suggested a return visit and some further discussion with residents about what new things might be attempted.

Philly belonged to the Jubilee Association, residents loosely forming round the local Catholic church and a Credit Union. They took on the idea of the *Neighbourhood Talent Survey*, teamed up, in pairs usually, an oldie and a youngster, male and female. When you go door-knocking, partic-  ularly in the flats where no-one opens the doors to outsiders if they can possibly help it, it helps to have someone else in support.

 Philly and her partner went round with their newborn daughter in the pram, and later on when we met in a disused shop, the temporary base of the Jubilee, Philly made a beeline for the back kitchen to cook up snacks that tempted people to stay and endure all the talk which followed.

Everyone agreed that a place was needed, not just a derelict shop in a building which could be easily broken into. And it should have enough space for different kinds of activity. Workshops, a sports area, an office, and, said Philly, *a kitchen and a proper café* which would serve meals for the elderly, and snacks for passers-by.

Back-door reconnaissance

Everyone knew exactly where to look. The Birkenhead College of Art was built in the heyday of Merseyside ship building, and was known by its principal donor, Cammell Laird. It looked out over that beautiful park. Its official entrance was up broad tessellated steps to the double doorway guarded by two voluptuous stone ladies supporting the porch roof.

That was no longer the way in, because everything had been boarded up by the Council when its Education Committee found it could no longer support the art school there. Philly's cousin's husband, living just up the road, knew how to get in by the back way, with a borrowed key.

Our first reconnaissance was just a few weeks after the place had been closed down. Inside, the rooms and the passages and the broad staircase were still graceful and intact. Down in the basement the cupboards were open, but there was modelling clay, still soft in its wrappers, and half completed sketch books lying open on the benches. There were no bodies about, but it felt as if the place had been visited by the Plague.

We discovered that the Education Committee had no idea what to do with this beautiful building. We learnt from the Chief Executive that it was up for grabs. Or it might be. More reconnaissance with the borrowed key as Philly and the others began to stake claims: spaces for a kitchen and a cafeteria (of course); and for try-out workshops down in the basement for fledgling enterprises. In the studio where once the College life models had reclined, just space enough for badminton and old-time dance sessions.

Upstairs, room for local clubs to meet, office space and an interview room for an Enterprise Advice Unit, but not one whose official appearance might frighten people off. It would be next door to the sitting-out space in the café, and people could drop in without making elaborate appointments, put up ideas of their own for enterprises and maybe take a look at those which were already underway downstairs in the basement.

Almost all this actually happened.

Eventually, the *Laird Enterprise Trust* scheme gained a national award for community enterprise from the Prince of Wales. Philly went to London to receive the plaque from Himself.

But not for a long, long time.

The right-hand man

The house-to-house survey showed where to contact the wasted talent: people with a lifetime of experience, on the rocks because dock work and shipbuilding were going down the drain. Youngsters pitched out of school which they had been taught to think of as a preparation for the world of work, and finding it was an introduction to the scrap heap.

We got the proposals together in a photocopied brochure with a free cover design from the Council, and outline costings from a local architect, all in a matter of weeks. The Chief Executive commended the brochure to his successor, and bobbed out into retirement.

But fortunately for us, he left behind his *right-hand man*. This was a back-room boy who knew everyone in all the departments scattered amongst the various municipal buildings. Nobody minded him because he had no department of his own, so he couldn't be seen as a threat to anyone else's empire. But he had his finger on the pulse, and he was free to do good by stealth.

He worked behind the scenes on our behalf, negotiating with the Education Committee and the Finance and Resources Committee, tapping into the Council's Community Chest, making many encounters with officials from the Department of the Environment. All this — to secure the release of the premises, and a little money — about £7,000, to make good some wear and tear and a patch of damp in the basement.

Without his efforts, the project could never have survived the interval between putting forward our first detailed propositions and getting the green light to move in and take over.

Time lag

That *interval* lasted sixteen months.

In the early autumn a few tramps had found their way in out of the chill, and made a fire or two to keep themselves warm. Nothing really bad, but enough to discolour those graceful walls and ceilings.

We borrowed a key (officially this time) and over three weekends Philly and the others went in with brooms and dustpans to clear up the mess. We all breathed in soot and dust and went around with sore throats. But by Christmas the place was at least tidy, and the word was going round that the various Council officers and politicians were in favour and something was bound to happen soon.

There was an attempted break-in one night in November, but that was forestalled by Philly's cousin who made her husband get up in the small hours, go down the street with a coat over his pyjamas and frighten the intruders off.

Just after Christmas residents nearby said to each other *It's happening at last!*
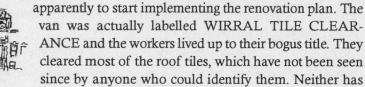
They had seen a van draw up and workers enter the building, apparently to start implementing the renovation plan. The van was actually labelled WIRRAL TILE CLEARANCE and the workers lived up to their bogus title. They cleared most of the roof tiles, which have not been seen since by anyone who could identify them. Neither has Philly's partner. She was left holding the baby.

For the next six weeks, whilst the Council (who still owned the premises) got round to treating it as an emergency, the once-beautiful building was left wide open to snow and rain. Pigeons and the occasional seagull from Merseyside roosted in the rafters. Then the roof was temporarily patched.

The place stayed damp and dirty for the best part of a year until in the fullness of time the Council committees and the Department of the Environment hierarchy, prodded on by the Chief Executive's right-hand man, gave their approvals.

By then of course, £7,000 did not go very far, so there were more costings, bids, negotiations, appeals to outside charities as well as to the Government and the Council; and a year's renovation work.

Meanwhile, room by room, we managed to get small enterprises going, an office for the Advice Unit (financed as a pilot venture by the government's new Training Agency) and upwards of a hundred small-scale local enterprises helped on their way. Philly turned up, with occasional help from her cousin, to improvise a kitchen in a disused cubby hole, to feed the haphazard trainee repair squad, and the slightly more dependable fledgling enterprises.

The new Chief Executive expressed interest, especially around the time we got our Award from the Prince. The right-hand man continued to be a friend, but he was finding less scope to do good. The Council's structure was being reviewed, re-arranged, and gradually de-personalised. But he helped to tempt a couple of semi-retired Councillors, one Left-wing, one Right, into joining the residents to form a *community company* that would run the whole enterprise as a joint operation between Us and Them.

He bent the ears of other Councillors, but they were mostly far too busy to pay much heed. The limelight had shifted to the Council's lavish Business Enterprise Scheme in brand-new premises, safely outside the area of greatest deprivation. The new centre would cater for up-and-coming entrepreneurs, a different class from the jobless, nearly hopeless, residents who dropped in on The Laird for a cuppa, and could be coaxed to stay on, shape up their own ideas, and get a fledgling enterprise going.

The residents' group that had survived, rather fewer than those who had started out, was somewhat bewildered by the shifts in the Council's policies. There was another re-organisation and the friendly right-hand man found his own position had melted away. He didn't much like the alternative offered and took early retirement to cultivate his garden and watch the birds.

Other Council officers came and went, said nice things to the residents, promising to put their proposals across to the appropriate Committees. But when these reports came up for Committee consideration, the residents' proposals were rather low down on the agenda, and more weight was given to schemes in which there was a stronger Departmental interest — like the new Business Enterprise Park.

Send-off

At long last, four years after that first back-door reconnaissance by the residents, Philly's modest dream took shape. A spacious upstairs room redecorated as the café, and her precious kitchen beside it, moved upstairs from its cubby hole, cooker, sink, fridge, deep-freeze and all.

The local MP gave us a send-off. Local pensioners had their first dinners. The enterprises in the basement were going full swing. Philly was now on the Board of the company, saying most of what she had to say before or after the formal meeting which she found quite hard to cope with, but in common with the other members, feeling rather pleased. This was in spite of having no guarantee of the future beyond what could be raised from the cafe and from the modest rents charged to the basement enterprises.

A month after the opening the ceiling fell in.

We discovered that the premises were seamed with the dry rot that had developed during those sixteen months whilst the project was the prey of the bureaucrats. After nearly a year more of temporary repairs, technical survey and negotiation it was decided that the cost of making good the dry rot was more than any of the funders could afford. The building was closed.

The Board continued to meet, now in Philly's flat. The kitchen equipment and the files were stored in her broom cupboard. There were fewer residents willing to press on, but the two Councillors continued, along with a couple from the Credit Union, and, on and off, Philly's cousin. They all edged Philly into taking on the Chair. That gave her an excuse for not talking much during the proceedings, except to move the discussion on. She rescued her committee papers when her small daughter turned them into scribbling pads. The discussions centred on prolonged negotiations to get an alternative building. A local clergyman half-offered premises, but there was always something to postpone commitment (it turned out he was angling on behalf of the church for sale to a developer). Council officers responded less to the two Councillors on the Board, who no longer had influential seats on sub-committees.

Philly and the other residents had only a shadowy notion of what went on in the Council, and even less of an idea of how the Council plans were affected by the Government. It became harder and harder to plan ahead with any prospect of success. Council officers left to work in other authorities, and those who succeeded them seemed constantly to change roles as departmental divisions shifted. Meanwhile the area, they felt, was going downhill.

Philly's flat was two stairs up in a dingy block down the main road from the Park. As time went on the stairs grew worse, first with litter, then with louts. One bunch became threatening, the police when contacted would make a fleeting passage past the block with lights flashing, and get back to base. Another group of youngsters came to her defence, but she no longer cared to be out in the evenings and return home after dark. The neighbourhood was no longer the place it used to be; the Laird building had given it heart once, but now it was derelict once more.

That summer the company disbanded. The photograph of Philly shaking hands with the Prince of Wales remained on her living room wall, for her nine-year old daughter to show off to her friends. The Award plaque stayed safe in the broom cupboard.

✧ ✧ ✧

So of the four weddings, that's the one that ended in a funeral.

2 • Boston, USA

Dudley Street lies in the heart of Roxbury, part of Greater Boston, Massachusetts. When I walked up the hill, the air was fresh. Nine years back, in the summer heat, the stench was overpowering.

> *"This neighborhood had become the city of Boston's dumping ground. It was an assault on us by outsiders — any contractor that wanted to be rid of garbage came in the middle of the night and dumped it here, bags of food, rotting carcasses, old refrigerators, boilers, toilets, abandoned cars. People themselves starting dumping their own rubbish. There were rats the size of cats and dogs walking all over the neighborhood. Kids were getting bitten by mosquitoes that bred in puddles of water in the empty canisters on these garbage piles.*
>
> *I remember talking to a mother who said in the heat of summer she had to choose — either open up her windows and have her children vomit, I mean vomit, from the stench created from the smell, or she could close her window and have her kids suffocate in the heat. Those were her choices."*

That was Andrea Nagel, from Chile, remembering how it was when she first came here to work. Further up the hill, I met Dennis and his kids getting ready to plant out an empty patch beside his house. The house that had been on it had been dynamited, years back, when this part of Boston was the prey of racist attacks, and unofficial *clearances* by speculative landlords, and headlined as the ARSON CAPITAL OF THE NATION.

> *"When we came here,"* said Dennis, *"this city lot was totally uncared for. Vehicles, abandoned and burned out, two, even four on every block. Picture neighbors fearful of one another, not knowing one another. That's the way it was."*

Salvation plan

In fact, there were several outside agencies attempting to care. Their leaders decided something must be done. They spent six months working out their salvation plan. Then they invited everyone to a public meeting at the local Catholic church. It got the biggest attendance Andrea could remember, 200 people packed into the pews,

> *"African-Americans, Latinos, Irish, Cape Verdeans — all colours, all backgrounds. I was absolutely floored by the attendance and the diversity of people."*

It could have been the turnout for a popular wedding, but actually the business end of the meeting looked more like the Last Supper. Seated on the raised platform with their backs to the altar, behind a long table, facing the congregation, were the directors of the support agencies, mostly men in suits, who had come to do good.

"They stood out like sore thumbs. They didn't belong. People began to say, 'What's going on here, you're presenting your ideas like we are the last to be consulted.' This sounds a little too funky, you know, the kind of promises that politicians and government officials have made to us so often, and then broken. There's no reason we should believe anything that's being said in this room.

But I remember some people sitting in the back of the room, with their arms crossed, looking like they were saying, 'I'm here, and I'm sure this is going to be no different from anything else that's happened. But I'll stay and see.'"

Awkward questions

Residents began to ask awkward questions. Earl Coleman, a hospital lab technician first, then Fadilah Mohammad and Ché Madyun, two Muslim women, both active in the local mosque. Ché had never been involved in any community organisation before.

"Actually, I came to the meeting because I was just curious. Sat there, listening to people talk about how they were going to revitalise the neighborhood and they wanted the community to be involved, and the next word out of their mouth was 'Let's vote for a management board.' Four community people seats out of a 23-member board. So then I raised my hand and asked a question: 'How can you say this is community involvement? You're asking us to vote for people to represent us on the committee, and how can we do that when we don't know each other? We don't know our neighbors. I don't know anybody here. I wouldn't know if they were the right person who's going to look out for the interest of my neighborhood.'"

Others said the same, and *their ideas resonated*, said Andrea.

"They really pushed the agency directors to show what they were made of, and much to their credit, I think, these directors said, 'Let's put this plan aside, we made a big mistake.' And they owned up to the fact that they should have included the residents from the very beginning in discussing what ought to be done. Ché and others saw that when they spoke their minds, they were being taken very seriously. The tables had already turned at that very first meeting. If they hadn't been taken seriously, that would have been it."

Jorge Fidalgo was working in the local store (he runs it now) and remembers people's mixed feelings.

"After the meeting that day, a lot of people were disappointed, they said, 'Nothing is going to happen, it was just a bunch of talking, just talking, talking.' But myself and a lot of other guys, we thought it was a serious meeting, and we were all part of it."

✧ ✧ ✧

Re-vamp

A local charity whose representative had sat with the other outsiders also decided to take it seriously and funded the newly-constituted community organisation — 31-strong, including 16 residents, and before long with Ché as president, and then as Chair. (She enrolled herself, part-time, on a two-year management course in order to learn the tricks of the trade.)

Andrea was appointed as organiser. On her very first day, she started going the rounds, knocking on doors and *talking to folks*.

Two overriding concerns. Crime and garbage. Many people were afraid to report crime direct to the police, or couldn't speak enough English to explain themselves. So volunteer interpreters came to the project office, and complaints were passed on by telephone. The police authority began to respond, with more cops on the beat.

Meanwhile, the *Dudley Street Neighborhood Initiative* as they now call themselves mounted a massive anti-trash campaign with the slogan, *DON'T DUMP ON US!* and signs that people held up saying, *DON'T BURY US ALIVE*.

All this got a lot of media attention. As someone said, *The squeaking wheel gets the oil. So we squeaked.* Boston's Mayor Flynn had been elected on a *Neighborhood First* ticket. He turned up in front of the television cameras, went away, and suddenly,

> "we had a line of dump trucks, huge yellow public works dump trucks rolling down the street. People came out onto the streets saying, 'We've never seen so many garbage trucks in this neighborhood in our lives!' The drivers got paid double time because we wanted them on Saturday, when all of us could turn out and do the clean-up. Although the drivers were getting paid that hefty amount, they did nothing but sit in their cabs and wait for the residents to throw the huge bags of garbage onto the trucks."

The drivers handed the volunteers 100 rakes and shovels to shift the muck, not expecting to get any of the tools back.

At the end of the day, the muck was shifted, and 96 pairs of tools returned. On Sunday, three more were handed in, and on Monday, the last pair, with an apology from a local mother whose son had broken the rake handle.

Eye-opener

> "When you're blinded by a mountain of garbage that has been there for 20 years, it's hard to envision anything different. It becomes sort of insurmountable to think of a playground or a house or a park. Once those lots were cleared, all of a sudden people started saying, 'Why don't we do this, why don't we do that?' The ideas created a new campaign to wage, a planning process to free up people's creativity."

They looked around for technical help and used their charity funding to employ two experts who set up an office on the spot, walked up and down the streets, got to know what people really wanted.

> *"We don't want to stop development. We need development, but we want development that's going to benefit us. We don't want development as defined by the city planners, or by commercial interests which are very different from our own.*
>
> *There was a leak to the* Boston Globe *that said they had a $750 million Revitalization Plan up their sleeves, with hotels, office towers, and a housing development that would displace most of the residents who had been there originally. So we decided we needed to be in the driver's seat."*

Take-over

They put together their own *Dudley Street Neighborhood Initiative Revitalization Plan* for 507 acres, estimated cost $135 million over five years — to get *development without displacement* by *mobilizing the untapped resources* of the people living in the Dudley Street Triangle, the heart of the area. They persuaded Mayor Flynn to look in on their annual multicultural festival, unveiled their Plan, got his endorsement, and more. He promised the City would take it over.

That was not quite the same as having residents in the saddle. By now, there were other experts within call — a high-profile legal firm giving free advice *pro bono*. Its leading partner, walking around the site with Peter Medoff, the project's director, hit on the notion of *eminent domain*. This was the power, which up to now had only been possessed by State governments or major public utilities, to take over vacant land in the public's interest, making a compulsory purchase at the ruling market price. He put forward the extraordinary notion, unprecedented, that this power should be transferred from the Boston city authority to the Dudley Street Neighborhood, set up as a legal corporation, and able to vet any new development, whoever financed it.

There were two powerful departments within the city administration, whose Directors were at loggerheads over *practically everything, including the time of day*. With enormous perseverance, each was won over and they found themselves collaborating, to their surprise, in pushing forward this bizarre proposal.

The Boston Redevelopment Authority (BRA) would have the last word, however, and its five members looked down their noses at the very idea of ordinary residents taking over. Minutes before the BRA's meeting, Mayor Flynn came to the rescue like the US cavalry, storming out of his office, red-faced, and bringing the BRA board reluctantly to heel. For the next three years, the *Dudley Neighbors Incorporated* could exercise its *domain*, unchallenged.

❖   ❖   ❖

It had the power, but not yet the money to do anything with it. Those three years were taken up in negotiations with the Ford Foundation for a $2 million loan at 1% interest to buy up vacant sites. By the time the money was released, the *eminent domain* period had expired. More negotiation — and it was extended a couple of years. The cheque was paid over, and a giant blow-up of it went on display for everyone to sign their endorsements. Soon after, a federal housing grant of $2.3 million was released for low-interest second mortgages. In November 1994, the last month of *eminent domain*, when I visited the site, the first buildings were already up and occupied.

Winning over

The wheeling and dealing had to be done at top level, with the help of the legal eagles and the won-over officials and politicians. The winning over was done partly by the full-time paid workers the residents chose, and partly by volunteers like Ché. These moving spirits were beginning to take stock, wary of the danger that they would lose touch with the run-of-the-mill people.

The building work was waking everyone up. How to keep them involved? The answer was already to hand, and had been almost since the project took shape. Youngsters themselves were besieging the little project office, day in, day out. As Ché said,

> "We haven't involved youngsters, youngsters have involved us. They started coming into the office, sometimes just to sit around and talk, or to try and type something for us or for themselves. They wanted credibility, and they followed our example. We'd go downtown to the city authorities and tell people what we'd want, and how we wanted it done, and insist on it being done our way. Well, the young people used the same approach with us. They were here all day and all night."

On the back of Jorge Fidalgo's store, there is a big blank wall. The youngsters were invited to paint an enormous *diversity mural* — showing residents of all the races with roots in the community, sitting around in the sunshine, listening to a young drummer. Over the years (like *Forty-Odd* in Meadow Well), the mural has stayed intact.

Each summer, youngsters have come together with some expert adult guidance, working on empty sites to prepare the soil, plant flowers and shrubs, put up benches for people to sit out and take the clean air. Neuza Sokaida, from Cape Verde, at fifteen the newly-elected Co-chair of the *Nubian Roots* youth group, got involved as a 13-year old in painting the mural and went on to help redecorate the project office, and to join in the annual trash clear-up, and the grass cutting and the planting.

> "We were out there in the summer, 90 degrees weather, they knew we were sweating. It's when you actually feel the sweat and you know you're doing something that the community will like and we all working as a team — that's the best part about it."

There are still plenty of other youngsters growing up with drugs and violence. I heard about one nine-year old shot dead the day before I talked with Neuza. But her group have got hold of an address list and are systematically contacting every youngster in the community, phoning them up, door-knocking, sending flyers, painstakingly winning them over. To what *could be*.

> *"The community was surprised, because they felt that youths don't really care, don't participate nothing in the community, just mess it up, but that's not true. We're proving to the older people that we're trying our best to fix the community up, they're beginning to believe that we are capable of doing things."*

Jorge keeps an eye on the mural on his store wall and makes comparisons:

> *"People used to be afraid of talking to each other. They were just minding their business, sticking to their own ethnic group. Now people are reaching out there together, as one family, I would say."*

There's still a long way to go, but Ché and the others know the route.

> *"I'm not one of those fast thinkers, I'm a slow and methodical thinker. I guess I would tell anyone to be patient, that's all, be patient, be patient. It's not just changing things visibly that we see around. It's also working to help people to change parts of themselves inside, that's the real challenge."*

✧ ✧ ✧

3 • Gulbarga, India

When Indians took over from the British Raj, they inherited the traditional approach to *know-how*. To amass the expert knowledge required to run a country meant issuing questionnaires and undertaking surveys. The people who organised this were undertakers in a double sense. They went to residents, with questionnaires a mile long, extracted the bits of information required to fit their survey forms, and returned to base with an embalmed version of village life and prospects.

Some of the researchers were Westerners, some Indian, but they were a class apart from the people they surveyed. Most of their material was obtained by what their critics called *development tourism* — a visit, preferably when the weather was good, lots of nice statistical souvenirs to carry home, seeing people pretty happy at the harvest season, with no idea of what they were up against during the bad times. Excellent number-crunching fodder for accountants and statisticians; but for anyone wanting to get at the nub of local problems, such methods were:

long drawn-out, tedious, a headache to administer, a nightmare to process and write up, inaccurate and unreliable in data obtained, leading to reports if any which were long, late, boring, misleading, difficult to use and anyway ignored.

Robert Chambers's views on traditional number-crunching came from his inside experience as a civil servant. There were several other professionals equally exasperated, and beginning to experiment, unobtrusively, in alternative ways of getting information worth having.

Jimmy Mascarenhas was particularly concerned with the effect of the top-down approach on local people. He is a senior official, university trained, brought up in cities, and heads up a team charged with *integrated rural development*. In practice, that meant finding out how villagers in a drought-stricken area could be helped by planting more trees and constructing better storage tanks to improve water supply. The problem he described to me seems almost universal:

> *"There has been a breakdown and no longer does the community believe in the outside system. They are not confident that it works any more. Villagers are sort of aloof because they've lost faith in the system."*

He had heard about Robert Chambers, already widely known and respected, summoned up courage and invited him to come with the team and camp outside one of the villages.

Discoveries

They stayed just outside the village of Kalmandargi in the district of Gulbarga, which is in Karnataka state. Without making an official fuss, they began asking people not just for bits of information, but for their expert advice.

> *"We sought out the local experts in the village, some have very specialised knowledge on trees, some know about animals and diseases, some know about crops, and on that first day, we asked younger people to guide us to those experts. We went to them and made appointments for the next day, just as we might ask the manager of some company to give us an interview. I think they changed their attitude towards us from that moment. We were treating them not as inferiors, more as superiors and people with a lot of knowledge.*
>
> *The nice thing was that in the evening, after we'd cooked our meal together, we went into the village and presented the information we had collected to everyone. That meant that we got in deeper more because there would be somebody there who could throw a little extra light, or even question some of the information.*
>
> *We came back very humble because we'd learned so much, discovered so much. All our minds were blown. We said, 'My God, this is just the tip of the iceberg, what have we been doing all these years!'"*

The villagers helped them to piece together a chronicle of events since the Great Drought of 1972. That had forced villagers away during the bad season to seek work in the city. Ever since they had gone each year for casual work in Bombay. Back home, still desperate to make ends meet, they had cut down the trees, and when they lost some of the good crops, they introduced hybrids which were shorter and gave less straw for the cattle.

The government replaced the lost trees with eucalyptus, but the villagers explained to Jimmy and the others that they needed a variety of trees.

> *"They named trees like mango, neem, tamarind, and we said, 'Oh, mango is good for fruit, isn't it? And they said, 'No, it's good for house construction, because we make our doors out of it.' And we said, 'OK, neem — it's good for disease control?' And they said 'Yes, it's good for disease control, but it's also good for house construction, because we use it to make the frame of the house.' And we found that each tree had many specific uses. They showed us a bullock cart, and its wheels were make out of teak, the beam was made out of jack fruit, the sides were made out of bamboo. Altogether they used seven different species in the construction of it.*
>
> *These were discoveries for us because we were blind, and our eyes were opened a lot that day."*

The team was able to compare the picture that the experts back at the base had of what was needed with the reality as the villagers knew it.

> *"They explained to us about cattle coming on heat. Indian cattle are still in a wild or semi-wild state and they will breed only once a year, like sheep. But our veterinarians were organising fertility camps in an effort to bring the cattle on heat throughout the year, pumping the animals with hormones, whereas all you needed to do was to wait for the months of March and April when the animals came on heat, and you get better calves. And we had kept missing that.*
>
> *We began to get a very good relationship with the community, because up to then they had only had government departments dealing with them in a very slipshod fashion and we as a group were living beside the village, and would be there in the morning and the afternoon, talking about crops, and water supply, and so on."*

Planning ...

> *"I remember one date very very clearly, 27 October 1989. We were saying, 'How do we go about planning for the watershed?' So somebody had the idea, 'Why don't we do a model?' And we asked the farmers and they said, 'Yes, no problem, we'll get some sawdust.'*
>
> *Now, in India, it's very traditional that every morning, every woman outside her house makes a very colourful pattern outside her house; each neighbour makes a different pattern, with coloured powders, blues, purples, greens and yellows, very cheap. So someone said, 'Why don't we get hold of these powders?' And they began to colour the sawdust, and in about two hours' time, the farmers had made a beautiful model which showed the farming land, the grazing land, the streams, the roads, the electric lines and the houses.*

They put in a stone for the temple, and later on a woman was passing by and she picked out the stone and threw it off. There was a big hullabaloo and they said, 'You've thrown away our temple', and she said, 'I didn't know it was meant to be a temple. But it was so ugly on that nice model of yours, I just took it and threw it off.' So she made a nice paper cut-out of the temple and put it there.

That night turned out to be the most animated discussion that we'd had because it was their village, their watershed. So we asked them, 'It's like this now, what would you like it to be in 20 years' time?' And then it was quite chaotic because everybody had ideas, and they were bringing specimens of different species of trees and suchlike to show on the model where they wanted to plant tamarind, or whatever. And someone was saying, 'I put a check dam here, and another there to conserve the soil. And that's the place where we can get good drinking water.' And we noted down all these suggestions very carefully.

And that was the very first time the model was used. It gave us a lot of thought because this thing happened without any real planning or intention. It just flowed from the whole business of trying out things in the community.

The model is in a way the most important breakthrough, I would say, in rural development. Very powerful because it's there, it's neutral, you can look at it objectively and discuss it. You can show on it the houses, with different coloured seeds to show the men and the women in them, and you can find out where there are handicapped people, and poor people, and nursing mothers, where the children ought to get their immunisation. And the land-based things include crops, trees, livestock. And you can show where there are skills, crafts, businesses."

Just as we had been finding back in the UK with *Planning for Real*, the communication gap and the confidence gap were narrowing. Local people were getting more interested, more and more responsive. The fieldworkers were discovering that when they asked people for their own observations, they got better results, because people were beginning to *own* the process. The traditional questionnaire was the outsider's property, and he took your information away from you and used it to suit himself. But when village people were sizing up their own situation, the conclusions they reached were entirely theirs. And the more they saw of themselves and their surroundings, the more they thought about what *could*, and *should*, be done.

... *for Real*

So the next stage was to weigh in on government departments, putting forward a plan of action agreed with the villagers. Not just agreed, but also budgeted.

"Groups of farmers sat and worked out the cost of developing their landholdings, and we also asked them to say how much they could contribute towards the development programme. And a sort of prioritisation takes place, short-term, medium-term, long-term; zero cost, low cost, medium cost, high cost. And so all the activities are worked out like that.

*Then we say to the government, 'Look, if we are serious about this programme, and it is agreed for instance that we introduce mango fruit trees into the area — then we must have a sign of faith that **in three days**, the fruit trees must come.'*

And the people also agree that they must dig their pits to be ready by that time. So we draw up an agreement which is signed by all the partners — the government, the farmers, and us.' "

Rewarding first steps, taken quickly. Small-scale. Quite unlike the mega-schemes that had been promoted by the Government, under pressure from the World Bank. Both government and World Bank have taken *Participatory Rural Appraisal* (PRA) on board, although, says Jimmy, they are *totally nonplussed* about how to go about it.

The villagers understand it very well indeed.

"We have such a strong demand, it's unbelievable. You get a group of farmers coming to say, 'Look, we'll give you 60 acres for tree-planting.' At first, we were paying them, but now they're saying, 'We will pay part of the cost ourselves.' So we're helping them to shift from subsistence crops to a more stable tree economy, which will help them in the long term, and stop the degradation. So we are always looking at things that harmonise, which fit with what people want and with what the environment, the earth, needs.

Q: 'Do you think the villagers were surprised to find they could take over and manage their own affairs?'

*A: 'They're not surprised they can manage their own affairs. What surprises them is that these changes are coming about, that what they dream of is happening **for real**.' "*

Jimmy Mascarenhas had felt himself a stranger, a townsman, a graduate official, and now he began to feel accepted.

"When you go into the village, you find a little girl coming and putting her hand in yours and walking with you and telling you everything that's happening. Or you'd find a little boy saying, 'I kept a few custard apples for you, after you've finished I'll be waiting here with them.' Five years ago, if they saw me coming on my motorcycle, they would run into their houses and hide in their mother's skirts."

When the older people had to go off to Bombay for casual work, the old people and the children and the teenagers were left behind. And the teenagers were going wild, out of the elders' control. But now they came up to Jimmy and the others complaining because they were being left out of the new programmes. At the same time, their fathers were complaining that youngsters nowadays were unwilling to work on the land, and just wanted white-collar jobs.

Job search

"So we sat down with the youth, and gave them cards and said, 'Each one of you write what you'd like to do.' Some wanted to be a driver, some an electrician, and some to be veterinary doctors. So we said, 'Do you really think there are opportunities here for a veterinary doctor?'"

No hesitation. It had all been figured out.

"'Our village has got 1,000 animals, and the next village has 200 animals, and another has 800; and so on. So I can be of service to nearly 7,000 animals in the area. Even if only 10% of the animals are sick and I charge one rupee per animal, then I'll make so much per month.'

They gave us a very good cost-benefit analysis which no expert I think would have given them. It's because it's their environment and they can see the opportunities.

So we began to organise courses — for the drivers, and the electricians, and the bus conductors, and shoemakers — who built a shed for themselves and we gave them working capital, and they're making and selling a lot of leather handicrafts. As for the veterinarians, we got them on short courses and that's created a lot of confidence."

It was mind-blowing all round. Not just for the professionals coming into the community from outside, but also for people from the surrounding villages, asking for someone to come and start programmes in the same way for them.

"So we say, 'We're not going to come to you. You ask one of the people from the village we've been in. Get him to come, and pay him, and he'll show you.' So there are people who have been through this experience over the last 4 or 5 years, and they're getting somewhere. The whole of India is not like this, but it's happening in pockets, and it is very very exciting for us."

There's still a need for outsiders to start the process. At first, when Jimmy went recruiting to the universities, he drew a blank.

"The cleverest students all went on for more academic studies, or went abroad, or got jobs in big companies. But two of us would go round the campus talking to students, getting them interested, selling it to them as an adventure. And eventually one chap came and worked with us, and he had a good experience, and went back to his college and got two of his friends, and they've gone back in their turn, and now we have a waiting list of people, students who want to go into rural areas.

With some of them, they've had a struggle to get through their courses, their parents were poor, they came from rural areas, father had to sell some land to put them through, they've got no connections, no influence. But we found that they learn fast, they could relate to rural situations, a little bit of investment in training — how to ride a motorcycle, how to conduct a meeting, how to draft a letter — and I've got an excellent core of people, they are real gents, I can't put it higher than that. These are our own Indian youth and it's a totally new experience for them."

✧ ✧ ✧

Three *professional inputs* so far.

The right-hand man in **Birkenhead** threading his way through the administration labyrinth to conjure up — for a time — a sensible response from the authorities to the community's practical proposition.

The well-meaning support agencies in **Roxbury**, wrong-footing themselves at first, then taking on new roles as expert advisors, like seconds at the ringside, helping the community to *take on* the authorities, nose to nose, and gradually *take over* the decision-making and the work of carrying out decisions that hitherto had been reserved for *Them*.

The rural development team discovering how to learn from local people and then how to enhance the knowledge and skills that already existed within the community.

Which brings us to

4 • Karachi, Pakistan

...where some professionals have been using their own expert knowledge to bring about a marriage between Us and Them that seems likely to last.

Karachi has 10.5 million population, three and a half million housed in squatter settlements, the *katchi abadis*, where incomers of many races had paid through the nose for land on which to put up single-storey houses. There was no money to spare for more than the bare necessities. Some of those were missing. Buckets and soakaways instead of toilets. An open trench running down the street for the sewage. Children playing and defecating in the open by day, adults making their way to the railway track or the bank of the nearest pond to do their business by night. Slender earnings from piecework, farmed out by rapacious firms. Much of the money spent on medicines, doctors, quacks, to cope with dysentery, diarrhoea, malaria, typhoid that thrived on the filth in the streets and the stagnant pools.

The largest of the squatter settlements in Karachi is Orangi Township, three-quarters of a million population,

a specially explosive area because large numbers of Pathans, Mahajirs, Biharis, Punjabis, Sindhis and Baluchis live in close proximity to each other.

A major international charity proposed a programme of *social welfare* for Orangi Township, to ease the pain. It approached Pakistan's leading social scientist, Dr Akhtar Hameed Khan, to undertake the work. He accepted on condition that the Orangi Pilot Project (OPP) should go to the roots of the problem:

We are all living through a period of social dislocation. Where people have been uprooted from their old familiar environment, this dislocation is especially acute. They have to re-establish a sense of belonging, community feeling, and the conventions of mutual help and co-operative action.

A small professional team under Dr Khan's leadership set to work on a programme of action research. The team had no time for conventional surveys to identify the problems. Having contacted

> university professors and leading Karachi consultants and experts, it discovered that they ... were not particularly interested in lowering cost, and did not take into consideration the constraints small contractors and poor quality skilled labour would have in implementing their designs. The reasons for [this] ... were that these leading professionals ... had never worked with people or on shoestring budgets.

The problems were obvious: sanitation, housing, health, jobs, education — in roughly that order.

Money down the drain

The team found that the cost of introducing proper sewerage was beyond ordinary people's resources, mainly because

> professional charges paid to international consultants and their Pakistani counterparts are extremely high... Cynicism and resentment is created all round, and this in turn erodes the authority of the professionals. The number of consultants is usually unnecessary high and most of them carry out studies and surveys that have already been carried out before.

The engineers and accountants in the team broke down the cost of underground sewage systems as charged by the authorities:

> It was about seven times the actual cost of labour and materials. Where foreign financial assistance was involved, costs went up by 30-50%. Where international tenders were called, it went up to 250%. In the end, the user was being asked to pay 25 rupees for something whose actual cost was only one rupee. These high costs, it was established, were due to high overheads, excessive profiteering by contractors, kickbacks to government officials, and fees to foreign consultants who came with the loan package.

They came to the conclusion that

> if costs could be brought down to only those of labour and materials, an underground sanitation system could be affordable to the residents of Orangi, and if money to build the system could be provided by the people before construction began, it would overcome the problems involved in acquiring and repaying loans to international agencies.

To do this meant a year's hard work researching better and simpler methods of sanitation; and then explaining to local people what could be done, and inviting them to make their own decisions.

How to get that message across?

There were two levels of local representation. The upper level, which included local councillors and other worthies, was unsatisfactory because there were quarrels and personality clashes. The next level down was the *panchayats*, village committees run by leaders whose office was hereditary. Their scope was to sort out family quarrels and rule on land disputes, not to do anything drastic about the place itself. Besides these, there were umpteen *anjuman-i-falah*, local societies and clubs sharing particular interests, and often voicing local anger at the failure of local authorities to deliver. Raising voices, but not used to taking action.

Lane management

The team decided to bypass such organisations and go direct to the residents themselves at the lowest possible level — *the lane*.

No-one living in the lane was used to the idea of getting together with the next-door neighbours to change things. The tradition had always been that others higher up should make such decisions. The team members had an uphill job to begin with, contacting residents who were suspicious of all outsiders, and judged outside help in terms of what money could be handed over. But they began a series of *motivational meetings*, painstakingly explaining how people themselves could build their own pour-flush toilets and lay the drains from their houses to connect with a common sewer which everyone in the lane would get together to build below ground. Each lane had to elect its own lane manager who would collect money, not too much, perhaps the equivalent of a month's earnings, from each householder, and, with expert help from the OPP team's engineers, supervise the whole operation. It would be

self-financed and self-managed without the corrupt exorbitant middlemen.

The only additional costs — the OPP team's professional charges — were covered by the charity funding, but amounted to

less than 10% of what is normally charged by professionals working for internationally-funded projects.

An underground sewerage system is a complex affair, and developing one lane at a time, without a master plan, was considered by planners to be an invitation to disaster. However, ... no disaster took place.

Where a site office was needed, it was *austere*, without frills or air conditioning. So people began to respond. In the first year, just one lane organisation took shape. In the second year, six. Soon after, scores. Then hundreds.

Students venturing outside the classroom

In the second year, a distinguished Karachi architect, Arif Hasan, was brought in as consultant to the Project. At the time, he was also teaching in the Department of Architecture and Planning at Dawood College. He told me that in those days, he did not think very much of his college commitment, or of the quality of the students he taught. But things changed when he persuaded a whole course at a time to get out of the lecture room and into the lanes.

Most of the students proved good at getting on the right side of the lanes people. Several learned enough from this experience to revise their own ambitions, and to sheer away from the goal of smart money architectural practices serving affluent clients. *Two or three out of every twenty students*, Arif Hasan reckons, have been worth all the effort, and have become exponents of the OPP approach, elsewhere in Karachi, and in other cities in Pakistan.

The student volunteers were especially useful in the early stages, spotting those in each lane whom the OPP calls *social organisers*, described by Arif Hasan as *sort-of-experts*. None had previous management skills, many were housewives, but they had

"the know-how to motivate people, understand what is involved in developing plans and estimates (though they cannot do it scientifically themselves)."

Maybe we should call them *moving spirits*.

They were the ones who coaxed their neighbours to come together for the *motivational meetings*, and gradually took over from the OPP experts, explaining what could be done about sewerage in the first place, and before long, about housing, health, family planning, family-based enterprises, and education.

Once the underground lane drains were done, they could be linked to a large-scale system to be built or adapted by the local authorities. They had to be persuaded, but gradually became convinced by the example set by the lane pioneers, backed by the patient diplomacy of the OPP. The laying of the lane sewerage *showed* what people could do. And it also *showed up* what the authorities had failed to do so far. Now they could hardly do less than respond. The local work, carefully costed by the OPP professionals, was paid for by the lane association. And OPP was determined not to provide more than technical guidance. In the first thirteen years,

Orangi people have invested 52.97 million rupees, ... they have constructed sewerage lines in 4,552 lanes, and sanitary pour-flush latrines in 71,127 homes.

Technical breakthrough

As the process developed, more and more residents picked up additional skills. OPP introduced them to better ways of mixing concrete and making building blocks. Local masons were given courses in improved construction techniques and better use of tools. OPP engineers designed a block-making machine which could be made locally and operated cheaply. They rented out tools and shuttering. Materials, tools and accessories had previously been retailed by the *thalla walas*. OPP persuaded them to improve the standard of their products, and to negotiate more acceptable prices.

> The machine-made blocks were four times stronger than the handmade blocks, but were sold at the same price because mechanization trebled daily production.

The new blocks were now used by people wanting to expand their houses with a second storey, without the risks of the walls giving way beneath the added weight.

So more and better houses were built. 94,122 new houses in just on ten years, without any assistance from the authorities.

Arif Hasan talks about *the snowball effect*, which is difficult to visualise in a hot country. What happened was that people in adjoining lanes followed the pioneers' example. Then others from outside Orangi Township took up the idea, and came to the OPP headquarters from elsewhere in Karachi, and from Sukkur, Hyderabad and Lahore to seek support and guidance. Instead, OPP suggested they should get the expert advice they needed from the local lane organisers.

Women's work

OPP workers had noted that from the early days, it was usually the women who unobtrusively took the lead in forming lane associations, and getting the sewerage schemes under way.

People in Orangi had for the most part made a poor living as outworkers for textile firms which exported yellow dusters, shopping bags and towels to Europe and America. Women did much of the work as *stitchers*, and had little or no say in negotiating terms. Negotiations were more likely to be done by the males in the family; and in any case, the outside firms had the whip hand.

> The traditional viewpoint about women is that women should remain in Purdah (segregation), while men should feed and clothe them. A wife should regard her husband as "majazi khuda" (human god). She should produce as many children as possible, and she should firmly believe that good God will always provide for every one of them. ... Segregation makes illiterate or semi-illiterate women almost inaccessible to outside agents of change.

OPP were learning how to challenge this situation.

Women were beginning to recognise their own capacities as *family activists*. OPP responded by helping to form *Women's Work Centres*, and *Stitching Centres*, each one based in someone's home, where other women could feel safe from male interference. Gradually, they began to sort out the outside contractors, ignoring the rascal middlemen, going direct to the exporters, and negotiating more acceptable terms.

As in our country discretion is the better part of valour, we did not tangle with our male chauvinists, but left them to be tackled by their wives.

Females are becoming active economic partners instead of remaining servile dependants. In the family enterprises, which are sprouting in every lane, girls form the majority of workers... Now there are hundreds of women-managed stitching centres. They have ousted the old male contractors who used to cheat and harass the poor stitchers.

The Women's Work Centres were gradually becoming powerhouses, economically self-sufficient, where the moving spirits (with the OPP professionals on tap but in the background) could spread information about preventing disease, improving diet, family planning, and growing vegetables in the back yard.

There has been a great thirst for better schooling. Particularly for girls, who had been kept at home rather than attend schools where male teachers dominated. The earliest independent school in Orangi came about because a civil servant wanted to do something useful in his free afternoons. He started as an amateur teacher with five children. In a few months, he had a hundred. He survived attacks from drug peddlers and the school grew to 830 students (430 boys and 400 girls), with two male and 23 female teachers. More girls were coming forward as teachers.

The dominant presence of lady teachers in the school removed the traditional Muslim inhibitions against sending girls to school.

More schools were set up with the help of OPP, 509 independent schools, maintained by residents themselves, compared with 76 in the state system.

Most Orangi parents no longer insist on separate schools for girls. Most of the schools are co-educational, even at the secondary level.

Guidelines

Arif Hasan and Dr Akhtar Hameed Khan, looking back over the first thirteen years of the Pilot Project, have come to some conclusions.

Just for Orangi Township, or for the projects following that example in Hyderabad, and Sind, and Lahore? Or could they perhaps apply elsewhere too?

• *The scale of the problem is far too large to be tackled without effective government participation. Rehabilitation programmes should develop strategies that can be integrated into the planning mechanisms of the government.*

• *There is no doubt that the poor people want to become partners in their own development if the planners would only take the trouble of inviting them to participate.*

• *Eminent professionals who have not worked with people are not competent to understand and cater to the requirements of a development project which is financed and managed by communities. They need to be exposed to local social and economic conditions. But first they must accept the need for it.*

• *Middle-level government officials do not accept new approaches by being ordered by their superiors to do so. Nor do they accept them by being formally lectured to. If they do not accept them, then they subvert them.*

• *A lot of innovation may be required. ... Government professionals are quite capable of this innovation once they get into the spirit of this form of development. ... [There is] an immense longing to do some useful work. ... [If they] are involved from the very beginning in dialogues and discussions on new approaches and their benefits, they become their supporters and promoters, provided they are assured of an important role.*

• *Support organisations must keep a low profile. People should be supported to take decisions and act on them themselves. Only then can they be empowered in the real sense of the term... People maintain the system they have financed and constructed themselves.*

• *The level of organisation needs to be small. ... The understanding is better, conflicts are less, disputes can be easily resolved, the trials and errors can be controlled.*

• *In contrast to what the poor people managed to do for themselves, government planning for the poor seems slow and sterile. [This] indicates the vitality of the poor and their skill in the art of survival. ... And the growing consciousness, especially among the younger generation, of their collective vote-power and street-power.*

Sound horse sense, you might think.

And could such lessons apply **closer to home?**

Progress on the jigsaw so far...

We've put together a framework of sorts: the capacities that have been common to the human species since time began and which we still have going for us:

• **the strength we derive from familiar surroundings, a place we belong to and which we feel belongs to us, the neighbourhood;**

• **the kick we get from doing things as we want them done, achieving our personal best;**

• **the support we get from others in a group;**

• **our childhood zest for trying things out in order to answer the questions we ask ourselves.**

Within this framework, there are faces in the crowd

• **those *moving spirits* — among both Us and Them — who can break through the crusts of apathy, suspicion and self-doubt;**

- the *onlookers turned doers*, who begin to <u>show</u> what can be done, not just shout about it.

As you will have noticed, our own experience isn't unique. It's not all happening on Home ground. Events and people Far Away come into the picture. Unimportant people, like ourselves, but faced with far worse problems; yet managing to overcome them. People who could sometimes teach us a thing or two.

◇ ◇ ◇

There's a stage in every jigsaw when what seem to be the key pieces are identified, and some of them in place; but there are baffling clusters of other pieces which seem to contain elements of more than one feature in the total picture.

Jigsaw pieces are not neat rectangles which can be labelled and arrowed like the boxes in a block diagram. Even when you guess roughly which part of the picture they fit, each piece may show an odd mixture of colour and pattern. That red patch — part of someone's cloak? A bit of the carpet? Or the curtain? And what's the grey-blue streak along one edge? The sky seen through the open window? The glint of gun metal?

- **The pace of change in our world is unprecedented. All sorts of unexpected innovations are erupting independently of each other, and they overlap.**

- **What's happening to us now is tangled up with what happened then, a lifetime ago, maybe half a millennium ago.**

So the next chapters are about this blend of forces and events; far away and close at hand; the way they took shape, and how, quite suddenly, they have begun to affect our lives.

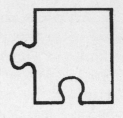

10C Family feeling

H ere's another inside story — or as far inside as an outsider can get. It's meant to show how little time it takes to cross from one kind of society to another — and what that devastating change implies for us.

Remember those Igbo bridge-builders in Uzuakoli?[1] I met them half a life-time back, at the time of Nigerian Independence. What they were doing seemed to me to make a bridge in time.

I met them because my Igbo friend, Oke, came from the same village. A local boy who had made good.

I first met him in the TV studio, way back in the days when Alexandra Palace was the beacon of the BBC. It was for a pilot programme in the world's first Schools Television project, piped to half a dozen schools in the neighbourhood. I called it *'Black and White in an African Village'* and meant it to show how Western skills were being gradually taken over by village people. With a slender budget, many of the shots showed little more than hands, white then black, wielding  hypodermic syringes, writing words and figures on slates, operating hydraulic pumps. Oke was one of the faces, confronted with a white interviewer quizzing him about the ability of black Africans to fend for themselves. As a light-hearted doctor, fresh from a postgraduate course at Hammersmith Hospital, he was finding that not so funny. I got the camera zooming in to show the vein throbbing at his temple as he answered.

Nine years later, I met him at home with his family, celebrating the birth of their fourth child, in the year when Nigeria declared its independence.

He was the country's best-known gynaecologist, delivering the babies of the new Cabinet.

Ten more years on, and his four children were living with ours, sent for safety to England by their parents in the middle of the Biafran war. Then back home with the uneasy peace to mingle as teenagers with Nigeria's young, upwardly mobile glitterati well-supplied with cars, TV, smart clothes, drug problems, security guards, crime waves, beggars in the streets, financial scandals and political skulduggery. Everything you might expect in the civilised West, but perhaps a shade more so. Nigeria had become the biggest, oil-richest free-market state in Africa. A customer, a supplier, perhaps a threat.

In less than a lifetime, Oke's family had jumped a thousand years of Western history, without the Western world quite realising what had happened. With Oke's help, I pieced together the history of that quantum leap.

It begins in soft focus, like a bedtime story told by your Gran. *When I was very little, I remember that my Dad ... and my Grandad....*

It ends in the harsh glare of modern times.

✧ ✧ ✧

Once upon a time, but this is a true story...

Oke came from a medical family. His ancestors had been hereditary medicine men, as long as the clan history records. Not that the record goes back very far. Beyond Grandfather's day, history is shadowy, there's just tradition. And beyond that, legend.

The oracle

Legends live long, and take powerful hold. The most potent was the legend of Aro Chukwu, the goddess daughter of the sky god Obassi, and the earth goddess Ala. She spoke to the four million people living in the Igbo heartlands. Her words were conveyed by an oracle hidden within a cave seven feet high on the bank of a small island. It was flanked by a steep gorge that could only be reached along a narrow, winding path beside the little river that flowed through the Aro villages.

Oke's Grandfather only once visited the cave of Aro Chukwu, but he never forgot it. As a young man, he was chosen by his village to escort a suspected murderer to the oracle for judgement. When he got there, he handed the prisoner over to one of the guardian priests of the oracle and told him all that was known about the crime.

On a day when the omens were favourable, the suspect was led to the mouth of the cave where the oracle dwelled. The priest recited the story of the crime in a loud voice, and then called on the prisoner to answer. The prisoner was frightened almost to death, and confessed his guilt.

From within the cave came a voice denouncing the crime, and giving sentence of death. All the onlookers were dismissed. The victim stayed, abject.

As the onlookers fled up the sides of the ravine, they could see that a torrent of water had been let loose from a cleft in the rock where it had been dammed up. The last they heard of the prisoner were his cries as the torrent swept him away, through a grove of trees and stunted bushes beyond the cave mouth.

Downstream, outside the ravine, the watchers turned again to look. There was no sign of the victim's body, but the waters that flowed past them were now blood-red.

Grandfather went home and told everyone:

"Chukwu akola."

The Goddess has declared. The village was happy, now that the shadow of uncertainty had been lifted, and they knew where the guilt had lain.

They met together round the threshing floor, and the oldest and wisest considered the next step, with everybody else clustered round.

There was a customary answer to every problem that arose in the village. The elders' job was to fit the right custom to the matter in hand. Crime was a family matter, like everything else. The guilty man's household was a part of him, it had helped to make him the man he was. So those closest to him were responsible for his behaviour and must make good the damage.

The council decided that the murderer's wife had been a bad wife to him, and they sent her back in disgrace to her parents. They awarded her children to the family of her husband's victim. The children would strengthen the household that had been damaged. The brothers of the murderer had to pay compensation to the victim's widow so that she should not go in want during the time when her new children were too small to work for her on the farm.

The women

Afterwards, fetching the drinking water from the pool outside the village, all the women talked it over and approved. Earlier, it was the women who had laid the information which had narrowed down suspicion and given Oke's Grandfather the facts to pass on to the priest of the Goddess.

Igbo women knew their place, and their rights. They could abandon their husbands if they proved to be thieves, or summon them to a tribunal for ill-usage. Any trading profits they made were their own. They arranged the marriages, sorted out domestic differences (or just occasionally blew on the embers and helped things flare up).

As a young man, just beginning to follow the family practice of medicine, Oke's Grandfather had singled out the girl he intended to have for a wife.

Through his parents and her parents, he let this be known to her. When she in turn admitted that he would be — *acceptable,* the family heads negotiated a bride-price — an insurance (repayable in case of serious complaint) that she was chaste, healthy, and reasonably good-tempered.

The wedding feast was a landmark. It changed, by a little, the face of the village. All the able-bodied wedding guests helped build the newlyweds' house. It was done in a day, with the most skilled thatcher astride the roof-tree. He plaited the palm leaves handed up to him by a chain of young men, full of the bridegroom's palm wine, all doing their best to keep the palm leaves moving faster than they could be tied to the rafters.

The celebration was a family affair, which is to say that it was a village affair. Everyone was related. The guests touched each other's hands and arms and shoulders and faces as if to remind themselves that cousins and cousins' cousins, they were all one flesh and blood.

As Oke's father, the first child of the marriage, grew up from babyhood, the family surrounded him like the air he breathed. Until he could walk, the daylight hours were spent on his mother's back, or slung on her hip, as she cooked, or worked the market garden. She went on suckling him for nearly four years. As soon as he could toddle, he began to help. In a very small vessel, he carried some of the water that had to be fetched each day. He gathered kindling for the cooking fire. He tried his hand at shaping wet clay round a curved stone to make his own special cooking pot. He learned which were the growing plants, and helped to weed them.

If he got bored with any of these little chores, he found himself unpopular. Not so much with his mother, who was kind to him whatever happened, but with all the other little boys and girls, brothers and sisters and first and second cousins growing up beside him. Each one's behaviour was shaped by all of them together. Whatever he did, good or bad, was the concern of everybody else. Like the murder, and the wedding feast, and the new house.

The children were involved in everything that happened, everywhere — funerals, quarrels, market bargaining, feasts. They looked after their elders, and were looked after in their turn.

The moonlit nights

On the moonlit nights, in the village centre, *mbara ama*, the children played and learned alongside their age-mates. Their elders taught them, male and female, about their difference; alongside the essential facts of the plant life and the animal life around them, and the stories handed down about Ananse, the Tortoise, always up to mischievous tricks, always outwitting the pompous and respectable.

The story-teller would begin his story when the mood took him, but always with the time-hallowed beginning:

It is not so, it is not so, it really is not so...

And the more far-fetched Ananse's adventure became, the better, because *it is not so, it is not so, it really is not so...* But for all that, the qualities in the stories were not imaginary: strength, cunning, generosity, courage, laughter. These were the weapons of the village against the unseen forces of darkness, the devils lurking in the shadows, the life after death.

Sometimes, when the story was over, the village drummer would begin dreamily to caress the skin of his drum, and gradually the others would join in, sing together, and dance.

The words they sang and the actions they mimed in their dancing recalled the triumphs and the sorrows of the past. They were remembering what had been remembered for generations back. Living memories blended with what had been handed down from five hundred or a thousand years. The slavers who had come collecting *black ivory* for Portuguese freebooters four hundred years ago were remembered in the same breath as the Arab raiders whom David Livingstone had denounced, but who paid their bills in sovereigns minted with the head of Queen Victoria.

Flight from the slave raiders, victories over hated rivals, floods, famines, bumper harvests, heroic deeds or betrayals, everything happened *once upon a time*, and that time seemed only the day before yesterday.

Memorials

Landmarks were when someone in the village felt the time had come for a celebration, *mbari*, something to bring together all the notable things in life. A few others would join in modelling a cluster of pictures and statues, a stage set, in a makeshift house of their own — gods, goddesses, animals, scenes of family life, scandals, tragedies, happy events. It might take a year or more to put it all together, and then it was like a marriage feast, or the gala opening of an English War Memorial Hall. It brought everyone together and lasted on as something the whole community could be proud of.

Nobody in this little neighbourhood was really a stranger. Within it, you couldn't feel lost, or out of touch. It was a world in which you could feel at home.

Only death could shatter the pattern. Then the familiar world gaped open and let loose the terrors of the unknown.

At such times, Oke's Grandfather, the medicine man, was out of his depth. His herbs and earths were useful in treating barrenness in women and infidelity in men; in easing headaches and purging stomach pains. But he was no match for death.

Death and the unseen world were the concerns of the man whom outsiders might call the *ju-ju man*, the *witch doctor*. He was more a priest than a healer.

Unseen forces

When something went wrong, like a miscarriage or a bad harvest, he could work out why it went wrong. It was because of some word or deed that was unnatural, unusual, not according to custom. Anyone whose milk teeth came first in the upper jaw was suspect. Or perhaps there was a mistake in preparing food, or siting a new hut, or the way a cloth was worn, or a gesture or a look even. Whatever the trouble, he had to smell it out and so prevent a worse disaster.

If a crime was committed, and it was not important enough to be referred to Aro Chukwu, the witch doctor tried the suspect by ordeal. He put up a concoction of sasswood, esere beans, strong enough to poison the suspect who swallowed the dose — unless he proved his innocence by vomiting it back at once.

So it paid to be friends. The witch doctor could help innocence establish itself by mixing an emetic with the sasswood. In time of difficulty, he could summon the powers of darkness to keep a man in health or to make him ill; to bring a woman love and fine children, or to estrange her and make her barren.

Most of the time, the village preferred to manage without calling him in.

Death, infirmity and feeble-mindedness were part of the natural order of things. The flies that clustered round the eyelids of the babies, the stink of the living quarters, growths, ulcers, blindness, old age, childbirth, were part of everyday life, to be accepted like food or drink or laughter.

Getting up

The main thing was to get on with everyone else, and to *get up*. **You helped each other to *get up*, and everyone helped the whole village, to *get up* and to go one better than the village next door.** There were leaders, sometimes young ones, who were accepted because of their ability to do great things for the village. That might mean that the young men went raiding, and returned with heads as trophies. That showed their village was superior, but it did not mean taking over subject villages and creating a little empire. **One village was enough. People said** *A tall tree does not span two towns.*

At home in the village, it was the present that mattered. Anger, envy, joy or grief gripped as suddenly and as completely as desire. But once over, they were forgotten. They were kinks in the rope which the years pulled straight again. The rope itself was made from what alone endured, undemanding, uneventful, unadventurous family life, that tethered everyone within a familiar world. Within the limits of the village neighbourhood, everyone was free to move as they pleased. Beyond it, hardly anyone wished or dared to venture.

✧   ✧   ✧

Only the witch doctor and the medicine man had the right, by custom, to move freely far and wide. Oke's Grandfather had a kind of diplomatic immunity. He had free passage even when villages in the district were at war with each other. He belonged to the *Dibia*, the guild of all the healers, diviners, clairvoyants and other priestly people in the region. The entry fee for a new member was reduced for the sons of former members, though Oke's Grandfather had to spend heavily on a feast to which all the *Dibia* was invited. Still, it was worth it. In return, the other members of the Medical Association passed on some of their professional secrets, and helped him to collect his first supply of herbal medicines.

At the age of 12, the boy who would one day be the father of Oke was apprenticed to carry Grandfather's medicine bag. He was shown where to find medicinal herbs and roots. He learned to be a dispenser.

But before the old man had taught many of these precious skills, he died.

Oke's father had to decide what to make of his future. According to Oke, his dad was an impudent sort of fellow, always up to something, with a liking for variety. Faced with choosing for himself, instead of having his choice made for him by his father, he decided he did not want to fit into the *Dibia*. He considered an alternative, suggested by his uncle who was guardian of the skull hut of *Ekpe* — the Leopard Fraternity. This was an exclusive and powerful society with its own rituals, and a freemasonry among its members which helped along anyone with a career to make — provided he belonged.

Oke's father decided to make as much as he could of his family connections, without getting too tightly involved.

Free enterprise

He had the itch to travel. He had got used to moving about among the villages where his father practised; he got on well with strangers. His world was already much bigger than the familiar world the rest of the village knew. He could see that there were opportunities further afield which a bright young man could seize. He kept up the medical work after his father's death, but began to use his contacts in remoter villages to do a little business.

At first, the trade was in cloth and coral beads. Later, by arrangement with his uncle and the Leopard Fraternity, he was able to deal in a more rewarding product.

Slaves.

Far away, over two hundred miles along winding bush footpaths, were the peoples of the Coast. Here, villagers lived a less restricted life. There was scope for enterprise. Elders with exceptional power and influence called themselves Kings. Occasionally, there were disputes between them over the sharing out of the trade with the foreigners who plied up and down the coast. Sometimes the disputes turned into little wars and the Kings showed their power and cleverness by selling up their defeated enemies.

The slaves could be traded with European dealers for guns; or they could be sold through the Leopard Fraternity, inland. The Igbos were usually the middlemen, without a great deal of contact with the foreigners on the coast. The slaves might be well treated in good times, almost as members of the family. In bad times, they were useful bargaining materials to buy off the powers of darkness. Any new enterprise needed some sort of sacrifice, as a kind of insurance premium. If you could afford a human sacrifice, so much the better.

As Oke's father got older, he learned that things were not always as they seemed to be. In his travels, he sometimes came across the priests of Aro Chukwu, the guardians of the Oracle. Surprisingly, away from their base. They too were into the slave trade. But they were not buying slaves to appease the Goddess. They were sellers.

Their stock-in-trade were the convicted criminals who supposedly had been executed outside the cave of the Oracle. The cries of the victims had been genuine alright. Like everyone else not in the secret, they thought the river waters were sweeping them to their death. But in most cases, it was not their blood that stained the waters, but an infusion of red ochre, mixed in under cover of the trees, for the benefit of ignorant onlookers. The victims became saleable livestock.

Oke's father was clever enough to keep silent on such matters. But he was full of funny stories and the latest gossip. He would show up at the courts of the petty Kings on the coast, flash his wares, crack his jokes, and move back again into the bush. This quicksilver stranger relieved the monotony, and won his way to respect, even friendship, by his very impudence. So the young man thrived, and his business deals grew bigger.

Taking over from the oracle

One day, on the Coast, he met his first white man, a trader from Liverpool moored off the coast of Calabar. To a salute of gunfire, he was brought by canoe to a formal dinner with the local chiefs. He sold them guns and brass bars for palm kernels and palm oil. The guns were not only for ceremonial use. If anyone defaulted on the deal, a boarding party came ashore and seized hostages who were kept in irons on the ship until the debt was paid.

Oke's father was fascinated. Not so much by those strong arm methods, which were customary amongst Coast people. What he took to show back home in the village were the fantastic things that the white man made: a perfectly reflecting mirror, a piece of cloth of a weave much wider than could be had from any village loom, a thin-bladed knife that kept its sharpness.

White people were not content to stay in the normal line of business. There were white soldiers, white teachers, elbowing out some of the traders, interfering. Soon, they were establishing themselves inland, along the courses of the great rivers. On the Coast, they broke the power of the little Kings and enslaved the slavers. Oke's father decided he had better readjust some of his business activities. Slave-dealing was getting to be risky.

Then came the news that white soldiers had journeyed to the Oracle of Aro Chukwu, killed or captured the priests, chopped down the sacred grove, and blocked up the little cave.

And the Goddess had done nothing.

Carve-up

From 1900 to 1914, the British made 21 military expeditions into Igbo country. Almost overnight, it seemed, they had become a new power in the land.

Fifteen years earlier, the European powers met in Berlin to divide the loot in the *scramble for Africa*. Or, to put it more tactfully -

"under Lord Salisbury's management," said a leading English historian, *"the African continent was divided among the Great Powers by peaceful agreement."*

Lord Salisbury, the incoming Conservative Prime Minister, making the speech of the evening after a well-lubricated Mansion House dinner, explained what the Great Powers had all been up to:

"We have been engaged in drawing lines upon maps where no white man's foot ever trod; we have been giving away mountains and rivers and lakes to each other, only hindered by the small impediment that we never knew exactly where the mountains and rivers and lakes were."

The lines on the maps were drawn to suit European military and commercial interests. They lumped different tribes and cultures together, or sometimes split them asunder.

There were upwards of 400 different languages spoken in the British protected territories which were named Nigeria. To ease the white man's burden, a tidy-minded administrator, Lord Lugard, came up with the notion of Indirect Rule. Wherever there were *native rulers*, his idea was that they should be paid to stay *on seat*, and see to it that their subjects toed the British line: safe passage for traders, civil servants, and missionaries, along roads and railways to be kept in good repair, with native soldiers and policemen under British officers to preserve the peace. Most of the rest of everyday life could continue on traditional lines under the local ruler.

Throughout the north and in many parts of the west, the old order continued under the sway of Sultans, Emirs, and hereditary Chiefs — all great believers in strong government from the top down and no unsettling innovation.

The Igbo lands were different. Here, authority was more likely to come from the community as a whole. There were leading citizens, sometimes called Chiefs, but they could be put in their place, and dropped if need be.

Now, everyone had to get used to dealing with an unassailable outsider who, they learned, had arrived in the region to *protect* them.

A new oracle

Even the stay-at-homes got the chance to see this white man for themselves. The village was visited by an almost godlike creature who spoke with the elders and told them what they should do.

They learned that it was for their sake that their Oracle had been destroyed. And now there was this replacement Oracle, the District Officer. Soon, the D.O.'s effigy would figure as one of the statues contrived at the next *mbari*-celebration, complete with his peaked helmet, his pipe, his bicycle and his police orderly.

The new Oracle had a lot more to say about the way the village should live. The bicycle itself was an eye-opener to people who in a thousand years had not made use of that kind of wheel (though they were quite used to grinding corn with a horizontal millstone). Farmers scratched the soil with a wooden plough, pushed along by hand. Cattle were hoarded as a token of wealth and importance; no-one knew how to improve a strain by breeding; none of the wise old women thought to use cow's milk to nourish the grandchildren they doted on.

Now there was a lot of new advice to absorb. Some of it good — like keeping the head free of lice, which saved the women hours of going through the children's hair. And then in the same breath, white people were telling everyone to wear a lot of clothes, instead of letting the air caress the skin and saving good cloth for special occasions. They explained how to get better results in farming, but they spirited away some of the young men who should have helped to do the work to become porters, soldiers, houseboys, handymen in trading posts and mission stations, contract labourers on new roads and railways to replace forest paths.

The village elders were disturbed by all these changes. But Oke's father had knocked about the world and knew a thing or two. He could see that more changes were on the way, and was ready to make the most of them. He had also glimpsed what lay behind white people's mystery. Like the Oracle of the Goddess, there was more than met the eye. White men of different nationalities were in competition, and before long, at war. More young men were recruited to fight for them. They did not rule by divine right, they were vulnerable like other men.

Half-way through the white people's war, in 1916 or thereabouts, Oke's father married a local girl. Beginning to raise a family, he came to another decision. As a youngster, he had chosen to fend for himself instead of accepting the path charted out for him by his elders. Now he made up his mind that his own sons should be equipped to make their own ways in the new times.

He determined to give them a future.

To do that, he decided the village must have a school.

He spoke with white missionaries he had met on his travels and persuaded them to come home with him.

Dignified, bearded, gracious, they impressed everybody. When they entered his house, he paid them more deference than he ever gave to the Kings on the Coast, whilst the villagers crowded round the open doorway and drank the strangers in.

Fans

Afterwards, everyone discussed the new idea. Some of the elders reckoned that it would lead to more young men drifting away to seek their fortunes in the towns. But they were overruled.

Everyone else, like Oke's father, had become fans. Whatever white people did or said had virtue and was worth imitating. Tools, clothes, sermons, laws — and above all, education: — you couldn't have too much of them.

The elders set aside a piece of ground, where the teacher could live and set up his school in the shade of the obeche tree. The children sat spell-bound before the blackboard and listened to the black teacher the white people had sent. Their fathers set to work as if for a wedding feast, and built the teacher a house to make every other village wild with envy.

Oke was born just after the Great War ended. By the time he was old enough to attend the school his father had helped to found, schooling had lost its novelty, but not its attraction. No-one went unwillingly to school. Children from other villages walked in daily from up to fifteen miles away, though they had to listen to jeers from Oke and his friends for belonging to villages that weren't up to having schools of their own. Nobody played truant; coming to school was a privilege.

He went on to the Middle school, too far away to be a day-boy, so he lived in. Many of the teachers were white, and their skills could be passed on direct. You couldn't have too much. There was a story about one inexperienced headmaster who told the school at Morning Assembly that there were too many late-comers. If there was any more backsliding, there would be punishment — such as an extra hour of arithmetic. Next day, the whole school turned up late and demanded their rights.

When Oke came home for the holidays, he was somebody out of the ordinary: his head was in the clouds, the bag on his shoulder was stuffed full with homework which kept him busy when the other kids were just loafing about, taking things as they came.

Igbos had always been footloose, and not too set in their ways. They were like the Scots, self-reliant, ingenious, tough; and usually good at a party.

Increasingly, the young men drifted away to the barracks and the offices and the mission stations in the towns and cities. They picked up new skills, and made money. Back in the village, there were fewer husbands to go round.

Good timers

Some of the girls joined the young men in the towns, for the Good Time. There was money to buy clothes that put them a rung above the village stay-at-homes. Once upon a time, ceremonial trappings had been ostrich plumes, leopard skins, cowrie shells. Now they were trilby hats with sweeping brims, flash ties, shiny shoes with soles two inches thick. And the girls matched their fellows with costumes based on the dresses that the Governor's lady and her friends had worn at presentation parties.

The Good Timers tended to live in cliques. Different parts of the town became the stamping grounds of rival groups. Neighbourhoods were in fashion, and so were village feuds. But the village traditions lingered. There were *contribution clubs* to gather savings and make loans; social clubs, often based on age groups, that met to help each other, have fun, and raise funds to help the home village to *get up*. Each club was determined that their own village should have, sooner or later — not a collection of enemy heads — but, in these days, its own school, market hall, water supply, health centre, a proper road — maybe a bridge.

This went counter to the policies of many British administrators. They wanted resources concentrated at suitable centres of government where they could take *an overview* of nice big office buildings, parade grounds, shopping marts, mission stations, maybe even a Staff College one day. But Igbos persevered (with occasional help from an enlightened D.O., like Chadwick in the Udi District), raised their own money, gave their own labour, and made sure that most of the benefits went direct to the villages and little towns, where everyone could see the results.

Separate lives

In such matters, the town groups were in tune with village life. But the music was fading. In the cities, the Good Timers were losing their roots, out of their element. They were getting used to white people's ways, the paperwork, the polite behaviour, the official rituals. They liked using the tools and materials and the fancy goods.

They often had great respect, and sometimes affection for the white people they worked for, or who taught them. But it was difficult to get much further. They tended to know white people from the feet up. There was good money shining shoes at the railway station; those feet crossed roads which had to be swept with care; in the evenings, white clubmen's legs were spread-eagled in repose, to be negotiated carefully by club stewards bearing the drinks that crowned the day's imperial work.

Some might claim that the poor African was being downtrodden beneath those well-shod feet. But not many people on the spot would have agreed. The money seemed to be good, the hours were good, the pickings were good. It was just that, although in the crowded city you lived on top of one another, there was a charmed circle within which white people had their own lives. One lot were the fish in the tank, the others were those swimming around outside in the pool that contained it.

Here and there, a white teacher ran a youth club; or a church fellowship tried to get white people and educated Africans to rub shoulders. But those who came to the youth club were mostly students or skilled apprentices. And no labourer found himself at home in the severely English atmosphere of the white people's church. It worked the other way as well. There were plenty of African chapels and tabernacles in which a vivid, colourful, enthusiastic religion came near to reflecting the warmth and familiarity of family life back home. White people *looked in* on such places, tourist-fashion.

Western style

Oke went on to the University and things began to be different. Tutors talked with their students as well as at them. It came more naturally to ask awkward questions, and to come out with independent views. People from all over the country were getting used to each other, and feeling they belonged to something bigger than a village, or even a clan. Independence was just round the corner. He won a scholarship and came on a postgraduate course to England, where I first met him.

There was a feeling that spring was busting out all over, just like the song in 'Oklahoma!'. Everything was on the up and up. There was a new kind of Good Timer. The bright young people who filled the hostels in London, Birmingham, Edinburgh, Paris, Berlin, Chicago, were educated persons, not ignorant peasants. They were above crude imitation of white people's clothes. They wanted more than gramophones and radio sets, or even motor cars.

They wanted the power enshrined in paper.

Power to secure influential jobs with the help of diplomas and degrees. Political power to be had by knowing how to handle facts and figures and voting strengths; advertising power to select, distort, promote.

The Good Timers on the street corners back home had dressed, *western-style*, to impress. In the same fashion, these educated young persons abroad picked up the latest styles in western institutions, the trappings of modern government, the tricks of company promotion.

Then they went back home to set up shop on their own account. But they found that their qualifications did not get them equality. Foreigners, whose paper qualifications were no better, got more pay, and better status.

Up to now, most people had wanted to be like the white man, meaning *as good as*, and in the long run, *as powerful as*. But there seemed to be a scam. The paper qualifications white institutions awarded were not getting their full value.

The white institutions themselves were unreliable. Or at any rate, unsuitable. What was needed were black institutions, right across the board. Black nationhood.

Looking afresh, they began to see through some of the white Oracles. They could see opportunities up ahead of them that white people had begun to lose. New nations were coming of age. New electorates were ready to be blooded. **Good works or smart deals, it was a free-for-all. The white man's world was their oyster.**

Independence

I saw Oke and his family on their home ground, with their new baby arriving just before the birth of the new nation.

There was a feeling in the air that all things were possible. Something like our own landslide election in 1945 which swept out the old régime and opened up what promised to be a new age.

Radio was reaching out to villages as well as towns. TV was a wonderful new toy in the cities. The new Prime Minister visited the Nigerian Broadcasting display at the Independence Exhibition, and we coaxed him into handling the one and only television camera we then had operating. The broadcasters trumpeted the good news and gave heroic commentaries (carefully rehearsed beforehand) as Parliaments were opened and dignitaries installed.

After that first year, things began to change. When I came out from England again in 1963, there was a taint in the air. Difficult to identify. Perhaps the Igbos were doing too well. They had always been great traders, making their number with traditional Hausa peoples in the north, and outdoing the Yoruba business people in the west. And not only traders. There were Igbo station masters, postmasters, long-distance lorry drivers, school teachers, office managers. Wherever there were new jobs going, it seemed, there were Igbos and probably their families, *getting up*, working round the clock to gain the commercial edge. There were thriving schools in Igbo territory a generation before the more conservative Northerners got round to it.

Igbos made no bones about the fact that they could do things a lot better. But the balance of power lay with the emirs and sultans who ruled the north, with 54% of Nigeria's population, but only 2.5% of the children in secondary schools.

Oil money

Regions were reviving tribal loyalties and competing desperately for contracts with Western entrepreneurs. And now, with Independence firmly established, Western oil firms had begun to trigger off an oil bonanza. It was only five years since the first oil supplies had been shipped abroad. Now, oil was becoming by far the country's biggest source of wealth. Strictly speaking, the oil deposits, and the outlet ports lay outside the traditional Igbo homeland, in the Delta where the Ogoni people lived. But Igbos were right up front when Western firms set up the new refineries.

A lot of *dash* was changing hands as Western oilmen, the representatives of the Seven Sisters — made deals with Government — in particular, with the Central Government, though even here there were Igbos making a fast buck wherever they could.

Central Government was riven by faction-fighting, increasingly inefficient and corrupt. A small group of middle-ranking army officers, mainly Igbo, decided to make a clean sweep of the *enemies of the people ... the political profiteers*. They were led by a devoutly Christian Igbo, Major Chukumma Nzeogwu. Overnight, they killed the Prime Minister and four other northern leaders. (Nothing very new in this approach; it was the seventeenth military coup to take place in newly-independent African states in under six years.)

The new Prime Minister, an Igbo general still loyal to the old régime, was assassinated in his turn, and another northern general, a Christian, Yakubu Gowon, took over. The killings had created a shockwave which shook every tribe and institution, and sparked off racial riots. In the north, massacres of Igbos on the strength of a false broadcast about anti-northern riots — which later took place in Igbo towns for real, in retaliation.

The temperature rose. The easterners could see what was coming. Over the next few months, upwards of two million Igbos began to return home, leaving their properties in ruins from the northern riots.

Their homeland, the East Central State, had a population of about five million. The central government was weak. Most people had preferred it that way. It seemed better sense to have a loose federation of the different cultures which had existed before the Europeans started drawing lines on maps. But now three of the four regions into which Nigeria had been divided began to think of opting out. Lieutenant-Colonel Chokwemeka Odumegwu Ojukwu, the Governor of the East Central State, demanded home rule. General Gowon, a cautious, moderate man, dug his heels in and countered by splitting up the country into twelve smaller regions. Igbos found their Eastern region divided into three, with their own homeland split off from the Delta area — which just happened to contain most of the oil.

Backed by leading Igbos, Ojukwu declared independence. The old Eastern region became the Republic of Biafra. Within its territory, foreigners decided it was time to leave.

To the outside world, Biafra was not just a small nation trying to achieve self-determination; it was also a people who had shown themselves able to move out of the past, to fend for themselves, clear of the domination of traditional Emirs and Chiefs.

The oil men, and their shareholders, saw it differently. The oil interests of the

 Seven Sisters had begun to feel the heat of competition from an assertive newcomer — Libya — now increasingly stroppy under the anti-imperialist Colonel Qdafy. Control of Nigerian oil had become very important. Western investment in Nigeria was tied in close with the federal government. Ninety-percent of Nigeria's wealth was in its oil, and two-thirds of the oil production was in Biafra. Gowon consulted the two most influential Westerners — the US Ambassador, and the British High Commissioner. They told him that if Nigeria split up, it would get *Not one dime, Not one penny* more of foreign aid.

War of independence

A war of secession, like the American Civil War, began. For once, the old Cold War got sidetracked. The Soviet bloc provided General Gowon with most of his airforce. The British supplied his guns and armoured vehicles, unobtrusively at first, but two years later a British Minister admitted *We have been supplying Nigeria with pretty well all its military equipment.*

Two years! To most people, the war had seemed certain to finish in a couple of months. Biafra was David against Goliath, with no stones for his sling, on a hiding to nothing, with the big battalions, the military hardware, and soon the oil installations, in federal hands. In the first ten months, more were killed than in the first three years of the Vietnam war.

I heard from Oke about the situation, and we managed to get his four children evacuated to live with us in London. The siege of Biafra went on, recalling the feelings that the British had in the worst days of World War II when Hitler dominated the rest of Europe. We saw in the Igbos the same kind of do or die exhilaration.

The Igbos had little more than their skill and adaptability.

They set up the Science Group, 100% black (including a few Yorubas who had come over to the eastern side). The Group was a higgledy-piggledy collection of everyone who had any kind of scientific or technological background, teachers, engineers from the railway and from the oil installations, research chemists formerly employed by Western firms, and with them artisans from the shopfloor, craftsmen, and what were known as *wayside mechanics* — the people who coped with your truck, on the spot, when it broke down on the corrugated laterite road.

They scratched around to make the most of local raw materials, crude sulphur, lead, brine, to make nitric acid and sulphuric acid. They invented the *Ogbunigwe*, the new bomb, encased in a milk churn, *that kills by numbers*. In the railway yards, they converted tractors to tanks. They set up makeshift factories, some of them in the bush. They ran a radio station from a Land Rover. They tapped oil wherever they could, and *backyard oil refineries* sprang up. Palm oil mills were converted to produce petroleum. New furnaces produced castings for the flame-throwers and the napalm bombs. An electronics group went into production. Cholera vaccines were made, and mosquito repellent was produced from dried orange peel. All products were *subject to quality testing and certification* by the newly-established Research and Technical Services Division.

The land area under Biafran control was shrinking all the time under the military onslaught, with fewer farms to supply the food. Most of the primary food protein had traditionally been imported — meat, millet, maize, fish and legumes. Women's organisations spearheaded a Dig for Victory campaign. The scientists encouraged them to use the leaves of cassava, pawpaw, hibiscus, coco yam, and to dry and press them. Salt, in short supply, was refined from brine taken by tanker to evaporation plants. A poultry industry was developed. Small rodents became part of the menu.

The Igbos continued to hold out for another two years. By that time, two million people had died, mostly those living in Biafran territory. The war was lost by starvation more than by force of arms.

General Ojukwu, a bit like Bonny Prince Charlie, went into exile, leaving his loyal supporters behind.

A teenage Yoruba who had been away in Ghana throughout the war went to visit the defeated state. He told me,

> *"No-one who wasn't there would believe the destruction. The shattered buildings, the maimed people. So many of them were half-starved, and had lost a limb. I went to one old woman who had lost a leg and was about to cross the road, with a baby in her arms and a load on her back. I offered to help. She politely refused because, she said, 'I am used to it, I can manage.'"*

Self-discovery

So far, there's been no attempt to remake that part of history. But for the Igbos, like the Scots, the Irish, and any number of other independent-minded groups throughout the world, there has been a moment of truth.

An Igbo journalist wrote:

> **"We have been purged of old delusions and illusions. Shut up in our country, faced by starvation, disease and death, ... taking stocks of ourselves, our possibilities, our limitations, our desires ... We have faced reality — raw reality. The result is ... a discovery not only of our goals, but also of our souls, the souls of emerging black men in a world of white men ... It is not just the newly-invented processing plants. It is not just the complete running of our country without one foreign expert ... It is the knowledge that these have been achieved by us. We too can fly."**

Two academics wrote, ten years later, in the officially-approved chronicle of Nigerian independence: Biafra, they said, was

> *'the first truly indigenous technological civilisation in Black Africa'* — *'The war led to the flowering of indigenous genius.'*

And what were the fruits?

With the support of a series of gimcrack military governments backed by British and American politicians, the oil men were able to *develop* the oil-rich territories on the Niger Delta (where Ken Saro-Wiwa and the Ogoni people lived).[2]

By the 80s, oil had become Nigeria's biggest cash crop, with Britain Nigeria's biggest single trading partner. But as the Ogonis were finding out, it was at the expense of their land and livelihood. Throughout Nigeria, military intimidation and political corruption were tearing the country apart. Those who made most out of the oil boom were foreigners and the officials and politicians on their payrolls. But the oil production figures began to be matched by the increasing number of hostile, but fairly non-violent, Ogoni villagers, coming together in 1990 to form their Movement for the Survival of the Ogoni People, with Saro-Wiwa as President. By 1993, Ogoni resistance forced Shell to suspend oil production in the Delta.

Those in the Federal Government who managed to stay above the battle could see what was going wrong. Senior civil servants reported:

"Crude petroleum production and sales on which our economy now mainly depends and which gives the false sense of wealth, depends in the main on imported technology, imported equipment, and significant expert foreign personnel to put them to work ... This should be a cause for concern."

The recipe for recovery:

"Priority should be shifted to stimulate investment in rural and cottage industries to service the first step in setting up local industrial infrastructures ... The experience of the scientific and technological effort in Biafra during the civil war should serve as a model.

For the first time in Nigeria, local scientists and technologists achieved technological feats without the guidance and assistance of foreign experts ... through a process of learning by doing. ... It was self-reliance in practice.

George Santayana, the philosopher, has correctly said that 'Once you make people think, you cannot stop them'."

Getting up — again

Three kinds of *self-reliance in practice*. The Biafran War, fought to a standstill; the Ogoni non-violent resistance — still surviving with most of the leadership dead or on death row. And the third?

Go to the Ojo Alaba International Market, in Lagos, the one time capital of the Nigerian Federation and still its financial and commercial centre. Look around, and almost every stall is owned or run by Igbos. There is more money circulating in that market alone than in the whole of the Nigerian Stock Exchange. The Igbos there have links with Igbo traders back in their homelands. They are used to relying on each other. You might call them a kind of *Dibia*, bang up-to-date.

At first, they were trading in foreign products. *Lately*, says a seasoned western Nigerian, whose work takes him all over the country, and to other parts of Africa as well,

"people talk of anything new as 'Aba-make', or 'Onitsha-make', or comprising all such places in former Biafran territory, 'Igbo-make'. The new things are made cheap, often with sub-standard materials, but they sell everywhere."

The Igbos continue to take things apart, find out how they work, copy the components and go into production:

"Nowadays", he says, "they go off to Taiwan to contact the producers of high-tech electronics, drugs, anything new that will sell. Sometimes they just copy and pass the products off with a Japanese or an American label. Often, they tie in with the Taiwanese manufacturer. They've reached the stage at which the Japanese were in the 1930s — producing cheap imitations. It won't be long before they go one stage further, and corner the market for the things they produce on their own account."

Already, Igbos are dominating the leather trade, producing handbags and shoes and no longer needing to stick foreign labels on them. Recently, they have been buying up old fridges in the UK, bringing them back to recondition. Before long, they will be turning out fridges, audio, video, TV in their own right. Buyers are beginning to come to them from Taiwan, China, Korea, Hong Kong, Thailand, Brazil, Venezuela, Mexico. Nothing great yet, but at the present rate of development, Igbos could be the industrial core of central Africa, by the end of this century.

Does this mean they will become a Biafran nation once more?

Probably not, judging from the attitude of Igbos to the Nigerian Federation. They want more small states. Each one able to fend for itself, without feeling threatened by outsiders. Able to take a *sidon-look* — a sit-down view of what everyone else is up to, including the Ogonis. But with a dyed-in-the-wool commitment to free-standing local independence. After all, as the people in Oke's village used to say, *A tall tree does not span two towns.*

The Biafran War made people in the Igbo homelands aware that they were *one people*, and yet could be many. They had a common cause, and by the end of the war, the men in Onitsha who used to think of themselves simply at *Onitsha men*, thought of themselves as Biafrans. As members of the Igbo people.

More determined than ever to *get up*. Waiting their turn to do business (like Oke's father) with all comers, including those Ogonis on the coast.

This *self-discovery* did not shred away with the end of the war. Perhaps the opposite has happened. Maybe the Igbos are ahead of the game, and can see the shape of things to come, not just in black Africa, but in the rest of the world as well.

So who was it lost the war?

Self-determination

No question about Igbos' or Ogonis' *determination*, in war or peace. It locks into the jigsaw with scores of others: Tutsis, Hutus, Tamils, Kurds, Basques, Kashmiri, and — yes, Geordies, Scousers, East Enders, and the citizens of Tennessee.

In varying degree, they share a sort of family solidarity, reinforced by memories and traditions handed down the generations:

Don't meddle with us. We're something special. Always have been, always will be. Whaur's better!

It's a common bond, that survives defeat.

Consider the Scots — two and a half centuries ago. People with clan loyalties, not much attracted to large institutions. Rallying to a romantic leader, proclaiming their independence. Defeated at Culloden by superior fire-power. And then? Ranging the world as engineers, lighthouse builders, traders, scientists, farmers, fishermen, writers, creating their own distinctive neighbourhoods wherever they come to rest.

Many Scots will tell you that clans are old hat. Fit to sell tartans to tourists, or attract North Americans in search of their past. What matters is not that you are a MacSporran or a MacIntosh, but that you are a Mac — one of Scotland's sons or daughters. That's someone with roots, in touch with tradition, sharing some common feelings.

Right now, how does Scotland compare with the rest of us? As demoralised? As clueless? Or on the way to a new kind of nationhood that leaves us... wondering.

And the *self* in Self-Determination?

Self-discovery? Self-expression? Self-sacrifice? Self-fulfilment? Self-respect?

Self-interest?

We're finding that the motivating forces in human nature are a threat as well as a promise:

Doing your own thing		Power lust/addictive greed
Joining in		Gang law
Trying things out		Weapons research
Family feeling		Ethnic cleansing

Harnessed, those forces *could be* the making of us. Let loose on their own, they are as menacing as the Four Horsemen of the Apocalypse.

Harnessed? Doesn't that smack of outside interference? The kind of *intervention* that sets limits to free-range, independent-minded self-determination?

Suppose instead that there's a natural order into which everything fits? A *system* that balances these conflicting forces and determines everything for the best in the long run — without the need for any of us to get involved?

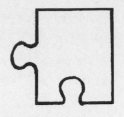

The mean machine

Four thousand years ago, the builders of Carnac and Stonehenge seem each to have been possessed by the same idea: to suss out the system which governs the Universe. They built giant clocks, the standing stones whose shadows plotted the positions of the earth and the sun for the benefit of Bronze Age mathematicians.

Overlapping with our own civilisation, the Maya people of central America devised their own stone wheel mechanical calculators to check back on the past and to work out the future — the time it took for a year to pass, accurate to 0.000198 of a day per year; the time to expect each solstice, each eclipse, centuries ahead.

Anyone who lives off the land has to think hard about when to plough and sow and reap and store. So it's reassuring to know where you stand: that there's an immutable order to the universe that you can rely on.

If you can predict the behaviour of the stars and their courses, the same must surely be true of human beings. There must be natural laws that shape and govern us. Find out how those laws operate, and everything will drop into place.

In our own, city-bound day, we are just as heavily into enormous calculating machines: the office towers that house the number-crunchers — the banking and insurance corporations, marketing conglomerates, tax administrations, property exchanges. All dedicated to estimating costs and predicting trends.

Until recently, those predictions have been largely governed by the calculations of a distinguished Scottish academic with a bee in his bonnet about the way nations enriched themselves.

Searching for a system

In the 1760s, Dr Adam Smith was about half-way through his lifework, *The Wealth of Nations,* a book which would set out the laws by which economic behaviour can be predicted; the guarantee that in the long run, everything comes out right.

Like those old Bronze Age and Mayan mathematicians, he was looking for a universal pattern, true for all time, determining how human societies pay their way.

*A system of behaviour which tends to promote the happiness either of the indi-
vidual or of society... The beauty (of the) well-ordered machine.*

He was a kindly man, and had recently expressed his fellow-feeling for other
people in his *Theory of Moral Sentiments*. Like Dr William Harvey a century
earlier, he wanted to chart a circulation system. Not blood, but money.

He reckoned to have found what was at the heart of human behaviour, its
mainspring,

human sympathy — the faculty for feeling other people's ills as pain.

However, the more he studied the lessons of the past, and looked around in
his own country, the more he felt that sympathy and goodwill were not enough.
In fact, he came to believe that they were almost irrelevant.

In much of Scotland, the land was held by clan chieftains with powers of life
and death, backed by armed retainers, leasing small farms to *tacksmen* who
sublet to cottagers making a hard living on stony ground. The clansmens's loyalties, their *fellow-feeling*, worked both ways. Chieftains claimed total allegiance,
but were looked up to as protectors of their people: against other clans; and
against the English, until their overwhelming defeat, twenty years earlier, at
Culloden in 1746. Tacksmen and cottagers stood by each other in the clan feuds
and the English wars, but they went on scratching a living from rocky soil
without joining together to improve the land, or the cattle. There had to be
something stronger than fellow-feeling to bring about prosperity.

The balanced economy

Dr Smith had just taken on the tutoring of the young fifth Duke of Argyll,
on a two-year European tour to improve minds and broaden horizons. From
what he knew of his country and what he saw of Europe, he concluded that the
economic answer was to go all out for whatever you could do best. *Specialise*. Let
the cobbler stick to his last, and leave others to trade their skills in return.

*"The tailor does not attempt to make his own shoes, but buys them off the shoe-
maker. The shoemaker does not attempt to make his own clothes, but employs a
tailor. The farmer attempts to make neither the one nor the other, but employs
those different artificers. All of them found it to their interest to employ their whole
industry in a way in which they have some advantage over their neighbours...*

*It is not to the benevolence of the butcher, the brewer, or the baker that we expect
our dinner, but from their regard to their own interest. **We address ourselves not
to their humanity but to their self-love.**"*

The system that ensures universal prosperity is the *division of labour*. The
power that makes it work is *self-interest*.

✧ ✧ ✧

The old clan economy, where the chieftain took the lion's share of local produce, but guaranteed security for everyone else to make a living, was already shredding apart as the English conquerors took over. Private armies were made illegal, chiefs executed or exiled if they would not submit, or won over with jobs for the boys. The surviving chieftains continued to be the landowners, but with a lot less family feeling for the rest of the clan. They did away with the old forms of tenure as a reward for faithful service. They changed the terms on which their followers had their holdings. They put the rents up.

They had become developers.

Kelp

This change got a boost from the discovery that you could make an awful lot of money from seaweed. No need to cultivate it, the sea delivered this kelp to your coastal borders, piled chest-high. All you had to do was to get it cut up, leave it for three days on the rocks above the tideline to dry, and then cart it to the great stone kilns to be rendered down over a peat fire to a brittle, blueish product that was in great demand down south as an ingredient in glass-making and soap-making, and as a fertiliser.

All a bit time-consuming — *labour-intensive* — but that was easily remedied by upping the rents of the peasant clansmen, creating a *more competitive labour market*. In order to make ends meet, they were forced to gather the kelp on their landlord's terms.

The Dukes of Argyll, one of the great Highland land-owning families, managed this transformation extremely well. Over about 20 years, the market price for a ton of kelp rose from £6 to £9. Over the next, it went up to £18 or even £20. Of this, £1 or £2 per ton went to the families gathering and roasting the kelp — earning about £5 a family over the three months in the season. Another one pound 12 shillings went on transport. The rest was landlord's profit.

By the mid-1760s, the kelp market was booming and the Argyll estate was making a packet (rather more than was morally justified, Adam Smith was inclined to think, though he probably did not say so to the fifth Duke in as many words). Making the best possible deal was in your own interest. Self-interest was the immutable law. So better not interfere.

Besides, it boosted employment. Kelp production brought in more people, outsiders from other parts of Scotland coming in to swell the army of kelp gatherers to around 10,000 families at the height of the kelp boom. But some of the locals had second thoughts. It was *a dirty and disagreeable employment*, poorly paid, and many Highlanders began to emigrate to America. The landowners,

seeing their cheap labour disappearing, did their best by legislation to prevent

"that pernicious spirit of discontent against their own Country and rage for emigrating to America, which has been raised among the people."

An Act was passed under the guise of regulating conditions on passenger vessels, but actually designed to push up the fares beyond the capacity of emigrants to pay.

Then, when the wars with the French ended and trade became freer, the kelp trade began to suffer from foreign competition. By this time the 7th Duke was on seat, and thinking seriously about a change of product which would revive the family's fortunes. (The 6th Duke had been particularly *self-interested* and had blued £2 million of the family's assets in making his number as a big spender in the fashionable drawing rooms and gambling parlours of Edinburgh, and at the English Court.)

Wool and mutton

The alternative growth industry — already well-developed by landowners further south — was the Big Sheep. Well-bred Black Face and Cheviots — wear them, eat them, let them roam. Lay out a bit on fencing, employ a full-time shepherd and some casual labourers for the shearing season, send the products on their own four feet to market, and the rest is profit.

The production which best suited the Duke's tenants on the other hand, was raising black cattle for dairying and for sale down South. Eked out with spinning and a bit of fishing, a family might just get by, with all hands fully employed.

From the Duke's point of view, all that made very poor economic sense. Much better to have a few well-heeled tenants who could afford to pay high rents for sheep runs which allowed them to *live and make rich with very few* workers on the payroll.

You had first to *restructure the workforce* so that the sheep could take over from the people. In 1841, the 7th Duke explained his position:

"My object is to get the farms divided into large proportions and have proper tenants on them, and the rest of the tenants to be provided for by emigration or induced to go to the low country."

He was able to restyle the economy, in favour of the sheep, with the help of the potato blight which brought famine to his poorer tenants. And a particularly effective management style was applied on his behalf by his factor, Mr Campbell, in the lands held on the Ross of Mull. Whenever the tenants' cash flow dried up, and they got into arrears with their rents, Mr Campbell seized their cattle, their one and only tradable asset, in lieu of payment.

In 1847, the 8th Duke succeeded, and was waited upon for his views by the Inspector of the Central Relief Board for the Highlands. It was the time of the Hungry Forties, when down south the Rochdale Pioneers were setting up their co-op shop and evolving their own policies for economic expansion, creating jobs, and profits, side by side.

People

The Duke had a different viewpoint. His people, as such, were a diminishing asset. A liability, really. So he talked to the Inspector *of the absolute necessity of removing a considerable number of them to some other locality or abroad. It would be attempted next spring.*

Next year, he kept his word. Tenants who could not pay their rents, as well as some who could, were *cleared*. Most were shipped to Canada (with the equivalent of redundancy pay in the form of a one-way ticket). There, if they had survived death by cholera en route, they arrived for the most part in rags, destitute, as objects for Canadian charity.

Those that remained had their rents increased twice in five years, so they had every incentive to get on their bikes and look elsewhere. Many ended up in Glasgow, desperately competing for unskilled factory jobs with refugees from the Irish potato famine. Behind them, half destroyed by the Duke's security people, they left the wreckage of their homes. Most have stayed that way ever since.

Towards the end of the last century, with the estates *improved*, the family sheep business well established, the 8th Duke was at pains to show how well everything had turned out, for other landowners as well as for himself. Adam Smith, if he had still been living, might have had reservations. His own book denounces

*"the mean rapacity, the monopolising spirit of merchants and manufacturers ...
though it cannot perhaps be corrected, may very early be prevented from
disturbing the tranquillity of anybody but themselves..."*

Adam Smith couldn't see how to *correct* that mean rapacity once it had taken hold. And to *prevent* it ever happening? Well, that has to be left to the *invisible hand* of Providence — the immutable law which guarantees that if you think and act hard enough in the interests of Number One, it will all come right in the end. Individuals may suffer in the short term, but nations are bound to prosper. Just so long as they specialise and drive the best bargains with each other that they can.

Cash crops

The Dukes of Argyll, like most other Scottish landowners, were greatly encouraged by Dr Smith's Good Book.

His prescription had been taken up by other abroad as well as at home, in what were then colonial territories; local people were persuaded, or forced, to give up their smallholdings in order to work for employers who concentrated on producing one marketable *cash crop*. The owners of booming factories, mines and plantations could see that it was all Providential, really. All you had to do was to follow the Doctor's instructions, look after Number One, concentrate on developing your *personal incentive*. And then, by the design of that *invisible hand*, the economic clockwork would keep everything in order.

By the beginning of this century, the benefits that could be achieved by specialising in this way — at home and abroad — were there for all to see. Mines and plantations overseas and sheep runs back home paid for great houses, fine living, university endowments, the rebuilding of churches, charity schools, investment in railways and manufactures, pomp and circumstance. And some loose cash to spend on horses, cards and women.

And the cost?

Now, a century later, we are just becoming aware.

The trouble is that crops like kelp and coffee can't be relied on to yield the same amount of cash from year to year. **It's all or nothing for the people who cultivate the crops or work the mines. If there's a glut, or fresh competition, there's no money to spare to buy the things that their ancestors used to grow for themselves. And they can't eat the copper or clothe themselves with coffee beans.** So when the owners find they can't sell as much as they would like, and see that it

is in their interest to *rationalise*, the labour force finds itself *down-sized*, like the kelp gatherers. They starve where they are, or drift away to the cities, desperate for even a dead-end job. Perhaps a service job, cleaning house for the well-to-do, or running errands for shopkeepers; perhaps a job as a beggar or a thief.

Holding things down

Newly-independent governments may find themselves in the same kind of trouble. Things are not running as smoothly as they did in the old colonial days. Not always because the new civil servants are any worse than the old ones, or the new business people any more corrupt than their foreign partners. But people are less sure of their prospects. Departing colonial powers left the new nations dependent on the deals they could get for the goods they needed from overseas. If the whole country is mainly dependent on a single crop — cocoa, or coffee, or sugar — everyone is in trouble. Government officials are desperate to win foreign deals. They need to squeeze the money to buy machine tools and technical advice to set up new industries and develop other crops. But the bargaining power is with the well-heeled foreigners, able to bribe their way to contracts which profit them and the officials they deal with, but are made at the expense of the local economy.

The fledgling governments invest early in printing presses, radio and TV to get their messages across to the voters. But there are awkward comparisons. People are getting wise to the difference between their own living and working conditions and those of the people on the telly — the well-fed, well-housed, well-furnished people in the sitcoms and on the talk shows.

Here and there, the news slips through to reveal the mismatch between what government claims to do, and what it actually achieves. Enlightened professionals like Arif Hasan and the others in the Orangi Project beaver away to reveal the difference between actual costs of labour and materials and the prices paid to smart foreign operators and corrupt local officials.

People lose confidence in the powers-that-be, and in their own ability to make a reasonable living. Racial and religious tensions take over. Many of those opposing corrupt or incompetent governments are at odds with each other, and without experience in developing the political machinery of opposition. The alternative is to go underground, or to get out and organise the overthrow of an evil régime from somewhere relatively safe, making the most of information technology to reach the people by satellite dish or smuggled cassette; and, if all else fails, to destabilize by assassination and the terror bomb.

Faced with economic uncertainty and political unrest, governments are driven in on themselves, under siege. And they turn to foreign arms traders who are only too willing to supply them with the means to stay in control.

Dispossessed

Those who can see the economic and political chaos looming try to get clear while the going is good. Like the Scots whom the 8th Duke of Argyll cleared away to make room for his sheep, they are forced away from home because there are not enough jobs, not enough food to go round.

Pioneer-minded or just plain desperate, they find somewhere to settle down, mopping up what dogsbody jobs can be got, making the best living they can. And before long, they are resented. As Winston Churchill MP put it, preparing to pocket several million pounds in exchange for his grandfather's papers, *more and more hungry mouths and hungry bellies* are on their way, *legally or illegally*. They should be turned back. (Grandfather's papers do not however include immigration passes for the time he spent in South Africa. But then, he seldom had to go hungry.)

Sometimes the incomers, honed by their wanderings, seem to have the edge on the locals, they make a sharper impact on the local economy. They get blamed for competing for jobs that our jobless should be having, suspected (usually unfairly) of jumping the housing queue and cashing in on benefits which come from the tax and insurance payments local people have been making.

They face the threat of conflict wherever they go.

Turnaround

At the receiving end, in what we have been used to thinking of as our own *developed* countries, people are also uncertain of the future. In the UK, we are finding that Germans or Japanese or Taiwanese are as good as us in making cars or videos. They even set up their factories here because, with less of the bargaining power British workers once had, we seem to be more biddable.

The Asian Tigers along the Pacific Rim have learned how to process their own raw materials. What's more, instead of buying the processing machinery from us as they used to do, they are building their own industrial plant as well. They are freeing themselves from the cash crop straitjacket, diversifying, selling shoes and designer clothing as well as cars and videos. And because they can draw on jobless workers drifting to towns, desperate to make ends meet — they're doing it on the cheap.

We have become anxious to please. We are no longer sure of jobs or homes. We are also under some stress because of changes that have been happening in our surroundings. Crime, pollution, kids running wild — nothing much compared with the traumas of the so-called developing countries; but because they're new to us, these changes seem ominous and make us jittery.

The economic see-saw begins to shift. Our manufacturing base has got smaller. It's important to expand it. But we're told we can't afford to be choosy.

Vital interests

The arms trade, politely called the 'defence' industry, requires pushy sales people with the political backing that allows them to pave the way for arms contracts by peddling overseas aid.

Any reservations on, say, humanitarian grounds?

We have too much already invested. Think of the *defence* jobs that would be lost. Adam Smith's *Moral Sentiments* are all very well, but the *bottom line* has to be his call for *self-interest*, which tips the balance.

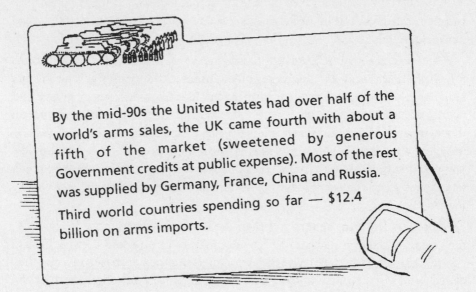

By the mid-90s the United States had over half of the world's arms sales, the UK came fourth with about a fifth of the market (sweetened by generous Government credits at public expense). Most of the rest was supplied by Germany, France, China and Russia. Third world countries spending so far — $12.4 billion on arms imports.

"The trade ought not to be abolished… It ought to be preserved and protected as well as any other." [Lord Maitland]

'No other measure could inflict so deep and lasting a wound on the commerce of this country." [Mr Rose]

'We must not sacrifice to … benevolent emotions the dearest, and most valuable commercial interest to this country, and thus rashly and precipitately extinguish a trade so essentially advantageous as a branch of our national commerce." [Alderman Newnham]

Sorry. We seem to have jumped a cog. Those were the arguments advanced in May 1789 when William Wilberforce first tried to introduce his Bill to abolish slavery (which then accounted for 18% of Britain's *National Product*). Alderman Newnham went on to appeal to the hearts of the fellow MPs. He warned that to abolish the slave trade, on which so much prosperity depended — in Bristol and Liverpool as well as in London —

"would fill the City with men suffering as much as the poor Africans. It would render the City of London one scene of bankruptcy and ruin."

To say nothing of the plight of *our seamen,* jobless if the *carrying trade* were to be curtailed. On such issues, we have to be *realistic.* A vibrant economy must surely be in everyone's interest. We simply can't afford to allow *benevolent emotions,* however attractive, to get in the way.

Roots of prosperity

Such economic realism goes a long way back — at least to Good Queen Bess. When the first free-booting adventurers found their ways round the world, their discoveries, and their booty, made marvellous economic sense to the City merchants back home in London, Lisbon and Madrid — and to their royal masters and mistresses.

Queen Elizabeth I of England, having heard from Captain John Hawkins how he had acquired 300 Negroes on the Guinea Coast *partly by the sword, and partly by other means* and exchanged them in Haiti for hides, sugar, ginger and pearls, was sure that such trade was *detestable, and would call down vengeance* on those who plied it. But when she saw the balance sheet, she had second thoughts. On Captain Hawkins's next voyage, she was one of his shareholders and profited from his visit to the coast of Sierra Leone, anchoring off Sanbula Island and *going ashore every day to take the inhabitants with burning and spoiling their towns.*

Dutch traders with better ships than the British began to move in. In 1619, they brought the first slaves to be landed in America and sold them to British colonists in Jamestown. Forty years later, Dutch ship-owners based in a city they called New Amsterdam (known now as New York) controlled most of the North American slave trade.

The other Europeans were doing their best to keep up.

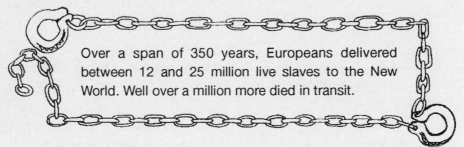

Over a span of 350 years, Europeans delivered between 12 and 25 million live slaves to the New World. Well over a million more died in transit.

The Merchant Adventurers, as some of them called themselves, found they could pick up other trade goods, mighty cheap. Local people on the Gold and Ivory Coast of Africa, in the Indies, and Latin America, were fairly easy to con. They didn't realise the value of their own resources — the precious metals, the spices — and at first seemed please to swap them for not very much in exchange.

Later on, the exchange rates were even more favourable, on account of the European buyers settling down, with their own *peacekeeping forces* and taking over, lock, stock and gun barrel. A precedent had been set 150 years earlier when Christopher Columbus and his management team had discovered that Indians on Haiti could be put to work for 14 hours a day, panning gold dust. When they revolted, *disciplinary action* was taken: they were massacred. But one colonist, Bartolomeo de las Casas, went home and petitioned Charles V of Spain to spare the poor Indian. So he did that, by granting to a favourite the concession to ship 4,000 Negro slaves from Africa to the West Indies to do the work instead.

All sorts of Europeans saw the point of establishing their own mines and plantations, where local productivity could be increased with the use of native labour, conned or coerced into working long hours for low wages; or by bringing in forced labour — African slaves, or poor whites conscripted as *indentured* workers from the home country.

Well before Adam Smith began writing about it, the city merchants and the adventurous colonists had understood that to be an effective developer you have to keep both eyes on the main chance, consolidate, specialise. Coffee, cocoa, tea, sugar, rum, rice, spices, tobacco, cotton, and later on, rubber — concentrating on just the one crop made things so simple. Planting, cultivating, picking, packing and exporting, all to a set routine with a few knowledgeable overseers and a great many farm hands who needed to know no better than to keep in line and obey orders.

Unemployment? Nil. Unless rival plantations cut costs further, or new territories were opened up where the climate was better or the transport cost less or local labour was even more gullible. Then there might suddenly be a glut, a slump in prices, and the painful necessity to *downsize, lay off* — to tide things over *until the economy rights itself.*

By and large, however, everyone who had put *money* into the business — right down to the humblest suburban shareholder — could see that, in the long run, it all made sound *economic sense*.

Until now.

About the time when young John D Rockefeller was selling turkeys for pocket money, some tightlipped New Englander surveying life from a verandah rocking chair, coined a new word:

come-uppance

It's what comes up, out of the blue, to crown a career that had seemed pretty tarnation smart, so far. It hits us between the eyes, like the handle of a rake when you fail to look where you're going.

Be done by as we did

Five hundred years of adventurous self-interest gave Europeans and North Americans the produce of the rest of the world, pretty much on their own terms. Buying cheap and selling dear. But saddling their countries with mounting debts to the money lenders to pay for the arms they needed to fend each other off those overseas possessions, and to keep the locals biddable.

Over the last 50 years, the debts have piled up, all round, along with the surplus *defence* gear now being scrapped or sold off to tyrants or smuggled out to terrorists.

The paper money has stacked up, too. More of everything to buy and sell, and most things priced up to extract a bigger cut for the go-betweens.

Money means a lot to those who spend their time in dealing with it.

Manipulating it brings them mounting self-satisfaction, but, as with the other sort of wanker, it does damn-all for anyone else. And because of these ups and downs, money itself has become less dependable. Its fluctuations create a fantasy world, *virtual reality*, where it's possible to ignore what is actually happening to real people.

A smart operator nowadays can gamble a fortune on a second's variation in the money value of a single commodity. But it's beginning to appear that the commodities themselves don't belong to us any more. It's not always clear who does own them. Until, let's say, the Organisation of Petrol Exporting Countries gets its act together, raises the price at source, and stops everyone else in their tracks. Then it begins to dawn on us that decisions about the food and fuel we buy in, and the raw materials for what's left of our industries — are slipping out of our hands.

Come-uppance.

✧ ✧ ✧

Some side-effects of self-interest have begun to show. Colonial possessions that used to be ours are being *re-possessed* by other self-interested people, overseas. *There's been a takeover.* The new owners may be a multinational consortium answerable to no-one but themselves, or smart local operators on the make, or popular governments struggling to catch up on western standards of living, or a mixture of all three. **The main thing is that a larger and larger share of the proceeds is straying outside our control.**

Profits are still pretty high for whoever handles them, because the people who produce the goods are doing the work for a lot less pay than Europeans and North Americans and Australians and New Zealanders get back home. And those goods include the sort of products we used to sell to them. Now, they have begun to outsell us, on our home ground. The Asian Tigers, with India and China coming up close, have taken a leaf out of the western form book and begun to sell westerners cars and videos and shoes and designer clothes.

Doing unto us what we used to do to their grandparents.

The business people operating in these new nations are also taking on enough new technology to begin *downsizing* **their own workforces.** *Productivity*, **we used to call it. More products, fewer jobs that you can rely on. Plantations swallowing up smallholdings. Lumber camps reducing forest cover. Factory effluent poisoning water supplies. Land hunger setting Hutus and Tutsis** **at each other's throats in Rwanda and Burundi. Job hunger peopling already overcrowded cities. Gun law.**

More discarded people to swell the armies of the dispossessed.

In the old days, when such things were happening a long way off, it is true that we had slums and unemployment of our own, but not on this scale. We got by, in one way or another. There were always wars or preparations for war to divert attention, and take up the slack. And more of us were making a living from producing something worth having, that you could handle (as distinct from paper money or the *virtual currency* which flashes up on the computer screens).

Like the Dukes of Argyll, it suited us, once in a while, to allow in cheap labour. And if sheep replaced kelp in the economy, we could always export our jobless to foreign parts. Now things have gone into reverse. We have the poor world on our doorsteps, in our own overcrowded cities, desperately competing for the jobs we reckoned were just for us.

Come-uppance.

What the doctor ordered

In the world of the 1980s, Dr Smith's doses of self-interest continued to be swallowed whole. In the 1990s, we are experiencing disturbing side-effects.

● The *mean rapacity* of the slave-traders and the arms dealers has sown minefields of fear and anger wherever displaced peoples have settled. They find themselves resented and before long harassed by the communities in which they have taken refuge.

● Specialisation has narrowed the choices open to the lively entrepreneur. It's all or nothing. To make ends meet, you have to sell an awful lot of whatever it is that you make or do. If competitors have cheaper labour on tap, there's only one choice open: go under and leave the market to them; or slim down your own workforce (until your own workers and ex-workers can no longer afford to buy the products and services which others in the community depend on to make a living).

All this goes under the heading of **market forces**, as if these were something cosmic to rely on — like gravity or the movements of the sun and stars.

It ain't necessarily so.

A new word has shamefacedly crept into the medical vocabulary:

IATROGENIC

It describes the disease created by what turned out to be the wrong medical treatment.

It's time we changed the prescription.

When in doubt, ask the patient

We know where it hurts. We can describe the signs and symptoms of the sickness.

We aren't as confident in the doctor as we used to be.

It's all good value for a comprehensive moan.

The time could be better spent if we go further than just patching up the effects of the disease.

It's time we took a fresh look at what it takes to be in health; and what we already have going for us:

- **what we have done so far with the resources within our reach,** and
- **what *could be* done to make them life-preserving, life-enhancing.**

A fresh look, from a different angle.

12 Time and money

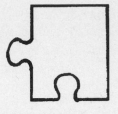

Let's start with a bit of problem-solving by Francisco Gangotena in Ecuador. He was village born and bred and his family have always had their own smallholding, so he knows how much it costs to make a living from a little patch of land. For twenty-five years, now, he has worked for foreigners — *SwissAid*, a worldwide relief organisation trying like *Oxfam* to help people help themselves. So villagers come to Francisco not just for advice, but for practical support. Recently, he's been dealing with 120 families in the village of San Nicolas de Tunshi. After four or five years of agitation they got some land which they can look after on their own account, instead of working for greedy landlords. Thirty hectares now, with luck they'll end up with 120, a hectare each. They want to find a way to make a living, and at the same time to work off the debts that have piled up, because the cost of land in these parts is very high.

"So they came to us asking for a tractor. They didn't want to hire one because that meant that the money just leaves the community. They wanted a tractor of their own.

When I went to the field, the first thing that I saw was the huge pile of fertiliser that they had bought. I asked them how much they'd paid for all that manure and they told me. Then I asked how much the tractor would cost. They reckoned it would come to around 35,000 dollars. So I said, 'How many oxen would you be able to buy with that amount of money?' Answer: 'About 70.' 'And how much manure and urine would you get from a single ox each day?'

I knew all about that from my own smallholding. They estimated you could get 40 pounds a day, which I reckon is an underestimate, though it depends on whether you have it concentrated in a stable or spread around in the open. So then we began to work out some figures and we came up with something like 15,000 sacks of manure from the 70 oxen during the year. And they suddenly realised that the value of these 15,000 sacks was already half the price of the tractor.

So the discussion ended with them saying, 'We'd better have the oxen instead.'

But then they came back again and said, 'We've been thinking it over. How about buying cows, and some oxen as well? We can keep 70 oxen and cows in 120 hectares, and besides the manure, we'll get the milk.'"

Of course, it takes more time to plough with oxen, and even more with draught cows. Time is precious. You could save a lot of it with a tractor. Get someone in the driving seat, working full-time, and the rest of us could be looking for jobs. We'd need to find them, in order to pay for the fuel and the repairs, and of course all that imported fertiliser. And to put something by to replace the tractor when it dies. The problem about tractors is that they don't calve, and you can't skin the carcass for leather jackets and gloves. And the overriding consideration —

"One old guy said it all. 'The reason we won't use tractors is because they don't shit!' "

Guaranteed inheritance

It all depends on the way you look at the time you spend. Most of us are born with masses of it in hand. In the Western world, with people's working lifespan from, say, 15 years old to seventy plus, and after taking out time for eating, partying, sleeping and having a contemplative shit like Martin Luther, most of us can expect about (52 x 55 x 12 x 7 = 240240) working hours before we're written off. Those peasant farmers in South America, like others in Asia, Africa, India, the Middle East, starting work around twelve years, with a life expectation of something nearer sixty, they're getting (52 x 48 x 12 x 7 = 209664) hours on their credit account.

Time is an asset, you go on using it, lifelong. As a measure, it's dependable; it doesn't fluctuate. On top of that, it's renewable — we keep producing babies with their own built-in inheritance waiting for them to spend.

❖ ❖ ❖

For a long spell after the last Ice Age, people had time on their hands. A few clans free-ranging over familiar land, the weather mainly good, meat and poultry, fruits and tubers, within easy reach. About three hours a day, it took, on average, to make a living. So they could spare the time to plan ahead, to organise the transport of those huge monoliths by rafts and log rollers, to make their mathematical calculations and invent their machines to measure the future. Shorter lives, with less security from natural disasters and human anger, but interesting and perhaps fulfilling.

Of course it's quite different for us. Our brain capacity hasn't altered much, but we have some thousands more years of experience to draw on, backed by laptop computer power that does some of our brainwork for us.

More and more

And what is that brainwork achieving, just now?

For a start, it produces a lot more information than anyone has ever produced before, and is doing it much much faster. More cars and trucks, more motorways, more jumbo jets, longer runways; more oil rigs and refineries; more chemical fertilisers; more fridges, TVs, ghetto blasters, music albums and sports magazines;

more computer networks; more digital watches, fine furniture, designer jeans, Doc Martens, and cosmetics; more smallpox vaccines and antibiotics; more landmines, handguns, incendiary bombs and CS gas; more hard drugs.

More food — in Northern countries, where grain stores, milk lakes and butter mountains have accumulated to the extent that farmers are now being paid real money to stop producing so much food, and to *set aside* arable land and sell it off or rent it out, if they're lucky, as theme parks and caravan sites and out of town supermarkets.

More famine — in Southern countries, where parts of the forests are being ravaged to satisfy the Northern love of elegant hardwoods; where some of the rivers are poisoned by industrial effluents; where civil wars have sown the fields with landmines and driven away the peasant farmers from the land they tilled.

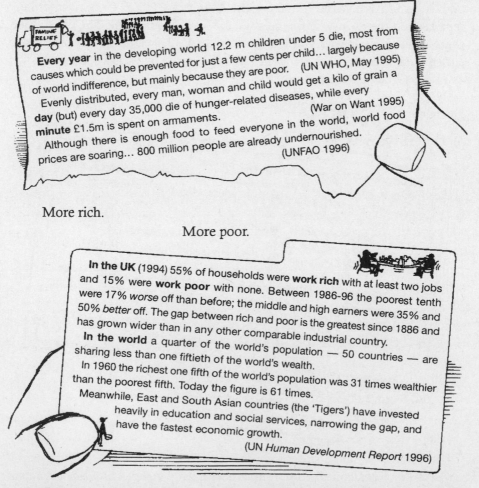

Every year in the developing world 12.2 m children under 5 die, most from causes which could be prevented for just a few cents per child… largely because of world indifference, but mainly because they are poor.   (UN WHO, May 1995)

Evenly distributed, every man, woman and child would get a kilo of grain a **day** (but) every day 35,000 die of hunger-related diseases, while every **minute** £1.5m is spent on armaments.   (War on Want 1995)

Although there is enough food to feed everyone in the world, world food prices are soaring… 800 million people are already undernourished.   (UNFAO 1996)

More rich.

More poor.

In the UK (1994) 55% of households were **work rich** with at least two jobs and 15% were **work poor** with none. Between 1986-96 the poorest tenth were 17% *worse* off than before; the middle and high earners were 35% and 50% *better* off. The gap between rich and poor is the greatest since 1886 and has grown wider than in any other comparable industrial country.

In the world a quarter of the world's population — 50 countries — are sharing less than one fiftieth of the world's wealth.

In 1960 the richest one fifth of the world's population was 31 times wealthier than the poorest fifth. Today the figure is 61 times.

Meanwhile, East and South Asian countries (the 'Tigers') have invested heavily in education and social services, narrowing the gap, and have the fastest economic growth.

(UN *Human Development Report* 1996)

It's what is called economic growth, and the trick is that it's all done with fewer people, in half the time.

Earning

What sort of people get the jobs available?

The senior appointments? No doubt in the Bronze Age there were arch-priests who could take their time, sit around, think mathematical thoughts, dream up plans and issue orders. The plans and the orders became more complex to match the increasing sophistication of everyday life. Everyone, apart from the thinkers and dreamers, found themselves with a full-time job to get on with, day in, day out (festivals excepted).

Today, we have a mixture of well-paid *executive directors* and *non-executive directors*, most of them quite busily wheeling and dealing with each other.

Some are workaholics who get to their penthouse offices before their PAs and office staffs arrive, and carry on the good work over business lunches and brainstorming dinners far into the night. Others are the *non-executives*, usually representing the money or the prestige the firm depends on. They earn their share options, perks and stipends with rather less sweat, and still manage to enrich their declining years with directorships paying up to £50,000 for as much as 21 days of their time in the year.

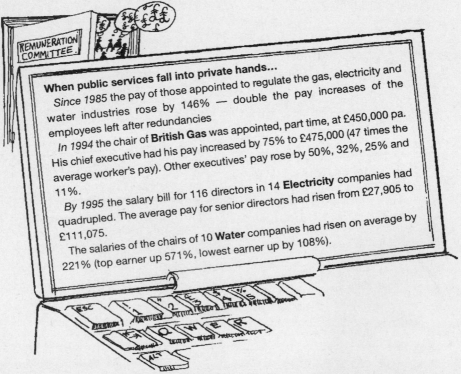

REMUNERATION COMMITTEE.

When public services fall into private hands...

Since 1985 the pay of those appointed to regulate the gas, electricity and water industries rose by 146% — double the pay increases of the employees left after redundancies

In 1994 the chair of **British Gas** was appointed, part time, at £450,000 pa. His chief executive had his pay increased by 75% to £475,000 (47 times the average worker's pay). Other executives' pay rose by 50%, 32%, 25% and 11%.

By 1995 the salary bill for 116 directors in 14 **Electricity** companies had quadrupled. The average pay for senior directors had risen from £27,905 to £111,075.

The salaries of the chairs of 10 **Water** companies had risen on average by 221% (top earner up 571%, lowest earner up by 108%).

How does their contribution compare with the people who *execute* the actual work — who make things, research new methods, operate services, inform and promote, package and deliver?

There are two main varieties here too.

The *core workers* are skilled in their crafts as accountants, legal eagles, production managers, research scientists, sales experts, tool-makers, fitters, caretakers, long-distance truck drivers. They know the ropes, and what the job really takes. They know they're pretty well indispensable, and so does the top brass. So their terms on pay, working conditions and insurance will usually be met; and when the firm thrives, many of them will be on overtime.

The other kind of worker can't take so much for granted. He (more often than she) holds on to a job which might quite suddenly become *marginal*, or *down-sized*. Maybe there is less demand for the product. Or those research boffins have come up with a device that does with less *manpower*. Or one of the results of those business lunches and late night get-togethers is a merger between competing firms, or a sell-out to some developer who wants to *pick the low-hanging fruit* — sell off part of the site, *restructure* what remains in order to *cut the fat*, and get the business looking *really mean and lean*. (Those who use this language find it pays to avoid emotional words like *sacking people*.)

So some of these marginal workers are *surplus to requirements*, and others find themselves reduced to *casual labour*.

This is where women (more than men) find themselves in demand. They can be persuaded to accept part-time work. Some, with small kids to look after, want nothing more. But part-time work doesn't guarantee all the same rights: holiday, sick pay, severance benefits, pensions. And as computer technology spreads, there are more opportunities for firms to save on lighting and heating and accommodation, by *outsourcing* the work to homeworkers who pay their own fuel bills, and can usually be replaced at nil cost if they go sick or need a break.

❖ ❖ ❖

This does at least spread the work around. Part-timers replace full-timers, and there are still heads to be counted when the government compiles its employment statistics.

"Look! Unemployment figures going down! More in work!"

And what's more — *productivity is up!* There's more *gross domestic product* — those trucks, planes, Doc Martens, chemical fertilisers, antibiotics, landmines, etc. — and it takes fewer working hours to make them.

All in all, with fewer people in factory jobs, part-time or full-time, we're getting roughly the same *manufacturing output* as we had, when there were many more people in employment, before the recession.

Fewer full-time jobs, less wages, lower overheads: so we can cut costs and compete with all those sweatshop industries that threaten us from China, Japan,

the Asian Tigers, and the others around the Pacific Rim. And before long, from those ingenious Igbos *getting up* in eastern Nigeria. And if humanly possible, our government would like us to have the edge on the European competition by undercutting the Spaniards and the Germans and other continentals who have agreed together on minimum wages and conditions as part of the Social Chapter.

Spending

What sort of work gets done?

Well, there's the arms trade. And all those who are into food production (but not too much or it might blunt our competitive edge). And transport, which gets a rough ride because there's an uneconomical use of public transport in order to boost the profits of the private operators.

What else? In this country, a lot more hours spent on hairdos, pressure advertising, taking people on tours, offering expert advice, moving money around.

Rather less on making things to use, homes to live in, clothes to wear.

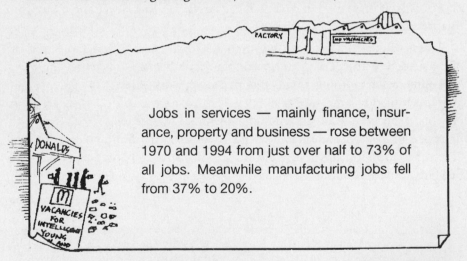

Jobs in services — mainly finance, insurance, property and business — rose between 1970 and 1994 from just over half to 73% of all jobs. Meanwhile manufacturing jobs fell from 37% to 20%.

In the 80s, there were lots of things that people wanted to buy — cars, hi-fis, designer clothes, package holidays in the sun. In the 90s, our priorities have shifted. **We still want those goodies, but other more pressing needs are appearing. Safety on the streets at night; even in the daytime, in the shopping malls. Opportunities for children in school to make the best of themselves, without fear of bullying, or the temptation to take drugs. Better job prospects, free of nagging doubts about redundancy; almost any kind of job, as an alternative to endless, unrewarding leisure.**

These needs come high, and are getting higher. The difficulty is to know how you pay for them to be met.

Can you do it just with money?

Compare the time that's already melting into legend, when we were *really* up against it. How did we get by then?

Surviving

In the 1930s, just before World War II, we found ourselves watching from the wings, insecure, without much confidence in the authorities. We had huge unemployment, a weak government, a widening gap between the well-to-do and the very poor.

 Those who were well-off had little idea of what it was really like living on the dole. Occasionally, there were glimpses — the Geordies from Jarrow came hunger-marching to London; a documentary film called *'Housing Problems'* showed a gaunt, cloth-capped slum householder saying a semi-scripted piece, and pointing out the slimy wallpaper and the jam-packed family bedded in the living room.

There were awkward facts: Sir John Boyd Orr, Chief Medical Adviser to the Minister of Health, showed that in families on the dole, there wasn't enough money to feed children properly. Malnutrition was on the increase. The economic Depression had widened the gap between rich and poor. Disraeli's Two Nations still existed. For the most part, the better-off people preferred to look the other way. Just as they did when incoming refugees talked of the atrocities in the concentration camps. Besides, a few prominent Cabinet ministers and newspaper owners discounted the atrocities, spread a little anti-Semitism around, and said a good word for those architects of *strong government*, Adolf Hitler and Benito Mussolini. People could *leave it to Them* to solve economic problems and get the unemployed off the streets — and into the army.

The Nazis and the Fascists needed their armies: to go into the empire-building business, catch up on the colonial gains that other countries had acquired in the past; and to put other European countries in their proper place, as satellites not competitors.

France and Britain were too big to be satellites and their political leaders decided that the best policy was to stay clear. *Non-intervention*, in the hope that the new oppressors would be content with their new powers; and maybe even go east into Russia and benefit the rest of *Western civilization* by taking out the Reds. The British Prime Minister, Neville Chamberlain, said of Czechoslovakia, the latest state to be absorbed, that it was *a far-off country, of which we know nothing*; and he came home from his negotiations with Adolf Hitler bringing *peace in our time*.

The phoney war

It was a phoney peace. The aggression didn't stop. Next year Germany made a pact with the Soviets, invaded Poland, and we went to war.

Then for nine more months, it was a *phoney war*. We watched more catastrophes taking place, just across the sea — Denmark, Norway, Holland, Belgium, France.

The government took steps: the first call-ups for the armed forces. An issue of gas masks for everybody. Censorship. Black-out curtains and strips of paper to be pasted across the windows to stop the glass splintering from bomb blast. A few Conservatives hoped that such warlike gestures would be enough, and that Hitler would be encouraged to make peace with us, break his pact with Russia, and go east.

All that ended in the summer and autumn of 1940, with the Battle of Britain and the Blitz. A friend and I had a vacation job as caretakers for a four-storey building owned by the Independent Labour Party in Clapham North. We got the top floor free in return for keeping the other three clean for meetings of trades union branches and suchlike. In the first week of September, being very short of funds, we heard that you could get 50 shillings a week for cutting logs in the woods outside York. So we got someone to stand in for us, and hitchhiked there on the Saturday. On the way up, a lorry driver said he had heard there had been *a bit of activity* over London.

For the next five days, we were up early and crashed out at the end of the day, so we didn't hear what was really happening to London until Thursday. We waited until we could collect Friday's money, and hitched back, in time to climb onto the roof of our four-storey building for a grandstand view of the air raid going on round us.

Seats of government

The next day, we crossed to the East End of London where we'd heard there was most of the action. Eventually, we found our way into Shadwell, and a place called *Paddy's Goose*. It was an ex-pub, nicknamed for a drunken Irishman's description of *The Swan*. It had become a complex of youth clubs serving those who lived along the old Ratcliffe Highway, where Jack the Ripper once stalked.

Now it had become, overnight, an all-purpose centre of *local government*. One of the first bombs in the Blitz had destroyed the district telephone exchange, and soon after another dropped on the Council offices and took out the filing system.

Government had suddenly become very *local*.

Local people — a mixture of youth club members, social workers, clerics, trades union organisers — were improvising every kind of service out of next to nothing. We were welcome to join in, and found ourselves sharing overnight accommodation on the concrete floor of the Gents in the basement with, amongst others, a young Communist disabled from work in the tobacco warehouse and a green-turbaned beach-pyjamaed Baroness with extreme right-wing views, drawn in because she was a Patron of the youth club and wanted to *do her bit.*

There was everything to be done, literally from the bottom up. One of the first jobs we tackled (we were soon a little bunch of pacifist volunteers) was to empty the shit buckets into the nearest sewers. The buckets stood, unprotected, on the floors of shelters that had mostly been improvised at the last moment. The arches that bore the railway eastwards across London were bricked up and people were sleeping on what used to be the road and the gutter, with the narrow pavements a privileged berth. Others found their way to the crypts of local churches, and slept beside the coffined bones of their ancestors. Dockers working in the big warehouses let their families in on the ground floors. Some camped out in the brick shoebox shelters that the government had built, here and there, in the middle of the back streets. Those living along the Commercial Road, where there were semi-basements, went downstairs and camped out there — they were the lucky ones in reach of the loo. On the other hand, there wasn't a great deal of protection, even though they had managed to scrounge sandbags to protect the windows. (It turned out that strips of paper weren't all that good.)

Ferrying the shit buckets to the nearest available manhole depended on achieving access to the local authority — a petrol permit for our dilapidated second-hand Austin van, a regular supply of bug powder and disinfectant to treat the shelter floors, and most important, a key to open the manhole covers.

The Town Hall had shifted for the time being to the People's Palace. For days on end, there were queues of bombed-out people wanting help. The auditorium was screened off into many cubicles where officials tried to cope with the confusion, and sometimes made it worse. In the early days, someone worked out that you had to walk eight miles from one office to another in the Borough to get all the forms you needed to fill in.

Everything depended on these officials because a few months earlier, following allegations of corruption, the Council had been displaced and power handed over to the Town Clerk. There he was, up on the stage, alone, surrounded by paper, looking tired and bewildered. It seemed best to make for him direct. I had an old leather briefcase still bearing the inscription *Presented to the Reverend J Clark Gibson* (my father) *by Officers and Members of the Onward Youth Club.* With some boot blacking, and well-stuffed with newspaper, it looked quite imposing, tucked under my arm, so I made it to the Town Clerk and got his signature to everything we needed, on the spot.

Others at *Paddy's Goose* were doing likewise. They made expeditions to the West End and returned with van-loads of food supplies, conned out of the big stores. They raided government warehouses for bedding. They collected Primus stoves and storm lanterns to make good the loss of gas and electricity.

There were half-a-dozen other outfits like *Paddy's Goose*, formed round a Jewish centre or a Presbyterian or a Catholic church, all places where lay people were used to sharing responsibility with the clerics. Each one became a rendezvous for other volunteers, and the one place you could turn to in your immediate neighbourhood for help.

Fair do's

Within the shelters, people got together and put a stop to quarrels about bedding space, and the occasional knife fight. They elected their own shelter committees which made sure that the space was properly shared out, and the bedding that people carried in from their homes was not tampered with. In the mouths of the shelters, a few stalwarts lingered, with stirrup pumps at the ready, to nip out and douse incendiaries before the fires took hold.

Before long, our little van was doing treble duty, shit buckets in the morning; essential furniture salvaged from bombed-out houses in the afternoon (including the occasional piano); cans of cocoa at night. And when it was safely parked in the lee of the local church, we went off again as a medical foot patrol to go the rounds of the shelters and treat all comers.

None of that was much protection from the bombs. The great fires spread, and were fought back by the Auxiliary Fire Service, hastily recruited and semi-trained during the phoney war to back up the existing fire service. The Rescue teams tunnelled through the rubble to get out the living from the ruins of their homes, and to take the dead to the mortuaries. The Ambulance teams picked up the casualties where they could, along with the victims of the diphtheria epidemic that swept through some of the shelters, and took them to hospitals that worked round the clock, and were still only partly protected. (I was one of the diphtheria patients, and our only protection from flying glass — apart from the strips of paper — was to sleep with our heads beneath the wooden trays that were put across our beds to hold our dinners.)

✧ ✧ ✧

Siege economy

1940 had changed a lot of things. The old government was scrapped and a new coalition formed from all the main parties. They all shared in the war work, with Winston Churchill, as Prime Minister, concentrating on waging the war,

Herbert Morrison, Deputy Leader of the Labour Party, in charge of the Home Front, and Clem Attlee, the Labour Party Leader, inconspicuously oiling the works.

The operations of the German U-boats and the laying of magnetic mines cut back the supplies we used to rely on from those overseas plantations of ours. Particularly the 60% of our food supplies that used to come from abroad. *County War Agricultural Committees* were set up to make sure that land was used effectively to grow food. If the owner was incompetent, the land was taken over, *for the duration*, and the farming done properly. Besides the farmers, there were thousands of Diggers for Victory making the  most of allotments, back gardens, former municipal flowerbeds. A lot more people kept chickens, and rabbits.

People who had lost their homes in the raids were rehoused — in the houses of people in safer areas. The local billeting officer acted on behalf of a committee of locals who saw fair play, and helped to sort out clashes of temperament between the incomers and their hosts.

Clothing supplies were rationed, everyone had the same ration, but with scope to choose how best to use it. Alongside, there were innumerable knitting circles and clothes recycling groups.

There was a strange flowering of the arts and education. People with time on their hands, in the Forces as well as the civilians in the shelters, were exposed to all sorts of free entertainment and information — some of it voluntary, most of it subsidised, nearly all of it unexpectedly fun. Entertainers — comedians, classical musicians, engaging talkers on Current Affairs — went the rounds meeting people on their own ground, carrying with them their props, scenery, visual aids and travelling libraries (with a spate of cheap paperbacks, packed tight with print to save paper).

People found themselves rubbing shoulders with those they would never have given a nod to in the old days. They had neighbourliness forced on them, and in the long run, mostly found it good.

There were *spivs* around, at all levels, from the *Dad's Army* type who knew where to get packets of fags and nylon stockings, to those at higher levels who wangled generous petrol allowances. People laughed at them, tolerated the small operators, but found the others disreputable and reported them to the authorities if they caught them out.

Fair shares all round meant more than trying to see that no-one got a fatter ration than anyone else. In a siege economy, you have to pool everything you've got.

Work share

The government planned the *direction of labour* — down the mines, into the factories, into the Forces. Everyone was fully employed for the duration. And fed, and clothed, often with the rations or the uniform thrown in with the job. Very slender rations, eked out with unlimited supplies of bread and potatoes, but just enough. The government doubled the income tax, stripped the economy down to bare essentials, *lean and mean*, by vigorous competition — not between rival firms, but within each organisation, to beat the previous month's production record. Park railings and aluminium saucepans were gathered in, marginal land was ploughed up, manufacturers were told to stop advertising their rival brands. Posters on the hoardings either asked you *IS YOUR JOURNEY REALLY NECESSARY?*, or challenged you to greater efforts, with the help of giant portraits of Winston Churchill (*LET US GO FORWARD TOGETHER*) or of Herbert Morrison (*Three Words to the Whole Nation: GO TO IT*).

The message was that we were all in it together. The government was in charge, and responsible for feeding and clothing and housing everyone. But it was the people who got things done.

They were not just a liability, they were a resource.

Central and local government was being forced out of some of its old habits and attitudes. It still spawned paperwork in all directions. Petty officials still got everyone's back up. Bureaucrats earned a bad name from which they have never really recovered. But under the impact of war, government just had to delegate.

Adapting

The people who took over, sometimes as volunteers, sometimes as part-time or full-time employees in auxiliary services, were operating at the *Paddy's Goose* level. Sometimes a bit on the bossy side, but tolerated on the whole; they were the *moving spirits* in each locality who didn't mind what they did in order to get whatever was needed, done.

The *Paddy's Goose* situations got formalised, losing a little spontaneity in the process, but not much. By and large, although drained out at the end of a long day or a long night, people stayed willing, even eager in a laid-back, jokey kind of way. They responded to Herbert Morrison's slogan on the hoardings — and *Went To It*, grumbling.

In time of war, everything necessary gets commandeered sooner or later. There were not many half-measures. Plans were made at the highest level and the people at the top were in charge.

So was this a *command economy*?

The top people did not see it quite like that.

The government provided guidelines, set limits, shared out available resources, but it gradually learned to leave the real decision-making, at their discretion, to the people at the coalface.

Official systems began to adapt. They took back some of the responsibilities that local people had taken over when the raids first broke the old systems down, but they still left plenty for people to get on with in their own sweet way. So long, that is, as they got on with it together.

It was a coalition government, Conservative Churchill and Labour Attlee, both believing this was the only way to win through.

The effect of all this, was that we survived the raids and the U-boat attacks — and by the end of the war, surprise surprise, our children's health was better than it had ever been.

Nobody at the time called it *state socialism*.

After World War I, a civil servant, Humbert Wolfe, scribbled his comment on the fruits of peace:

> *Here in this village churchyard snore*
> *The businessmen who won the war*
> *Whilst by the foreign seas they crossed, it*
> *Happens, lie the men who lost it.*

They were not the only losers. In the 1920s, many of the warriors who survived found themselves jobless, selling matches in the gutter. Unemployment disfigured Britain for the next 20 years.

After World War II, when the Labour government came to power and the Forces began to be demobilized, there was the same threat. But instead of becoming another army of the unemployed, everyone continued working flat out to rebuild the economy. Dole queues — almost nil. Some of the factories were converted from war production to the making of prefabs to house the homeless. Clothing was still rationed, and so was food. At one point, even bread went short. But health continued to improve, and at the end of the first five years, all-round productivity was up.

So was the war debt...

ran out; farmland that used to produce food, now *set aside*. 700,000 hectares of derelict, underused or neglected land, according to the *Groundwork* survey in 1995.

● **WASTED ENERGY: heat loss because poor people can't afford to insulate; traffic jams for want of public transport; hot air from endless talking shops that never reach conclusions.**

● **Above all, WASTED PEOPLE.**

In the public eye: derelict people living in cardboard boxes, footloose youngsters hanging about on the street corner — sights which the media seizes on, because these are people who have been abandoned, and nobody has managed to reclaim them.

Mostly out of sight, there are others. Some on the government's unemployment list, just visible once a week in the dole queue. Many more have given up hope and opted out of the system. Others persuaded to retire early, quietly rusting on the shelf. Young and old, male and female, another army of wasted people, wondering what to do, *killing time*.

Time has always been our biggest resource, and it can't easily be split up and pigeonholed. The work we do, or *could* do, flows through our everyday lives. It's making things or providing services that we can sell, bringing up children, looking after people in need, creating entertainment. It's what gives us *job satisfaction*, whether or not it happens to be paid for in money.

It's a resource that's wasted because, it seems, there aren't the means to make use of it.

The means? That's the money. We can't afford to make use of the resources we have because nobody can spare the money to pay us to use them.

The money minders

As a nation, we have been making use of the never-never for centuries. Whenever we needed to cope with an emergency or to set up a new enterprise at home or abroad, we borrowed the money.

Somehow, we managed to match our needs to our resources. Can we still do it?

We are in the wings, as we once were in the 30s during the phoney peace and the phoney war, watching distant disasters coming nearer. Watching other nations being torn apart, monitoring the movements of people dispossessed, who now threaten our prospects because the market forces we helped to unleash are forcing them to work for sweatshop wages that begin to force us out of the market.

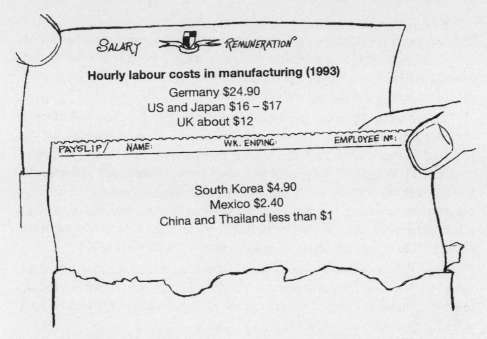

SALARY → ← REMUNERATION

Hourly labour costs in manufacturing (1993)
Germany $24.90
US and Japan $16 – $17
UK about $12

PAYSLIP/   NAME: WK. ENDING: EMPLOYEE N°:

South Korea $4.90
Mexico $2.40
China and Thailand less than $1

We are lenders as well as borrowers. There's a lot of money swilling about. Most of it belongs to ordinary people, but it's looked after by the money-minders — the banks, the building societies, the pension funds, the insurance companies. They rent it from us. Just as if they were using our basement, or a slice of the back yard. The name they give to this rent is — *interest*.

The way these minders use our money is largely up to them, so long as they keep paying the interest. That's not much by comparison with the rents they get when they sub-let: maybe four or five times as much for the money of ours they lend out as they ever pay us for lending it to them in the first place. There's not much we can do about it, apart from making a fuss at Annual General Meetings, already well-packed with more substantial investors.

Then there's the tax money and the community charges which we hand over to the authorities in return for their promises to deliver what they say we want from them.

Value for money

Some of the enterprises that are financed in this way are respectable. House-building, railways, farms and fisheries, at home or overseas. There are big overseas development schemes which seem admirable, from a distance. Bridges, dams, processing plants which are meant to transform the prospects for poor people in ex-colonial countries. But people like Arif Hasan and his colleagues in the Orangi Pilot Project have taken a professional look at the books. It appears that these monster schemes do best for the well-heeled foreign firms which undertake the work, and pay only the going rate, a shade above starvation, to the people on the spot. And in any case, what those people need most is help at local level in getting the basics, a reliable supply of clean water, sewerage, a bus service and better local roads to make it easier to get locally-produced food to the market and back again.

The big national and international spenders are losing the confidence of the people whose money they use. Governments seldom manage to get the backing of more than half the voting population, let alone persuading anything up to half of the rest of the adult population to get as far as the polling stations. People don't think they're getting value for their money. Maybe they're wrong, but they can't get enough inside information to make a fair judgement. And if they're right, they can't see how to do anything about it. They can't get a grip on management. It's all too big.

Look at it the other way round. The money-minders themselves — bankers, insurance fundholders, government — hold back from putting serious money into local schemes. They're much too small. Fledgling enterprises with no track record aren't *creditworthy*.

Well, that depends. Plenty of small businesses go bust either for want of business nous and a reliable market, or because there's not enough cash flowing to tide things over the early stages. It's not the size that matters...

Starting from scratch

Mrs Debbie Bennett gave up being a secretary in Carshalton, Surrey, to bring up the children. When the family was on holiday in Wales, they stopped off at a notice advertising organic food fresh from the farm, and loaded up. When she got home in Surrey, she got to thinking about organising a regular supply locally. She found an organic firm ready to deliver in bulk, £50 delivery charge. So she got four friends to join in and arrange regular deliveries; before long to the spare room they hired one day a week in the back of a local shop.

They branched out into bulk buys for fresh vegetables from local people's back gardens and allotments, dried foods from further off, opening the room once a week — in the morning for people to bring in their produce, and in the afternoon to sell it to members. Then home baked cakes, honey from local bees, and an arrangement with the local bakery to bake their bread for them, with organic flour they supplied.

An old man turned up at the shop and was overheard offering the shopkeeper free-range eggs, half-a-dozen at a time. So Debbie went back with him to check that his hens really were free-rangers, and then offered to take over his whole output, ten dozen a week. She found he had several acres of land, which were used to pasture a few horses he kept for hire, along with some sheep and some geese. He had a couple of polytunnels, but since his son had died he'd lost interest and wasn't growing much. Debbie persuaded him to revive cultivation, got some of her friends to come over and help with the digging and the planting and cropping, making the most of the chicken shit and the horse manure. So now there are tomatoes, courgettes, cucumbers, marrows growing inside the tunnel, plus leeks, runner beans and winter cabbage in the open air. Half the battle was to stagger the planting so that things ripened in succession, instead of all coming together at once and being sent to the market.

Progress? About forty members in two years, averaging £10 a week each for their purchases. Debbie does the pricing, a few pence above those in the local greengrocers' shops, so that people pay a shade extra for organic, and don't put the local shops out of business by undercutting.

Forty members is about as much as Debbie can manage on one day a week. But she's heard about a Japanese housewife with no track record, who started off her fledgling enterprise by organising her own direct milk supply. That was in 1965 in Tokyo, and it began with a group of twenty clubbing together in a bulk-buy scheme. It got bigger and bigger, food, clothes, cosmetics, all bought wholesale from established distributors. Then they got through to the farmers and fishermen themselves and took over distribution of rice and meat and fish.

Thirteen years on, they set up their own Club headquarters in Setagaya, and the housewife who had got it all going was elected to the local government. Since then, thirty more members of the Seikatsu Club have been elected to local government in the area, and the Club carries out national campaigns against detergents that have been polluting rivers and lakes. With a turnover of 40 billion Yen (that's between 320 and 350 million US dollars), the Club packs a punch.

❖   ❖   ❖

In 1976, Dr Muhammad Yunus was leading a fairly sheltered life as a professor in the University of Chittagong, Bangladesh. His subject was economics, and he found himself outside the campus one day, taking a fresh look at it. The University was on the edge of the city,

"so I could walk out of the University and into people's everyday lives. I met a widow woman, Sufia Khatum, who was making beautiful bamboo stools for less than a penny and a half a day. She had to borrow 15 pence to buy bamboo and in return, had to sell to the trader who lent her the money.

My students got involved and we found that there were 42 people in the same village needing a total capital of $30. So I gave $30 to my students to distribute as loans."

What banks are for

"Well, this was just an emotional response. It shouldn't be me, it should be the bank. That's what banks are for. So I went to the Bank on the campus. The manager fell from the sky, 'We can't possibly lend to such people. They have no collateral.' I said, 'There are rich people with lots of collateral who default on the money they borrow.' He still would not lend and referred me to other banks. They were no good either. Finally, I offered myself as a guarantor and the bank reluctantly agreed. I signed papers and the loans were made. I was told, 'You'll never get your money back!'

Surprise! They all paid back on time.

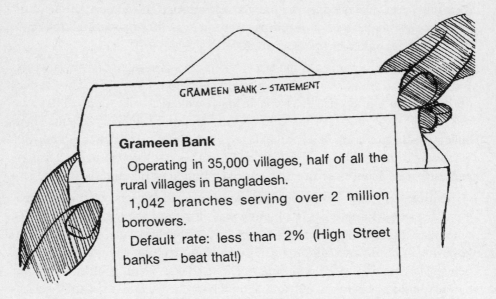

Grameen Bank

Operating in 35,000 villages, half of all the rural villages in Bangladesh.

1,042 branches serving over 2 million borrowers.

Default rate: less than 2% (High Street banks — beat that!)

I did this for two villages, five villages, fifty villages. The banks were still not convinced. Finally, I went to a new district to prove it still worked. It worked beautifully. We went on and did it in five districts. The banks were still not concerned. So I decided to do without them. I knocked on many doors and finally, in 1983, got the OK to set up our own bank. We began to expand. People said, 'If you expand, it will explode like a balloon.' Well, it hasn't exploded yet.

*Grameen troubled the minds of people all over the world. They thought it must surely be fishy. So we became the most researched institution you can think of. **But the results have shown that poor people are more creditworthy than the rich.**"*

Creditworthiness

One of the secrets of Grameen's success is that each borrower must be one of a group of five who take *collective responsibility* for repayment. Nowadays, nearly all members are women. (That compares with the banks in Bangladesh where women borrowers are less than 1%.) Why?

"Money in women's hands gets spent on the children and the household. They're borrowing for a cow or a sewing machine or a farm tool. Men suit themselves first and they want things on short-term. Women have longer vision, they want to build for the future."

Grameen loans are made on conditions. Members attend weekly meetings to discuss neighbourhood improvements; they promise not to demand a dowry for sons or give a dowry for daughters. They plant at least one tree every year (seeds provided).

How does this compare with other kinds of economic development?

"75% of the money lent by the richer countries to the poorer countries goes to paying fees to their own consultants and to local advisers in the cities. Meanwhile, in the villages, many are still poor without enough to buy a pennyworth' of kerosene to lighten the home in the evening.

Our main need isn't for expensive new machines to fit expensive new technologies. Grameen has taught us that conventional wisdom is not as infallible as people said.

It's very easy to design a Grameen bank. All you need to do is to look at conventional banking and turn it upside down."

The Grameen Banks, like the lane sewerage schemes in Karachi and the community newspapers on Merseyside sparked off by Chrissie Maher's *Bugle*, catch on because they provide working models which others can copy. By 1995, there were 168 more projects on similar lines elsewhere in the world — 52 countries, including America.

President-elect Clinton said America could learn from Bangladesh about regenerating its inner cities. He had. The good faith fund of Arkansas's South Shore Bank is modelled on Bangladesh's success in lending to people ordinary banks would not consider.

The Grameen Bank puts into practice the ideas about empowerment and encouraging initiative that Mr Clinton says a Democratic administration would use to rebuild America's inner cities.

The Grameen idea is big enough to become a model for the rich world. It's small enough to catch on via the grapevine.

It's no surprise that President Clinton wants to tap the experience of the Third World for the benefit of the American economy. And Britain? In 1995, Oxfam, after a year's deliberation, decided to extend its fight against poverty to the *14 million people in Britain on less than half average income and one in four families on income support. The scale of poverty is different*, said Oxfam's Director, David Bryer, *the impact on individuals is remarkably similar. (We have) much to learn from third world communities who have managed to stand on their own feet...*

The grapevine

Aid workers who operate at ground level already know that the best way to get ideas and experience across is to put communities in touch with each other — best of all when the communities themselves make the contacts. In South Africa, in the 90s, nearly 200 squatter settlements have been linking up to form *Umfe' landawonye waBantu Basemijondolo* — the South African Homeless People's Federation, built round five city federations and three regional federations; each federation made up of at least five savings groups.

Those *housing savings collectives* — anything from 12 to 500 members — took shape in much the same way as the *lane management groups* and the *women's work centres* came about in Pakistan. Most of the motive power comes from women, who understand about housekeeping, and the need to put money aside to keep the wolf from the door.

One of the settlements I went to see was in Langa, Cape Province. I particularly wanted to meet those who had made an even bigger bridge with other communities — in India. In 1993, they were members of a group which went from the squatter settlements in South Africa to meet and learn from their opposite numbers, *the barefoot housing experts* of Bombay:

"We were really shocked and bewildered. We saw the people living in small shacks right on the side of the busy streets, ... the Pavement Dwellers, ... and similar rows of houses along the railway tracks. ... Some of us wept because we'd never imagined there were others in the world whose living conditions were worse than ours. ... We were so angry and so sad."

A series of exchanges had been going on since March 1991. Some of the Indian *Pavement Dwellers* had come to South Africa, and there had already been  one return visit to India. The South Africans learned from the Indians at first-hand, in an informal training scheme based in the Indian squatter settlements. Then they went back and trained 40 leaders of their own federations. They saw how Indian groups were mapping their neighbourhoods, surveying needs and resources, using lifesize models (sheets tacked to a wooden framework) to work out and display the possibilities for housing design in their own self-building schemes.

They took those ideas home and added some of their own, using cardboard boxes to experiment with building designs (much as the children did when we were piloting the *Living Space* experiments back in the UK).

Women have taken the lead, *participation is women*, said one of the leaders. They set up BIT centres (for Building, Information and Training), making their own bricks with hand-operated machines and *whilst they make their bricks, they talk, so the dialogue goes on.* Visitors from other BIT centres help to produce *cross-pollination*, and this is backed up by the Utshami Newsletter, which reports how the revolving fund for small starter loans is working, and uses as its slogan *The grass is talking.* Grass-roots, springing up in 250 places, involving 15,000 families, all within the last three years.

In Langa, I saw some of the results — the group, some 90% of it women, had secured a patch of wasteland, saved enough to start brickmaking, made cardboard models of the houses and the layout and were about to start building for themselves. The project was frequently visited by others in South Africa wanting to follow suit. The links with *Mahila Milan (Women Together)* in India continue, with more training visits —

> to strengthen settlement residents in their negotiations with the relevant authorities … (and to) educate, inform and mobilise the residents as the process of self-determination rolls on. **All knowledge and information gets transferred horizontally**, from one community to another.

The South Africans' slogan *Amandla Imali Nowlwazi* stands for *The Power of Money and Knowledge*.

● **Poor people's money in the savings collectives.**

● **Poor people's knowledge bought over time, the hard way;**

● **and exchanged for free.**

Balancing act

In South Africa, *unimportant people* are showing how they can draw on their own resources to spearhead the changes they want to see.

All over the world, for good or ill, there is a growing disillusionment with *Them*, the *people in power*. Even Nelson Mandela's government is on probation.

That still leaves most of us with a pretty dim view of the prospects for advancing people's own power to the point where the balance shifts.

There's *the System*, upheld by and upholding the powers-that-be. They may not be up to much, but *they're still there*, in government and the finance houses and the mass media and the multinational trading corporations — running things their way. Not a bit keen on anyone else taking over.

That's true, so far as it goes, but it's misleading. **The glitch is in that Biblical phrase — 'the powers-that-be', *the authorities* as we call them now. The power, the authority, is lumped together with those who hold it, and would like to hang on to it for keeps.**

Even to think of power as a sort of trophy, to be hung on to or wrested away, could be wide of the mark.

Power as we know it in our own lives isn't like that. It's a means of getting something done by yourself or someone else, or of putting a stop to what someone else is doing. It's winning someone over, or putting someone down. It depends on the love, fear, loyalty, hatred, self-sacrifice, self-interest that we managed to arouse in others. *That's what empowers Us.*

Or the love, fear, loyalty etcetera that others manage to arouse in us. *That's what empowers Them.*

To work out what that implies, we need to look first at the sources of power, and the strengths of those who hold it now.

13 Sources of power

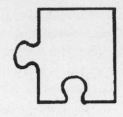

Five resources on which powerful people can draw:

- ☞ know-how
- ☞ other people's loyalty
- ☞ solidarity
- ☞ discipline
- ☞ authority

1 • Know-how

Those people at the top — politicians, financiers, media moguls, info-highwaymen — reckon to have a near-monopoly. At first sight, information technology seems to be reinforcing them. *Knowledge is power*, and they are in the know.

In the know about us. We're on file somewhere; our phones can be tapped; our earnings assessed; our foreign travel recorded. Shop in the supermarket, and the checkout scans your bar-codes, at present just one item at a time; before long, in an instant by the trolley load. Whether you like it or not, that information is briefing headquarters on your tastes and purchasing power; and if you use a credit card, your buying behaviour will be under scrutiny as you respond over the weeks and months to their sales techniques.

Power for the top people depends on getting at the facts, and then being able to keep them to oneself.

Joe Stalin's hold on power rested on a fact-finding and fact-concealing system which worked on a scientific as well as a political level. When the Soviets made their breakthrough to space flight in the 1950s, they were able to exploit and refine transistors, which made for miniaturisation. Part of this success was due to a backbreaking collection of information, the hard way, by gathering together 9,000 foreign scientific and industrial journals, month after month, picking out the relevant bits, translating them, and then getting them out to research establishments all over the Soviet Union, and re-distributing the fruits of their own research workers within the network.

Nothing faxed, no modems, not even a telephone network. Simply a continuous postal flow. Within the system, the information could flow freely, researchers were not just hugging each batch of new data to themselves lest a competitor gets hold of it; instead, comparing findings, egging each other on. But keeping the rest of the world in the dark.

When the Soviets grew their own computer systems, the hardware in the early days was in some cases even larger than that produced in the West. Size in the systems at base did not matter. At first, the main requirement was to transmit instructions from headquarters to an obedient satellite, or a biddable Regional Commissar.

Centralised co-ordination of information allowed the Soviet government to overhaul its key industries, steel in particular, and at the time, to peg level with, or even surpass, the production techniques of Western competitors. But as the technology developed, and the information spread sideways, it began to pose a threat. Stalin put the brakes on Soviet cybernetics, denouncing it as *a prostitute on the payroll of world imperialism*. The trouble, as he saw it, was that the technology was getting out of hand.

In particular, **out of his hands**.

Seven league boots : feet of clay

The trouble is that information networks are neither foolproof nor leakproof.

Taurus, the London Stock Exchange's pet share settlement system, 15 years on the drawing board, had to be scrapped at a cost of around £400 million and a loss of about 350 jobs. *Socrates*, the French railway high-speed booking system, cost about £146 million, and worked so fast that it booked or double-booked the wrong tickets, charged the wrong fares, and at one point booked up a non-existent train. A £48 million system designed to make sense of 82 Training and Enterprise Council schemes in England and Wales produced 7,000 errors and was finally scrapped because it would have taken another £71 million to put it right. As for the London Ambulance Service call-out computer, that suffered cardiac arrest on the very first day.

To complicate matters, there are ingenious loners invading other people's systems to deposit stink-bombs in the shape of *computer viruses* which vandalise or destroy. In 1992, when *Michelangelo*, the *Dark Invader* and the *Maltese Amoeba* were on the rampage, the cost to Britain of the virus epidemic was reckoned to be £1 billion.

The boys and girls in the back rooms battle on to penetrate each other's counter-systems and protect their own.

Meanwhile, the quicksilver information is slipping away from the traditional centres of Western industrial power. When the age of the microchip began, in 1978, it was estimated that information technology, in one shape or another, was occupying 65% of all those who were employed or self-employed in the UK — in printing, banking, broadcasting, office work. As the technology has developed, that has put most of those people at risk, at one time or another. Manual skills as well as clerical skills have been taken over by the technology.

Watchmaking, cash registers, TV sets, have drifted away to the Pacific Rim, China, South-East Asia, where wages are lower, but assembly workers' fingers are just as nimble.

The giants and the beanstalk

That still leaves the multinational giants surveying the world market from their positions at the top of the tree. The *infotech revolution* has accelerated the information flow and made it easier to implement decisions, worldwide, and from the top down.

Computer systems make information accessible as never before. But information is a very slippery commodity. Other people get to know.

Suppose you are a *middle manager*. At this lower level, you may be nearer reality. You can see where the facts are coming from. And you may have your own informal network with others like yourself. Not only within your own organisation, also through the everyday contacts you have with your opposite numbers in other outfits.

Inside government, just as inside industry, there is less job security than there used to be. Everyone's future is *on hold*, dependent on decisions higher up about *restyling, outsourcing, slimming down*. So there's more incentive to keep an eye open for a job elsewhere. It pays to stay on friendly terms with the competition.

There are conferences, seminars, trade exhibitions, where people rub shoulders and drop hints. So inside information spreads. It is no longer flowing along carefully guarded channels. It slops around.

Middle management gets to know what, in some cases, top management does not fully grasp. It could be information crucial to the whole organisation's future. One division of an American bank was transformed on the initiative of a secretary who understood better than anyone else what was wrong with the old system and how to put it right. On the other hand, the top brass in Barings Bank only managed to catch on to what was happening lower down when it was too late to save their bacon (roughly £500 million had vanished overnight).

Power-wise, the tycoons are losing touch. Money-wise, they may still help each other, on *remuneration committees*, to over-generous servings from the trough; but the work that makes the money is done, and better understood, lower down.

This makes giants vulnerable.

The bigger the system, the more cover it provides for those lower down. Besides the moderately loyal members on the staff, there may be enterprising outsiders on the prowl, exploring and perhaps manipulating for their own gain.

The giants can't be sure that further down the Beanstalk there aren't these nimble Jacks (or maybe Jills) hacking their way through the foliage to threaten their security.

The tighter the security, the greater the tension. It's not the tension of a well-sprung machine so much as the nervous tension of someone on the verge of breakdown.

Loyalty becomes a key word.

2 • Loyalty

Two ways of looking at it. The view from the top, and some way down as well, is that loyalty means being faithful to the organisation, and in particular to those who run it.

Others lower down may partly share this *team spirit*. But what brought them in and holds them fast is partly that they like what their organisation is doing, or is meant to do.

In either case, there is an element of protectiveness about it. The key decision-makers at the top should not be disturbed whilst they make up their minds. And when these political, financial, industrial powers-that-be come together to *explore the options*, their privacy must be protected.

Their henchmen like to be seen as in the service of the public, accountable to society as a whole, not only to shareholders or to those voters who elected the party in power. In practice, of course, they are only answerable to their superiors.

This creates problems when someone important lets the side down through incompetence or corrupt behaviour. If this should get known, the reputation of the Department or the firm might suffer. It will become less effective. So *damage limitation* requires that those who are in the know should *soft-pedal*, *draw a veil*.

There may also be shortcuts, sharp practices even, which allow the organisation to save time, avoid controversy, cut costs.

Those priests of the Oracle of Aro Chukwu, for instance: smoothly operating a widely-appreciated public service in the punishment of crime. If they secretly sell off offenders instead of judicially executing them — well, that makes the whole thing more *cost-effective*, doesn't it?

Beyond that, there are the corporate lies — sorry, *disinformation* — smart advertising designed to distract from the effects of smoking, official gobbledegook to conceal dodgy arms deals. How do the people with the inside knowledge feel about that?

If their offices are somewhere along the corridors of power, and they share the loo with the Permanent Secretary or the Deputy MD, it's very difficult to decide between loyalty to one's mates, so to speak, and some vague feelings about Departmental integrity. Departmental *interests* come first. So, as the wartime posters used to tell us, it's best to *Keep Mum*.

This can get out of hand. It is interesting that in Naples, the Latin word *humilitas*, which once meant being humble as a servant might be, became converted in Neapolitan slang to *omerta* — the key word for the professionals of the Mafia and the Camorra. *Omerta*, says the Italian dictionary, is solidarity in concealing the identity of those who commit an offence on behalf of your organisation — which is to say, act in its interest.

In countries where political power has been concentrated in relatively few hands, this tradition, dressed up as Official Secrecy, has disguised whatever skulduggery politicians, or their officials, decide on *in the interests of the Service*.

This policy probably works for most of the time. *Probably*, because there's no knowing how much concealment successfully conceals. All we have to go on is the rare case when someone slips up, or else deliberately flouts the house rules and lets in daylight.

Letting in the daylight

This isn't necessarily a dramatic affair. Some insiders are simply wanting to draw the curtains back a little, to show the thoroughly legal workings of the system to ordinary people so that they can make better use of it.

Within the toils of most public systems, there are people like that *right-hand man* in Birkenhead who helped to make residents' vision of the new-look Laird Centre a reality (until the dry rot nourished by other officials' sloth brought the whole system crashing down).[1] The closer their work brings them to the people the system is supposed to serve, the more likely that these moving spirits within the system will see how daft it is to keep such people in the dark, when they could be allies. So they ferret out helpful information and convey it across no-man's land to the rest of us.

Most of the information is uncontroversial. It was just gathering dust in the vaults. Nobody minds it being passed on, and when a local community responds by using it constructively to do things for themselves and save public money, everybody smiles to the camera.

---

1 That story started on page 142.

The crunch comes when one of those moving spirits comes to the conclusion that information being kept under covers is a *cover-up* which threatens the very things the system exists to serve.

 It is more than their jobs are worth to let the facts be known, but the skulduggery is more than they can stomach. Someone says *ENOUGH IS ENOUGH!* and blows the whistle.

So long as there are photocopiers and fax machines around, no authority can keep itself entirely to itself. Somewhere in the system, there will be *moving spirits* — Mordecai Vanunu, Cathy Massiter, Clive Ponting, Graham Pink — whose loyalty is of a different kind from the rest.

You can't budge them. They have *staying-power*, come what may. These Jacks and Jills with minds of their own, strip away some of the disguises, kick up a dust. They make a stand, put up a marker, inflict a flesh wound or two; they are seldom giant-killers. When the dust settles, the powers-that-be are still there.

Dead weight

This is because the authorities' power base, the source of their strength, is, surprisingly — the community. It is the unimportant people who tolerate the VIPs. They may be increasingly contemptuous of them, with or without good reason. In most countries of the world, they reckon that government has failed to come up to the expectations they might once have had. Government is *Them*, and this often includes the official Opposition, which differs mainly in respect of the personalities of its leaders. Even the personalities are difficult to tell apart. They're all concerned with *meeting the challenge* of the problems which everybody knows about, and has probably experienced at close hand for donkey's years. Poor housing, food costs, pollution, not enough jobs to go round. Fear and suspicion of people of a different culture who appear to be muscling in at the expense of everybody else. Meeting the challenge, so long as it doesn't involve anything unpopular. Nobody dares to *tax and spend*, at a national level, although locally when a few people — like the Rodney Street Raiders — decide that something good needs doing, nobody baulks at the idea of a whip-round, in cash or in kind or in people's time, in order to get it done.

Nationally or internationally, you can pay tribute to what needs doing, sound off about it, but take no risks that might lose votes. People, sometimes no more than a minority of the adult population, get as far as the polling stations and then give a rather tepid support to one or other of the parties on the ballot paper. Others stay clear.

This apparent indifference gets described as public apathy. In fact, it is more likely to be frustration at the absence of a believable alternative.

Those problems that the politicians confront are undermining many people's confidence, in society as a whole, and in themselves as being unable to do much about improving it. So the active politicians are left for much of the time to manage or mismanage on their own. They carry on with the grudging *consent* of people who put up with them for want of anything better.

3 • Solidarity

Once in a while, someone seizes this opportunity, builds on that frustration and contempt and persuades people to try something different, because it couldn't be worse than what they have had so far.

In the 30s, the Nazis used the pre-war equivalent of today's Murdoch press to make a double-edged appeal to Germans' gut feelings: their distrust of old-style party politics, their longing for jobs, and safer streets and better living conditions. And their willingness to put the blame for past corruption on religious, racial or political outsiders. Germany became a vast national exclusion zone. The younger generation, reacting against the failure in peace and war of their elders, kindled to the idea of a society built to new specifications, serving an Aryan race that they would help to breed. *Deutschland erwache!*, the fascist equivalent of *Arise ye starvelings from your slumbers*. Yesterday was discredited, today was challenging, *tomorrow belongs to us*.

✧ ✧ ✧

My school had an arrangement to exchange visits with what had once been a Lutheran school in Ilfeld in the Harz mountains in Germany. In September 1938, it was my year group's turn to go and stay with our opposite numbers, the German sixth-formers. By then, it was a Lutheran school no longer. It had been taken over in the first year of the Hitler régime and turned into a National Leadership Training School. Their lot had come over to us the previous term, matching our black blazers and school ties with their brown tunics and swastika badges.

That year group had entered the school before the Nazis took over. The sons of politically dubious parents had been purged, but those who survived still had some of their natural disrespect intact. So we got on quite well together. They took us behind their cycle sheds to smoke an illegal fag, and to make elementary jokes. One was about the ceremonial knives they wore in their stockings, each blade engraved with the words **Blut und Ehre**, *Blood and Honour*. They told us that the actual use was for **Brot und Käse** — *bread and cheese*.

They were the last in the school who could make that sort of joke. The year group below them, and all the others, had been hand-picked, and more thoroughly brainwashed. They included the son of Von Ribbentrop, who was shortly to negotiate the Nazi-Soviet pact which ushered in World War II, and the two nephews of Field Marshal Goering, who masterminded the Luftwaffe which next year bombed the Poles to smithereens and went on in 1940 to win the air war in France and fight the Battle of Britain.

Individualism was a minus. The plus was to be part of a great and glorious whole. *One Race, One State, One Leader.*

School sports were warlike. Instead of putting the weight, you threw a dummy hand-grenade. There were day-long manoeuvres between rival groups roaming the countryside to try and ambush each other and *take lives* by breaking the enemy's woollen armband. The English tended to bunch together in a lively rugger scrum in the course of which some *lives* might be lost, but a good time was had by all. The younger Germans took it much more seriously. One broke his ankle at the beginning of the exercise, and dragged on for the rest of the day, lest honour should be tarnished.

The prospects of war were on everyone's mind. I went with a German class-mate to see a film of what was then the Great War (merely World War I to us nowadays). Its heroes were of course German, and British Tommies were shown surrendering with their hands up, mouthing *Kamarad*. Walking back from the cinema, I mentioned another Great War film I had seen, based on the best-selling novel by the German, Erich Maria Remarque, *All Quiet on the Western Front*. It looked on the war through German eyes, but, it seemed to me, not in terms of heroes and cowards, but of ordinary people, perhaps doomed people, perhaps like ourselves. The last shots showed the survivor of his year group edging partly out of his trench in pursuit of a butterfly perched on the parapet. Cut to a sniper, aiming. Cut back to the butterfly and the enticing hand, which stiffens as the shot is fired.

My companion's comment was simple: *Remarque — he is a Jew!* That disposed of him and everything he had to say.

We English used to sneak off to the picturesque little town below the school grounds to buy sweet cakes to offset the cheese-impregnated potato which dominated the school menu. Local people were quite happy to chat, if they were on their own with us. Otherwise, they clammed up.

We came back from an excursion late one night, edging our way through darkened streets in a practice black-out; stumbling into the gallery of the school assembly hall to find the whole school ranged before a giant picture of Adolf Hitler, listening to his radio denunciation of Czechoslovakia. The school, boys and masters together, wrapt as one organism: *Ein Volk, Ein Reich, Ein Führer.*

We got back to London in the middle of the *September Crisis*, to find soldiers filling sandbags to protect the entrances to government buildings in Whitehall, whilst Prime Minister Chamberlain hurried away to Munich to make his deal with the dictators at the expense of the Czechs.

Six years later, with Hitler's armies beaten back and German cities bombed into submission, our school magazine featured a report from one of our party who had found himself back as an officer in the occupying Allied Military Government in that picturesque little town. Its name was Nordhausen, a ten-minute bus ride from the concentration camp Dora Mittelbau, a feeder camp to Buchenwald.

In our time there, work had already begun to dig out the interior of the mountain to shelter the production of Hitler's *wonder weapons*, the V1s and V2s, which were his last resource. The inmates of the camp provided the slave labour to hollow out the rock. 50,000 of them died in the first phase. They suffered *Vernichtung durch Arbeit — extermination by work*.

And nobody in the little town next door appeared to notice.

Like many others before and since, they preferred not to look. Sometimes, people find blinkers reassuring (who wants to know what it's really like on the other side of those grim prison walls in Risley, Holloway or Strangeways?)

How did we acquire them? That's very hard to say. Our upbringing at home and school? Religious doctrine? The media? The main thing is that we get used to them, and with a one-track mind, it doesn't do to look sideways.

So long as there's someone right behind us in the driving seat, who knows where they're going, we can feel secure. All power to them!

Such power works in both directions. Those in the driving seat certainly have it: on the strength of the consent the rest of us give to what they do on our behalf. But they also give authority to what we do. Things we might never have ventured to do on our own.

4 • Obedience

"I acted as directed, carried out orders."

This explanation was given by a soldier who had just admitted that he had killed a five-year old child. The child belonged to *Pinkoville*, which was the name given to a pair of villages in Vietnam which were to be targeted by Company C for Charlie.

There were about a hundred young Americans in Charlie Company, mostly in their late teens and early twenties. 87% of them were high school graduates and they had all done well in Vietnam so far. The night before they went on this assignment, their Captain had passed on his Colonel's orders. The local people were suspected of harbouring Vietcong guerrillas. According to Sergeant Hodge and others,

> *"The order we were given was to kill and destroy everything that was in the village. It was to kill the pigs, drop them in the wells... Someone asked if that meant women and children ... and the order was 'Everyone in the village'... It was quite clear that no-one was to be spared."*

When C Company arrived, all they found were women and children, and old people, unarmed. They killed them wherever they found them — over 200 it was estimated — and at times went back to finish off the wounded:

Nineteen-year old Varnado Simpson said:

"That day in My Lai, I was personally responsible for killing about 25 people. Personally. Men, women, from shooting them to cutting their throats, scalping them — to cutting off their hands and cutting out their tongues. I did it... I just went. My mind just went. And I wasn't the only one that did it. A lot of people did it. I just killed. Once I started, ... the training, the whole programming part of killing, it just came out..., it just came. I didn't know I had it in me."

Sergeant Hodge said:

"I was very pleased with the way they turned out. They turned out to be very good soldiers. The fact that they were able to go into My Lai and carry out the orders they had been given, I think this is the direct result of the training they had... As a professional soldier, I had been taught and instructed to carry out the orders that were issued by superiors... At no time did it ever cross my mind to disobey or to refuse to carry out an order... I felt that (Charlie Company) were able to carry out the assigned task, the orders that meant killing small kids, killing women, because they were soldiers, they were trained that way. I feel that we carried out the orders in a moral fashion and the orders of destroying the village, of killing the people in the village, I feel we did not violate any moral standards."

Getting away with murder

Sergeant Kenneth Hodge was not a special case. When the truth about the My Lai massacre emerged — because Henry Clowers Thompson, piloting a reconnaissance helicopter, landing twice to observe the massacre at close hand, his report side-tracked by his base commander, decided eventually that he could not stay quiet — no-one from President Nixon down was fully prepared to recognise the facts. There were inquiries which published the evidence, but only one man, Lieutenant Calley, who was in charge of C Company, was convicted and his sentence was only partly carried out. Lieutenant Calley was put under

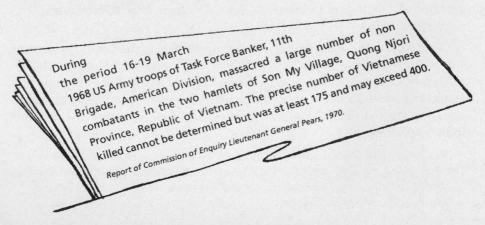

During the period 16-19 March 1968 US Army troops of Task Force Banker, 11th Brigade, American Division, massacred a large number of non combatants in the two hamlets of Son My Village, Quong Njori Province, Republic of Vietnam. The precise number of Vietnamese killed cannot be determined but was at least 175 and may exceed 400.

Report of Commission of Enquiry Lieutenant General Pears, 1970.

comfortable 'house arrest', and before long freed to become a prosperous small trader, with a sympathetic fan mail.[2]

LIFE Magazine estimated the cost of killing a single Vietcong guerrilla averaged $400,000, which included 75 bombs and 150 artillery shells. By the time of the My Lai massacre in 1968, Robert McNamara, the US Secretary for Defence, stepping out of his job, reckoned that more bombs had been dropped in Vietnam than on the whole of Europe during World War II. America was spending $2 billion every month, and failing to defeat a guerrilla enemy which had hardly any transport apart from bicycles. Thirty years later, he got round to admitting it was all a great mistake.

The mistake involved the killing of between 3 million and 5 million Vietnamese and 58,000 American war dead. Soldiers were not expected to reason why. Perhaps because no civilised reason could be offered.

For Jung Chang, twelve years old in the ranks of the Red Guards, it was Mao Ze Dong, the Great Leader, who knew best what was good for all of us. He wielded the *authority* which welded together family feelings, companionship, the feeling of awakening to a new life, the satisfaction of a job well done — total absorption in something bigger than oneself. The challenge was to clear the way for the Cultural Revolution which would set everything right, once those non-conforming reactionary rightists were forced into line or put out of the way.

Nothing new about such feelings. They are common to most world-shaking movements at some stage. They separate the sheep from the goats, the heretics and infidels from the true believers.

The golden invitation

Afterwards, perhaps, when the conquests are completed, the mood changes. One of Mao Ze Dong's predecessors, seven centuries back, had inherited the lion's share of the largest empire in the known world, carved out with disciplined savagery by the Mongol hordes, under the leadership of Ghenghiz Khan. The empire spanned most of central and northern Asia, extending westwards into European Russia, eastwards to the China Sea. It was held together by the fastest communication system yet known — a network of courier stations twenty miles apart along good main roads, with fast riders waiting to carry news from point to point, 500 miles in a day. It was an empire bigger than Islam and Christendom put together, (yet almost unknown to either). The sort of empire that in our day Rupert Murdoch might bequeath. Kublai Khan inherited a technically advanced society, at peace with itself, centuries ahead of every other civilization, with block printing, paper money, porcelain, magnetic compasses, gunpowder hand-

---

2 Evidence quoted in Michael Bolton and Kevin Sims, *Four Hours in My Lai*, Penguin.

grenades. His court brought together the best of scholarship and the arts.

Now he wanted to widen the horizon and add to the little he had heard about Christianity. He had a good impression of a couple of Italian merchants, Niccolo and Maffeo Polo who had made the long journey to his court in search of silks and spices. He asked them to return home, with a golden tablet giving them safe-conduct, and an invitation to the Pope to send

"some hundred wise men, learned in the law of Christ … fully capable of entering into discussions and clearly proving to … people of other persuasions … in the light of reason, that the Christian law was better than their own."

When the brothers reached home, everything was at sixes and sevens. A three-year argument was going on about who should be the Pope. The fourth and last Crusade had petered out with nothing gained on either side. The only notable achievement in 200 years of crusading had been a sideways swipe at two sects of non-conforming Christians, the Albighensians and the Waldensians, land-hungry aristocrats and independent-minded weavers and shepherds who were named *false Christians* and butchered, village by village, man, woman and child.

The Polo brothers hung about whilst the leaders of the crusade continued to quarrel about who should be Pope. When the new Pope was at last elected, they went to collect the 100 Christian teachers who might between them win over the leadership of the greatest empire in the world.

The new Pope spared them just two.

Then, early on in the journey, hearing rumours of a border war ahead, those two dropped out and went home. Maffeo and Niccolo, bringing Niccolo's seventeen-year old son Marco with them, continued three and a half years on the journey, through crowded Persian cities, across deserts, over mountain ranges,

 enduring *the snows and the rains and the vast rivers and the furious winds* until, forty days distant from Khan-Balicq, they were met and welcomed by messengers whom the Khan had sent when his courier service informed him of their approach.

All they had to say on their arrival was that the supreme head of the Christian church had failed to muster a single teacher willing to go the distance to honour that golden invitation.

The Great Khan deserved his title. He did not reproach the unsuccessful go-betweens, but honoured them. He made young Marco his special envoy, travelling throughout the empire to gather in fresh knowledge of the way people lived and loved and worshipped.

The Khan's favour and friendship survived even the revolt of a Christian convert, Naian, whose troops marched behind the banner of the Christian cross. Kublai outmarched, outmanoeuvred, surprised and overthrew the rebels.

"After the Great Khan had done this and won the battle, the different kinds of people present, Saracens, Idolaters and Jews, and many other people who do not believe in God, mocked the Cross that Naian had borne on his standard. And they said to the Christians who had been present: 'See how the Cross of your God has aided Naian who was a Christian.

The mockery and the jibes were so loud, that they reached the ears of the Great Khan. And ... he angrily rebuked those who mocked. Then, calling many Christians who were there, he comforted them, saying 'If the Cross of your God has not aided Naian, there was good reason for it; ... Naian was a disloyal traitor ... and the Cross of your God has done very well in not helping him ... for, in that it is a good thing, it cannot do but what is good.' "

Afterwards, dictating the account of his *Travels*, Marco Polo kept coming back to this strangely tolerant *authority*, so nearly Christian, and yet so far from the loyal single-mindedness that Christendom demanded.

The trouble about Christendom, as with other single-minded empires, was that question of authority. Or, to be more accurate, the *authorities*: the religious and political leaders who over the centuries have unfurled their banners — Cross, Crescent, Hammer and Sickle, Swastika, Market Forces, and the Rising Sun.

Authority, if you recognise it, requires acceptance. The authorities on both sides in the Crusades believed that their truth should be all-conquering and must demand surrender. Christians and Muslims alike understood very well that if you accept what has been laid down as truth, that requires obedience. The word for *submission* is *Islam*.

OK to obey

Through the ages people have tended to take on trust what the authorities — in the name of Party, Church, State, and the Market — have told them was the proper thing to do.

So it's OK

- to kill about 3 million women as witches over a span of 250 years
- to allow 2,345 Afrikaner civilians, 1,500 of them children, to die — in a single month — in the world's first concentration camp, British Army-operated, during the Boer war
- to kill 6 million Jews by starvation or by cyanide gas, with the help of obedient prison officers
- to let 16,000 Commonwealth troops and 100,000 Asians die working on the Burma raliway
- to kill 1,000 Vietnamese non-combatants each week with the help of the workforces back home, loyally manufacturing landmines, cluster bombs and napalm
- to atomise 92,000 Japanese in Hiroshima

- to create the Hamburg firestorm which, in 3 days and nights, killed 42,000 civilians, 8,400 of them children
- to stone adulterers, and to kill schoolgirls without a headcovering
- to shoot anyone trying to cross the border from east to west Berlin
- to dispose of delinquent teenagers from broken homes by shooting them (in Bogota) or locking them up with active drug peddlers and sadistic bullies (in Britain).

It's not a comprehensive list! I'll leave space for you, reader, to add your own.

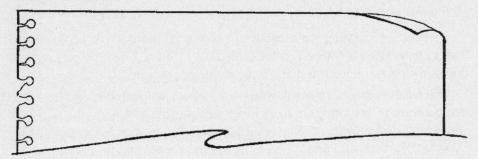

Of course, we wouldn't do that sort of thing ourselves. Not nowadays. Not knowingly...

On the other hand, it doesn't seem to be our business to rock the boat, disturb the peace, ask awkward questions of the people in charge. After all, they're in a position to *know* what's best. That's why they're there.

5 • Authority

An American researcher, Stanley Milgram, wrote a book about some experiments in *Obedience to Authority*. He set up a dummy laboratory in which shock treatment was apparently being administered as part of some experiments about learning. Outsiders were roped in, at a four dollar fee, and invited to act as *teachers* administering shocks to help a *learner* (an actor, really) to memorize. The experiments went far beyond expectations. *The subjects* — the people who were asked to help administer the shock treatment — had too much respect for the authorities — the professionals they thought were in charge — to question what they were told to do.

The actor was at first mute. In later experiments, he screamed. Still, nobody felt it was their place to interfere.

> The victim claimed heart trouble; subjects still shocked him on command. The victim pleaded to be let free... Subjects continued to shock him... The final effort to establish a limit (to obedience) was the Touch-Proximity condition. (In other words, sitting next to the person giving the shocks.) But the very first subject in this condition subdued the victim on demand... A quarter of the subjects performed similarly.

The results, as seen and felt in the laboratory, ... raise the possibility that human nature, or — more specifically — the kind of character produced in American democratic society, cannot be counted on to insulate its citizens from brutality ... at the direction of malevolent authority. ... **A substantial proportion of people do what they're told to do, ... without limitations of conscience, so long as they perceive that the command comes from a legitimate authority**.

Afterwards, Stanley Milgram kept asking himself how his laboratory experiment was matched by people's behaviour outside, in the society we take to be civilised and democratic.

The importation and enslavement of millions of black people, the destruction of the American Indian population, the internment of Japanese Americans, the use of napalm against civilians in Vietnam, all are harsh policies that originated in the authority of a democratic nation, and were responded to with the expected obedience. In each case, voices of morality were raised against the action in question, but the typical response of the common man was to obey orders.

I am forever astonished that, when lecturing on the obedience experiment in colleges across the country, I faced young men who were aghast at the behaviour of the experimental subjects and proclaimed they would never behave in such a way, but who in a matter of months, were brought into the military and performed without compunction actions that made shocking the victim seemed pallid. In this respect, they are no better and no worse than human beings of any other era who lend themselves to the purposes of authority and become instruments in its destructive processes.

What makes authority *legitimate*?

Where does it get its power?

Perhaps the power and the authority are God-given. That's what we are told. Who by? By the chap who tells us it's what God told him, he thinks.

Perhaps he was right?

How do we *know* he's right?

Common sense

God-given, or the fruit of evolution going back to an infinity we can't conceive, one thing the human species has in common is the urge to make sense of our surroundings, ourselves and each other. Try as we may, we can't stop thinking about it.

You can't think unless you change your mind. Anything else is biologically impossible.

Peter Abelard drew students in their hundreds to his theological lectures in mediaeval Paris. In an Age of Faith he had the courage to talk about doubt:

By doubting, we learn to enquire. By enquiring, we perceive the truth.

14 Self-evident truths

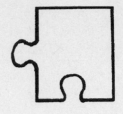

In New Orleans, an unemployed, homeless street beggar called Michael Dennis goes to the rescue of an elderly couple trapped in a burning car. Afterwards, he says he couldn't do otherwise:

> "It wasn't no big deal. It was just the right thing. I saw two old people burning up. You can't just ignore that."

Of course, we can be brainwashed, or intimidated, into standing back; even aiding the blaze if someone tells us the victims are witches or heretics or infidels or Iraqi losers in the Gulf War trapped in their cars on the Basra road. But there's a gut feeling that leaves us ill at ease.

Charles Darwin, reporting his investigations into the human species, said that we respond by instinct, and used the example of the passer-by who sees a house on fire.

Alternative 1: **he risks his life and goes in to try and make a rescue.**

Alternative 2: **he doesn't, and feels guilty.**

No-one tells him to do it. There's no penalty involved, except the danger to his life.

No-one tells the three-year-old, walking along the garden wall, what balance 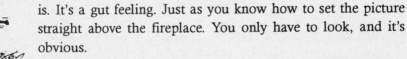 is. It's a gut feeling. Just as you know how to set the picture straight above the fireplace. You only have to look, and it's obvious.

Earlier in this book, I described how people in many parts of the world have sized up their own situations, and begun to set matters straight for themselves. **There has first to be an eye-opening process which makes people aware of their own value, and from that, of their own power.**

In this respect, women are a special case. For most of human history, they have been at the receiving end of male dominance. Set aside from formal decision-making, not expected to take the initiative. This has meant exerting all their powers from behind the scenes, sorting things out before the men really get round to it, like the Igbo women in Oke's village. Being valued, perhaps, as something precious to be kept apart. Or just *used* to do the donkey work.

This century has seen something more than the *Emancipation of Women* that the Suffragettes set out to achieve. It's one thing to fight for equal status, the vote, equal pay, entry to the professions, rights over motherhood. It's another to become the kind of *moving spirit* that people like Chrissie Maher represent. These are people who have understood what needed to be done, sketched out roughly, and then put into effect with increasing precision; who could see clearly the obstacles (often, but not always, male) standing in the way, and were able to stir things up to the point at which all sorts of other people began to get moving.

It seems likely that the next century will see that process gathering strength. If so, it will be because people, especially women, have begun to understand themselves, and their capacities to be *agents, not victims*.

Coming out

The way this is happening may not be spectacular. In Pakistan, Arif Hasan observed the effect on women in purdah when they had the opportunity to get something done together. At first, it was a matter of joining in to the *lane organisation*, collecting contributions for the work in hand. Then it was coming together in each other's homes to set up alternative ways of defeating the rapacious middlemen and getting a fair deal for their piecework. Then exchanging information about hygiene and family planning.

All that led to more and more girls venturing to become teachers, and more parents being willing to send their girls to schools. And the schools becoming co-educational, where boys and girls could be on an equal footing.

✧ ✧ ✧

In India, Meena Bilgi is visiting one village after another where neither the men nor the women have really thought to compare the way they go about making a living together.

Here she is describing her visit to Jambhar Village, Netrang, in Gujarat:

"The road was washed away due to heavy rains the previous night... We walked down to Dilipbhai's house (the man who was Secretary of the village group). ... About 15-18 women came along. We introduced ourselves, and started asking them about their village and if they could draw a map of their village.

Dilipbhai, who was listening to the conversation, said: 'Oh! These women do not know anything. It won't be possible for them to draw a map...' Taraben, a young pretty woman who had studied up to fourth standard, was sitting in the *front. She was reluctant even to touch the pen to draw the map. She said: 'I have lost the habit of writing, and do not feel confident. Let Kamlaben draw the map, we will help her.' Kamlaben, a school teacher, willingly started working on the paper.*

We found them getting much involved in discussing among themselves — asking each other the number of wells, hand pumps, biogas plants, whose agricultural land lies where, etc, etc.

I kept on observing women's face expressions, listening to their talk, amazed at the way they were discussing, arguing."

Eye-openers

Later that day, after the meal break —

"Taraben again sitting in the front, ready with a pen in her hand (interesting!).

Taraben said: 'What shall I draw on it?

I said: 'But in the morning, you said you feel nervous picking up the pen.'

Taraben smiled and said: 'I will write now.

It was 3.30 pm. Meenaben arranged tea for us. She said: 'Women have to work a lot, isn't it!' The other women said: 'Yes! We cook, wash clothes, utensils, clean up the house, take care of our children, bring water and fuel, take care of animals, work on the fields — ' so I said: 'Can we write all this down?' Taraben, again ready with pen, started writing. The chart was divided into five spaces: household work, work outside the house, animal care, agriculture, rest/sleep... and the time spent was worked out according to the seasons — monsoon, summer, winter (when, the women said, we have to collect more fuel wood)."

Between them, the women worked out the hours spent and totted them up to make *15 hours a day* in the monsoon, *17 hours a day* in summer, and *18 hours a day* in the winter.

Soon after, Meena went to meet the men of a nearby village, Boripitha. They were asked how much time their wives and daughters normally worked. Meena got them, too, to draw a chart on the ground, with spaces for each kind of work. A boy ran for a bundle of leaves, one leaf for each hour spent. Gradually they worked through the day — $^1/_2$ a leaf for cleaning, $^3/_4$ of a leaf for water collection, the same again for grinding flour, a whole leaf for cooking the morning meal. Meena asked what about the fuel for the cooking? They had forgotten to mention firewood collection.

*"Then they discussed among themselves and decided to put two more leaves to indicate the time spent by women in taking care of animals, and going to the forest for fuelwood. The men kept on adding leaves for the various activities carried out by women during the day — carrying the food to the fields, working in the fields for $3^1/_2$ hours, taking animals for grazing, cutting fodder for animals, collecting water, grinding, cooking, serving food to the family members. At the end of the exercise, when they calculated the total number of hours, it came to be **19 hours**.*

Margiabhai said: 'You mean to say women work for 19 hours a day!' I said: 'I'm not saying, you are all saying this.' Margiabhai said: 'If women worked for 19 hours, they would not be able to get up the next day.' The other men agreed and said: 'Yes, women will fall ill if they work so much.' So I said: 'What do you want to do now? You gave this information.' The men said: 'We would like to do this exercise again. Definitely, we have made some mistake.' They started reducing five or ten minutes here and there. They seemed quite baffled. When they calculated the hours, they found they could only reduce by one hour.

Fatehsinghbai said: 'But their work is much softer, our work is much harder.' ... All the other men nodded their heads and said: 'In cooking and washing, not much labour is involved. These works are much easier than ours.' So I said: 'Let us talk about each activity of women.' "

And so, patiently, she got the men to admit that their women have to walk long distances often barefoot to fetch wood from the forest and risk snakebites and rude passes from forest guards, that  a lot of smoke gets into their eyes while cooking, that they have to carry big bundles on their heads, that their hands get rough with washing, that they have to stand in a queue to get water, and to pull up the buckets on a rope.

"The men took a lot of time to come out with this, as if they were thinking it for the first time."

Women are beginning first to see themselves in a new light; and then to open the men's eyes. With some difficulty.

Reclaiming the faith

What would Muhammed ... think of the way Muslim men have, over the centuries, distorted his ideas for their unjust and sexist purposes?

Born poor, orphaned young, ascetic and sensitive, Muhammed grew up on the side of the dispossessed. He revolted against a society where girls were often buried alive at birth, or bought and sold like chattels; where women were disinherited and disenfranchised. Where a man could rape with impunity, or take as many concubines as he pleased, sometimes into the hundreds, discarding them at whim, penniless and helpless.

Such abuses needed stopping, and Muhammed was determined to stop them. Since no society loves its reformer, patriarchal Arabia rose up in arms against him. But its slaves and its women, for the first time hearing themselves spoken of as free human beings with inalienable rights, flocked to become the first converts to Islam, understanding it to be a compelling force of emancipation. ...

My interpretation of women's rights in Islam, like the interpretation of countless other Muslim-born feminists, clashes strongly with the conservative, official interpretation that has always been subsidised by regressive governments to please the egos of reactionary rulers.

It is high time we demanded our religion back from their treasonous hands. ...

The heavy veiling that we see across the Muslim world and among Muslim communities elsewhere is certainly not Islamic: it is a dead relic from Byzantium, which the Arabs took on when they conquered my native Damascus soon after Muhammed's death and saw fit to ape the conservative customs of the Christian élite they there displaced. ...

A Muslim reformation is in the making, and it is Muslim women who are at its forefront.

The Muslim woman who wrote that, Rana Kabbani, is speaking for — how many millions? — who have not yet found the way to make themselves heard.

What is it about universal religions that has made them survive? What is it in them that strikes a chord in us, in spite of the terrible things religious leaders persuade us to do in their name?

It is not necessarily a set of laws, the *sharia*, or the Ten Commandments. They set down a fixed code of behaviour which the authorities administer (with occasional readjustments to suit the powers-that-be — when, for instance, *Thou shalt not kill* is out of kilter with a *Just War*, or a judicial execution).

Islam itself, with men in the lead, has been a world-shaker for at least 1,000 years; never more so than now. It has shown up the self-doubts and the overblown self-satisfactions of the Western world. It has turned deprived and oppressed people into first-class citizens, who feel themselves to be the children of God.

Like other world faiths, it survives in spite of its pious betrayers.

Seeing is believing

> One of the unexpected things I have learned in my life as a Quaker is that religion is basically about relationships between people. This was an unexpected discovery, because I had been brought up to believe that religion was essentially about our relationship with God.
>
> George Gorman, 1982

At the heart of the matter, it isn't the rules that carry conviction, but the pattern of life that people live. When we come up against heroines, heroes, saints — we can feel the quality. Not just the big names, the cult figures, glamorised in the media or the history books. Ordinary-seeming, unassuming people, whose lives glow, who are fun to be with. They show in themselves without fuss or self-glory what it is to be generous, compassionate, merciful, unselfish, steadfast, just.

They are the evidence.

Our judgement has little to do with the law, and everything to do with our own instinctive awareness of what is there in them and may be lacking in ourselves. They are the reminders of what we *could be*.

What we see in them is *self-evident*. It doesn't have to be proclaimed, or fitted into someone else's system. We can see it, feel it, for ourselves.

The man who coined the phrase about *self-evident truths* was a young American lawyer brought up in comfortable circumstances, inheriting his share of the family plantation, slaves included. Thomas Jefferson became a human rights fighter in his twenties, and in his thirties a revolutionary, one of the founding fathers of American independence. He wrote the first draft of the Declaration of Independence by the United States of America:

> … We hold these truths to be self-evident: that all men are created equal; that they are endowed by their creator with inherent and inalienable rights; that among these are life, liberty and the pursuit of happiness; that to secure these rights, governments are instituted among men, deriving their just powers from the consent of the governed; that whenever any form of government becomes destructive of these ends, it is the right of the people to alter or to abolish it…

Self discovery

Jefferson had steeped himself in the writings of the great thinkers of his day, from Locke via Adam Smith and Montesquieu to Rousseau and Tom Paine. But when he came to draft the Declaration, he *turned neither to book nor pamphlet*. He wrote what he felt was *an expression of the American mind*, the self-discovery of people who had begun to think for themselves: who had got the measure of a cloth-eared King and a sleazy government that cared only about raising taxes to pay off the mountainous war  debts run up in the process of becoming the world's biggest military and naval power.

That armed might was wielded by a top-down régime which had eliminated Scottish and Irish opposition, outgunned the French, the Spanish and the Dutch, and drew its economic strength from possessions spread across the known world.

It seemed — like other vested interests before and since — *invincible*.

Except to those independent-minded Americans — at most no more than a third of the New England population — who decided that *ENOUGH IS ENOUGH!* and were no longer prepared to do as they were told.

What made them take that awful step, renounce allegiance to the Crown, risk their lives and liberties?

The records show that people were divided, uncertain of themselves, endlessly debating what action to take, until almost the last moment. What brought them to their feet and got them moving was an anonymous pamphlet called *Common Sense*. Tom Paine[1] had only been in the country sixteen months when he wrote it A few weeks before it came out, according to one New Englander,

> *"the public sentiment had shuddered at the tremendous obstacles.*
> *(Now) it overleaped every barrier."*

It was read aloud to those who could not afford the shilling it cost. And it went through 56 editions in less than a year. It stripped away the public relations hype which surrounded *the present race of kings* and traced them back to

> *"the principal ruffian of some reckless gang, whose savage manners or pre-eminence in subtlety obtained him the title of chief among plunderers; and who ... overawed the quiet and defenceless to purchase their safety by frequent contributions.*
>
> *... England, since the conquest, hath known some few good monarchs, but groaned beneath the much larger number of bad ones... William the Conqueror ... a French bastard landing with an armed banditti and establishing himself king of England against the consent of the natives, is in plain terms a very paltry rascally original."*

✧ ✧ ✧

Returning today, Tom Paine might think that old-style royalty has done for itself without the need for further attention. Instead, he might be exposing the addictive greed and the power lust of oil czars and media emperors; putting out his message in a flash on the Internet (following the example of the Mexican Zapatistas). But the mind-blowing force of *Common Sense* has never been merely to show up false oracles and their priestly spin-doctors.

A modern historian said,

> *"It would be difficult to name any human composition which had an effect at once so extended and so lasting ... It worked nothing short of miracles."*

Knocking down Aunt Sallies is often useful, and fun too. There's plenty of it most nights on TV. But *miracles* only happen when someone manages to *speak to our condition* as Tom Paine's Quaker parents would have put it. To let us see ourselves in a new light:

> **"Time hath found us**.
> **We have it in our power to begin the world over again. A situation, similar to the present, hath not happened since the days of Noah until now. The birth-day of a new world is at hand."**

---

1 Remember? Turn back to page 67.

The birth-day of a new world

And who was he saying that to? A rag-tag-and-bobtail of farmers, fishermen, craftsmen, lawyers, merchants, journalists, ne'er-do-wells — and their wives and daughters — facing experienced British officers and well-equipped German mercenary troops. Facing them with pitchforks, stones and blunderbusses. Plus an *info-network* of laundresses, potboys, odd-jobbers and chambermaids who between them fed *early and authentic intelligence* on British military plans hours before the troops got their marching orders.

General 'Gentleman Johnnie' Burgoyne, surrendering to the rebels at Saratoga in 1777 complained that *wherever the King's forces point, militia to the number of three or four thousand assemble in a few hours.* One of the German mercenaries later explained:

> *"It is almost impossible to surprise the enemy because (from) every house that one passes … the farmer, or his son, or his servant, or even his wife or his daughter, fires off a gun, or runs by the footpath to warn the enemy."*

Between them all, that rabble took on the Colossus and showed the others on the sidelines that, once in a while, this vastly more powerful force could be repulsed, and in the end defeated.

They had one advantage over the ingenious Igbos in the Biafran war nearly 200 years later. They had room to manoeuvre; they couldn't be boxed in. But they won through because, like the Biafrans, they had ingenuity and endurance, and a new view of themselves.

Well-born Jefferson, who called tearaway Tom Paine his friend, wanted above all to have men see each other in a new light, and to deal with each other on a level footing.

> *"The mass of mankind has not been born with saddles on their backs, nor a favoured few booted and spurred, ready to ride them …"*

As for *womankind* — well, women's rights were not so much on people's minds, though he sympathised with the idea. What mattered first and foremost was freedom to think for oneself, *man, woman and child.* He got Congress to pass a law upholding religious liberty, with his own preamble to it:

> … The opinions and beliefs of men … follow involuntarily the evidence proposed to their minds: that Almighty God hath created the mind free, and manifested his supreme will that free it shall remain by making it altogether unsusceptible of restraints… and finally that truth is great and will prevail if left to herself … errors ceasing to be dangerous when it is permitted freely to contradict them.

When Jefferson became President, he went on trying to free people to think for themselves.

Jefferson believed that *the liberties of a nation ... are a gift of God.* That included the freedom owed to the slaves which he wrote into his draft for the Declaration of Independence (probably with the help of Tom Paine). But that he found was the sticking point: the blind spot in the vision of independent-minded, freedom-loving Americans. People could feel the force of the big idea within the pattern of their everyday lives. But when it came to applying generally, with a bit of lateral thinking, that gut feeling was no longer strong enough to engage their minds. The argument for self-interest took over.

In England, Lord Dartmouth advised his government that the American colonies must not at all costs be allowed *to check or discourage a traffic so beneficent to the nation.* On this issue, the merchants and the great plantation owners of the Southern States thoroughly agreed with him. They drummed up enough support to force emancipation out of the final Declaration. They figured the economy simply wouldn't stand it.

A false economy if ever there was one. Jefferson lived on another 50 years, as Governor of Virginia, and twice as President of the United States. He kept trying to make the legislators see further than their short-term profit. The state of Massachusetts — where the Revolution started — was the only honourable exception. The rest allowed slavery to fester. In Jefferson's lifetime, there were slave revolts followed by judicial hangings in Louisiana, Virginia, North and South Carolina, New York, Pennsylvania, New Orleans and Maryland. Ninety-six years after his first, unsuccessful, emancipation bill, at the price of 623,000 lives in the Civil War, slavery was at last outlawed throughout the United States (as it had been, two generations earlier, in the British Isles).

Paying back

The idea that *All men are created equal* was *self-evident*, a marker that most people could recognise from then on. But recognition of what's been wrong isn't the same as reparation, restitution, putting things right. Self-interest gets in the way. We have inherited the fruits of that self-interest. Not slavery itself, but its after-effects. Something is owed to the victims which has not yet been paid. All over the world, the descendants of slaves, by and large, have had the worst deal in housing and schooling; and as a result, the worst qualifications in the competition for jobs.

In this they are like others who have lost out on their inheritance. American Indians, Australian Aborigines, South African blacks, the Jews displaced by Hitler, the Arabs displaced by Jews, the peoples of Azerbaijan and East Timor — you can fill out the list from every day's reading of the news.

Together, they make up those armies of the dispossessed — ethnic and economic migrants who have never forgotten their roots and are now re-discovering themselves, self-evidently, as the equals of those who dispossessed them.

Neighbourhoods are where that re-discovery takes place. It's here that the false economy of the money market and the arms trade and the cash crop can see-saw the value of a house or the prospects of a job. Where cut-throat competition for overseas markets begins to force down wages and job security; where there are not enough homes and jobs to go round; where schools are overcrowded and teachers over-burdened; where parents' anxieties begin to sour home life; where fear and uncertainty can spawn the drug culture and where addiction depends on crime to obtain the makings.

It's where children are at risk: because parents lack the time to understand them and schooling underrates their hidden capacities, their need to try themselves out, to break new ground, to get a kick out of doing things together; where teenagers, fed on junk food and tele-pap, denied much of what family life could give, cheated of the chance to fulfil themselves at school, end up in dead-end jobs or on the scrap heap.

It's here that people, seeing for themselves that society has let them down, decide to take it out of someone else within easy reach.

We know all this. As couch potatoes it's all happening before our very eyes. We feel bad about it. But maybe we can't take it. Best look the other way.

I grew up with a picture of a friendly man on a seashore who seemed to be some kind of Arab. He had a long robe like the Arab warriors mixed up in my box of tin soldiers. There were children playing all around him, and one small girl in high spirits had grabbed his robe, braced her feet against his heels, and was swinging to and fro behind him. The man was listening to a question put to him by a more sober character, leaning forward and looking up with a long finger stroking his pointy beard. The question he was putting was the title of the picture — *Who is my neighbour?*

Did he really want an answer, or was he simply concerned to catch this Jesus out? In the end, he had to provide the answer himself. But first came the story.

A man gets mugged and is left for dead. One after another, two respectable people come down the road and pass him by. The Priest and the Levite, reliable establishment types, conscientious about their duties, but in this situation, not wanting to get involved.

Then along comes this dubious Samaritan character, not short of a bob or two but belonging to a tribe which had intermarried with the occupying force, sold out, traitors to the Jewish race and religion. In Belfast, it might have been a Prod or a Provo, depending on which side of the Falls Road you lived;

or a Brit soldier off duty. In Bosnia, or Rwanda, a target for ethnic cleansing.

And this is the fellow who risks attack from muggers who might still be lurking, rescues the man in the ditch, gets him fed and looked after, and promises to follow up and see that all is well when he next comes by.

Who was the *neighbour* in all this? Well, you couldn't dodge the fact that it had to be that Samaritan.

And what about *human nature*? The Priest's? The Levite's? Keeping themselves to themselves, looking after Number One, as most of us are inclined to do, but maybe afterwards feeling what a mediaeval writer called The Ageyn-bite of In-Wit — *the Remorse of Conscience*. Or perhaps not. Maybe they were quite used to passing by on the other side.

The Samaritan acted on impulse, but didn't leave it at that. He followed it up, to make a good job of it.

The lawyer who asked Jesus the question probably went off with a flea in his ear, or perhaps a nagging doubt at the back of his mind about what he'd been brought up to believe in.

The conversation had started with another question, *What shall I do to inherit eternal life?* Very personal, self-centred, you could say. And the question was put back to him, *What has the law to say about it?* Being steeped in the Jewish law, he has the answer, pat. It's a modern answer, that doesn't quite correspond with what was written in the old books. The old version was that you must love the Lord your God with all your heart and all your soul and all your strength. And (in a separate set of instructions) — your neighbour as yourself. That's as far as it went. The version that the lawyer quoted might well have been a repeat of what had been said on some other occasion by Jesus himself. Picking out those two commitments from the mass of Jewish law, locking them close together — and adding something entirely new:

*"Love thy God with all thy heart and all thy soul and all thy strength **and all thy mind."***

I shall not cease from *mental* fight

Not a bad vow for women, and schoolchildren, to take on when they sing Blake's *Jerusalem* at the Women's Institute or the school Prize-giving.

About time the men amongst us joined in (perhaps spurred on by the likes of Meena Bilgi).

It is as much a part of human nature to face facts as to dodge them. It may take someone else to make us look at them, but when we do — when *the minds of the people at large* are illumined, and they have *knowledge of the facts* — there's a sporting chance, as Jefferson believed, that they will *exert their natural powers*.

It is our powers that are in demand now. Revolutions are made from below, because there is a stirring in people's hearts and minds which revolutionary leaders understand and build on. Revolutions are betrayed when those leaders forget what made them. Revolutions can only be made whole again when ordinary people regain confidence in themselves and their abilities to make changes, or preserve them.

✧   ✧   ✧

That story about the Samaritan. Looked at closely, it might seem out of place in this book about neighbourhoods.

What sort of neighbourhood was that? Because of the muggers, the road from Jerusalem to Jericho was almost a no-go area. Not the place that anyone would choose to stay around in. The man in the ditch was so knocked about that he might well have been unrecognisable. Who knows where he lived? For that matter, where did the Priest, where did the Levite come from? And the Samaritan, no-one knew him from Adam. You couldn't locate the four of them in any neighbourhood on the map. And there wasn't a *neighbourhood support group* in sight.

Yet it's a story that for most of us strikes home.

It's about choice.

"We are at the dividing roads of Good or Evil."
Willy Brandt (the former West German Chancellor)'s dying plea for the United Nations, three years after the destruction of the Berlin Wall.

Driving force

We are driven by two motivating forces within ourselves, the instincts that Darwin and Adam Smith identified:

- **self-interest, self-preservation, let's-not-get-involved;**
- **integrity — being able to live with what you do and who you are.**

Half the time, we teeter between the two.

There's another choice to make. Between doing something on impulse — like the first time Chrissie Maher dumped her rubbish — and thinking it out beforehand.

Too often, the think-piece becomes an elaborate excuse for not doing very much until it's too late. It's using your intellect to devise an elaborate analysis of what's gone wrong, having *meaningful discussions* with all the other theorists, and in the end, coming out with a critique instead of a plan of action:

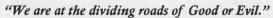

- a plan of action, thought through.

Words alone won't get you far. We've had more than enough of them. What matters is to **see** our way, step by step, with short-term achievements building confidence to go further. The neighbourhood becomes the proving ground for bigger things. Its boundaries may not be precisely on a map. It may be more a network of people with a common cause, a *cybernetwork* even; the foundation on which to rebuild the structures of political and economic power. Wherever it is, it works because there are moving spirits, who **show** what needs doing and persuade the onlookers that between us it *could be* done.

Acting on impulse at least starts you off. Where would Chrissie Maher have got if she hadn't decided, on impulse, *ENOUGH IS ENOUGH!* and got weaving?

Impulse and staying power

You have to turn on the ignition before you can get a move on. But if you're going to get anywhere, there has to be staying power, and that does not come so easily. Maybe you're the sort of person who goes it alone, and has the stamina and the single-mindedness to go the distance. In which case it's on the cards that you end up as a hero or a martyr or a dud, with a lot of followers dependent on you, who may lose their bearings if you're the only one with a map and you keep it to yourself.

What's needed is a share in the thought as well as the action.

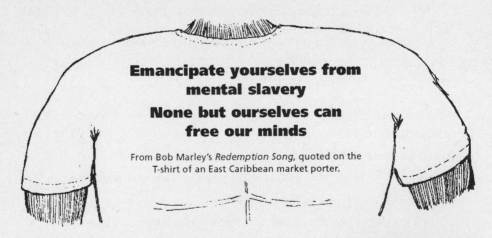

Emancipate yourselves from mental slavery

None but ourselves can free our minds

From Bob Marley's *Redemption Song*, quoted on the T-shirt of an East Caribbean market porter.

Thinking things out, together. That's how the Rochdale Pioneers managed it. When people are credited with the ability to sort out their own ideas, however rough to start with, and fit them together, they suddenly gain confidence in themselves and in each other.

What they make between them is *common sense* — the name Tom Paine gave to the book which helped to launch the American Revolution; and gave it *common purpose*.

✧ ✧ ✧

Some people would argue that there's no real choice. We're in the grip of a master plan, pre-ordained. Or we're programmed to respond to the market forces of addictive greed. There's nothing we can do to change the system.

> *There was a young man who said Damn!*
> *At last I know just what I am.*
> *All I do is to move*
> *In a pre-destined groove,*
> *I'm not even a bus, I'm a tram.*

Believe that if you choose, with the prospect that the tram is en route to the breaker's yard. But if you choose otherwise, then it's time to take the initiative, break new ground.

No easy choice, you might say. Things have gone wrong, and there's not much time left to put them right. *So who am I to do it?* Then there's that gut feeling, that, like love, takes risks. Brenda Cooksey, on Lightmoor, knew how it felt:

"I've got the panic within myself, that it's got to work, it's got to work."

This chapter is not meant to leave us in a rosy glow, floating about 18 inches above ground level. Uplifted perhaps, by the evidence that across the world, all sorts of ordinary people are choosing to do extraordinary things. People in suits as well as people in anoraks. Not necessarily fitting in with a body of doctrine or a formal system. But responding to something within our hearts and minds that says: *ENOUGH IS ENOUGH!*

When I was a fourth former, an earnest fifth former lectured us all about winning the swimming competition. He said we needed a slogan, and he had one all ready:

"We strive, we conquer and we go on forever!"

I think he probably ended up either as a Downing Street spin doctor, or a soccer commentator.

But a very small third former offered an alternative:

"Sink or swim!"

We don't have to be grandiloquent, or exclusive, so long as we get together with whatever moving spirits are in sight.

Professionals built the Titanic.

Amateurs (with a bit of expert advice) built the Ark.

Job in hand

We have got to build it right.

The nearest I got to building a boat was building a boat shed. I had two goes at it.

The first was shoring up a century-old lean-to against the wall of a ruined byre. Old ship's timbers supporting a turf roof. A lot of tinkering and patching up — and it lasted ten years or so, leaking more and more as the gales blew and the years rolled by.

Then, when the roof threatened to collapse on the little boat below, I decided to start all over again and build a free-standing boathouse which would weather every storm.

To be near the sea, we had to build it on sand. First, the footings, concrete piles 18 inches deep to support the base frame. Then the walls bolted to it, then the roof. Afterwards, some massive doors, hurricane-proof, opening most of the time on an inner door to let in light and air when the sun shone.

Building materials? Some new timber, with a tendency to warp. Some seasoned timber, gradually accumulated over the years. Some rough old beams salvaged from the ruins of the first boat shed.

Well, you can probably see my drift. It's about structure: something more than impulse and staying-power. It's the hard-thinking commitment to take on the powers-that-be on their own ground; and with the help of those moving spirits on the other side to re-structure or replace the top-heavy systems that they operate.

We have to build, or re-build, societies which are long past their prime. There's a choice. Some still have a limited life. We can patch and prop them up for the time being. Others have rotted away and are on the verge of collapse. They'll have to come down, one way or another.

Wherever we are in the world, it pays to improvise. Not for keeps, but to get something done in a rough and ready fashion now — makeshifts to tide things over whilst we get on with better structures that will stand the test of time.

First, the footings. Those elements in human nature which endure: the DIY urge to make our mark with something that shows our mettle; the kick we get out of doing things together; inbuilt curiosity — the urge to ask questions and try out something new; our sense of belonging — to a place, a race, a family, that gives us identity and personal worth.

Then there's the timber for the framework and the cladding. Some brand new ideas, with a slight twist to them perhaps; some institutions salvaged from the old structure — solid, reliable, but riddled with the old quarrels and mutual suspicions which crop up in every seasoned community, and the departmental rivalries which get in the way of effective action by the authorities: rusty nails that must be dug out or hammered in hard or they'll destroy the cutting edge of the plane.

Dealing one way or another with the old structures of society is hard going. There are so many built-in prejudices to get rid of, so much toxic greed. The temptation is to scrap the lot.

It's easy to develop a bulldozer mentality which can't see beyond conflict, confrontation, the need to destroy.

Three hundred or so families have set up an informal settlement, Misamu Yethu, near Houf Bay, in South Africa. They had twice been forcibly evicted from previous sites, but with the coming of Independence, they now have legal rights. One of their leaders, Kenny Tokwe, an unemployed garage attendant, took me round.

Some houses had been built with walls and roofs of salvaged plastic sheeting, nailed to a wooden framework with bottletops as washers. Others were walled with solid sheets of tin or hardboard. Kenny, there from the start, had gone through both these stages, at each point replacing makeshifts with better materials he had saved up to buy. Now he was in his new house, built in two weeks; ship-shape, sound materials fitted well together on a concrete base. A solid roof, a power point, and before long as the community gets its act together — a mains water supply, proper sewerage and a retraining-for-jobs scheme on a vacant lot.

Gugile Nkwinti, long-term resistance leader in the ANC's fight against apartheid and now Speaker of the Eastern Cape Parliament, had told me two years earlier:

"The change we have to be making now is from street resistance to street regeneration."

From street level, all the way up.

15 Common ground

From now on we are fitting together jigsaw pieces which have figured earlier in the book. For the benefit of readers who have dipped and skipped there are bracketed page references to check back.

Moving spirits like Kenny Tokwe, Chrissie Maher and Zhou Wen, and on the other side of the Us and Them divide, Arif Hassan and Jimmy Mascaranhas are often seen as leaders; without them, people think, nothing will happen. And if they fail, or move on, everything peters out.

Even with them in the lead it's all too easy for the rest of us to stay at home and leave it to them. We've all got round to seeing what changes are needed. We're all in favour. Joining in — that's different. There are too many wolves about and the global weather isn't like it used to be.

What's needed is some neutral ground where people come together, as a matter of course, without having to sign on, make promises. No commitments until they're ready for it.

It's fine to have a friendly meeting place for the active few, like James Smithies' digs in Rochdale, nicknamed Henland [p60], where the in-group can hatch plans together.

That's not quite the same as a place where people can get used to each other, pick up the gossip and the vibes, size up the situation in a non-committal sort of way. It has to be common ground, wide open to all; where no one feels particularly threatened and everyone belongs.

The old industrial communities, where almost everyone in the neighbourhood had someone working up at the mill or down the pit, were places where you could have a sing-song as well as a ding-dong argument, where everyone could be in the know about what was going on, and who was responsible. As manufacturing gets de-centralised, down-sized, dispersed, it's much harder to find that common ground where everyone meets on roughly the same footing

In Europe, in the Middle Ages, the obvious meeting place was the church, where you could sometimes hold a dance as well as a harvest festival or a service for worship. From its earliest days the church was an *ecclesia*, the old Greek word for an assembly of people. In much the same way Jewish communities used the word synagogue, which simply meant *gathering together*, and the mosque in Islamic cultures is the place where everyone comes to share in worship and good works.

Until the cracks in religious institutions began to open up — the sectarian divisions which bedevil most of the great faiths — such places brought everyone together, high and low; belonging together as *members of one another* as they used to say.

Today in multi-cultural communities, and even in some with the same ethnic roots, that common ground no longer exists. Religious self-righteousness puts even colour bars in the shade. Some religious people do their best, in an ecumenical way, to get together from time to time; but for many being a true believer means meeting apart, separating from the rest. In one small Caribbean village I went to recently, there were seven different churches and chapels, each looking slightly askance at the others. **The only place where everyone could be on the same footing was the school**.

Going to the roots

Back in the time of the American Revolution, when some sects had already begun to breed discrimination, Jefferson [p247] saw that schools could provide the common ground where people could put down roots and grow together, within one small neighbourhood:

I have two measures of heart without which no republic can maintain its strength. (1) general education to enable every man to judge for himself what will secure or endanger his freedom. (2) to divide every county into hundreds, so that all children will be in reach of a central school.

Jefferson was on the side of growth. Not size for its own sake. Not administrative empire-building, but down to earth in *the hundred* (the neighbourhood of a hundred families or so where people were used to fending for themselves and keeping the peace). He liked to get his hands dirty working with his flowers and vegetables. He cared most about *cultivation*, the process by which a patch of ground becomes fruitful.

Going for the hundreds — not thousands or millions at a time — meant getting to the roots of good government. Not in isolation. Not exclusions zones. Simply places where people could feel at home; and with luck and perseverance feel at home with each other; sharing their experience and on occasion their feelings, too. Fellow-feelings: which slowly or suddenly bring about a change of mind. Enough is Enough!

In the State of Massachusetts, where the American Revolution was born, there were none of the great slave-owning estates that had been planted in the South. The countryside was dotted with small townships and villages where farmers and shopkeepers met on level terms, in the church or the alehouse. They provided the Minute Men, who worried Gentleman Johnnie Burgoyne, volunteers who undertook to get together at a minute's notice to defend the community.

(Their right to bear arms, built into the US Constitution, had little to do with the arguments put forward by today's Gun Lobby. It wasn't primarily for personal protection, or to make a man feel macho, or to hold the rest of society at bay, or to fatten the profits of the small arms industry. The right to bear arms was the right to participate in the revolution which had been won because people got together, arming themselves as best they could to defeat the mercenary armies brought over by the British, and to create a new government of their own.)

Their power (not just their fire-power) lay in their loyalties to each other, to people they knew as, roughly, their equals. They allowed, a bit reluctantly, that this could extend to the top brass and the high command. As independent-minded neighbours they combined forces to defeat the first world-wide Great Power.

Their folk heroes — their moving spirits — who took horse and rode through enemy-occupied country to mobilise volunteers through a network of other neighbourhoods were Paul Revere, a middle-aged silversmith, and later, Sybil Luddington, 16 years old, borrowing her father's best horse, Star, riding post-haste, like a courier from Kublai Khan [p237].

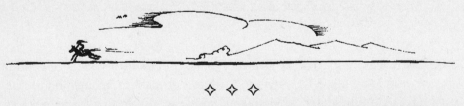

✧ ✧ ✧

Jefferson's idea of the school and the hundred made schools the nodes, the cross-over points, the knots in the network — each little neighbourhood tied in with the others.

As strong and as flexible as chain mail.

Does that still apply in our day? If it doesn't, could it?

Mixtures

Schools then were natural meeting places, as they still are in America where parents reckon the way the school is run needs to be watched as least as closely as the way the garbage is collected.

Elsewhere in the world the dividing lines between school insiders and everyone outside are sharper. In some UK schools there used to be a white line painted across the playground, beyond which parents were not allowed to venture when they came to fetch their children. It's better now, since the government (for dubious party political reasons of its own) decided to weaken local councils by transferring power to parent-governors.

The governors are still getting wise to their higher status, and may find themselves thinking and talking gobbledegook, speaking of children as AWPUs (*Age Weighted Pupil Units* whose education attracts more government funding as they gain grades and progress towards the sixth form — all at the expense of those little beggars in the Reception Class whose entry to school life is often crucial to the way they look on themselves and the rest of the world, ever after).

Getting in the money. What could possibly matter more? Three examples to be going on with:

● On Merseyside, one Middle School Head, seeing what a local *Planning for Real* [p129] scheme was doing for the adult community, decided to introduce his staff to a schools version in which we drew heavily on the techniques developed in the *Living Space* [p88] experiments. Reaction from the Maths and English and History and Geography and Science teachers: *Sorry Headmaster, can't possibly spare the class time.*

So, regretfully, he settled for the two classes which didn't really matter so much, Reception and Remedial (for the kids who couldn't keep up). Three weeks after the start of term the Head left a message asking me to visit the school. I turned up thinking something had gone wrong. Quite the opposite. He took me to a spare classroom in which the neighbourhood model made by those two classes was laid out. The walls were covered with maps, graphs and house designs, interspersed with written transcriptions of tape recordings the children had made when (as part of the project briefing) they went to interview the older generation to find out what things used to be like, and what scope there might be now for improvements.

All this just the work of the Reception and Remedials? No, they did their share, but the word had got round and the other teachers had involved their own classes in *number work*, and *spatial recognition*, and *language development*, and *social awareness*, because with the help of the children's example they had tumbled to the fact that the study of the neighbourhood meant that they were not only practising the skills they were trying to teach, but making them relevant.

The interviews that went on, back home and with neighbours next door, also helped to bring about a sort of ripple effect in the catchment area of the school; people liked to be asked about their feeling and memories, and the changes they wanted to come about in the neighbourhood as a whole. Youngsters and oldies got a fresh view of each other.

● In Glasgow, early in 1996 during the Islamic fast and festival of Ramadan, David Gordon the Headmaster of a secondary school with a large proportion of Muslim children decided to make a token fast himself, and to encourage other non-Muslims to join in as a way of getting across the Islamic idea of self-denial and concern for the needs of others. Ramadan and what it stood for became a focal point for the whole school and a step towards bridging the suspicions and enmities outside it.

"Senior students, where their suspicions were just based on ignorance, were genuinely moved. We already had a multi-racial committee — now we made the jump from tolerating other kinds of people to sharing with them. People have stopped talking about each other as 'Them'. Pupils have actually begun to motivate the staff in some ways, to ease them out of prejudice which they hardly realised was there, subliminal feelings.

We've been able to celebrate together.

That's really important if we're going to get schools opening themselves out to the rest of the community. We're bringing parents in, at first just to see their children at work. That's a halfway house to getting parents to help, — hearing children read for instance, — so that teachers have more time and scope to take the children further. We have to create a triangle of strength: teachers — pupils — parents."

● A junior school in Chapeltown, in the heart of the multi-racial district in Leeds: some mums were bringing their school age children to the school, and gossiping when they came back to collect them in the afternoon, coping with the toddlers they had to bring with them. One bright spark propositioned the Head and secured the use of a vacant classroom where they could all sit together and maybe use a handy gas ring to make a cup of tea.

So they started meeting, and instead of going home in the mornings, some of them stayed around, with occasional interruptions to do the shopping. Then they thought it might be an idea to have a snack together. The gas ring came into use as they took turns to make a proper meal, curry one day, sweet and sour another, in between a scouse or a Lancashire hotpot. Variety is the spice of life. Nobody needed to sound off about inter-racial co-operation. The toddlers played around, the parents talked and someone mentioned that on Saturday afternoons you could buy eggs cheap in the market if they were cracked. So the *Cracked Eggs Co-op* took shape, with someone going down to bulk buy, on the group's behalf; — eggs first, soon after, cheap cuts of meat. An object lesson in home economics.

Nothing to do with schooling, you might say, but a lot to do with what schools are partly for: discovering and enjoying what it is that makes people different. Not just tolerance, appreciation. *Vive la différence!* as the little boy and the little girl in the French cartoon said to each other when they looked inside each other's bathing trunks and made comparisons. Discovering new resources; learning how to make the most of what is available to suit what people need; and having a bit of fun in the process.

✧ ✧ ✧

Why all this fuss about schools? They've taken some knocks over the past twenty years — from Black Paper academics, from government, from the media, from some parents, and not least from many children who show their feelings by playing up or opting out.

But stand back for a moment and take a hard nosed business look at the school as a resource:

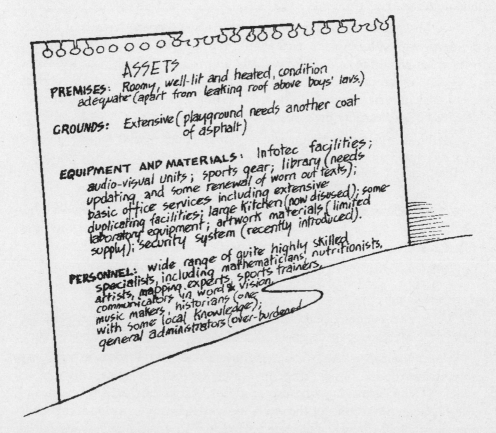

Ripe for takeover?

Not on your life, say the hard-pressed teachers. *Well, not in school hours,* say the administrators. And outside hours available resources should be reserved for out-of-school clubs — *Wish there were more of them but we're short staffed, and a bit tired.* Sure, there is a real need for a whole range of motivating, body-building, mind-blowing activities for the under-achievers and the latch key kids; let alone the bright ones who get bored with marking time in order to slow down to the pace of the average children, and are liable to throw over the traces and be up to devilry for want of something lively and challenging to stretch them a bit.

The needs are there but there's a limit to what staff can be expected to spare on top of government form-filling and marking scripts, and assessment meetings, — and, oh yes, of course, teaching in class, trying against the odds to imbue the children with the values, interests and enthusiasms teachers have, or had once before it all got too much.

So the physical resources, outside school hours, tend not to be fully exploited. (Besides, where's the money coming from to pay the caretaker's overtime?) And all those expert human resources seem strangely to be over-stretched and under-used.

Yet those teachers and administrators are also shoppers, tenants or householders, commuters, users and sometimes providers of entertainment, concerned about the care of the very old and the very young, worried about drugs and crime and the spoiling of the environment, exasperated by political confidence tricksters, turned off by talking shops, afraid that things in general may be taking a turn for the worse.

All this they have in common with the families and the next door neighbours of the children they teach.

Schools matter not for what many of them are at present, but for what most of them could be, and some are already. More than any other institution in modern society, schools are, potentially, powerhouses for change.

Three good reasons to be going on with; a fourth comes later.

1. Meeting point

A school is neutral ground where people rub shoulders, swap experience, voice concerns. It lets us get acquainted, comparing notes, glimpsing possibilities.

Most of us tend to be very cautious about what we let ourselves in for. So it's important to be able to size things up — and that includes getting wise to each other — without making any rash promises. But you can't help seeing and hearing about what some of those moving spirits are up to, inside and outside the school itself. And when they are getting on with things that obviously need doing, and you are not asked to make long-term commitments — it becomes the sociable thing to join in.

The time? Well, it's actually there, buried beneath the everyday frustrations and self-doubts that turn human beings into couch potatoes.

Parents find themselves joining an informal class, outside school hours, where they can pick up tips on how to help their children back at home with the 3 Rs; perhaps becoming a bit more literate and a bit more numerate themselves in the process.

They may even be allowed into the classroom (or the corridor outside) to hear children read or to thread needles and help them sew. They come out on to the playing field to do a bit of coaching. Some actually join the cast, paint the scenery and fix the lighting for the pantomime — teachers, parents, children all in it together. Others help with the 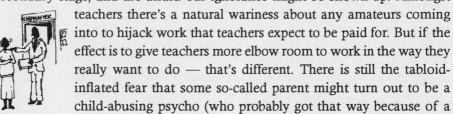 school garden, and the pets' corner over holidays and weekends. They go along on local visits to see how things in the neighbourhood compare with the way they used to be. They save up to go further afield on school trips abroad to sample other cultures, other attitudes.

Of course it doesn't all happen at once. Not by a long chalk. There's still that invisible white line that separates professionals — the teachers — from the rest of us. We feel a bit out of our depth, by the time our children are at the secondary stage, and are afraid our ignorance might be shown up. Amongst teachers there's a natural wariness about any amateurs coming into to hijack work that teachers expect to be paid for. But if the effect is to give teachers more elbow room to work in the way they really want to do — that's different. There is still the tabloid-inflated fear that some so-called parent might turn out to be a child-abusing psycho (who probably got that way because of a rotten up-bringing). But once the school becomes the sociable meeting place it deserves to be — there's safety in numbers, when it's people we all know and everyone is under everyone else's eye.

2. *Vantage point*

Schools set out to be more than force-feeders of the 3 Rs and a mish-mash of useful information about getting on in the world. That basic knowledge is the necessary bread-and-butter of everyday life. It's not a body and mind builder.

Finding Out is what we all get used to doing at school, though the danger is that the habit wears off. For children it's about *thinking,* not just looking information up in books. It's drawing conclusions from first-hand observation: rainfall, traffic counts, animal and insect behaviour. And in collaboration with others outside the school it could extend a little further — traffic danger spots, garbage collection, shopping services, local transport, the distances old people have to go to find a chemist when they want to fill their doctor's prescription.

Schools draw their sustenance from their own neighbourhoods — the everyday experience of buying and selling, communicating, getting from A to B.

So there is scope for fact-finding about the place as it is — good bad and indifferent; and as it could be.

School is there to offer an independent perspective: to feed our curiosity and our inborn capacity to ask usefully awkward questions; to sharpen our vision of the new world around us and of the old world we inherit; to develop the intellectual muscle for all kinds of demanding creativity: writing letters, stories, songs, poems, plays; making pictures, designing clothes, furnishings, menus, team-play and computer programs; finding out facts and weighing them up — as scientists, mathematicians, debaters, historians, geographers, home economists. *Seeing oursels as ithers see us,* understanding our own humanity.

We need this perspective, and these insights, to see through shoddy art and dodgy logic. To be less often bamboozled by slick advertising and headline journalism. To steer clear of the blinkered thinking of religious fundamentalists, the racists' twisted patriotism, the Party spin-doctors' manipulation of our hopes and fears.

In all this — getting a better idea of what *work* really means when it's not just a bread-and-butter job; sorting out what needs to be done *Now, Soon or Later,* [p134] deciding who's going to do it; marshalling the evidence before jumping to conclusions. Bringing to bear our common sense.

When these habits of thinking spread inside school, children tend to carry the contagion home. And it works the other way too, enriching what goes on in school with the hard graft of family comment and experience, back home.

3. Power base

There's more to this than cultivating a generalised, sanitised, detached view of the rest of society and what *other* people should be doing about it.

As parents, along with other residents, we start taking stock: not just of the way the school runs, but of the long-term purpose it serves — preparing the next generation to cope with change, get a livelihood, feel both adventurous and secure, make a go of the lifetime left to them.

We can see what needs doing, pronto, about our immediate surroundings; we can feel what is missing in our quality of life; we can judge the shortcomings of the systems that society runs on.

Or to put it bluntly, we can all get together and have a good old moan.

But that's where the moving spirits come in to make the crucial difference. Somewhere among those parents clustered at the entrance waiting to fetch their children; and among the teachers and administrators taking a coffee break; there are those moving spirits who see what is going on, recognise danger/opportunities and don't turn their heads away.

The inner strength of a local school as Maria Montessori [p82] discovered in the San Lorenzo slum is that it is one of the few institutions which belong to the community[1] — parents and children in the first place, but in the long run others too. Young singles; middle-aged with their life skills and experience still intact, but no longer in demand; elderly on the shelf before their time. There are common concerns, not just about the children's present life styles and future prospects, but about opportunities to widen one's own horizon, catch up on the way others find enjoyment and increase their range. Maybe even join a club or sign on to an evening class.

Underlying this heightened interest it's possible to see that we have a common cause as well as common ground: between us we could be, should be, doing something now about our immediate future, not just the children's, but our own, since events are moving so fast that the next decade or so may decide whether we have a future at all.

There is a deal waiting to be made: between the school people and the rest of the neighbourhood. It's OK. Teachers (and their unions) begin to recognise that parents' help is worth having and can be accepted without giving any footholds for the government's hatchet-men. The moving spirits (on both sides) establish the principle that the school, accepting the help offered it, owes the community something in return.

Parents and some of the children are allowed to use the school's duplicating gear at weekends (with insurance cover and something extra for the caretaker) to produce a community broadsheet — their version of Chrissie Maher's *Tuebrook Bugle* [p22] with news, views, sports tips, niggles, corny jokes and cartoons. They run off the enquiry forms for residents' own house-to-house, face-to-face *Neighbourhood Talent Survey* [p132] (collated and analysed on the school's computer; results displayed graphically to all comers with the help of the Art Department). They stage a *Planning for Real* event coupled with a Fun/Fund-raising Day in the school grounds to muster practical support for things that can be done, inside or outside school, without waiting for the bureaucrats.

The bureaucrats, so-called, can be brought into the act. Local Education Officers are obliged to meet school staffs, see children at work, and increasingly,

---

1...Apart from those schools which opt out in order to meet the demands of the well-to-do, or of members of exclusive religious sects; both imposing a self-inflicted apartheid on themselves and their children — cutting them off from the chance to mix in and make the most of other kinds of people. As yet, thank goodness, these deprived schools are only a minority and with luck such children will one day be reunited with the rest of our children in schools with enough resources to allow for — and celebrate — differences in background and varieties of skill and ability.

come to terms with parents. They know all about the workings of local government and the routes through the administration labyrinth. So there are the makings of a better understanding of what the bureaucrats (poor things) are really up against; as well as what they and their colleagues in other departments might come across with, in the way of practical support, if they understood neighbourhood needs and opportunities better.

Meeting each other informally (round the *Planning for Real* model, for instance) it becomes easier for both sides to get used to each other, tap each other's resources of knowledge and experience, see the lie of the land.

Inside or outside the school premises, the moving spirits are having a stab at doing some of what's needed. They draw on the findings of the talent survey to recruit people with job or hobby interests to help run children's out-of-school activities (given up to three months delay while the tortoise-like police computer vets them for paedophiliac tendencies). They drum up customers for adults' sports and social activities (which produce the revenue needed to pay the caretaker's overtime). They follow Roxbury's [p148] example and do something drastic about the unofficial garbage tips; maybe clear a derelict site for a five-a-side. They borrow a minibus and go off to see what others are up to: a self-build housing scheme like Lightmoor [p43] an energy-saving domestic insulation project, home safety installations for the elderly, a women's refuge from alcohol-abusing macho males (and maybe an alcoholics' group where they can sort themselves out), a parents and toddlers' group that runs its own bulk-buying scheme [p262]. They give a fresh face to a boring wall with a multi-coloured murals [p136-7]. The school gets a reputation: it's a hive of activity, a source of fun-and-games as good as honey. And its pollinating bees go far and wide to help bring other schemes to fruition.

Schools aren't the only starting point. They just happen to be within reach; and can gradually be won over to the idea of becoming the heart and soul of the community. Other institutions with deep local roots, like some Settlements and some outward-looking religious bodies, can do much the same. Or, as it turned

out when Chrissie Maher and her friends got going, one small initiative by a handful of determined housewives turns into a cluster of others — the gobbledegook translation centre, the anti-rubbish and the playground campaigns, the *Tuebrook Bugle* itself — a web of activity which draws in many sorts of people.

People getting together locally to confront or win over a local authority may achieve great things, at micro level on their own patch. Not all at once, but bit by bit, according to whatever concern comes uppermost and impels someone to say *Enough is Enough!*, make the first move, and get others joining in. They stop a school being closed, they hang on to a local post office, they get road plans altered to calm local traffic or make life difficult for kerb-crawlers [p131]. They link up with local producers of crops and livestock [p220]. They persuade the authority's Economic Development Unit that there are local enterprises to be developed by collecting usable waste for recycling, they set up a LETS scheme [p50] to swap skills within the neighbourhood, they organise a Credit Union [see Appendix 3] or a Rastafarian Pardner Fund or a Grameen Bank [p221] to keep money circulating within the community instead of subsidising national banks or local loan sharks.

Loads of possibilities and they need not be intimidating. It's just a matter of lending a hand for the time being. Not getting committed for life and burning out in the process. But small scale involvement, with a bit of fun thrown in, gets to be *addictive*.

That's where the power lies.

 **16**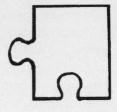

Mind blowing

This chapter fits together more jigsaw pieces which have figured earlier in the book. For those who have dipped and skipped, there are bracketed page references to check back.

Power? *Neighbourhood power?* People beavering away, all over the world, to change their surroundings, re-structure their lives; and making some headway here and there, in spite of the obstacles.

But what does all that amount to compared with the systems which dominate? The multi-nationals shifting their weight and their workforces from continent to continent? The media moguls, psyching up their readers and viewers to back whatever trend happens, for the moment, to be commercially and politically profitable? The other kind of pushers, the drug cartels, turning the punters in on themselves, sapping the will? And, lagging behind in the power stakes, the politicians, anxiously trimming their policies to match the opinion polls?

We've all been brought up on stories of Jack the Giant Killer, and braw young David the shepherd boy who went down to the brook, picked five smooth stones, shook free his sling and with the first stone slew the armour-plated, earthshaking Goliath.

That was then, and maybe the stories have gained in the telling. This is now, when the giants and their systems shape the events which govern our lives. What are we compared with Them?

System failure

I was struggling with those last paragraphs as a rail passenger on the New England Express, speeding towards New York, trying to work out how to convince anyone that *Small* is not merely *Beautiful* in Schumacher's words — a local initiative that makes local sense — but is also a source of power, that could be world-shaking.

Then the train grinds to a sudden halt. The temperature rises. The lights go out and it gets dark. Nothing happens.

After sweating it out for an hour or so, the conductress comes along to tell us why. Some kids had thrown stones and hit an oil pipe which took the engine out, along with the public address system, the electric light and the air conditioning. In turn we held up half a dozen other mainline trains in Penn Station.

The knock-on effect.

(Whilst we waited for the relief engine to turn up and haul us in, my mind switched back to another train journey: a Japanese lorry fitted with railway wheels and hitched to four wagon loads of passengers; crossing the North China Plain during the Civil War, breaking down in bandit-ridden territory. No radio communication and anyhow no prospect of a relief. So we got out, upwards of 200 of us, and *pushed* our train back to the nearest strong point, where those with a mechanical bent helped the driver to strip down the engine and repair it, in peace.)

We've got used to depending on high-powered systems, world-wide, which keep on getting upset by things that the system builders didn't really bargain for. People react in exasperation, anger, anxiety, dismay: losing faith in those systems and in the people who operate them. Nothing spectacular apart from the occasional riot. Just a gradual rotting away of such links as there were in the neighbourhood until poor people, like the rich, wall themselves up behind bars of their own making, on the watch for the wild ones that roam the streets and get their own back on the rest of us, whichever way they can.

What's to do about that young stone thrower who stopped the locomotive in its tracks? Armour the train? Patrol the track? Seek out the teenager who did the damage? Not easy, maybe one in ten gets caught, and the authorities, bowing to the version of public opinion currently presented in the tabloids, *get their own back* on the delinquents by locking them up with others like-minded, who, the figures show, will probably reinforce their skills and their anti-social feelings, the urge to *get even*. (They already had it in for society when they discovered that their schooling was a confidence trick: preparing them for the *world of work* only to land them on the street corner or in the queue for short-term, dead-end jobs).

"Our biggest problem is fear — we close the doors and keep the children in. There is a culture of suspicion and fear and our own young people are so alienated that their only reaction to anything that happens — is violence".
Julie Fawcett, Chair, Stockwell Park Tenants' Association, South East London

"These are ordinary youngsters with time on their hands."
Councillor Barbara Graham, a governor at a North London comprehensive school, commenting on the teenagers who had invaded the school and attacked examination pupils with knives and broken bottles, in June 1996. Six months earlier the head teacher of a neighbouring school had been stabbed to death by youngsters when he intervened in a fight outside his school gates.

Tabloid headlines about FAMILY VALUES or YOUNG THUGS don't quite fit. The alternative? It happens, here and there. In Rodney Street, Jamaica, [p14] remember? Youngsters managed to get themselves some attention, to prove themselves, show their mettle by fixing up the place instead of tearing it apart. They got a hand, early on, from one or two of those moving spirits. They got some credit for what they were doing, and some job satisfaction. They're still vulnerable to invading gunmen and trigger-happy police. But in their own small neighbourhoods, at ground level, slowly the climate of opinion begins to change.

Small neighbourhoods. *Yes,* you might say, *We know that a few moving spirits can get others joining in the make a local impact. But that's not the same as moving mountains.*

In other times and places — Jefferson's America [pp247 & 259], Mao's and Jung Chang's China [p104], Oke's Biafra [p167], and even tousel-headed Billy Cooper's Rochdale [pp59 & 67] — local initiatives combined to change the social and economic map. For good or ill. Tributaries swelling the Yellow River to overflow its banks and devastate the countryside; or to power the turbines and irrigate the crops.

How is it going to be done, here and now?

History is made under the pressure of events, from the Black Death (which created a shortage of labourers — and shoved up the bargaining power of the survivors) to the Information Revolution (which provided electronic substitutes for people, and shoved it down again). We change our minds about ourselves and our surroundings. Either because we give up and yield to the pressure, or because we take a hand in pushing things along for ourselves. It all depends on that climate of opinion.

Mind sets

Another name for the climate of opinion is the *mind set* we have been brought up in: what we take for granted about ourselves and our surroundings. Mind sets vary. The native Red Indians of North America, like the Maoris of New Zealand, had a feeling for the land and the lakes and the rivers, as living space to be respected, enjoyed free-range, but not interfered with. Incoming Europeans saw it as territory to be occupied, fought over, bought and sold, cultivated and developed.

Mind sets are not set in concrete. Suddenly or slowly we find ourselves changing our minds, for better or worse. Granny thinks nothing of scorching down the motorway at rather more than 70; her own grandmother would have had a fit. Young couples nowadays live together and raise families without feeling that they are living in sin. And we have all been having *second*  *thoughts* about feeding sheep's brains to grass-eating cattle to make a killing for the factory farmer; as well as about rainforests, tower blocks, animal welfare, the pollution of land and sea and air.

The Great War, as people called it then, World War I as we know it now, took most people out of themselves, often out of their normal surroundings, made them feel at times heroic. But when it ended, the mind sets changed again. Heroism was out, in its place a kind of retreat. The New Jerusalem wasn't going to happen after all. Lawrence of Arabia, legendary desert leader, who could have swayed men's minds, despaired of them and chose instead to vanish from public life.

> *"When we achieved and the new world dawned, the old men came again and took from us our victory and remade it in the likeness of the former world we knew."*

Governments, usually reflecting the anxieties of the middle-aged and elderly, prefer to play it safe, damp things down, keep things stable. In Saxon times, priests and lawyers set down the *rectitudines singularum personarum*, to establish an order that was not meant to change. *Rights-and-duties* carefully balanced, rather like the *communitarianism* recently evolved by Amitai Etzioni and other American academics. When he met some of us, on a missionary visit to the UK, he explained this in terms of the bicycle: lean over too far on one side and you fall flat.

Fair enough, so far as that goes. But try balancing on a bike that stays still. Watch any roller blader weave and glide. It's the momentum that keeps us up and going.

We have to be on the move. The only alternative to being taking over by events is to take them over; and that's not easy.

Frame of mind

The changes being forced on us at this moment in history are mind-blowing. There's not much we can take for granted any longer. This is neither a minus nor a plus; it's a fact of evolution which happens, unlike any previous stage in history, to be breath-takingly sudden. How we react to it, whether we find this depressing or exhilarating, depends on our present *frame of mind*.

That's difficult to describe, but it's important nonetheless. It is to do with attitudes, how you react to the situation as you understand it. Cautious or adventurous; laid-back; up in arms; gung ho; or undecided.

The mind set is the collection of beliefs and assumptions on the strength of which we size up our situation. The frame of mind is what determines whether we actually *do* something about it; whether we become agents instead of victims; whether we take courage or take fright.

In the years between World Wars I and II, Germany defeated and deprived of many of the overseas possessions it had partly lived on, had six million unemployed. The Nazis were able to exploit the general disillusionment by shifting most of the blame on to the Jews. They reinforced the racist mind set that already existed, and then began to change the frame of mind. *Enough is Enough!* they said. *Don't put up with it any longer! Deutschland erwache! Wake up to a new view of your destiny.* That new view excused pogroms and concentration camps as necessary evils in the transformation of German society. It was that blind conviction that seized the minds of the youngsters I met in the Nazi school in Ilfeld [p233] and blocked the minds of their elders, living and working in Nordhausen next door to the death camp of Dora Mittelbau, on the road to Buchenwald.

When World War II broke out and the British Expeditionary Force was defeated in France and Belgium and Holland, and the air raids began, the people who sheltered by night in the church crypts and the railway arches and the warehouse basements, had also begun to change their frame of mind. They responded to the government's exhortations to GO TO IT, but they put their main trust in each other, and found in places like *Paddy's Goose* [p210] that they had a kind of solidarity, a belief in themselves, a communal strength.

So too did the Jews, survivors of persecution, returning to the lands where their ancestors had lived, setting up their State of Israel in the teeth of local opposition and outside invasion. And in their turn, so too did the Palestinians, the locals, who found out the hard way how to fight back, not with conventional forces but by boycotts and guerrilla war.

So too did young Chinese like Jung Chang — the generation that grew up after their parents had brought about the Communist Revolution, needing credit and status of their own, dancing their way through Beijing [p114] to celebrate the cleansing of the city sewer. Later on, as Red Guards [p116] responding to Mao's appeal to *cleanse* the State of *counter-revolutionaries*. So too have the student dissidents of the '80s and '90s, risking persecution in order to promote a change of mind.

From acquiescence to intervention

We can be high-minded, or bloody-minded. Self-sacrificing or pulling the place apart. Or both together. The critical change is to move from acceptance — acquiescence in things as they are, to intervention — making change.

Remember Spencer Chapman and the Malayan jungle? [p3] What made the

difference between death and survival was not the physical surroundings — the jungle itself was neutral.
What mattered was the attitude of mind:

> Go on or go under.
> Get together or go it alone.

Nothing new about these conditions of survival. And not all that much
difference between the basic concerns that occupy our minds today and those
that bugged us when we lived in caves.

**Civilisations aren't created by the pronouncements of an oracle through
the mouths of its priestly spin-doctors; or by Act of Parliament. They grow
out of people's needs and resources, and the wit to put the two together.**

Go back a few inches on the timescale to those cave-dwellers. A clutch of
males and females, old and young, sheltering together against seen and unseen
dangers, concerned about food, weather, warmth and the kids. Finding that you
can't get far without coming to terms with the bunch in the cave next door.
Dimly aware of forces outside themselves which may, perhaps, be won over,
controlled. Immediately concerned with the here and now, but drawing inspiration with the help of poets and singers who tell of things past and foretell what
could happen, maybe, in the future.

It's the singers and poets, and in our days also the radio and television writers
and producers who may open our eyes to what is going on. But it's the moving
spirits, without much in the way of rhetoric or charisma, who *get up* (as the Igbos
[p197] would say) and **show** what could be done.

Seeing for ourselves

Showing what could be done means seeing for yourself how to do it. Most
of us are better placed to do this than we realise. So far as our surroundings are
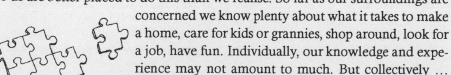 concerned we know plenty about what it takes to make
a home, care for kids or grannies, shop around, look for
a job, have fun. Individually, our knowledge and experience may not amount to much. But collectively …
Getting together, comparing notes, the jigsaw pieces begin to
fall into place. We can see what *could be* done about the neighbourhood, as a whole.

Neighbourhoods, yes. Livelihoods — the way we earn a living when we get
the chance? Surely that has to be left to the experts?

Not entirely. Where do those experts get their knowledge? Marketing advisors, productivity experts, management consultants — they earn their keep for
the most part by fitting together the information they glean piecemeal from the
people on the shopfloor, or in the research lab; plus what can be learned from
the people who might buy the end product.

They have to do a lot of consulting — asking around — before they can be any use as consultants — advising us what's best. The process begins to look suspiciously like someone who borrows your watch in order to tell you the time

Dead end

Take that part of most national economies which gets maximum attention these days: the 'defence' industry. In World War II it mopped up every spare worker who could be found. Afterwards the victors kept arms production going full blast, even expanded it, on the strength of the fears each drummed up about the others. The arms, and arms-making equipment went to any government, however corrupt, which could be aligned as an ally or a satellite.

When the Cold War petered out the more 'respectable' governments, on either side, had to face the fact that the arms trade they had built up had become part of the job-creating economy. Just like the slave trade [p197] used to be. But the arms stock-piled for self-defence produce no profits, just gigantic debts. And much of the weaponry for export has gone to governments needing them to maintain their grip on increasingly restive populations, who can't be relied on to carry on buying from us, once they take over.

Short term profits, bought at the expense of long term disasters. What's needed is some creative thinking in the work place, to bring the arms industry out of the Dark Ages, re-structure it, give it a new identity — without shedding thousands of jobs in the process.

Message from the shop floor:

We can produce Concorde, but not enough heaters for all the old age pensioners who die of cold every year …. We have a chronic shortage of all kinds of equipment to improve the quality of life. We have building workers on the dole, whilst there is a shortage of houses and schools. We have engineers on the dole when there is a shortage of simple urban heating systems and we've electricians on the dole when we need all kinds of transport systems that could make it possible to use the cities we've built …

In the Willesden Plant of Lucas Aerospace where I work we are …. working out a complete programme of alternative products which we would make in the event of a cut back in our traditional products, and we want these products to be socially useful … We are establishing a science and technology advisory service and corporate planning committees at national level to examine in detail what skills are available, and what means of production exist and above all what alternative work we could do that would be of direct use to the community.

The response — mainly from the technologists — has been amazing. We've got over 150 products on which we could be working in the event of redundancy. We have drawn up a corporate plan which embodies those, including radical proposals for retraining our people to perceive problems in the community — rather than just thinking in the narrow technological way in which they have been trained to deal with design and engineering problems ... We have in mind ... an integrated road/rail system with a lightweight flexible vehicle ... its power unit, also applicable to city cars, consists of a quiet, small internal combustion engine which, through a generator, charges the batteries continuously. Pollution would be reduced by 80% ... and the fuel consumption would be down by 50%.

We are talking about automatic fire fighting equipment ... wind power... and a whole range of proposals in the medical field...

Just the sort of creative thinking top management should provide. Should have provided long ago. *Top management* is a bit misleading. It gets applied to the people who manage the money the firm is making — looking after their share-holders' keen interest in a nice steady income, with a fast buck whenever it's safe to gamble.

Those detailed, technologically sound proposals were worked out over twenty years ago. Not by the top management but by those who managed to *make* the company's products — middle management, shop stewards, researchers, ideas people. They came together in the combined shop stewards' committee convened by Mike Cooley which covered all 17 Lucas Aerospace sites in the UK.

Top management's mindset, in spite of years of pressure, remained unaltered. It even tried to sell off their kidney machine production division because it was *not compatible* with the traditional product range. The trade union membership in the plant threatened industrial action and saved the product; but it could not cure top management's tiny minds.

Working it out together

Mike Cooley and his fellow shop stewards were ahead of their time. Their achievement wasn't to turn round the arms industry overnight, but to show that when people on the shop floor put their minds to it, and their heads together, they could come up with a collective answer that made sense then; never more so than now.

The way they pieced things together provides a working model which others can use, in their own way, to sort out the changes that need to be made in all sorts of out-dated organisations. They created a network of thought and action.

This is what most moving spirits eventually achieve. They begin on a very small scale, like Chrissie Maher [p20] on Merseyside, or the likely lads in T'oad Lane Rochdale (p59) in the 1840s or in Hull Giroscope [p70] in the 1980s and '90s. But what begins small, if it's thought out properly, can catch on.

There are also moving spirits among some of those professionals who stand clear of the rest of the community, as

 academics or government people. Arif Hassan [pp161 & 219] architect, helping to set up street working parties to build new sewers, lane by lane, in Karachi. Muhammad Yunus [p221] university teacher, handing out thirty dollars as the first Grameen Bank loan. Both working with students they managed to enthuse and involve. And that Right Hand Man at the centre of the bureaucratic web at Birkenhead [p144] who managed to leapfrog departmental barriers and make some of his fellow officers, in local and central government, for a while, see sense.

Working models

Those moving spirits are concerned with working models, pilot schemes which show how to go about tapping buried resources; Not only where to sink the oil drills, but also how best to refine the crude oil — by hard and sometimes bitter experience — and make it workable for light and power.

Locally, we begin to see the value of our time, our imagination, our understanding of each other and what makes us tick. We can see what needs doing, and that some of it is do-able, here and now, without waiting for the rest of the world to pay the living it owes us. The first covered-in sewage pipe in Karachi or the brand new houses self-built by the women of Langa [p224] in South Africa or the first barefoot village school created by BRAC [p81] in Bangladesh, and that makeshift Co-op in T'oad Lane — are there for real. Jeered at, perhaps, at first; but before long beginning to challenge imitation. **The locality is a proving ground**: *Will it work as well elsewhere? — maybe we should try it and see.*

So far, so good. But that may still leave most of the initiative on the shoulders of those few moving spirits whose frame of mind has always been pretty positive.

What about the rest of us, the born spectators? We can see, more or less, what needs doing. But we've always taken it for granted that it's up to someone else — whoever we choose to vote in — to do it on our behalf; or if they fail, to be grumbled at and replaced at the next Election.

It's that mind set again. There's the feeling that action, especially collective action, is *not on*. For those *activists*, the would-be giantkillers, yes, perhaps; but not for us normal people. Activity, on the other hand, is alright — support at the football match, or attendance, upwards of a million a week, at a rave — but it doesn't do to get *involved*.

Wait a minute. What's a rave if it's not an invitation to join in? So one way to begin might be to stage a fun happening that sparks the imagination, and sets people thinking (with the adrenalin of getting together to make things happen instead of the drugs required to keep everyone bobbing up and down, marking time through the night hours).

In July 1996 between five and seven thousand youngish people *Reclaiming the Streets* had a party to occupy a strip of the M41 motorway and undercover of the enormous skirt of a 25ft high fun figure drilled a hole in the road (the sound drowned by loud P.A. music) to plant some small trees as a symbolic reminder of the leafy thoroughfares that used to be.

Two months earlier four hundred British volunteers followed the example of the Diggers in 1649 who occupied St. George's Hill in Surrey to dig and sow, proclaiming that *the earth is a common treasury.* They cele-brated May Day 1996 (spelling it May DIY) with a squat in 13 acres of an abandoned distillery site in Wandsworth, South London; bringing their gardening and carpentry tools and a lorry-load of materials to build temporary homes and begin to farm the land. A demonstration — *This Land is Ours* — to contrast the common sense of using vacant land to house the homeless with the idiocy of 700,000 hectares of land still lying derelict in Britain.

Linking up

This is the moment when it makes sense to go a step or two further. To create *structures* which can act on behalf of most of those *ad hoc* schemes, to strengthen their bargaining power whenever deals are necessary with the outside world. The main thing is that people agree on a convenient framework for action: short-term or long-term.

✔ *A combined operation, one-off:* some forty Argentinean housewives living far apart from each other arranged that each should go to her nearest point on the riverbank, fill a jam jar with water, and get it analysed by the nearest chemist, so that between them they could demonstrate the extent of the pollution carried downstream from a local factory.

✔ *A time-limited company* — formed so that one particular job can be seen through, and be accountable for whatever is needed (people, materials, money) against an agreed deadline; and then wind itself up.

✔ *A community of enquiry* which sets questions and brings together the findings of community workers in many different areas, to tease out a particular problem — alienated youngsters for instance — and to test out possible solutions.

✔ *A Community Forum*, open to all groups and individuals living locally, which becomes a clearing house for bright ideas, complaints, information about local resources and requirements and how they might be met perhaps through a LETS system. It displays the findings of the *Neighbourhood Talent Survey* so that everyone recognises the wealth of skills and experience waiting to be tapped.

✔ *A Community Development Trust*, probably promoted by the Forum, with local representatives elected under the eye of an independent outside body. They set up a neighbourhood consultation (perhaps a *Planning for Real*) which sorts out possibilities, establishes a broad agreement on priorities and gives the Trust a head start in negotiating on the neighbourhood's behalf.

✔ *Negotiation from strength* as when the North Kensington Amenity Trust forged an agreement with the highways people so that in return for putting up with through traffic on the overhead Westway, the community was funded to develop a thriving market place for local enterprises, using the road as a canopy.

These structures take shape to suit local ways of doing things. That's part of their strength. If they are any good it's because local people see them as a direct expression of everyone's overriding concerns. Within each structure the various groups can function in their own sweet ways, not dependent on the others, but linking up whenever it's useful to make common cause.

Those links form the chain mail, flexible, strong, not easily damaged by ego-tripping at ground level or crafty manipulation from above.

Ad hoc

At first it's all small change. Everything is done on its own. That's a plus, not a minus.

Ad hoc means *for a specific purpose*. Each job is an end in itself. No messing about. It's tailor-made, custom-built, to suit the way people want to work with each other. It doesn't have to fit into some VIP's comprehensive Master Plan; so it may get a disparaging look from those who love block diagrams and can only think in generalisations.

A small-scale immediately practicable local initiative is unlikely to need a lot of advance preparation. It doesn't give anyone a power base. It makes the most of initial impulse. There are few if any bureaucratic hoops to go through. As the Rodney Street Raiders [p14] showed it's not all that difficult to raise what little money might be needed by having a whip round (or a Domino Bash, or a bingo session, or a sponsored Karate endurance test, or even a jumble sale). So, one after another, things begin to happen. Mostly they are visible. Seeing them every day, or displaying snapshots someone took at the time, hearing about similar efforts that others have made elsewhere — begins to change mind sets.

We're making waves....

Many small waves that come and go (not all those projects continue once the main objective is realised). But we're stagnant no longer.

That's the inside view. Now look through the eyes of an outside investor — a central or a local government agency, a charity, a commercial developer.

What any hard-nosed financial manager insists on is *growth and security*: the prospect that whatever money and facilities are put into the community won't just waste away, but will fund something that has its own strength and staying power.

People in the neighbourhood are seen to be on the move. Even though that consists of many, very small-scale initiatives, they are creating their own motivating power.

The mind set is changing: it becomes the in-thing to be in, not out. More people are concerned to safeguard what they have begun to achieve. All that adds up to what could be called *community collateral*. There's more long-term security, less risk.

Simply from that hard-nosed financial manager's viewpoint this investment of time and commitment by the insiders is what makes an outsider's investment worthwhile. More important, the insiders themselves are discovering their own strength, their bargaining power: first their time and their commonsense; then, gradually, their growing knowledge of the way things *could be*.

Time is bankable

The time required to turn society around and get it back on the right track is OUR time, and its value can be measured.

It's a long-term investment which in the long run overtakes the boom-and-bust short-term profit-taking of the money marketeers and the arms salesmen. Time which could be invested in jobs that really need doing. Time that could be spared whilst industries re-tool.

And how is it to be paid for?

Governments have survived so far by relying on the never-never, paying high interest to fat cats at home and abroad to cover the cost of past wars and present unemployment. The spin-doctors' term for each year's potential addition to this National Debt is the *Public Sector Borrowing Requirement*.

There's a limit to what any government can get away with before the interest payments on the Debt become too heavy to be borne any longer.

The money runs out; but the time is still there. Time unspent. If there's no money to buy that time, cash on the nail, it will have to be borrowed from those who own it. There's a **Public *Lending* Requirement**: the time and commitment invested by us on our joint behalf.

On what terms?

Some of us, with time on our hands, may put it into the community for love, or kicks. But later on, just keeping things going may demand a bit more than purely voluntary effort can sustain. Time can be traded through a LETS system allowing each person to be credited for the time they contribute with time they can draw on from someone else. Skills themselves can be enhanced from within the community: *I'll teach someone to bake bread if someone else will teach me car maintenance or book-keeping or drums.* Space can be traded — use of a room for meetings, or part of a garden for growing vegetables. So can materials — *Swap you a hundred bricks for your pressure cooker?*

We have a formula for this internal investment. Put in a N.U.T.S.H.E.L.L. it goes:

Neighbourhood Use of Time and Space
for Homes, Environment, Livelihood and Leisure

Pat Conaty and I came up with this in an early collaboration between the Neighbourhood Initiatives Foundation and the Money Advice service he was running at the Birmingham Settlement. Since then, in the course of launching the Aston Reinvestment Trust he has been fitting together the jigsaw bits to show how the process of **re-building** society can take shape. More on this in the Tool kit in Appendix 1.

Some people are far too busy on their own affairs to spare working time for the community. Good luck to them. If they prefer not to give time to parenting they can pay through the nose for an au pair or a childminder or a boarding school. They can buy their own housing, private transport, medical attention. In turn it is part of the deal that they pay full whack in income tax and contributions to everyone else's health insurance. Meanwhile others choosing to invest some of their time for the general benefit can have it calculated and credited to them. Tax breaks now, pension and insurance advantages later; maybe cash credits deferred (like the post-war credits in World War II) until after the present war on want is won.

This is the point at which government comes in; or perhaps prefers to stay clear. There have to be adjustments to laws and regulations. And it's all going to be *very difficult*, according to Them.

Us and Them

This Us and Them business needs reconsidering. Perhaps with the help of another parable from the immortal works of Laurel and Hardy which I first mentioned at the beginning of this book.

After, or maybe before they got involved with the jigsaw [p8] in that penthouse flat, they found themselves unexpectedly in charge of a large white horse which was feeling poorly. They got expert advice on administering suitable medication, in the form of a pill which had to be propelled down the horse's throat by blowing down a tube like an enormous pea-shooter. Stan Laurel, of course, gets the assignment: inserts the pill in the tube; puts it to the horse's mouth; prepares for action.

Mind-boggling pause. Harrowing gulp. Stan explains:

"The horse blew first."

Taking it at face-to-face value this is an argument for pre-emptive action, getting in first. But wait a minute. Just where do our sympathies lie? Is the horse representing Us or Them?

The old mind set assumed a trial of strength between Us in our small corner, at the receiving end, and Them, the providers, bungling the job, getting blamed for failing to deliver what we reckon we are entitled to as voters and taxpayers.

Most of us have put up reluctantly so far with whatever government we are lumbered with because there doesn't seem to be much to be done about it. *Let them get on with it!* (aka *Laissez faire!*). You change the caretakers every few years at a General Election but the place remains a dump.

The temptation is to reject the lot — get away from it all in a tax haven or a cult commune; or tear the place apart for the hell of it like a bunch of lager louts; or bulldoze everything that grows and turn the site into a shopping mall or a private car-park.

That's one side of the medal: people wanting to steer clear, fence themselves in, declare an exclusion zone. Pull up the ladder and let the others rot. After all, *self- interest, that's human nature, isn't it?*

On the other side, governments seldom dare to stick their necks out. They respond to pressure, when they have to. The strongest pressures, until now, have been from particular interests — oil, arms, the road lobby, nuclear power, factory farming, tobacco, the money market, the packaging industry — all claiming to be acting in the public interest; but turning out to be something rather different. All aiming to fence government in, keep it away from *interfering* with the market economy.

Appeasing greed

Non-intervention as a policy goes back at least to the Priest and the Levite passing by on the wrong side of the Jerusalem-Jericho road [p251]. It got serious political treatment by Prime Minister Neville Chamberlain (a pre-war version of John Major) who gave it an extra spin by making up to the Nazi and Fascist dictators, allowing them free rein in the hopes that they wouldn't bite back.

Today's governments are equally anxious to buy off the powerful — in this case the rich and even the moderately well-to-do — on the mistaken assumption that those who make, say, £30,000 a year are just as *rapacious* (to use Adam

Smith' word [p193] and Disraeli's [p61]) as those who get away with ten times as much. All such voters must be *appeased*.

This underestimates most people's capacity to make personal sacrifices for the sake of a better future for themselves and their children — once they see what's really involved.

A new kind of bargaining begins to take place. *We'll make and mend our neigh-bourhoods as best we can*, making existing resources stretch further with the time and effort we put in; *always provided that government responds*: tackles (with our backing) our concerns according to our priorities. And hands down some of the decision making. **If we have a hand in spending our money on the things that really matter to us, we'll put up with the taxes that are needed to see the job through.**

It's what Rousseau (who was probably top of Jefferson's and Tom Paine's reading lists) called the *Social Contract*.

Suppose there were a serious effort to transform the arms industry on the lines worked out by Mike Cooley and his fellow shop stewards in Lucas Aerospace? Or to allow farmers to think far enough ahead to accept less short-term profit so as to preserve the fertility of their land and the quality of their livestock? Or to wean the packaging industry from creating rubbish mountains by wrapping everything up and tarting it up so that we are all conned into thinking that there's more inside, and better, than there really is (— suppose those resources were diverted into more learning materials, bright and easy to handle, for toddlers, schoolchildren, apprentices, adults with learning difficulties?)

Don't look at me, **says Government,** *Think of the economic chaos which would result, the loss of jobs! People just wouldn't stand for it!* **Public opinion can be an awkward beast when roused. So feed it with tabloid titbits, dose it with soporific tax cuts and then —** *let sleeping dogs lie!*

Test case

There comes a time in every society when the drug wears off. Under the pressure of events we wake up and begin to realise that we can't afford to leave all the serious decision-making to Them any longer.

Schooling itself is the first test case (to highlight the difference between deep-seated public concern and a cost-cutting government's blue funk; or — hopefully not — *pink* funk): giving teachers access during their training to a wider range of experience, outside lecture halls and classrooms as well as inside them; backing them up in their work with children, reducing class sizes to give them time to consider individuals on their own merits; widening the range of subject matter to suit different skills and interests. All this costs mega money and *where's the profitability in such investment?* How on earth does that rate in comparison with the markets for fast cars, or Top of the Pops or second-hand battleships or hard drugs?

OK. We heard you the first time. *It's all going to be expensive and complicated and the electorate won't stand for it.* Excuse us: we *are* the electorate — we've changed our minds on this one. We might even be prepared (like the villagers in Bangladesh [p862] to make sacrifices. Making a bogey of *Tax and Spend* is a lot less of a frightener than the prospect of a younger generation turning sour because it can't cope. And then turning on us [p271].

All over the world we are getting wiser than we used to be. We can see what  we're in for if we let governments drift. The information revolution, coupled with the ordinary, everyday itch to get about in the world and compare notes, is allowing us to make links, across frontiers as well as within them. Word of mouth on exchange visits; words on faxes and over the radio; words and pictures on TV and the Web. Gradually people are becoming aware that their concerns aren't unique: bureaucratic inertia; the demoralising of young jobless; the backlash from unfairly treated religious or ethnic minorities; drugs peddling; arms pushing; the destruction of the rain forests, the exhaustion of the land, the pollution of the sea.

We need to create a new mindset. We have to convey to the peoples of the world the message that the safeguarding of our common property — human kind — calls for developing in each of us a new loyalty, a loyalty to mankind.
Professor Joseph Rotblat, Nobel Laureate, one-time member of the Manhatten Project researching the A bomb. January 23rd 1996

On Tuesday July 30 1996, at Liverpool Crown Court, four women belonging to the *Ploughshares* movement heard the verdict on their action in planning "criminal damage" to a military plane, part of a £500 million sale by British Aerospace to the Indonesian government, negotiated with the connivance of the Bitish government.

Three of them had cut through the security fence and used hammers and crowbars to do their public-spirited best to render the machine harmless. They explained that they were "using reasonable force to prevent a crime" — the continued oppression of the people of East Timor by the Indonesian military regime, responsible according to Amnesty International for nearly 200,000 deaths in the 20 years since the invasion and annexation.

A decade back, in the depths of Thatcherism, such acts and such arguments got short shrift. This time a jury of 12 *ordinary people*, 7 male and 5 female, on a majority verdict, acquitted the women on all charges — to the great satisfaction of local Protestand and Catholic leaders and rank-and-file.

A change in the mindset, perhaps?

We are making connections: between racism and genocide; inadequate schooling and alienated youth; office hierarchies and administrative sloth; cut-throat competition and sweated labour; financial greed and communities dispossessed; arms investment and military take-overs; religious bigotry and disabled minds (That's for starters. Add your own!)

In all this, youngsters — especially students [pages 27, 69, 77, 96, 102, 104, 107, 109, 118, 137, 152, 158, 162, 180, 221, 241] are ahead of the rest of us in recognising the issues that transcend party political manoeuvres. Along with the rest of us they are beginning to see through the dodgy claims of self-appointed oracles and corporate fat cats and party spin-doctors, that everything will turn out alright if we just *Leave it to Them.*

Comic relief

Leaving it to Them is a joke, shared by the moving spirits within these systems as well as those outside them. *Their* policies are daft, verging on the criminally insane. If only we could just laugh them off (with the help of TV satirists and seditious doggerel faxed in under the noses of oppressive governments).

Laughter helps. It undermines pretensions. It takes in oxygen. It is infectious, catching all sorts of people off their guard for long enough to see the funny side of what they used to take for granted. But it's no more than an cop-out unless it's matched with practical, common-sense alternatives to the nonsenses we're saddled with.

Common-sense requires that we put things together again, building replacements, mending what is still serviceable; not just scrapping the lot and reeling away in boozy triumph.

Renovation and re-building depends first of all on getting the priorities right: Beginning with the future of the human race. Otherwise known as bringing up the kids and keeping the planet intact for them so that they can make a better fist of things than we have done.

We begin with what's got to be done now, somehow. Swimming for our lives and heading for land. Not giving up until we touch solid ground. The objective comes first; then the hard slog to reach it.

Early in 1996 thirty-two of the organisations listed (and starred) in Appendix 2 at the end of the this book, came together to set out our conditions for survival in the *Real World*: the changes to be made in the teeth of opposition from those *particular interests* which profit most when the world is at its worst — the world as we know it now, arms-toting, trigger-happy, self-righteous, divided, desperately competing for whatever can be had.

No government, or group of governments, has yet proved able to stand up to those particular interests, on its own. But, here and now, the situation has altered. The basic problems are common to almost all of us, and we know it. Across the world there are the same glimmerings of self-confidence and mutual self-reliance, and slowly but surely — the same awareness:

We are not alone

We are beginning to see what it takes to replace the false economy of a divided, self-seeking society with the *real world economy* which matches needs with available resources (chief among them: ourselves).

Hit list

The *Real World*'s hit list is in Appendix 2. Are these targets *for real*?

That depends on who's aiming; and what with.

Who are *We*? The underclass? The threatened 'haves'? The office dwellers stabled along the corridors of power?

We are all those who share a common interest — the survival of our species; and who would quite like to do something about it. One way or another.

This includes most of Us and at least some of Them: as allies, not adversaries.

The idea of separate and conflicting interests between *Government* and *People* has screwed up our thinking ever since King John got clobbered by the Barons at Runnymede.

At first sight it seemed to be what Jefferson was on about nearly six hundred years later in drafting the Declaration of Independence. He was suspicious of too much intervention by the centre. But he wanted the kind of *strong government* which was the very opposite of top-heavy rule by a handful of grandees and a King whom no one had a hand in choosing. Instead he wanted a government whose strength was in its roots — *the hundreds and the schools*. Its *just powers* were rooted in the *consent of the governed*. The consenting parties were none of them to be sleeping partners. They were all in it together. They all had a stake in the community, slaves and women (eventually) included. As stakeholders they had the right to decide the ground rules for themselves; and then to take a hand in carrying them out.

Combined operation

The choice is between owning government and disowning it.

Remember Roxbury, the *Arson Capital of America*, its breathing spaces overgrown with weeds, a dumping ground for poisonous rubbish, people complaining because they could scarcely bear the stench, street crime making it a no-go area where government seemed powerless to intervene. But the moving spirits at ground level managed to locate the moving spirits within the government system and between them they shared out what had to be done: not only to clean the place up, also to keep it that way. A combined operation, built to last.

In many, perhaps most, modern societies, public apathy and government indifference have allowed the rotting carcasses of Nazi-ism and religious dogma to become breeding grounds for racism, fear, bigotry. Where private greed has spread like bindweed.

So what's to be done? Well, the site needs cleaning up, the rubbish cleared away, the weeds uprooted (without, if possible, rooting out whatever good stock is worth preserving).

We have begun to see that we ourselves, at first in our small ways, can make things happen. Our thinking, our mind set, is changing in the light of that first-hand experience. Little by little, we are all getting used to a double-edged conclusion:

● **Government can't manage on its own any longer. The resources available fall short.**

● **There are buried resources within the community: waiting to be unearthed. (That takes some doing: Top down as well as bottom up. But it's already beginning to work.)**

R & D

Remember Oil Creek Pennsylvania? [p101] Top down: bottom up. The puddles on the surface and the vast, untapped oil lake below.

People are a resource as potent and as little understood as the Pennsylvania oil before they drilled for it. Our most valuable, longest surviving asset, our time, counts more than anything else in a siege economy; as we were once and as we are becoming now.

Time measured as effort, endurance, commitment. Time as experience to be shared. Time used to improvise solutions without waiting for someone else to take action.

Time spent at the Paddy's Goose level.

There were all sorts and conditions of people getting together during the Blitz in places like *Paddy's Goose*. Middle-class do-gooders alongside dock workers and old-age pensioners on the poverty line. A mixture not unlike those nowadays assembled in an anti-roads campaign [p29] or those Wandsworth squatters proclaiming *This Land is Ours*.

In war time they were committed *for the duration* as the phrase went. Meaning that no one lets up until we win through.

The time we need to spend now is on what professionals call R & D — *research and development*. It doesn't yet alter the production figures, but it lays the foundation for changes which may prove world-shaking. It takes things one stage on from drilling for oil to setting up the refineries which turn it into sources of light and power. It's the very opposite of wasted time. Not treading water, but making waves. Big ones, now.

The build-up

Agenda = *Things to be done* (not just talked about).

The job in hand is to bridge the gap between that *Real World* wants list and its realisation. Two things needed:

1. To count the cost: the cost of what's gone wrong and what it will take to put it right. And to cost out the benefits that make the work worthwhile.

This is where R & D comes in: piecing together the jigsaw bits of evidence: what governments suppress and spin-doctors distort, plus the information which nobody as yet has brought to light. Investigation nationwide, world-wide as scientists trace the spread of TB or the origins of BSE; or as those Argentinean women charted the pollution of their river.

It also means counting our blessings in the shape of buried talent, working out how to build on them by better training, tougher thinking, closer collaboration, fewer bureaucratic delays; figuring out (as we all have to do in time of war) what it demands of us, the *blood and tears, toil and sweat*, to get from the shadows into the sunlight.

Mike Cooley and his fellow shop stewards set an example on the shop floor, systematically working out what it takes to shift from the self-destructive present to something job-satisfying, life-enhancing.

In other areas of our everyday life all sorts of fact-finders can be roped in — students (and some of their tutors); housewives (if it's not too sexist to admit this) used to organising time and budgeting for a rainy day, going the rounds, block by block in downtown Philadelphia to pinpoint people's concerns and priorities; setting up *Planning for Real* schemes to identify problems/opportunities and locate buried talent. Fieldworkers like Meena Bilgi [p243] , Francesco Gangotena [p203] and Jimmy Mascarenhas [p154] helping villagers to size up their own direct experience and tease out the implications for local action; and those moles inside governments and corporations and the media who can nose out the facts and the figures that some of their bosses would rather keep under wraps.

It's a new kind of Mass Observation (the infectious idea dreamed up by Charles Madge stimulating people all over the country to send in their own accounts of scenes and conversations as they came across them, day by day, making a living history of life in England in the '30s). Today it draws on everyday observers of what is going wrong, and where it's coming right. Feeding the facts to the national and international networks with their electronic outreach and analysis, marshalling the evidence to bring key issues into focus and *demonstrate* how to resolve them. Accumulating the clout to challenge governments and corporations to act or abdicate.

In hope and anger

Each of these investigations begins as what professionals like to call a *Feasibility Study*. It's a kind of benevolent confidence trick which starts with nothing more than getting together with others to gather information. No one makes promises, mind. Information in itself is neutral and doesn't commit anyone. But when between us we begin to sort it out it becomes pretty obvious what has gone wrong and what *could* be done to put it right. What *should* be done. What *must* be done! And buggered if we stop short now — let's start in and do it!

That's the confidence trick. From being uncommitted to getting stuck in. From staying in isolation to ganging up. Which brings us back to —

2. Changing the mind set AND the frame of mind. Showing what can be done when we put our minds to it and spare a bit of time. Using working relationships (not just talking shops) to put people wise to each other's backgrounds and abilities. Getting a kick out of joining in to make things happen.

A young fitness enthusiast in the poorest part of a small village in Barbados

 has spent most of his time organising a gymnastics club. Recently he and some others decided they had to have a real gymnasium instead of the back yard where they did their practising. Over many months they begged, scrounged and if absolutely necessary bought the raw materials. Then, in three weeks, they built their gymnasium from scratch: 40 ft. by 54 ft., with a beautifully sprung floor; everything up to competition standard; open and affordable to everyone in the neighbourhood. On the wall he has a list of useful maxims. Half way down, it says this:

Understanding comes by practice, not argument.

✧ ✧ ✧

Understanding that comes from *doing* things together is the glue that more often than not holds things firm when temperaments and backgrounds differ.

Action first on a local level: trying out pilot projects — in schooling, food producing, energy conservation, housebuilding, shopkeeping, sports training, transportation, music-making, money-minding, swapping skills — you name it!

Experimenting on a small enough scale to be able to get cracking without fuss, and to adapt in the light of experience. Saying to other people, *"Don't just listen to us telling you what should be done — LOOK, it's beginning to happen, here and now! Come on in!"*

Local initiatives are stepping stones (or sometimes, sling stones) that enable us to cross over and challenge Goliaths on their own ground.

Seeing for ourselves what we can do between us, on a small scale, here and now, is the first step. That's **the practice**.

Alongside is our second source of power — **the knowledge**. Chrissie Maher demystifying official gobbledegook, whistle-blowers exposing corporate skull-duggery. Painstaking collection of the facts from all over to **show up** the consequences of idiot policies. Making links like ALARM UK's South Coast Corridor [p31] and the Calder Valley alliances, formed to fight the motorways invaders. Taking the trouble to work out viable alternatives, the costs, the timetable, the shared responsibilities. Telling the world in precise terms what those *particular interests* are up to and how public or private greed, deception, sloth or ignorance is getting in the way. Using our networks to spread the word when something really works; and when it doesn't.

Getting more of Them in on the act, by sheer weight of public opinion, shifting the balance of political advantage, so that their mind sets are changing too. *No, Minister, the public mood has altered. You can't get away with it any longer.*

Bad governments survive by appealing to personal self-interest or fear: threatening the life or the belongings of each citizen. Governments are reformed or displaced when people discover a common cause and share the job satisfaction of achieving it together, step by step, however long it may take. They generate staying power.

 *Incremental change*, to give it a label, can span centuries, as the planting of many trees gradually changes the climate. Or it can occur overnight as bomber pilots demonstrated when they sowed many small incendiaries which between them raised the temperature to flashpoint, to create a fire storm, an inferno. Or as small acts of racial harassment and revenge build up via murder and counter-murder to riot and civil war.

Either way, the process is like that little experiment the science teacher shows on the elementary chemistry course: add pinches of the right kind of salt to a tumbler of liquid. Pinch after pinch until the solution is almost saturated. It is still no more than a mixture. Then one more pinch and a tap on the side of the glass, and hey presto! it crystallises. Transformed into something quite unlike what had gone before.

Good or bad, that depends.

It's easy to be doom-laden, to shut down because we fear the worst. Two years before Independence in South Africa, at about the time when Gugile Nkwinti was telling me that the time was coming when *street resistance* would change to *street regeneration*, an Afrikaner couple were debating whether to emigrate to Australia to avoid the coming blood-bath. They decided to stay on in hopes. On the night before the Election, they told me afterwards, they debated again *Should we go together to vote, or separate so that if a bomb kills one of us the other will survive to look after the kids?* They decided to stay together and next morning went to the first of several polling stations to choose from. The queue was so enormous that they went on to the next, and the next. After the fourth, they came back to the first and queued for four hours, blacks and whites jam-packed, with everyone laughing, joking, singing together.

It was what religious people call a sacrament — the outward and visible expression of something inward and spiritual — people's unquenchable desire to get things right.

Back in the '70s Dr. E.F. Schumacher's book, *Small is Beautiful*, made many of us jump to conclusions. Mass movements and mega structures were out. What mattered was to get things right, each on its own, at ground level where things work better.

We got him slightly wrong. He said later:

"The discovery and mobilisation of people's power may be nothing less than the condition of survival for the hitherto affluent societies of the West."

He was concerned with the **scale** on which people's power can be *mobilised*...

"what precisely is the right scale, I cannot say. **We should experiment to find out..."**

Using the tools to make it happen

The users...

... are the *moving spirits* perhaps encouraged by an outside *facilitator* (whom they can trust and who is able to put them wise to some of the possibilities they may choose to follow up, and some of the pitfalls they need to avoid).

The power tools...

... are mostly designed to suit people some of whom are still feeling their way, and don't want to let themselves in for more than they bargained for. The working situations allow people to

1. do things together which everyone can easily agree on,

2. produce eye-catching results which attract onlookers' attention,

3. allow newcomers to join in without fuss,

4. open up further possibilities to explore, once people feel sure of themselves and confident in each other,

5. make decisions and take action: locally/nationally/globally.

Here's a rough and ready programme: but don't feel tied to this particular running order.

MAKING THE PLANNING FOR REAL MODEL — perhaps including some youngsters from school, but hopefully involving a cross-section of adults drawn together because making the model is going to be interesting and fun. First, the outline map — either obtained by enlarging an existing local plan (with luck, done in the Council Planning department); or by improvising the outline, literally drawing on the experience of the group. To do this provide lengths of string to represent one or more roads that everyone knows, and (coloured blue) any local waterway. Members of the group lay down the 'main road' with one landmark — perhaps a cut-out model of the school building — adjusting the kinks and the straight bits until everyone reckons it *looks right* and can be inked in. Then add two or three other roads in relation to it, with similar adjustments, allowing people to set down the house cut-outs, beginning with their own. In an area such as a housing estate or a village this can produce a surprisingly accurate layout, with the bonus that everyone's experience has been committed, and consequently everyone owns the result.

The model can then be 'dressed' using the range of cut-outs provided in the

Neighbourhood Initiatives Foundation's 'Planning for Real' pack, but making additions, and colouring the base, with materials the group itself contributes as it thinks best.

TAKING THE MODEL ROUND — to places where people can be found at various times of the day, bus stop, market, school entrance, place of religious worship, Advice Centre, etc. Leaflets available to aid moving spirits who accompany the model in explaining that an Event is planned (date and place) where everyone can use the model, not just gaze at it. Meanwhile -

PLANNING THE SURVEYS — the same or a parallel group meet to sort out what skills *might* lie buried in the neighbourhood (perhaps using the Neighbourhood Talent Survey proforma provided by the NIF). The group may think the NIF proforma is enough in itself, but it's still useful to break down all the items it lists, on separate scraps of card, with blanks for others to throw in additional suggestions. The scraps are laid out higgledy-piggledy so that the group can look at them objectively, add or reject and arrange them in an acceptable order. Here too, the process helps people to think things out together and own the result — which then is photocopied for trial use: at first interviewing each other; then going out in pairs to a few houses in each of a few streets; coming back to compare notes and perhaps make adjustments. Then, as time allows, tackling every house in every street, beginning with those best known to group members, and branching out as confidence grows.

As results come in, someone posts them up, to show the scores for each kind of skill — from brain surgery to disc jockeying — on the nearest noticeboard.

Alongside it is worth recruiting youngsters to case the joint — i.e. scour the neighbourhood checking the whereabouts of materials, equipment, waste ground or empty premises, which might perhaps be brought into community use. (There's a set of instant survey cards which NIF can provide as a pattern from which to work.)

SPREADING THE WORD — moving spirits are well placed to tap into the grapevine. Either by organising a telephone tree (if telephones are available) with each person undertaking to contact half a dozen others to tell them where the Planning for Real model can be seen on its rounds and when it will be available for everyone to use as part of the Event. Failing the telephone, — face-to-face contact — which sometimes yields even better results.

INVOLVING *THEM*. — amongst the moving spirits there may be some with contacts in the media or the local authority, or in the management of local enterprises. With the model-making and perhaps the surveys already underway, they have a good excuse to put these contacts in the picture, and persuade them that it is in their interest to learn more and to see what is happening, by coming along to the Event.

STAGING THE LOCAL EVENT — the *Planning for Real* model is the centrepiece in whatever building is best known and most accessible to the community at large, perhaps the school. Around it there are opportunities for all sorts of activities reflecting different interests and enthusiasms. Refreshments, home-cooked according to various multi-cultural recipes; live music from local groups, face-painting, sports events, perhaps a tug of war, school children doing a puppet show.

'Outsiders' — from the local authority, charities, and other interests, are invited along as guests, on hand to be consulted about possibilities and constraints, equipped with labels (engagingly designed by local children, so you can't refuse to wear one) so that their kind of contribution can be instantly identified, but still leaving residents able to choose between options, rather than to swallow someone else's solution whole.

MAKING WAVES — all sorts of aids to publicise what is being revealed of the neighbourhood's needs and resources in the light of the surveys and the *Planning for Real* sessions;

✔ one or more **community noticeboards,** home made, graffiti decorated to order, with space available for additional suggestions and comments alongside the information presented by the moving spirits on progress so far.

✔ **photographs** taken of the survey workers in action, and of the *Planning for Real* Event, circulated to the media with a punchy press handout (preferably including a few **sound bites** from those involved).

✔ the first edition of a **newsletter**, perhaps made up of sound bites from various participants in the *Planning for Real,* coupled with the latest figures from the surveys and backed by jokes, sports tips, non-actionable gossip, recipes, thumbnail decorations and cartoons — gleaned from as wide a cross-section of the community as can be reached. Important to involve youngsters, in the layout as well as by contributing particular items, because they will then prove reliable distributors of the newsletter, house-to-house, letter box not litter bin.

SORTING OUT THE OPTIONS — using the NOW SOON LATER format [p134] with whatever variations in the labels at the top of each vertical column that the moving spirits and others now beginning to be involved decide.

This prioritising could take place during the main *Planning for Real* Event and/or could be set up as a sequel, with different groups forming to work out the priorities in different subject areas (Housing, Care, Traffic, Environment, Youngsters, etc.) More about this in the handbook on *Planning for Real* available from NIF.

In these sessions it is important to involve visiting experts, *on tap not on top,* so that everyone concerned is clear about both the possibilities and the constraints, including the time it will take to achieve any given objective (but excluding bureaucratic delays which could be short circuited when residents take over some of the work and do it themselves).

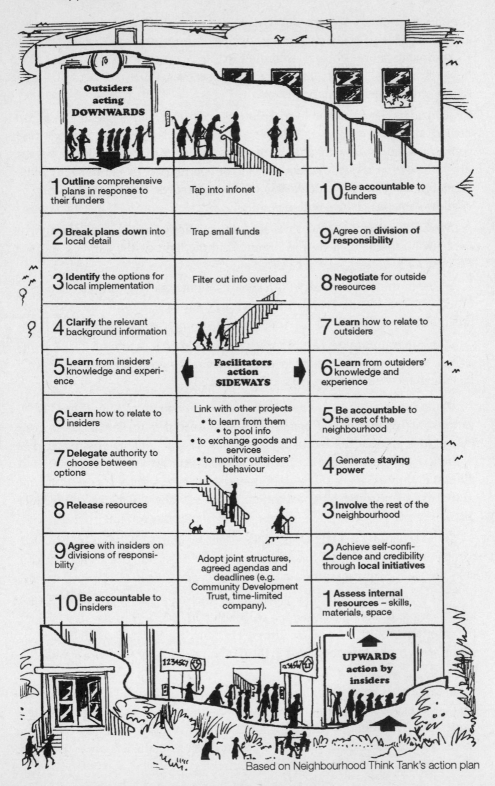

Outsiders acting DOWNWARDS

1 **Outline** comprehensive plans in response to their funders	Tap into infonet	**10** Be **accountable** to funders
2 **Break plans down** into local detail	Trap small funds	**9** Agree on **division of responsibility**
3 **Identify** the options for local implementation	Filter out info overload	**8** **Negotiate** for outside resources
4 **Clarify** the relevant background information		**7** **Learn** how to relate to outsiders
5 **Learn** from insiders' knowledge and experience	◀ **Facilitators action SIDEWAYS** ▶	**6** **Learn** from outsiders' knowledge and experience
6 **Learn** how to relate to insiders	Link with other projects • to learn from them • to pool info • to exchange goods and services • to monitor outsiders' behaviour	**5** Be **accountable** to the rest of the neighbourhood
7 **Delegate** authority to choose between options		**4** Generate **staying power**
8 **Release** resources		**3** **Involve** the rest of the neighbourhood
9 **Agree** with insiders on divisions of responsibility	Adopt joint structures, agreed agendas and deadlines (e.g. Community Development Trust, time-limited company).	**2** Achieve self-confidence and credibility through **local initiatives**
10 Be **accountable** to insiders		**1** **Assess internal resources** – skills, materials, space

UPWARDS action by insiders

Based on Neighbourhood Think Tank's action plan

ENHANCING SKILLS — using the findings of the surveys to pinpoint those who might be willing to pass on their own skills to others who are still beginners; or to exchange one kind of skill for another as part of a LETS network. Pulling in outside expertise to help people teach their skills effectively. Teaming up with other bodies to take part in joint skills training (e.g. through the National Tenants' Resource Centre, see Appendix 3).

SCALING THE LADDERS. Working out, as working relationships begin to form, what delegations of decision-making can be negotiated from Top Down; and what requests are worth making from Bottom Up for action and/or decisions at top level which those at ground level decide are beyond their own capacities.

See diagram on previous page. Any facilities available are helping to develop links at appropriate 'landings'.

ACTION PLAN. The moving spirts have increased, and perhaps by now involve some of their opposite numbers in the outside bodies known as *Them*. Everyone so far involved is getting used to a sorting out process (moving bits of card around until an acceptable pattern emerges) so that everyone can chip in without endless talk. At the same time even those who were non-talkers now have the vocabulary and the familiarity with the situation to keep their end up when talk is needed.

The Plan separates **Objectives** on one side of the NOW SOON LATER chart from **Outcomes** on the other side. In between, in more and more detail go all the actions which are necessary to implement what has been decided, step by step, coming down to who is going to see Who about What as well as When we are going to do this or that Where.

STRUCTURES. An umbrella organisation perhaps — an **Open Forum** as a sounding board and/or a **Community Development Trust** elected to wheel and deal. Particular organisations: a **Parish Council**, a **Neighbourhood Council**, a **Credit Union** branch, a **LETS network** of those wanting to trade their skills individually (arising from the findings of the skills survey), a **sports training club**, a **local enterprise** such as organising and recycling usable waste, a **bulk buy club**, an **environmental improvement group** (involving children — important) planting shrubs (which therefore will not be pulled up again) and perhaps embarking on murals, a **human rights group** concerned with victims of greed and discrimination, at home and abroad.

All sorts of structures appropriate to particular interests and dependent on particular enthusiasms. But between them raising the profile of the neighbourhood, as a power in the land, changing the climate.

RESOURCES BANK — The four bankable resources are spare time, raw materials that are about to be thrown away, land and workspace not in use, and spare money.

Particular structures such a LETS network, a Credit Union and a waste recycling scheme can reinforce each other.

A **local re-investment trust** enables people to sort out those resources and make them available within the community and on affordable terms. It's a new look to an idea that was first applied by some of Robert Owen's collaborators in Birmingham and London, way back in the 1830s. They set up the *National Equitable Labour Exchange* for raw materials, commodities and people's time (using 'labour notes' instead of pounds sterling). The UK Social Investment Forum [see Appendix 3] is developing the idea through the **Re-Building Society Network**.

LINKING UP — exchange visits with other groups to share experience on problems and possibilities. One possibility already being realised by **Out of This World** [see Appendix 3] is setting up 'the first ethical supermarket chain' — local stores, so far in Newcastle, Bristol and Nottingham), each drawing on local produce for 10% of its sales but bringing in other items that aren't available locally.

Spread the news of local initiatives on the Web.

Join national and international networks [see Appendix 3] to pool fact-finding, exchange resources, build up the pressure.

TELLING THE WORLD — Use those links to set up headline-catching **Events**, bringing people together from all over to stage a demonstration against what is going wrong; a projection of the way things should be. Candle-lit vigils, woodland occupations; derelict site transformation scenes. Casual onlookers attracted to seek further and hear more through on-the-spot contacts, leaflets and follow-up meetings.

CONCERTING ACTION — Find out from insiders what's gone wrong with those official, commercial, legal, financial, religious systems which no longer live up to what they profess. Sort and sift the evidence. Release it to the media, ram it home at public inquiries.

Hacking away at the undergrowth, **showing up what's gone wrong**, bringing pressure to bear on the giants at the top of the beanstalk — that's half the battle.

The other half is the hard graft of working out the practicable alternatives, fitting together working models drawn from all over the world; *showing what can be done together*; not just talking about it; putting professionals in the picture (*on tap, not on top*) — so they begin to see things whole and share with the rest of us the job satisfaction of making most of them come right.

Appendix 2

Targets: *The Real World*'s UK hit list

Action Programme for Government

✔ A £1 billion annual programme of public investment in local, community and voluntary enterprises, to create work opportunities and meet social needs.

✔ An 'ecological' restructuring of the tax system.

✔ A Bill of Rights, establishing in law the individual rights of citizenship, after wide public debate and consultation of its contents.

✔ Establishment of a time-table for achieving within ten years the UN development aid target of 0.7% of national income.

✔ A housing strategy to provide at least 100,000 affordable homes in the social housing sector each year for the next ten years.

✔ An integrated transport programme with the target of reducing road traffic by 10% from 1990 levels by the year 2010.

✔ A programme for the reduction of the UK's CO_2 emissions by at least 20% from 1990 levels by the year 2005, as a first step towards deeper reductions.

✔ Leadership at international level to promote an enforceable code of conduct on international arms transfers, incorporating a ban on the manufacture, stockpiling, export and use of anti-personnel mines.

✔ An integrated strategy to increase the consumption of fresh and nutritious food.

✔ Leadership at European and global levels to secure effective regulation of international trade and investment to safeguard social and environmental standards.

✔ Binding legal protection for Sites of Special Scientific Interest.

✔ Regular publication of a new measure of economic welfare which includes social and enviromental factors.

Appendix 3

Work mates: contacts to make with useful organisations

(Members of the REAL WORLD coalition are starred)

When danger threatens and opportunities beckon, there isn't time to dither. These organisations are all concerned with action here and now. You can join in.

They can provide information and may be able to put you in touch with like-minded people within your reach.

In turn you may be able to help them to get at relevant facts so that they can piece them together and get moving.

Before it's too late.

ACRE (Action with Communities in Rural England) Somerfield Court, Somerfield Road, Cirencester, Glos. GL7 1TW. Tel 01285 653477   Fax 01285 654537. Aims to improve the quality of life of communities and disadvantaged people in rural England, particularly through the support and promotion of its members, the Rural Community Councils.

ACTAC (The Technical Aid Network) 64 Mount Pleasant, Liverpool L3 5SD. Tel 0151 708 7607 Fax 0151 708 7606. National network of architects, landscape architects, surveyors, planners and community artists all committed to providing technical support to community based initiatives concerned with the design and development of neighbourhoods.

Action for Sustainable Rural Communities c/o Nicole Armstrong Lowe, 3 Crowns Yard, Penrith, Cumbria CA11 7PH. Tel 01768 863812 Fax 01768 890067. Aims to generate sustainable rural communities through community-led partnership development based upon ecological principles.

*ALARM UK (The National Alliance Against Road-building) 9-10 College Terrace, London E3 5AN. Tel/fax 0181 983 3572. The umbrella body for about 250 local anti-road groups; campaigns for a sustainable transport policy. (See page 29).

Amnesty International 99 Rosebery Avenue, London EC1R 4RE. Tel 0171 814 6200 Fax 0171 833 1515. Campaigns for human rights worldwide; seeks release of prisoners of conscience; works for prompt and fair trials for all political prisoners; opposes death penalty, torture and other cruel or degrading treatment of prisoners.

Association of British Credit Unions Ltd Unit 307, Westminster Business Square, 339 Kennington Lane, London SE11 5QY. Tel 0171 582 2626 Fax 0171 587 1774. Trade association for Credit Unions (financial co-ops).

Association of Community Technical Aid Centres The Royal Institution, Colquitt Street, Liverpool L1 4DE. Tel Fax

Aston Reinvestment Trust (ART) Swan House, Hospital Street and Summer Lane, Birmingham B19 3PY. Tel/Fax 0121 236 4808 Provides uncollateralized loans for the voluntary sector, small and medium enterprises and community businesses in Birmingham. (See page 148).

Ballsall Heath Neighbourhood Forum c/o St. Paul's Centre, Hertford Street, Ballsall Heath, Birmingham B12 8NJ. Tel/Fax 0121 440 4376. Umbrella body for various resident, tenant, voluntary and religious agencies in the Ballsall Heath neighbourhood of Birmingham; assists community regeneration through its members; represents and reflects local opinion to other bodies.

Bangladesh Rural Advancement Committee Public Affairs Department, 66 Mohakhali, Dhaka - 1212, Bangladesh. Tel +884 1807x 2007. Fax 880 2 883542. See p81.

*Birmingham Settlement 318 Summer Lane, Birmingham B19 3RL. Tel 0121 359 3562 Fax 0121 359 6357. Runs day centres, out of school clubs etc. as well as National Debt Line on 0121 359 8501 to provide advice with personal, household and business money troubles.

*Black Environment Network UK Office, No. 9, Llainwen Uchaf, Llanberis, Gwynedd, Wales LL55 4LL. Tel/Fax 01286 870 715. Promotes equality of opportunity within the ethnic community in the preservation, protection and development of the environment; maintains a network of individuals and organisations working for change.

*British Association Of Settlements and Social Action Centres (BASSAC) 1st Floor, Winchester House, 11 Cranmer Road, London SW9 6EJ. Tel 0171 735 1075 Fax 0171 735 0840. The national body representing over 70 settlements nationally - a network of multi-purpose community centres; works for urban renewal and regeneration.

British Trust for Conservation Volunteers (BTCV). Tel 01491 839766 Fax 01491 839646. Works to involve people in conservation activity in both urban and countryside areas; activities include practical projects, holidays and publications; network of local groups.

Building Services Research and Information Association Old Bracknell Lane West, Bracknell, Berkshire RG12 7AH. Tel 01344 426511 Fax 01344 487575. Tests anything which goes inside a building!

*CAFOD (The Catholic Overseas Development Agency for England and Wales) Romero Close, Stockwell Road, London SW9 9TY. Tel 0171 733 7900 Fax 0171 274 9630 Raises money for long-term development projects in the Third World, working in partnership with local organisations with the aim of helping people to help themselves; campaigns for change in Britain to benefit the world's poor.

The CAF Social Investment Fund Charities Aid Foundation, 25 Kings Hill Avenue, Kings Hill, West Malling, Kent, ME19 4TA. Tel 01732 520 000 Fax 01732 520 001. Aims to assist charities to borrow money; attracts returnable donations from individuals and companies to provide loans to charities.

Camcorder Action Network (See Undercurrents)

Campaign Against The Arms Trade 11 Goodwin Street, Finsbury Park, London N4 3HQ. Tel 0171 281 0297 Fax 0171 281 4369. Campaigns against arms exports.

*Catholic Institute for International Relations (CIIR) Unit 3, Canonbury

Yard, 190A New North Road, Islington, London N1 7BJ. Tel 0171 354 0883 Fax 0171 359 0017. An independent charity working for justice and development; specialises in skill-sharing, advocacy, information and analysis with , and on behalf of, its partners in the South.

Centre for Alternative Technology Plc Machynlleth, Powys, Wales SY20 9AZ. Tel 01654 702400 Fax 01654 702 782. Aims to inspire, inform and enable society to make the changes necessary to move forward to a sustainable future, via a seven acre site in mid-Wales, publications, courses and school visits as well as a mail order service.

CHAR (Housing Campaign for Single People) 5-15 Cromer Street, London WC1H 8LS. Tel 0171 833 2071 Fax 0171 278 6685. Umbrella body for organisations working for homeless single people; provides training, research and advice to its member organisations as well as campaigning on their behalf.

*Charter 88 Exmouth House, 3-11 Pine Street, London EC1 ROH. Tel 0171 833 1988 Fax 0171 833 5895. Campaigns for constitutional reform and democratic renewal; supported by over 60,000 signatories, it calls for a Bill of Rights, freedom of information, a fair voting system of proportional representation, reform of the House of Commons, a written constitution etc.

*Christian Aid PO Box 100, London SE1 7RT. Tel 0171 620 4444 Fax 0171 620 0719. The official relief and development agency of over 40 British and Irish churches; works directly with the poor in more than 70 countries world-wide through local organisations whose programmes aim to strengthen the poor towards self-sufficiency.

Christian Ethical Investment Group Secretary: Canon Bill Whiffen, 90 Booker Avenue, Bradwell Common, Milton Keynes, MK13 8EF. Tel/Fax 01908 677 466. Aims to increase awareness of ethical investment amongst churches, individual Christians and others.

*Church Action on Poverty Central Buildings, Oldham Street, Manchester M1 1JT. Tel 0161 236 9321 Fax 0161 237 5359. Aims to help poor people to speak out their own behalf via educational and campaigning work; has about 2000 individual and group members maintaining active links with all the main Christian denominations and other church-based and secular social justice networks.

Civic Trust 17 Carlton House Terrace, London SW1W 5AW. Tel 0171 930 0914 Fax 0171 321 0180. Advises local civic societies on a range of issues including traffic, environment and amenities.

Common Ground Seven Dials Warehouse, 44 Earlham Street, London WC2H 9LA. Tel 0171 379 3109 Fax 0171 836 5741. Campaigns for greater awareness of locality and local distinctiveness.

CommunityMatters 8/9 Upper Street, London N1 0PQ. Tel 0171 226 0189 Fax 0171 354 9570. Supporting democratically elected community organizations and linking up with local authorities.

Community Service Volunteers 237 Pentonville Road, London N1 9NJ. Tel 0171 278 6601 Fax 0171 833 0149. Finds placements for volunteers working with people including the homeless and those with learning difficulties.

Consumers' Association 2 Marylebone Road, London, NW1 4DF. Tel 0171 830 6000 Fax 0171 830 6220. Aims to put consumers in a stronger position to make wise, value-for-money choices, providing information via a number of publications including *Which?*; works to improve the lot of consumers by lobbying suppliers and government.

Council for the Protection of Rural England Warwick House, 25 Buckingham Palace Road, London SW1W OPP. Tel 0171 976 6433 Fax 0171 976 6373. Campaigns for the countryside through well-informed research and briefing of national and local government; range of issues includes agriculture, land use, planning, transport, minerals etc.; network of active local groups.

Cyclists' Public Affairs Group c/o Cyclists Touring Club, Coterell House, 69 Headrow, Godalming, Surrey GU7 3HS. Tel 01483 417217 Fax 01483 426994. Links the main cycling campaign groups for parliamentary and political lobbying.

Demos 9 Bridewell Place, London EC4V 6AP. Tel 0171 353 4479 Fax 0171 353 4481. Independent think tank which aims to help reinvigorate public policy and political thinking by drawing on ideas from outside the political mainstream, including people from business and science, community activists and environmentalists; carries out programmes of policy research , publishes books, working papers and a quarterly journal.

Development Trusts Association 20 Conduit Place, London W2 1HZ. Tel. 0171 706 4951.

Dudley Street Neighbourhood Initiative 513 Dudley street, Roxbury, Massachusetts MA 02119, USA. Tel. +1 617 442 9670. Aims to get development which benefits the local neighbourhood without displacement by mobilising the resources of the people living in the Dudley Street neighbourhood of Boston, Massachusetts. (See page 148).

The Ecology Building Society 18 Station Road, Cross Hills, Keighley, West Yorks. BD20 5BR. Tel 01535 635933. Provides a means of finance for the purchase of properties that give an ecological pay-back, such as small-scale workshops, back-to-backs, houses incorporating special energy saving or energy efficient features, etc.

*Employment Policy Institute Southbank House, Black Prince Road, London SE1 7SJ. Tel 0171 735 0777 Fax 0171 793 8192. Think tank focusing on the whole range of labour market issues; promotes policy options which would lead to a return to full employment.

Energy Advisory Associates 1 Moores Cottages, Bircher, Leominster, HR6 0AX. Tel 01568 780868 Fax 01568 780866. Energy conservation consultants working on buildings for a range of clients from private individuals to universities.

Environmental Transport Association 10 Church Street, Weybridge KT13 8RS. Tel 01932 828882 Fax 01932 829015. The green car and cycle rescue service; not members of the road lobby unlike RAC and AA, but instead campaigns for environmentally-friendlier transport.

Ethical Investment Research Services (EIRIS) 504 Bondway Business Centre, 71 Bondway, London SW8 1SQ. Tel 0171 735 1351 Fax 0171 735 5323. Undertakes portfolio screening for people who want to invest ethically.

European Network for Economic Self-Help and Local Development IFG Lokale Ökonomie, SEKR FR - 4 - 8, Franklin Strasse 28/29, D - 10587 Berlin, Germany. Tel Fax +49 30 31421117.

Family Service Units 207 Old Marylebone Road, London NW1 5QP. Tel 0171

402 5175 Fax 0171 724 1829. Provides support to families via a network of locally-based agencies.

Findhorn Foundation The Park, Forres, Scotland IV36 0TZ. Tel 01309 690 154 Fax 01309 691 387. Rural community with environmental, spiritual and agri-cultural interests; activities include running conferences, courses and growing very big cabbages.

*Forum for the Future Thornbury House, 18 High Street, Cheltenham GL50 1DZ. Tel 01242 262 737 Fax 01242 262 757. A new charity taking a positive, solutions-orientated approach to today's environmental problems; activities include a Best Practice Database across a range of sustainability issues, promotion of economic solutions to environmental problems, publication of *Green Futures* etc.

*Friends of the Earth (England, Wales and Northern Ireland) 26-28 Underwood Street, London N1 7JQ. Tel 0171 490 1555 Fax 0171 490 0881. Environmental pressure group campaigning on a wide range of issues including pollution, transport, energy, waste, habitats, forests and sustainable development; campaigns nationally as well as through over 250 local groups.

*Friends of the Earth Scotland Bonnington Mill, 72 Newhaven Road, Edinburgh EH6 5QG. Tel 0131 554 9977 Fax 0131 554 8656. Independent member of the Friends of the Earth International Network campaigning on a range of issues including energy, mineral extraction, climate change, trans-port, air pollution and local sustainable development planning.

Giroscope 46 Wellsted Street, Hessie Road, Hull HU3 3AQ. Tel 01482 223 376. Small co-op who renovate houses in Hull, then make them available at low rents to the single homeless. (See page 70).

Greenpeace Canonbury Villas, Highbury, London N1 2PN. Tel 0171 865 8100 Fax 0171 865 8200. Campaigns against abuse of the natural world through lobbying and non-violent direct action protests, which are backed by scien-tific research.

Highlands and Islands Forum David Whyte House, 57 Church Street, Inverness. Networks community development. Tel 01463 713531 Fax 01463 710965.

Homeless Information Project 612 Old Kent Road, London SE15 1JB. Tel 0171 277 7639 Fax 0171 732 7644. Aims to encourage the homeless or near home-less to work on self-help solutions on an individual and group basis; holds workshops and provides information packs with a self-help focus on many aspects of homelessness.

ICOM (Industrial Common Ownership Ltd) Vassalli House, 20 Central Road, Leeds LS1 6DE. Tel 0113 246 1738 Fax 0113 244 0002. National body for democratic employee -owned coops; can provide a list of Coop support organisations across the UK.

Intermediate Technology 103-105 Southampton Row, London WC1B 4HH. Tel 0171 436 9761 Fax 0171 436 2013. Booksellers and publishers specialising in the field of Third World Development.

*International Institute for Environment and Development 3 Endsleigh Street, London WC1H ODD. Tel. 0171 388 2117 Fax 0171 388 2826. Works for the recognition of the intrinsic interdependence between the environment and economic development; provides policy advice, information and technical help to governments, aid agencies, grassroots development organisations etc.

IPPR (Institute of Public Policy Research) 30-32 Southampton Street, London WC2E 7RA. Tel 0171 470 6100 Fax 0171 497 0373. Aims to contribute to the public understanding of social, economic and political questions through research, discussion and publications; provides an alternative to free market think-tanks.

Jigsaw 178 Campbell Road, Oxford OX4 3NR. Tel 01865 770833. Provides training in non-violent direct action.

*****Kairos** (Centre for a Sustainable Society) The Rectory, Glencarse, Perth, PH2 7LX. Tel/Fax 01738 860 386. Promotes a programme of community education and policy formation called 'Vision 21'; supported by the Scottish churches.

LETS Link UK 61 Woodcock Road, Warminster, Wilts BA12 9DH. Tel/Fax 01985 217 871. (See pages 50 and 297).

Lightmoor New Community Ltd (Contactable via Neighbourhood Initiatives Foundation — see below). A self-built, self-managing village near. Telford. (See page 43).

Local Agenda 21 UK LGMB, Arndale House, The Arndale Centre, Luton, Beds LU1 2TS. Tel 01582 451 166 Fax 01582 412 525. The project to implement at local authority level the policies and commitments arising from the 1992 Earth Summit; assists local authorities to consult their local communities, organisations and businesses and draw up a programme for action.

*****Media Natura Trust** 21 Tower Street, London WC2H 9NS. Tel 0171 240 4936 Fax 0171 240 229. Helps environment groups fight conservation problems with media resources, utilising expertise from the media industry; projects include video, design and print, market research etc.

*****Medical Action for Global Security (MEDACT)** 60 Holloway Road, London N19 4DJ. Tel 0171 272 2020 Fax 0171 281 5717. A voluntary association of doctors and other health professionals in the UK working for the abolition of nuclear weapons, the promotion of peace and global security, the protection of the environment and preventive medicine on a global scale.

National Council for Voluntary Organisations Regents Wharf, 8 All Saints Street, London. Tel 0171 713 6161 Fax 0171 713 6300. Umbrella body for voluntary organisations; provides a range of services including training.

National Federation of Housing Associations 175 Gray's Inn Road, London WC1X 8UP. Tel 0171 278 6571 Fax 0171 833 8323. Looks after the interests of Housing Associations in England; publishes *H A Weekly* and *Housing Agenda*.

National Food Alliance 5-11 Worship Street, London, EC2A 2BH. Tel 0171 628 2442 Fax 0171 628 9329. Umbrella body for 70 national organisations working on food and health issues from a public interest perspective; includes everyone from the Baby Milk Campaign to the BMA.

National Housing and Town Planning Council 14 - 18 Old Street, London EC1V 9AB. Tel 0171 251 2363 Fax 0171 608 2830. Provides a forum that brings together those involved in housing, planning and environmental issues, including individuals, local authorities and housing associations; campaigns for higher standards in this field, conducts research, organises seminars and conferences and publishes a journal, books and reports.

National Network of Community Businesses Society Place, West Calder, Scotland EH55 8EA. Tel 01506 871370 Fax 01506 873079. A network of communities acting for themselves to create jobs and provide services.

National Society for Clean Air 136 North Street, Brighton BN1 1RG. Tel 01273 326313 Fax 01273 735802. Aims to secure environmental improvement by promoting clean air through the reduction of air pollution, noise and other contaminants; membership includes Local Authorities and industry as well as individuals and other organisations.

National Tenants' Resource Centre Trafford Hall, Ince Lane, Wimbolds Trafford, Near Chester CH21 4JP. Tel 01244 300 246 Fax 01244 300 818. A resource centre for tenants' groups; services include a library, conference centre and training courses.

*****Neighbourhood Initiatives Foundation** The Poplars, Lightmoor,. Telford TF4 3QN. Tel 01952 590 777 Fax 01952 591 771. Helps to empower people to shape the future of their neighbourhoods using techniques like "Planning for Real" to encourage residents to participate in the identification of problems and the development of solutions; works with local authorities, housing associations, voluntary agencies and community groups. (See also Appendix 4).

New Consumer 52 Elswick Road, Newcastle upon Tyne NE4 6JH. Tel 0191 272 1601. Fax 0191 272 1615. Produces publications describing and making comparative evaluation of the social, environmental and ethical policies of companies and other organisations; aims to encourage companies to apply best social and environmental practice in their activities and policies.

*****New Economics Foundation** 1st Floor, Vine Court, 112-116 Whitechapel Road, London E1 1JE. Tel. 0171 377 5696 Fax 0171 377 5720. Projects include social auditing, formulating alternative economic indicators, energy conservation, researching links between economics, trade and the environment etc.

New Sector Society Place, West Calder, Scotland EH55 8EA. Tel 01506 871370 Fax 01506 873079. The magazine of workers' co-ops and community-owned businesses in the UK; promotes the principles of collective enterprise and common ownership.

Open Spaces Society 25a Bell Street, Henley-on- Thames, Oxon RG9 2BA. Tel 01491 573535. Campaigns for stronger laws to protect common land, open spaces and rights of way and to secure legal access to all open country.

Out of This World 52 Elswick Road, Newcastle upon Tyne NE4 6JH. Tel 0191 272 1601 Fax 0191 272 1615. A national chain of shops, owned by its members, which, through its products and policies promotes better health, environmental sustainability, fair trade, animal welfare and community development. (See page 298).

*****Oxfam** Oxfam House, 274 Banbury Road, Oxford OX2 7DZ. Tel 01865 311 311 Fax 01865 312 600. Works with poor people worldwide regardless of race or religious beliefs in their struggle against hunger, disease, exploitation and poverty, through relief, development, research and public education.

Permaculture Association PO Box 1, Buckfastleigh, Devon TQ11 OLH. Tel. 01654 712188. Active national worknet of practitioners of permaculture, which consciously uses ecological principles is designing self-sustaining food, fibre, and energy producing ecosystems; organises conferences, meetings, training etc.

Plain English Campaign P.O. Box 3, New Mills, Stockport, SK12 4QP. Tel 01663 744409 Fax 01663 747038. Seeks out gobbledygook and puts it right through rewriting and redesigning; runs courses in Plain English. (See page 29).

Planning Aid for London Calvert House, 5 Calvert Avenue, Shoreditch, London E2 7JP. Tel 0171 613 4435 Fax 0171 613 4452. Provides advice and practical support on planning matters.

Planning Exchange Tontine House, 8 Gordon Street, Glasgow G1 3PL. Tel 0141 248 8541 Fax 0141 248 8277. A company providing information on economic development, planning and housing issues to local authorities and private organisations.

*Population Concern 178-202 Great Portland Street, London W1N 5TB. Tel 0171 631 1546 Fax 0171 436 2143. Works in partnership with grassroots organisations in 19 less developed countries, helping women in particular to increase their opportunities and rights by providing reproductive health care, including family planning information and services.

*The Poverty Alliance 162 Buchanan Street, Glasgow G1 2LL. Tel 0141 353 0440 Fax 0141 353 0686. An alliance of community groups, voluntary organisations, local authorities and individual community activists which seeks to combat poverty through the promotion of strategic and collaborative action; activities include awareness raising, support and skills training for community leaders etc.

Public Concern at Work Lincoln's Inn House, 42 Kings Way, London WC2B 6EX. Tel 0171 404 6609 Fax 0171 404 6576. Provides free legal advice to people who have concerns in the work place about issues which threaten the public interest including fraud, malpractice and other situations which seem to be wrong, illegal or dangerous.

*Public Health Alliance 138 Digbeth, Birmingham B5 6DR. Tel 0121 643 7628 Fax 0121 643 4541. An alliance of organisations and individuals which promotes and defends public health, campaigning for health promoting public policy at all levels of government.

*Quaker Social Responsibility and Education Friends House, 173-177 Euston Road, London NW1 2BJ. Tel 0171 387 3601 Fax 0171 388 1977. Supports Quakers in Britain on issues of social and economic justice - including housing and penal reform - equality, democratic renewal, truth and integrity in public affairs and community care; presents Quaker views nationally.

*Real World Coalition c/o TCPA, 17 Carlton House Terrace, London SW1Y 5AS. Tel 0171 930 0375 Fax 0171 930 3280. A coalition of non-governmental organisations committed to raising the importance of environmental sustainability, social justice - including the relief and eradication of poverty, in this country and internationally - and democratic renewal in UK political debate. (See page 286).

Reclaim the Streets P.O. Box 9656, London, N4 4JY. Tel 0171 281 4621. Non-violent direct action group which organises dynamic street parties, and other actions against car culture; grew out of direct action around anti-road protests. (See page 279).

Reforesting Scotland 21a Coates Crescent, Edinburgh EH3 7AF. Tel 0131 226 2496 Fax 0131 226 2503. Aims to restore Scotland's natural resources so that future generations can continue to gain sustenance from the land; also actively involved in land use and land rights issues.

RoadPeace PO Box 2579, London NW10 3PW. Tel 0181 964 9353 Fax 0181 964 9353. The national charity for Road Traffic victims; supports families and friends of road crash victims; campaigns for better enforcement of traffic law and changes to legislation.

Royal Town Planning Institute 26 Portland Place, London, W1N 4BE. Tel 0171 636 9107 Fax 0171 323 1582. Has a network of planners across the country willing to give free advice on planning matters to community groups.

Rural Development Commission Dacre House, 19 Dacre Street, London SW1H ODH. Tel 0171 340 2900 Fax 0171 340 2911. The Government's rural development agency; works with the voluntary sector and others to high-light problems, create a climate in which rural businesses and communities can prosper and initiate action which will improve the economic and social development of rural areas.

Rural Forum Highland House, 46 St. Catherine's Road, Perth PH1 5RY. Tel 01738 634565 Fax 01738 638699. Alliance of organisations working to improve the quality of life of all who live and work in Scotland's rural areas; promotes the 'Personal Housing Plan' method of empowering individuals to secure best solutions to housing problems; Action Network provides support services, information exchange etc.

*Save the Children Fund 17 Grove Lane, London SE5 8RD. Tel 0171 703 5400 Fax 0171 703 2278. The UK's largest international voluntary agency concerned with child health and welfare; aims to influence policy and practice to make a reality of children's rights.

Schumacher Society (UK) Foxhole, Dartington, Totnes, Devon TQ9 6EB. Tel/Fax 01803 865051. Promotes good economic practice, ecological and spiritual values, and human-scale development; primarily concerned with educational work, including annual lectures and a mail order book service.

Schumacher Society (USA) 140 Jug End Road, Great Barrington, Massachusetts MA01230, USA. Tel Fax +1 413 528 1737.. (See above).

*Scottish Education and Action for Development (SEAD) 23 Castle Street, Edinburgh EH2 3DN. Tel 0131 225 6550 Fax 0131 226 6384. Looks at the common roots of poverty and linkages between experiences of development in Scotland and world's poorer nations; produces publications, organises conferences and study tours, runs campaigns, co-ordinates international network to exchange ideas for action on development, etc.

Seeds of Hope East Timor Ploughshares, Box 5, Queen Margaret's Grove London N1 4PZ. (See page 285).

Seikatsusha Network 2-18-1 Kyodo, Setagaya-Ku, Tokyo, Japan. Tel + 03 3425 0111 Fax + 03 3420 1450. (See page 221)

Shared Interest 31 Moseley Street, Newcastle upon Tyne NE1 1HX. Tel 0191 261 5943 Fax 0191 261 8759. Attracts investors' money from the UK to be re-invested in locally beneficial projects in the Third World.

Shelter 88 Old Street, London EC1V 9HU. Tel 0171 253 0202 Fax 0171 505 2169. Provides practical advice on housing matters and campaigns on behalf of homeless people.

Soil Association 86 Colston Street, Bristol BS1 5BB. Tel. 0117 929 0661 Fax 0117 925 2504. Promotes organic farming and gardening; awards a symbol for display on organic produce which adheres to certain standards; produces a range of publications; offers advice on organic practices.

*Sustainable Agriculture, Food and Environment (SAFE) Alliance 28 Ebury Street, London SW1W OLU. Tel 0171 823 5660 Fax 0171 823 5673. An alliance of farmer, environmental, consumer, animal welfare and development organisations promoting sustainable food production through analysis, research, education and information.

*Sustrans 35 King Street, Bristol BS1 4DZ. Tel 0117 926 8893 Fax 0117 929 4173. Designs and builds routes for cyclists, walkers and people with disabilities; has completed several hundred miles of traffic-free paths through urban and country areas and promotes Safe Routes to School.

TCA (Telework,. Telecottage and. Telecentre Association) c/o Wren. Telecottage, Stoneleigh Park, Warwickshire CV8 2RR. Tel 0800 616 008 Fax 01203 696538. Helps people working from home to set up resource centres which will provide access to computers etc.

Tenant Participation Advisory Service St. Peters, Bridge Road., Saltley, Birmingham B8 3TE. Tel 0121 327 3115 Fax 0121 327 3144. Offers training and advice to tenant groups, local authorities and housing associations on issues such as how to set up a tenant group, current housing legislation etc.

The Land is Ours East Oxford Community Centre, Princes Street, Oxford OX4 1DD. Tel 01865 722016. Campaigns to highlight ordinary people's exclusion not only from the land itself, but also from the decision making processes affecting it; organises events itself and provides media support, research and contacts for other groups. (See page 279).

*Town and Country Planning Association 17 Carlton House Terrace, London SW1Y 5AS. Tel 0171 930 8903 Fax 0171 930 3280. Campaigns for improvements to the environment through effective planning, public participation and sustainable development; membership is drawn equally from the corporate sector, local government and concerned individuals. (See page 43).

Traidcraft Plc Kingsway, Gateshead, Tyne and Wear NE11 ONE. Tel 0191 491 0591 Fax 0191 482 2690. Promotes trade based on fair shares, concern for people and care for the environment; imports and distributes a range of goods sourced in the 'Third World', mainly from community based enterprises and associations of smallholder farmers; mail order service.

*Transport 2000, Walkden House, 10 Melton Street, London NW1 3EJ. Tel 0171 388 8386 Fax 0171 388 2481. Campaigns for a coherent and sustainable national transport policy which meets transport needs with least damage to the environment; activities include research, reports, seminars, lobbying and supporting a network of local groups. (See page 30).

Triodos Bank Brunel House, 11 The Promenade, Clifton, Bristol BS8 3NN. Tel 0117 973 9339 Fax 0117 973 9303. A social bank lending only to organisations and businesses with social and environmental objectives; accepts deposits and investments from individuals, charities, businesses, voluntary groups and other organisations.

UK Social Investment Forum First Floor, Vine Court, 112 Whitechapel Road, London E1 1JE. Tel 0171 377 5907 Fax 0171 377 5720. Promotes ethical, environmental and social investments; runs workshops, seminars and conferences. (See page 298).

Undercurrents 16b Cherwell Street, Oxford OX4 1BG. Tel 01865 203661 Fax 01865 243562. Provides media support to campaigns through the use of video; activities include training, a news service and compilation/distribution of videos; also runs and supports the Camcorder Action Network - a network of people round Britain willing to take video footage of campaigning actions.

Unemployment Unit 322 St John Street, London EC1V 4NT. Tel 0171 833 1222 Fax 0171 833 1121. An independent organisation which researches and campaigns on the problems facing the unemployed; organises seminars, conferences and training events; offers free advice and information to unemployed people, trainees, researchers, local government and MPs.

*United Nations Association 3 Whitehall Court, London SW1A 2E L. Tel. 0171 930 2931/2 Fax 0171 930 5893. Aims to promote awareness and support of the principles and worldwide work of the UN in conflict avoidance and resolution, peacekeeping, economic and social development work etc; lobbies nationally and campaigns locally via a network of local branches.

Voluntary Service Overseas 317 Putney Bridge Road, London SE15 2PN. Tel 0181 780 2266 Fax 0181 780 1326. Links possible volunteers with opportunities in the developing world.

Walter Segal Self Build Trust 57 Chalton Street, London NW1 1HY. Tel 0171 388 9582 Fax 0171 387 3203. Assists self-build schemes by liaising between councils and self-builders.

Wildlife Trusts The Green, Witham Park, Waterside South, Lincoln LN5 7JR. Tel 01522 544400 Fax 01522 511616. Aims to create a UK richer in wildlife by protecting and enhancing species and habitats; manages nearly two thousand nature reserves; campaigns nationally and has network of local groups of volunteers who actively carry out wildlife conservation projects.

Women's Environmental Network Aberdeen Studios, 22 Highbury Grove, London N5 2EA. Tel 0171 354 8823 Fax 0171 354 0464. Aims to empower, educate and inform women who care about the environment; activities include seminars, public meetings, consumer action and representations on behalf of women; network of local branches.

World Development Movement 25 Beehive Place, London SW9 7QR. Tel 0171 737 6215 Fax 0171 274 8232. Campaigns on a wide range of aid and development issues including international trade, overseas aid, debt, famine and the environment; lobbies nationally and has a network of active local groups.

*World Wide Fund for Nature (WWF) UK Panda House, Weyside Park, Godalming, GU7 1XR. Tel 01483 426 444 Fax 01483 426 409. Works in over 100 countries to conserve biodiversity, promote sustainable development and reduce pollution and waste consumption; runs programmes for policy reform and education as well as undertaking or supporting thousands of practical projects mostly working with local communities.

...so published by Jon Carpenter

...mpact Development

...g and people in a sustainable countryside

...Fairlie

...mplete re-examination of Britain's planning system from the bottom up ...the point of view of the planned, rather than of the planner – is an ...tant contribution to the topical debate about the future and use of the ...ryside and what it means to achieve sustainability in the modern world.

...mon Fairlie argues that instead of excluding low income people from ...g and working in rural areas, planners should look favourably on proposals ...low impact, environmentally benign homes and workplaces in the open ...ntryside. Criteria for planning approval at present favour the wealthy ...mmuter and the large-scale farmer and discriminate heavily against (e.g.) ...allholders, low-impact homes, and experimental forms of husbandry.

The book is the result of much detailed research. It includes a number of ...ases studies of low impact developments, some of which received permission, ...ome of which failed. It includes illustrations; policy recommendations; guides ...to acts of parliament, government circulars and policy guidelines etc.; refer- ...ences; and explanatory appendices. It is an invaluable tool both for those who wish to live on the land in a sustainable manner, and for planners and politicians who would like to make it possible for them to do so. As well as proposing changes to planning law, the author shows how existing regulations can be used to enable many environmentally benign projects to take place.

Simon Fairlie is an editor of *The Ecologist*, and co-author of *Whose Common Future?* (Earthscan, 1993). He writes for *The Guardian*, *New Statesman and Society*, and *Perspectives*.

£10 paperback 1 897766 25 4 176pp illustrated

Books on these pages, together with additional copies of *The Power in Our Hands*, may be found in bookshops, or ordered post free from the publisher. Please make your cheque payable to 'Jon Carpenter Publishing' and send it to Jon Carpenter Publishing (POH), The Spendlove Centre, Charlbury OX7 3PQ. If you are ordering from overseas, please add £1 to your order towards postage, and pay by Eurocheque or by a cheque drawn on a London bank.

Prices and other information are accurate at September 1996, but may change without notice.

Appendix 4

Further reading

Sean Baine (ed.), *Building Community Partnerships* (Community Matters, 8-9 Upper Street, London N1 0PQ)

Michael Bolton and Kevin Sims, *Four Hours in My Lai* (Penguin)

Rachel Carson, *Silent Spring* (Penguin)

Robert Chambers, *Rural Development: Putting the Last First* (Longman)

Jung Chang, *Wild Swans* (Harper Collins Publishing)

Child Poverty Action Group, *Poverty — The Facts* (Child Poverty Action Group, 1-5 Bath Street, London EC1V 9PY)

Community Matters, *The What, Why and How of Neighbourhood Community Development* (Community Matters, 8-9 Upper Street, London N1 0PQ)

Suzy Croft and Peter Beresford, *Getting Involved* (Community Matters, 8-9 Upper Street, London N1 0PQ)

Guy Dauncey, *After the Crash: The Emergence of the Rainbow Economy* (Green Print)

Richard Douthwaite, *The Growth Illusion: How Economic Growth has Enriched the Few, Impoverished the Many and Endangered the Planet* (Green Books, Hartland)

John Elkington and Julia Hailes, *The Green Consumer Guide* (Gollanz)

Herbert Girardet, *The Gaia Atlas of Cities: New Directions for Sustainable Urban Living* (Gaia Books)

Peter Hudson, *Managing Your Community Building* (Community Matters, 8-9 Upper Street, London N1 0PQ)

Will Hutton, *The State We're In: Why Britain is in Crisis and How to Overcome It* (Vintage)

John Keane, *Tom Paine: A Political Life* (Bloomsbury)

Tim Lang and Colin Hines, *The New Protectionism: Protecting the Future Against Free Trade* (Earthscan)

Barbara Lowndes, *Making News: Producing a Community Newspaper* (Community Matters, 8-9 Upper Street, London N1 0PQ)

Nelson Mandela, *Long Walk To Freedom: The Autobiography of Nelson Mandela* (Abacus)

Andrew Marr, *Ruling Britannia: The Failure and Future of British Democracy* (Penguin)

Paul Medoff and Holly Sklar, *Streets of Hope: The Fall and Rise of an Urban Neighbourhood* (South End Press, Boston, USA)

Neighbourhood Initiatives Foundation, *Planning for Real Guide* and *Turning the Talk into Action* (specimen forms for neighbourhood surveys) plus a range of *Neighbourhood Action Pack*s — ask for current publications list

(Neighbourhood Initiatives Foundation, The Poplars, Lightmoor, Telford TF4 3QN)

John Pearce, *At the Heart of the Community Economy: Community Enterprise in a Changing World* (C.Gulbenkian Foundation)

The Real World Coalition, *The Politics of the Real World* (Earthscan)

Carol Riddell, *Tireragan — A Township on the Ross of Mull: A Study in Local History* (Highland Renewal, Knockvologan, Fionnphort, Mull, Argyll PA66 6BN)

James Robertson, *The Sane Alternative: A Choice of Futures* (J. Robertson, via bookshops or by mail order from the Old Bakehouse, Cholsey, Oxon OX10 9NU)

E.F. Schumacher, *Small is Beautiful : A Study of Economics as if People Mattered* (Vintage)

John F.C. Turner, *Housing by People* (Marion Boyars)

For further lists of books on a range of issues including environmental sustainability, social justice and local initiatives, contact either Schumacher Book Service, Foxhole, Dartington, Devon TQ9 6EB (Tel/Fax 01803 865 051) or WEC Bookservice, The Wadebridge Bookshop, 43/45 Molesworth Street, Wadebridge, Cornwall, PL27 7DR (Tel 01208 812 489; Fax 01208 815 705).

Also publishe[d]

Ethical Investment

A saver's guide
Peter Lang

The book for anyone with money to invest — whether [...] or many thousands — who tries to apply ethical standar[d...] but who doesn't have a detailed understanding of money [...] written in everyday language, free of the confusing jargon o[...]

Unlike the typical financial adviser, the author explains a[...] ethical investment opportunities, including those that don't [...] to 'independent financial advisers' for recommending the[m...] banks, building societies, and a number of funds and companie[s...] 'social economy', as well as the commission-paying unit tru[...] pension funds. There is also a discussion of the choice of insuran[ce...]

Ethical Investment explains how all these various investments [...] ethical pros and cons, and guides the investor through the questio[ns...] to be asked before deciding whether to sign on the dotted line.

Peter Lang pulls no punches in revealing

• why 'independent' financial advisers are not independent in the [...] might think

• why financial advisers are extremely selective in the investment[s...] recommend

• why many investment opportunities sold as 'ethical' are far from ethi[cal...]

• why pensions are unlikely to keep you in old age in the manner t[...] brochures suggest

• why a pension may not give you the best income in retirement

• why the best investment for your future might be to spend rather than save

• how companies make massive deductions from the money you invest

• the widely differing ethical criteria used by different 'ethical' funds

• where to find the information you need to judge a company's ethical record

Peter Lang is an environmental consultant and writer. He is the author of *Lets Work: Rebuilding the local economy*, the definitive guide to setting up and running LETS (Local Exchange Trading Systems). He is currently helping set up Britain's first ethical property company.

£10 pbk   192pp   1 897766 20 3

Low [...]

Planni[...]
Simon [...]

This c[...] — fro[m...] impo[...] coun[...]

S[...] livi[...] for [...] co[...] co[...] sm[...]

"This is the missing link in the debate about how we live.

It is the secret formula that our leaders consistently misunderstand. Tony Gibson's book is about people and power — and how the grassroots can effect real change. It's vital!"

JOHN VIDAL, *The Guardian*

The pace of events seems overwhelming: there's been nothing like it since time began. But we ourselves are much the same. And we're fed up with the blundering and blethering of the powers that be.

So here's the story of **ordinary** people doing **extraordinary** things all over the world, and back through time, and of how we're beginning to put things right — **homes, jobs, schooling, environment, human rights** — step by step, beginning on our home ground, gaining confidence, cutting the cackle, linking up with the moving spirits inside governments as well as outside them.

Sorting out what needs to be done, showing each other how to do it, spreading the news along the information highway, making waves.

The changes start small, but they end up worldwide.

LORD SCARMAN has delivered his judgment on the book:
"Invaluable … a joy. I find it inspiring … Gibson hits his target, and does so in a manner the reader can never forget."

Representatives of more than 20 leading campaigning organisations are also enthusiastic:
"This is a powerful and accurate portrayal of what can be done — an urgent and exciting prescription of what must be done. People are not the problem: they are the solution."

TONY GIBSON draws on his first-hand experience working alongside East Enders in the blitz, with Sicilian refugees, with both sides in the Chinese civil war, and with groups taking shape in different parts of Africa, Europe and the Caribbean; writing and producing for the BBC; initiating award-winning community self-help schemes in the UK; setting up the Neighbourhood Initiatives Foundation; and writing books about *Spare Time, Jobs and Careers, Breaking in the Future, The Use and Practice of Educational Television,* and *People Power.*

JC

£10
US $17.95

ISBN 1-897766-28-9

9 781897 766286 >